# INTRODUCTION TO THE HUMANITIES

*Painting, Sculpture, Architecture,*

*Music, and Literature*

# INTRODUCTION
# TO THE HUMANITIES

Painting, Sculpture, Architecture,
Music, and Literature

## DORIS VAN DE BOGART

*Formerly Assistant Professor of the Humanities*
*The University of Pittsburgh*
*Bradford Campus*

BARNES & NOBLE BOOKS
A DIVISION OF HARPER & ROW, PUBLISHERS
New York, Hagerstown, San Francisco, London

Printed in the United States of America

81 82 83 84    20 19 18 17 16 15 14 13 12 11

*To the memory of*
*my mother and father*
*who first awakened in me*
*a love of the arts*

consistent with the same may be said for all measures.

# Preface

The author recently heard a concert consisting of three of the Brandenburg Concertos by Johann Sebastian Bach, directed by Pablo Casals. The music radiated infectious joy, and was as alive, vibrant, and exhilarating as it was when Bach composed it over two hundred years ago. At the conclusion, the musicians seemed in no hurry to leave. They stood along with the entire audience, faces alight with smiles, and applauded as long as the eighty-eight-year-old maestro had the strength to return for one more bow. The solo violinist who had done such a superb piece of work on the Fifth Concerto picked up a viola and sat down on the very last stand of the viola section to play the Sixth Concerto, which calls for no violins. Even the conductor applauded his musicians before he turned to receive the tribute of the audience. Such is the joy inherent in great music for those who are receptive to it. And the same may be said for all the arts. It is the purpose of this book to increase that receptivity.

At long last, educators and public officials have come to realize the tremendous need for the arts. Stewart Udall, Secretary of the Interior, has written: "In America, culture has not kept pace with science and technology. Art is not an ornament to be worn for a day in its newest gloss, or a plaything of an intellectual elite, but an elixir that nourishes the best and highest impulses in man. We must recognize the difference between meaningful art that ennobles and entertainment that distracts. Not until the arts become a genuine need for the individual and the society can America think of herself as culturally mature."[1]

Historian Arnold Toynbee says that it is characteristic of advanced societies to substitute license for liberty, irresponsibility for obligation, comfort for challenge, and self-interest for brotherhood. With shorter work weeks, earlier retirement, and automation all providing more leisure, thoughtful people are wondering whether this leisure will be spent productively or for the gradual eroding of the individual's character. "Our educa-

---

[1] Stewart Udall, "The Arts as a National Resource," *Saturday Review*, March 28, 1964.

tional institutions," says Toynbee, "have largely educated people for work, and perhaps it is time now to spend part of our education in teaching how to use leisure productively. Leisure offers us an opportunity for personal self-fulfillment, for creativity, for service to our fellow men, but we need some training in these fields."[1]

To be sure, we live in a period of doubt and uncertainty, but every historical period has been a period of doubt and uncertainty for those who were living in it. The medieval Italian poet Dante began his *Divine Comedy* with these significant words: "In the middle of the journey of our life, I came to myself in a dark wood." The wood is always dark because we cannot see what is on the other side of it. What we need is a light to penetrate that darkness, and such a light can best be supplied by religion and the arts.

Loren Eiseley, well-known anthropologist, looks at the record of man's long and tortured history and yet affirms his faith in man's future. He says: "I have been accused of wooly-mindedness for entertaining even hope for man. I can only respond that in the dim morning shadows of humanity, the inarticulate creature who first hesitantly formed the words for pity and love must have received similar guffaws around a fire. Yet some men listened, for the words survive."[2]

There has been an unparalleled upsurge of interest in the arts in the United States since World War II. Course offerings like "Our Cultural Heritage," "History of the Arts," and "Humanities" are increasingly to be found in college catalogues. Symphony orchestras, opera societies, and drama groups which once struggled to maintain themselves in our largest cities, are now reaching down to the grass roots and finding enthusiastic audiences. There are more than twenty major music festivals going on every summer and as many drama festivals, some using barns and tents. New York is taking free drama to the most culturally deprived sections of the city on a movable stage. Many people are building their own libraries of fine literature in paperback form, their own collections of art prints culled from magazines.

Asks Dr. Adolf Grunbaum, philosophy of science scholar at the University of Pittsburgh: "What is the point of making a good living if a man can only enjoy the comforts of the lower animals? Once he has bought a house and furnished the place, what

---

[1] Arnold Toynbee, "Leisure," quoted in the Bradford, Pennsylvania *Era,* February 10, 1964.
[2] Loren Eiseley, "Our Path Leads Upward," *Reader's Digest,* March. 1962.

is he going to do? He has a comfortable kennel, what then? What if he hasn't furnished himself and is empty inside? What's the point? Does the psychiatrist get him?"[1]

Says Dr. Frederic Keffer, chairman of the Department of Physics at the University of Pittsburgh: "I don't know many scientists who aren't interested in some field of the humanities. . . . If any one wants to start a string quartet send him up to chemistry or physics. Some of our people are good enough to have considered musical careers."[2]

Major industries, not content with decorating their buildings with works of art, encourage their employees to form choral groups or brass bands. Indeed, it is difficult to avoid music and art masterpieces today. Television programs play the old masters either "straight" or "souped up." Rembrandt is helping to sell cigars, Grant Wood to sell breakfast food, and Botticelli's "Birth of Venus" to sell bras. Vicki Goldberg says: "Art has won the race for the most effective status symbol of the year."[3]

Sometimes a well-meaning person will say, "I enjoy Beethoven, but I don't like Bach." Or again, "I like Rembrandt's paintings, but I don't like those of Van Gogh." One cannot compare Beethoven with Bach, or Rembrandt with Van Gogh. Each is the product of a different stylistic period, a different cultural milieu, a different thought process. Unconsciously we tend to judge a modern artist by standards which have proved relevant in the past. This is often unfair to the artist. Similarly we are prone to judge an older artist in the light of his influence on subsequent men, or unfortunately, by his commercial value today. Such snap judgments must be put aside. We must endeavor to understand and enjoy each artist from the point of view of the age in which the artist lived. To do this adequately involves a vast amount of information: nothing less than the entire history of Western culture.

This book does not aim to be a history of art, a history of music, and a history of literature all condensed into one volume. Its purpose is to introduce a few key figures in each stylistic period in order to provide an intelligible perspective on the period. If it can give the reader an adequate picture of logical development, he can fill in the gaps by more detailed study or by his own continuing experience.

---

[1] Esther Kitzes, "Out of their Winter of Discontent," *Pitt Magazine,* spring, 1965, p. 7.

[2] Helen Knox, "The Literate Men of Science," *ibid,* p. 17.

[3] Vicki Goldberg, "Mondrian is a Paper Napkin," *Horizon Magazine of the Arts,* May, 1963.

It may perhaps be argued that English and American literature have been slighted in this survey. Thanks to English courses in our public schools, American readers are fairly well grounded in the literature of their own language, but they know very little about great literature outside England and America. Even people who have studied European languages in school have seldom acquired the facility to appreciate a piece of foreign literature in the original. Reading good translations is far better than not knowing great masterpieces from all sources. The arts of the Orient have been omitted from this volume because this vast field merits special study.

Certainly there is no dearth of excellent material on the arts available today. Literary masterpieces are nearly all obtainable in paperback at nominal cost. Very fine reproductions of art works are coming out all the time, but many books containing them are necessarily expensive. A number of students start their own collections of art reproductions clipped from magazines. To supplement the illustrations in this book, we have placed in the Appendix (see p. 382) a list of desirable art prints taken from the catalogue of *University Prints* (15 Brattle Street, Harvard Square, Cambridge, Massachusetts), the most inexpensive and comprehensive collection we have found. Each year its number of color reproductions is increased. For the beginning art student these are a real bonanza.

For the collector of musical masterworks the task is not so easy. Practically anything in the history of music is now available on long-playing records, and one can consult the Schwann catalogue which comes out each month. But how does one know which of a dozen listings of the same symphony, for example, is the best? Our advice is to locate a dealer who has access to the various recordings and whose opinion can be trusted as to the mechanical perfection of the recordings and the musicianship of the artists. Don't expect discounts from such a dealer and don't buy "bargain" recordings, especially when they do not list names of artists or conductors. There is no substitute for the best. We have listed in the Appendix (p. 381) a few unusual recordings which are especially valuable and are discussed in this book.

There is no substitute for "live" material. Hence, the student should attend symphony concerts, operas, recitals, art museums, and the theater if these are available to him. But he should be adequately prepared for what he is to see or hear. There is no reason why the study of the arts should not be both vital and stimulating.

Material in this book has been mimeographed for students of

*Interdisciplinary 81, the Humanities,* on the Bradford Campus
of the University of Pittsburgh. It is the enthusiasm of these
students which has prompted its publication. I want to express
my sincere gratitude to Dr. Donald E. Swarts, President of Bradford Campus, University of Pittsburgh, for his encouragement
in the undertaking, and to his office force, especially Mrs. Jane
Thompson, for typing and mimeographing the manuscript. I am
also grateful to my students for catching some inadvertent errors.

I cannot sufficiently acknowledge my debt to Dr. Paul Henry
Lang and his inspiring seminar in musicology at Columbia University for many of the ideas contained in this book, and for
stimulating my interest in the interrelationship of the arts. 1
also want to thank Mrs. Helen Nesselson for much helpful criticism and for compiling the index, Miss Jane Crosby, and Mrs.
Mildred Friedman for their many suggestions, and my inde-
fatigable editor, Miss Nancy Cone of Barnes & Noble.

# Contents

# List of Illustrations

# INTRODUCTION TO THE HUMANITIES

*Painting, Sculpture, Architecture,*

*Music, and Literature*

# Chapter 1 / The Meaning and Importance of the Humanities

The word *Humanities* comes from the Latin *humanus*, which means human, cultured, refined. The word has different connotations in different historical eras.

When the first medieval universities were established in the twelfth and thirteenth centuries, the professors, mostly churchmen, were interested in arguing about metaphysics and religion (Scholasticism). To them Humanities meant primarily philosophy and theology.

The Humanists of the Renaissance asserted the intrinsic value of man's life on earth, as opposed to the medieval interest in eternity. Hence Humanities included disciplines which would make man's life richer and more meaningful: the languages and literature of Greece and Rome, fine arts, music, and philosophy in its more traditional divisions.

The nineteenth century witnessed a certain loss of prestige of the Humanities to the sciences and social sciences, because many men believed that science could procure everything that man needed or wanted. Recently, there has come the important realization that science is not an unmixed blessing. The atomic bomb, insecticides, drugs, and other scientific inventions can ultimately destroy man unless they are controlled by individuals of high ideals, morality, and good will.

Another troublesome development has been the tendency to explore a field of knowledge in depth rather than in breadth. While this technique has produced amazing discoveries in all fields of learning, it has also produced the *specialist* "who knows more and more about less and less." Now educators, realizing that all fields of knowledge are interrelated, are beginning to believe that young students should be made aware of these interrelationships before they select the particular field in which to specialize.

At long last, the federal government has set up a Foundation of the Arts and Humanities to promote scholarship and progress in these subjects, and thus to leaven the alarming materialism of modern civilization. The emphasis has shifted to modern literature although masterpieces of philosophy, history, theology, and science are often included. Included too are critical and his-

1

torical studies of the fine arts and music with the emphasis on serving man as an individual rather than as a social being. Ideas and experiences in the Humanities have their full effect only when they are examined critically, evaluated, and appropriated by the student.

## The Artist and His Work

This book will survey the development of the arts (painting, sculpture, architecture, music, and literature) to help the reader appreciate our cultural heritage and to give him a background for understanding and evaluating the arts of our own day. We will try to discover what the arts can tell us about how men thought and felt in the historical period which produced them. Conversely, we will see how man's thinking and feeling are reflected in the arts which were produced in a given period so that we may appreciate a work of art in the light of the age which produced it.

This discipline should give us the historical and aesthetic background for a more comprehensive response to art in general. All this sounds very academic. In reality, a person who opens his home to the arts has never a dull moment, nor can he ever be lonely or bored. It is fascinating to see how each bit of new insight fits into the picture where it belongs like pieces in a jigsaw puzzle, but unlike the puzzle the picture is never finished.

We may examine a work of art as the record of a particular artist's vision. He has selected something he has seen, felt, or thought and has recorded it in an arrangement of design, color, line, mass, tones, or words which satisfies his aesthetic purpose. Hence, it is the product of his unique personality. But the artist has also been influenced consciously or unconsciously by many other determining factors: his environment, traditions, national traits, religious beliefs, economic condition, his patron, and even geography and climate have all influenced him. Hence, each work of true art represents the individual genius of its creator, and the general character of the age and locale in which it was born.

## Style

There are certain common denominators of subject matter, treatment, and emphasis which appear again and again in art works of a given epoch. These characterize the style of a period, perhaps the result of a certain community of feeling in the leading spirits of an age. The same cool classicism in the tragic dramas of Racine is to be found in the classic landscapes of Poussin. The violence in the life and narrative poems of Byron appears also in the paintings of Delacroix and the music of Berlioz. The massive grandeur and eloquence of Handel's oratorios have their counterpart in the façades and interiors of German Baroque churches. A number of factors determine a particular style.

**Historical Factors.** Most artistic creations of any one period have certain traits in common. When an artist searches for new perceptions, he is tied to the world around him. If he ignores or loses this tie, his work becomes unintelligible to his contemporaries. He is also affected by geographical and ethnic differences within the period. Early Gothic begins in French art about 1150, in German art about 1230. The Renaissance in Italy starts around 1400, some eighty years earlier than the corresponding period in the north. Indeed, Huizinga in his *Waning of the Middle Ages* [1] has been at pains to prove that the Low Countries (Flanders and Burgundy) remained almost exclusively medieval throughout the fifteenth century.

**Geographical Factors.** Artists are conditioned by their nationality. For example, artistic expression may be typically Dutch, French, or English. More particularly, in Italy they may be Florentine, Roman, or Venetian; in Germany, south German or north German. Of course, national characteristics are most extreme in literature because of the differences in language. It is easy to notice the difference between the French chanson and the Italian madrigal; yet both are Renaissance. Similarly, one can differentiate between English and Dutch landscapes of the seventeenth century; yet both are Baroque.

**Political, Psychological, and Sociological Factors.** Political systems and social patterns contribute to changes in style. In France, from the mid-seventeenth through the eighteenth century, art was the servant of king and court. Hence, personal vanity and frivolous rivalry were motivating factors. If an artist broke away from this environment, as Voltaire did, he had a rough time and might even be banished from the country. With social and economic change, the groups in a society which sponsor art also change. At different periods, art has been subject to the Church, the nobility, and the wealthy middle class (as in seventeenth-century commercial Holland, when the rich burghers delighted in paintings of themselves decked out in fine lace and

---

[1] Johan Huizinga, *The Waning of the Middle Ages* (New York: Anchor Books, 1954), p. 323.

velvets and seated at festive tables loaded with platters of fruit and fish).

**Ideational Factors.** Spiritual movements such as Christianity, the Renaissance, Humanism, the Counter Reformation, and the Enlightenment brought striking changes in social and political structures and they also influenced directly changes in art styles. The famous Bernini arcade in front of St. Peter's, which was built during the Counter Reformation, not only flings out its mighty arms to embrace the faithful, but it draws them right into the church.

**Technical Factors.** The importance of technique has been overemphasized in the past. Modern piano technique with its cult of the virtuoso could not exist before the modern piano was perfected. Landscapes painted out-of-doors were limited before light canvas and readily transportable oil paints in tubes had come into general use. But these technical and material influences are not nearly so important as other style-shaping factors.

## Words of Warning

Beware of generalizations; there are always exceptions. Heloise was a very modern French woman, but she lived in the twelfth century. Gesualdo da Venosa, sixteenth-century madrigalist, used chromatic harmony as daring as any exploited by Berlioz in the nineteenth century. Dr. Charles Burney, English music historian of the eighteenth century, said of Gesualdo: "It is extremely shocking and disgusting to the ear to go from one chord to another in which there is no relation, real or imaginary, and which is composed of sounds wholly extraneous and foreign to any key to which the chord belongs." What would he say today of Karlheintz Stockhausen? We think of the medieval period as Church-dominated until we encounter the love stories of Troilus and Cressida, Aucassin and Nicolette, and Tristan and Isolde.

Stylistic periods cannot be set off by any fixed dates. Any style is a transition period between the style that preceded it and the one that follows it. The roots of a new style are hidden perhaps a hundred years in the past and are slowly developing during the highest flowering of the current style. Just as almost any day on the street most people are dressed in this year's styles, a few may be wearing an advance model, while some little old lady comes along in a 1910 outfit, so in our work we must recognize stylisms of past, present, and future concurrently, sometimes in the same master. Haydn is not the "Father of the Symphony." He comes almost at the end of a long line of sym-

phonists, most of whose works have disappeared from the repertory. Beethoven marks the end of the true Classic development,
but there are traits in his late works that lead some critics to
call him a Romanticist.

In general, the greatest masters come at the end of a stylistic
period and often incorporate elements of the new style in their
work. Dante sums up the entire medieval period and foreshadows
the Renaissance; Michelangelo sums up the Renaissance and
foreshadows the Baroque. And as for Shakespeare, stylisms of
well-nigh every period, including the modern, can be found in his
work. He is the universal genius who speaks to every age and
race.

Our task becomes increasingly complex as we approach our
own period. The world moves ever more rapidly. Even in the
nineteenth century Realist and Impressionist styles were appear-
ing simultaneously. In the twentieth century, styles have changed
more rapidly than we could assimilate them. This fact accounts
for the general state of artistic confusion today. We can only
attempt to understand modern trends; we cannot prophesy which
will be significant for the future.

The following are the major stylistic periods (dates mark the
approximate outside limits of the period) :

| | |
|---|---|
| Greek Golden Age | 500 B.C.–410 B.C. |
| Hellenistic | 336 B.C.–A.D. 146 |
| Roman | 146–323 |
| Medieval | 323–1400 |
| Renaissance | 1270–1594 |
| Mannerist | 1530–1616 |
| Baroque | 1600–1750 |
| Classic | 1644–1793 |
| Rococo | 1715–1774 |
| Romantic | 1773–1848 |
| Realist and Naturalist | 1827–1927 |
| Impressionist | 1863–1900 |
| Modern | 1895 to the present |

# Chapter 2 / Basic Elements of the Arts

All arts have certain elements in common: rhythm, line, medium, structure, style, and, to a certain extent, color. Literature, painting, and sculpture have the elements of subject. Architecture has no subject unless you consider as subjects such terms as *church*, *dwelling*, and *factory*. Intrinsically, music has no subject, although a subject may be suggested in the title (for example, "Night on Bald Mountain").

Each art, like every other field of knowledge, has its own special vocabulary. One must learn to use certain terms intelligently in order to be articulate in discussing the arts. Such words as "pretty" and "beautiful" are not meaningful; avoid them. You might get away with "interesting" once but not more than once in a discussion. These words imply that you don't know enough about the subject to commit yourself. The latest catchword "empathy," meaning "feeling with" a certain artist, is already overworked.

## Elements of the Fine Arts

Basic elements of the fine arts (painting, sculpture, and architecture) include subject, medium, line, color, texture, volume, perspective, form, and style.

**Subject.** The subject provides the answer to the question: What is the painting or piece of sculpture about? Architecture has no specific subject, although architectural ends are sometimes served by bits of sculpture, such as the caryatids of the Erechtheum in Athens which hold up the porch roof on their heads or the gargoyles on Gothic churches which are rainspouts. In painting, subject is no problem if the artist has painted realistically. However, late in the nineteenth century artists began to distort reality, as in Henry Moore's "Family Group," and then to represent only an idea or feeling about a subject, as in Zorach's "Spirit of the Dance." Some modern painters have discarded representation altogether in favor of a pleasing pattern of lines, colors, or shapes; an example of this sort of painting is "Rhythm of Straight Lines" by Piet Mondrian. Another modern art form, Cubism, reduces figures and objects to geometrical planes in pleasing arrangement, as exemplified by William Zorach's "Still Life with Fruit and Guitar."

**Medium.** The term *medium* refers to the materials which an artist uses. Many mediums have been used by painters, but we shall consider only four: *fresco,* in which pigment is mixed with water and applied to wet plaster; *tempera,* in which the pigment is mixed with egg and applied to a very hard smooth surface, usually several layers of rubbed plaster *(gesso)* ; *oil* on canvas or prepared wood panel; and *water color,* which is pigment mixed with water and applied to smooth or rough white paper. Each medium has certain advantages and limitations.

*Fresco.* Fresco, the most noble and monumental, is adapted to large wall surfaces. It is the most exacting because it must be done quickly while the plaster is wet, and once applied cannot be changed. Only earth colors and certain others like cobalt blue will mix with the lime in the plaster; hence the colors are never intense but tend to fuse in a natural harmony. Again, plaster has a tendency to crack or is often ruined by dampness. The greatest frescoes lie well within the Renaissance: those of Giotto in the Arena Chapel in Padua, those of Piero della Francesca in the Church of San Francesco in Arezzo, Raphael's "Stanze" in the Vatican, and those of Michelangelo in the Sistine Chapel.

*Tempera.* Tempera painting, popular during the medieval and early Renaissance periods, requires the meticulous skill of a craftsman. The color is applied with tiny strokes of pointed brushes and dries immediately. Gold is often applied first as a background. Look at Simone Martini's "Annunciation" and notice the wealth of detail, the clarity of the colors, and the sharp lines of the figures.

*Oil.* Oil is the most popular medium today because the pigment comes ready-mixed in tubes. It dries slowly, so that if the artist is dissatisfied he can repaint his errors or scrape all off for a fresh start. Through the eighteenth century, most painters used a series of transparent glazes which produced a very smooth surface as you can see in any of Van Dyck's portraits. Later, the tendency has been to apply pure color directly from the palette to the canvas, even allowing the paint to stand out in great blobs or thick swirls as in Van Gogh's "Starry Night." This technique is called *impasto.*

*Water Color.* True water color did not reveal itself until the mid-nineteenth century. It is a very difficult medium, but in the hands of a master is both fluid and transparent. Since the artist must work rapidly and cannot change anything, there is a freshness and spontaneity in water color not felt in oil. Winslow

Homer's "Sloop Bermuda" is a masterpiece. Note how John Marin has allowed little dribbles to run down the paper so that they form part of the design in "Boat Off Deer Isle."

*Materials Used in Sculpture.* The materials used in sculpture are stone, wood, metal, and, recently, junk. Marble has always been the favorite material, especially in countries like Greece and Italy where there is a plentiful supply near at hand. Because of its hardness, it has great permanence, but when polished to a high gloss it looks soft and yielding as in Michelangelo's "Pietà." In western Europe, statues were frequently made of the same material as the church, usually limestone, or they were sculptured in wood and painted.

Of the metals, bronze has always been the favorite from the early Greek *kouros* (boy) down to the modern Picasso and Henry Moore. Working in metal requires a special technique. While the sculptor in stone chisels his figure directly from the block, the sculptor in bronze makes a clay model, builds a furnace around it, and pours the molten metal around the model. You can read an exciting account of the difficulties Benvenuto Cellini encountered in casting his "Perseus" in his *Autobiography*, Book II, chapters 72 to 79.

Up until modern times, architects have generally used the materials which they found readily available. In Italy, churches, public buildings, and even the country villas of the Renaissance merchant princes were built of marble. There is also in Italy an abundance of reddish clay called *pazzuolia* out of which roof tiles are made. When you look down on Florence, for instance, you behold a sea of red roofs. Against the green of the trees and the blue of the sky and hills, the effect is unforgettable. In low-lying countries like Holland and England, brick is generally used for dwellings because local clay is adapted to brick-making. Americans have used wood because it was plentiful.

In this century, however, structural steel, reinforced concrete, and glass have revolutionized architecture. In the future we may be living in plastic houses.

**Line.** The shape of a work of art is defined by *line*. The lines of a painting or sculpture tell us what the work is about. There are three kinds of lines: horizontal, vertical, and diagonal; consciously or unconsciously, our eyes must follow these lines. Both horizontal and vertical lines are in repose. But while the horizontal is more restful, the vertical is more forceful and dynamic. Diagonal lines are lines of action. Compare George Inness' "Lackawanna Valley" with Velasquez' "Surrender of Breda." In the former, the lines are predominantly horizontal, giving a peaceful effect; in fact, were it not for the vertical tree on the left, we might fall asleep. In the latter, notice the lines of vertical lances held by the Spanish soldiers. Both armies are at rest, but it is not difficult to tell that the Spaniards have been victorious. The action in the painting is expressed by the two generals in the foreground who form diagonal lines as they lean graciously toward each other.

**Color.** When we speak of *color*, we refer not only to hue but also to value, which means the amount of white or black in the hue, and intensity or brightness. Color is the decorative element in painting. When value and intensity are in a low key, all the colors tend toward gray or brown, and we say the painting is *monochromatic*. When value and intensity are high and all the colors are strongly opposed, we say the painting is *polychromatic*. Contrast Tintoretto's "Last Supper," which is monochromatic, with Raphael's "Madonna of the Chair," which is polychromatic. We also speak of warm colors (red, orange, and yellow) and cool colors (green and blue). Since warm colors, which tend to advance, are stimulating and cool colors, which tend to recede, are restful, an artist must balance his warm and cool colors carefully according to his purpose.

**Texture.** The term *texture* refers to the way objects feel to the touch. This is very real to the sculptor and architect because marble, metal, wood, brick, and glass feel different as we touch them. To the painter, texture is an illusion. He must make an object look the way it would feel if we could touch it. The painters of the Low Countries were adept at painting texture. Study the "Portrait of George Giesze" by Holbein and count the number of different textures he has portrayed in this one painting.

**Volume.** The term *volume* refers to solidity or thickness. This is the architect's primary concern because a building encloses space. His problems are too technical for our concern here, but suffice it to say that the building must look shipshape from whatever angle the light falls on it or from whatever vantage point we look at it, inside or out. The sculptor is concerned with volume because his figures actually occupy space and are observed from any direction depending on where the beholder stands. Areas of light and shadow depend on the direction of the sunlight. To the painter, volume is an illusion because the surface of the canvas is flat. To give his figures thickness, he decides arbitrarily from what direction he wants the light to fall; then he paints the lighted portions bright and those in shadow dark. In general, the brighter the light the deeper the shadow. It wasn't until the nineteenth century when artists began painting out-of-doors in direct sunlight that they discovered that light is reflected off a bright surface onto adjacent objects and also that the shadows tend to take on the complementary color of the object. Study Van Gogh's "Bedroom at Arles" and Picasso's "Seated Acrobat" for these effects.

**Perspective.** To get depth or distance, an artist uses *perspective*, both linear and aerial. Brunelleschi and Piero della Francesca, who lived in the early Renaissance, had much to do with codifying the laws of perspective. By *linear perspective* we mean that objects become smaller as they recede into the distance. Parallel lines below eye level seem to rise to a vanishing point on the horizon, while those above eye level seem to descend to the vanishing point. By *aerial perspective* we mean that objects become fainter in the distance due to the effect of the atmosphere. Stained-glass windows should have no perspective because the window is an integral part of the wall. Similarly, Gozzoli's paintings on the walls of the Medici Chapel have no perspective, not because he didn't know any better but because again they are a part of the wall. Leonardo in his "Last Supper" and Raphael in his "School of Athens" solved the problem very well by carrying the actual architecture of the room into the painting. This procedure seems to increase the size of the rooms, and it does no violence to the architecture.

Another facet of linear perspective which applies chiefly to the human body is *foreshortening*. The more nearly an arm, limb, or body is placed at right angles to the observer, the shorter it looks. (You may have photographed someone lying on the beach, and found that you had recorded nothing but feet.) An extreme and rather gruesome example of foreshortening is Mantegna's "Pietà."

**Form.** The term *form* applies to the over-all design of a work of art. Favorite designs are the triangle, used by Raphael in his "Sistine Madonna," the circle used in Michelangelo's "Holy Family," and the rectangle in numerous paintings. When the elements of a painting are contained within the frame and lead the eye back into the picture, it is said to be in *closed form*. Conversely, if parts of figures are cut off by the frame and we feel that the action extends out of the picture, it is said to be in *open form*. A good example of closed form is Botticelli's "Birth of Venus" and of open form is Toulouse-Lautrec's "Circus."

**Style.** Every artist has a personal style which is the result of his temperament, outlook on life, and training. He tends to repeat certain stylisms that he has found effective. We recognize Michelangelo by his colossal, twisted figures, El Greco by his elongated, ascetic forms, Modigliani by his long faces which are usually turned "on the bias." But the artist is also influenced by the world around him, so that his work reflects the time and place in which he lives. It is this spirit of the times which determines the style of a period. The Germans call it *Zeitgeist*.

## Elements of Music

Music is often referred to as the "universal language." This characterization is false because only words can express concrete thought. Music is abstract. It appeals to us intellectually when we understand how the composer has manipulated his material, and emotionally when we apprehend the feelings he has expressed. Literature is the vehicle for telling a story, and painting for showing a picture. This is not to say that composers have not tried to tell stories and paint pictures in tone all down through the centuries. We even read of an ancient Greek musician who tried to represent a storm at sea, and of an astute contemporary critic who averred there was more storm in his mother's cooking pot than in this piece of music. If a musical work will not stand up as an aesthetic experience without a story or even a descriptive title, then it is not worth our attention.

Basic elements of music include rhythm, melody, dynamics, harmony, texture, form, color, and style.

**Rhythm.** The most basic element of music is *rhythm*, the over-all movement or swing. Long before the days of recorded history, rhythm arose, probably out of the fundamental movements of the human body: the march rhythm from walking; the dance rhythm from recreation; the lullaby from the swaying of the trees, the rocking of the boat, or the effort of the primitive mother to quiet her baby. *Meter* means measure and refers to the number of beats in a rhythmic unit, or measure. Western man seems to respond naturally to two-beat or three-beat measure or multiples of these. Five-beat or seven-beat meters have come into Western music from the Orient, and are more difficult for us to feel. *Tempo* refers to speed, whether the music moves fast or slowly. Some musicians erroneously use the word "time" to refer to all these terms.

**Melody.** By *melody* we mean an orderly succession of tones, or musical sounds. (A *tone* is a musical sound designating pitch and depends on the vibration rate per second.) The smallest melodic unit is the *motif*, which expands into a *phrase*, a succession of tones easily encompassed in one breath. The phrase usually rises to a high point from which it falls to a point of rest or *cadence*. An entire melody is formed out of repeated and contrasting phrases. Since we commonly identify a piece of music by its tune, melody corresponds to line in painting. In fact, musicians frequently refer to melodic line.

**Dynamics.** The term *dynamics* refers to force or percussive effects: degrees of loud and soft. *Forte* means *loud; piano* means *soft.* Dynamic markings were not written on musical scores until the seventeenth century.

**Harmony.** The simultaneous sounding of two or more tones results in *harmony.* Hence harmony is the musical third dimension loosely analogous to depth in painting. Before the seventeenth century, harmony was achieved by having two or more melodies sung or played against each other. This practice is called *counterpoint* or *polyphony.* In the sixteenth century musical theorists indulged in a pitched battle to decide whether to tune instruments by mathematical vibration rates or by ear (equal temperament). The advocates of equal temperament won out, and the modern science of harmony proper with the resulting interrelationship of keys was born. This system, generally called *tonality,* governed all Western music for one hundred and fifty years until certain modern composers, complaining about the "slavery" of the system, began to experiment with other systems such as *polytonality* (using several keys simultaneously), *atonality* (having no key feeling), and the twelve-tone row (see p. 293). However, even today, most music is based on the tonal system. In no sense did tonality supersede or abolish the use of counterpoint, which has been employed by all the great composers and is especially favored by modern composers, but it too was brought under the control of key relationships.

**Texture.** The term *texture* refers to the number of tones we are asked to apprehend simultaneously. In a Haydn symphony in which the texture is relatively thin, air seems to circulate freely between the tones, and we can hear clearly what each instrument is doing. This is impossible in a Brahms symphony, which is thick in texture.

**Form.** The *form* or structure is as necessary to a work of music as a blueprint to an architect or a pattern to a dressmaker. Without structure, the work would be chaos, lacking direction or finality. It is based on demands which seem to be inherent in man: repetition and contrast, tension and repose. Listen to a Bach fugue and notice the repetition when each voice enters with the same subject; note the contrast in the episodes between the various entrances and the tension of the conflicting melodic lines. But notice that the work does not cadence or come to rest until the end. This type of organization we call *open form.* Significantly, it was at its height in music at the very time when painters like Tintoretto and Rembrandt were painting in open form. Now listen to the third movement of Mozart's *Symphony No. 40 in G Minor*. Notice that it is organized in a number of short sections of first tune, contrasting tune, and return to the first tune. Enough tension is introduced into the harmony so that we demand a complete stop or cadence at the end of each tune. This kind of organization is known as *closed form*. The *rondo* form is like a circle because after every contrasting tune we come around to the first tune again.

**Color.** In music *color* is the result of the difference in *timbre* (quality of tone) in the various instruments and voices. You should be so thoroughly familiar with the quality of sound of each instrument of the symphony orchestra that you can pick them out even when the texture is quite thick. The composer has on his instrumental palette almost unlimited resources in combining instrumental colors to suit his particular purpose. The strings (violin, viola, cello, and bass) are the most human, can express the most poignant feeling, and can continue playing indefinitely without fatigue. The woodwinds (flute, piccolo, oboe, clarinet, and bassoon) are the most decorative, and because they are so different in timbre they contribute the greatest variety to the ensemble. The brasses (trumpet, trombone, and tuba) contribute strength, vigor, and energy to the tonal complex. Special mention must be made of the French horns, softest and mellowest of the brasses, which play in the middle register and light the music from within like indirect lighting in a room. The percussion instruments (drums, cymbals, triangle, etc.) are most often used for special accent and to mark the climaxes.

**Style.** What was said about style in the fine arts (see p. 10) applies equally to musical style. Each composer has his personal idiom, which differentiates his work from that of others, and he also reflects the style of the period in which he lives.

## Elements of Literature

Literature results from the communication of thought and feeling through consciously organized language. Speech is the basis of the written language. It is speech which makes us superior to the other animals because through speech we pass on accumulated wisdom from one generation to another. But this was a slow process until men learned to write.

In spite of the fact that spoken language is shifting and perishable, much beautiful literature has been transmitted to us by the ancient bards. Such are the stories of Homer and the myths and legends of the Celts, the Saxons, and the Teutons. The purpose of these oral storytellers was not only to entertain but also to teach the ideals and aspirations common to the race.

In the broadest sense of the term *literature* we have all been speaking and writing it for most of our lives, perhaps not with any great skill. The eighteenth-century French dramatist Molière points this out humorously in his play *Le Bourgeois Gentil-homme*. The hero, Monsieur Jourdain, is surprised to find out that he has been talking prose all his life without knowing it. Monsieur Jourdain's prose, or ours, for that matter, aims at communication, but it is not deliberately couched in such artistic language that it has permanent literary worth, or that it will bring enjoyment to the hearer or reader, which is the primary aim of all literature.

Inspiration comes to the writer of great literature in three channels: through the senses, through the intellect, and through the emotions. These then are the elements of literature. But what he senses, understands, feels, must be communicated. The art of communication constitutes the writer's craft: meaning and connotation of words; grammar, syntax, and form; color and rhythm of language. No matter how skillful the writer is, he cannot be a great artist without keen sensory impressions, profound thoughts, and powerful emotions to convey. But these are not present in the same degree in all types of literature. Reason and thought predominate in prose, while emotion predominates in poetry. And since man tends to feel first and think afterward, it is natural that poetry should develop before prose.

**Elements of Poetry.** The poetic experience which the poet seeks to convey is too complex a subject for us at this point, but we will try to sketch certain guiding principles in judging poetry. First, words are not only informative but also evocative in that they call up the same response in us which inspired the poet. That is, they make us share his experience. Second, since poetry is the most concentrated form of writing, we must be willing to dig deeply if we would penetrate the depths the poet has sounded. Third, when we speak of poetic rhythm we mean not the conventional meters but the entire thought and emotional flow of the poem. It is as inadequate to say that the rhythm is iambic pentameter as to say that music is in two- or three-beat measure. The rhythm is not regular like the heartbeat, but has infinite variety, breaking like waves upon the shore. It is this rhythmic flow that gives organic power and vitality to truly great poetry. Fourth, in good poetry there must be a synthesis of content and design: that is, a balance between what is said and how it is said. Fifth, the poetic mind expresses itself in images or, as Aristotle called them, metaphors, which clarify his experience. In fact, it is the symbols and images the poet suggests which give us the excitement of a sudden revelation of truth. Wordsworth's "I wandered lonely as a cloud" is more revealing than just "I was lonely." My heart "dances with the daffodils" means infinitely more than "the daffodils made me happy." Physical, mental, and emotional meanings are fused in one complete whole, and the images react upon each other like colors in a painting. These principles of great poetry are the same in every age because human emotions are unchangeable.

Poetry is usually divided into epic, lyric, and dramatic categories.

*Epic Poetry.* When a nation or an ethnic group begins to become conscious of its identity and seeks to perpetuate its ideals through pride in a great hero of its past, epic poetry arises. The Hebrews found such a figure in Abraham, the Greeks in Ulysses, the French in Roland, the Germans in Siegfried, the Anglo-Saxons in Beowulf. Stories of these heroes, chanted by the bards, were probably passed down in oral tradition for hundreds of years before they were written in definitive form. The *Iliad* and the *Odyssey*, however, transcend all other epics in literary value and seem to bear the stamp of one great poetic genius. The *Iliad* is a double tragedy, as relentless as that of *King Lear*, in which pride in the form of self-will leads to the inexorable destruction of the protagonists and antagonists. The gods may be considered personifications of sin and folly and flaws in human nature which precipitate disaster. The *Odyssey*, on the other hand, is a comedy, fantastic and sparkling, but so true to human nature that we cannot help identifying ourselves with some of its hero's foibles.

*Lyric Poetry.* Wordsworth in his Preface to the Second Edition of his *Lyrical Ballads* (1800) said: "Poetry should be the spontaneous overflow of powerful feelings." These feelings "recollected in tranquility" are evoked in the reader, whose sensibility is freshened, renewed, and purified. This means that if we enter into the lyric poem with all our intellectual attention and our imagination we shall find therein some new intuition about man and his world. It does not mean that we have to analyze its form or put its meaning into other words (if it has meaning). Many lyric poems are so highly concentrated that it takes several readings to capture their "intuition." Let me illustrate by quoting a little spring poem for children by E. E. Cummings, called "in Just"—

*in Just*
*spring      when the world is mud-*
*luscious the little*
*lame balloonman*

*whistles      far      and wee*

*and eddieandbill come*
*running from marbles and*
*piracies and it's*
*spring*

*when the world is puddle-wonderful*

*the queer*
*old balloonman whistles*
*far      and      wee*
*and bettyandisbel come dancing*

*from hop-scotch and jump-rope and*

*it's*
*spring*
*and*
*      the*

*            goat-footed*

*balloonMan      whistles*
*far*
*and*
*wee* [1]

First, the disjointed, uneven lines express the way you felt when you tried to pant out your story when you were all out of breath from running. *Mud-luscious:* do you remember how it felt when the cool mud oozed up between your bare toes? Or how you loved to swish through puddles? *eddieandbill* and *bettyandisbel* are two sets of "boon companions," always together. The first time the balloonman whistles "far and wee" he is coming toward the children; the last time he has left them and gone far

---

[1] Copyright, 1923, 1951, by E. E. Cummings. Reprinted from his volume POEMS 1923–1954 by permission of Harcourt, Brace & World, Inc., and Faber and Faber Ltd.

down the street. The poet has captured some of the pristine delights of childhood, and has expressed them in language which gives us joy whether or not we have shared these experiences. If we are to make the "meaning" of the poem our own, we must apply not only understanding, but also memory, emotion, and imagination.

*Dramatic Poetry.* It is well to remember that drama, whether in prose or poetry, is intended not to be read but to be performed on stage. Although many great plays (those of Shaw and Ibsen, for example) have been written in prose, most students of literature would probably agree that the greatest masterpieces of drama, especially of tragedy (including those of the Greeks, Shakespeare, Racine, and Goethe) have been written in poetry. The "majesty of grief" seems to demand the lofty dignity of poetic language. The playwright's task is primarily to present people in action; hence his chief concern is usually with plot, and all speeches and episodes bear upon the development of the action. That the theater should have such a powerful attraction for audiences is due to the skill of the playwright and our natural interest in seeing how people react to live situations.

Since the playwright cannot appear to explain the story (although a narrator is sometimes employed in that capacity) the situation, motives, and personalities must be explained by the characters themselves, in their speech, actions, and facial expressions. The actors must also make clear the author's purpose or idea. We see before us real men and women engaged in working out their destinies through choices, discussions, and actions which lay bare the deepest motives of their minds and the most profound feelings of their hearts. We, the audience, are quick to discern any note which does not ring true to our understanding of life. Even internal action, that is, thoughts and emotions which may not be expressed in words, must be subtly derived from what we do see and hear.

The illusion of reality is so precarious that any untoward happening on stage may upset the illusion and spoil the play. We have all experienced this with amateur groups of actors. The audience, a heterogeneous assemblage of people for the most part strangers to each other, must be welded together by the action on stage, so that when the final curtain falls, they leave the theater with an unambiguous, memorable impression.

The state of affairs which exists at the beginning of a play, including necessary incidents which have already transpired, is made clear by what is known as the *exposition.* The action begins when something happens to disturb the status quo. For example, King Lear has reigned for many years at the opening of the play. It is only when he decides to retire, so to speak, and to divide his substance among his daughters that the real trouble begins. This begins what is known as the *complication,* in which the situation becomes more complex and suspenseful until the *climax* is reached. The climax is the emotional high point of the play in which all the issues become most acute and call most urgently for resolution. In *King Lear* it occurs in that stupendous storm scene of Act Three when amid the buffeting of the elements, the tongue-lashing of the Fool, and the pretended madness of Edgar, Lear begins to recover his reason. This may be the most dramatic scene in all literature. Then follows the *denouement* (meaning unraveling), in which the tangled threads of the plot are straightened out and order is restored. In most plays the denouement is short, but in *King Lear* it involves the battle, the arrest and imprisonment of the King, his last meeting with Cordelia, and finally his death.

There are certain *conventions* of the stage which an audience must be willing to accept, and we do so usually without thinking about it. For example, a man and woman engage in an intimate love scene, or two men in a secret conspiracy within sight and hearing of an audience of five hundred people. Some people do not like musical theater because they cannot accept its conventions. That a man should sing full voice after he has been stabbed, or a woman should hit high-C when she is dying of tuberculosis strains the limits of their credulity.

Other conventions have arisen out of practical necessity in certain periods of the drama. The Greek chorus was used to explain the situation or to warn of impending disaster. The *deus ex machina* was a person or object sent by divine intervention to resolve a tangled situation. Shakespeare's stage had no scenery or curtain; his scenes are therefore short and dead bodies must be removed by servants or soldiers. Our "Theater in the Round" has removed some conventions and imposed others; hence you will still find conventions today if you set out to look for them.

**Elements of the Novel.** The purpose of fiction, whether long (the novel) or short (the short story), is to recount a narrative which brings us pleasure. As in the drama, the substance of a story is usually its *plot,* which concerns human activity and the changes which occur from the beginning of the tale to the end. Not all of the descriptions, the dialogue, or even the incidents actually concern the plot. Some are included to help establish a mood or to make the characters more vivid. The author can step into the story with ideas of his own or other matter which is not absolutely necessary. You may recall how often Melville does this in *Moby Dick*. The long sections on the whaling industry are not essential to the plot, but they serve to postpone the action and increase our suspense. The plot often contains a conflict or struggle, and so anxious are we to learn the outcome that some of us turn to the last pages "to see how the story comes out." The old rules of unity, coherence, and emphasis are common-sense rules of good storytelling, and blessed is the author who quits when he has made his final meaning clear. The ending may be surprising or unusual (as in O. Henry), but it must be credible.

Since there cannot be action without human beings, besides plot we must have *characters*. A character is not only a person who acts, but one who displays the moral, emotional, and intellectual qualities with which the author has endowed him. As in real life, character is very complex, not just good and bad. But at least we should be able to say: "Yes, I understand why he acted or spoke that way." Many modern authors are concerned with so-called "fringe characters," people who break the moral code either deliberately or because they cannot help themselves, and our attitude toward them is determined either by sympathy or by aversion.

As in real life we enjoy colorful characters, but we demand that they be consistent. This does not mean that a character cannot change as a result of the circumstances through which he passes. Eugénie Grandet has been conditioned by her father to a life of such extreme frugality that even after he dies and she has plenty of money, she goes on in the same way because she knows no other life. Madame Bovary, on the other hand, in pursuit of pleasure, money, and thrills, goes straight down the path of moral disintegration which ends in suicide. Both are consistent characters.

Insomuch as a person's actions are conditioned not only by moral and emotional attitudes, but also by thought, many modern novelists stress the thought processes of their characters. It is difficult to overemphasize the influence of psychology and psychiatry on modern fiction. Henry James was one of the first to attempt to capture the "atmosphere of the mind" in his novels. Even as early as *Portrait of a Lady* (1881) James showed his profound understanding of the psychological motives which determine action. His last novels (*The Wings of the Dove, The Am-*

*bassadors*, and *The Golden Bowl*) are more difficult to read because they involve opaque symbols and metaphors, thus anticipating the exhaustive psychological analyses of Proust and Joyce.

The race problem has inspired a rash of modern novels. If their purpose is propaganda rather than imaginative creation, these novels usually do not stand up as good literature. However, Alan Paton's *Cry, the Beloved Country*, which concerns the separation of the races in South Africa, is a sensitive, sympathetic novel and deserves to be read as a great piece of literature.

The environment or *setting* of a novel involves not only geography but also the entire climate of beliefs, habits, and values of a particular region and historical period. Unless one understands the privileged position of an aristocratic Southern lady, one cannot appreciate the sequence of events in Conrad Richter's *The Lady*. An understanding of Puritan New England is indispensable for an appreciation of Hawthorne's *The Scarlet Letter*. A great city like New York or Chicago often plays the role of antagonist, an obstacle to the fulfillment of the hero's desires. In *Manhattan Transfer* by John Dos Passos, the city might be called the real protagonist, shaping both character and plot.

It is an interesting but not indispensable exercise to try to put the theme of a novel into words. By *theme* is usually meant a universal truth of which the story is a particular instance. There may be almost as many themes as readers, because every reader has his own idea of what is universally true. Theme does not mean moral. The moral of *Moby Dick* might be "Don't tangle with a whale." The theme might be "To concentrate on revenge is madness" or "Pride is man's greatest enemy" or "All life is an unrelenting struggle against evil." No matter what the theme means for you, the book is one of the greatest pieces of imaginative literature ever penned. It has unfailing power to delight thoughtful men everywhere.

Since World War II, the novel seems to have declined somewhat in popularity. This decline may be due to a craving for sensation which is satisfied more effortlessly watching television and movies than in reading a book. But we believe that at least part of the fault lies in the writers themselves. The majority of thinking people still believe in the eternal verities of right and wrong, of human dignity and purpose in life. When these values return to literature, novels will find readers. V. S. Pritchett, American literary essayist, quotes these words by the Russian writer Maxim Gorki: "The redeeming points which may and must save humanity are enlightenment, beauty, and sympathy." [1]

**Elements of the Short Story.** The short story as an art form developed in early nineteenth-century America when a considerable segment of the population began to read magazines. It is a highly concentrated short prose narrative which in a single incident or situation reveals a character and clarifies some truth about external nature or human nature. Granville Hicks says that a good short story is "an attempt to make the reader share in a unique moment of insight." [2] This moment continues to reverberate in the imagination of the reader. The good short-story writer never throws this truth at you. If you don't get it the first time you read the story, read it again—and again.

**Elements of the Essay.** Essayists write because they enjoy giving their opinions on a variety of subjects. What they write may be purely entertaining like James Ramsey Ullman's "Victory on Everest," provocative like Helen Keller's "Three Days to See," informative like Stewart Edward White's "On Making Camp," or didactic like Howard Pease's "Letter to a Fan." Incidentally, this last essay has some good suggestions on how to read a novel. Whatever the writer's purpose and whatever his subject, the essay should be clear and stimulating, and it should tell us something of the writer's personality. The inventor of the essay was a sixteenth-century Frenchman by the name of Montaigne, whom we shall meet later. According to publishers' statistics, essays seem just now to be more popular than novels. The magazine with probably the widest public today, the *Reader's Digest,* consists largely of essays.

**Other Languages and Translations.** Since you will read in translation many of the literary masterpieces discussed in this book, it seems necessary to say a few words about the difficulties and limitations of the translator. If you have some knowledge of the original language, by all means put your knowledge to work by reading portions in the original. The dual-language books are excellent if you can get them because you can read the original until the going gets rough, then look across the page at the English translation.

A translator's task is very difficult because each language has its own beauties and its own peculiarities of syntax, idiom, and

---

[1] V. S. Pritchett, *The Living Novel and Later Appreciations* (New York: Random House, 1964), p. 429.

[2] Granville Hicks, "The Art of the Short Story," *Saturday Review,* April 13, 1963.

expression which cannot be translated literally into another language. This is especially true of poetry. The translator may keep the literal meaning as close as he can and ignore the poetic beauties, or he may make a poetic translation which is often far from literal. Most translators try to compromise, sometimes with superior results.

Like English, the European languages are continually changing. After the revolutions of 1830 and 1848, the European workingman had a right to express his opinions. He did so in slang and in vulgar expressions which, although not acceptable in polite society, are found in some modern literature. The French Academy has only recently accepted the words *chic* and *épatant* as good French. But even one who has had long familiarity with German and French cannot understand the jargon spoken by young people on the streets of Berlin and Paris.

The difficulties are not all on our side of the language barrier. English gives foreigners trouble too. The Romance languages, for instance, have no way of distinguishing between *house* and *home* or between *sky* and *heaven,* and so people accustomed to French or Italian may find the English distinctions puzzling.

In general, languages, like German, which have an abundance of consonants and consonant clusters are less aesthetic in sound than Italian, Spanish, and French, which have an abundance of pure vowels. This is because vowels are easier on the vocal apparatus both in speaking and in singing. Intonation, pitch, and relative speed also affect quality of sound. Modern French, like the classical languages, has quantity (duration of sound) but not accent. Hence we will look in vain for our four poetic meters in French poetry, which still uses predominantly the twelve-syllable Alexandrine line. The inflexible rules for word order which make German prose difficult fortunately do not apply to German poetry. The same figures of speech we use are found in all European languages. Standards of unity, coherence, and emphasis are also universal.

### Judging a Work of Art

Students often ask: "What makes any work of art great?" This is a legitimate question, but the answer is not easy. It involves the whole science of aesthetics, a discipline which has engaged great minds down through the centuries. The simplest answer is to say that it is art which has stood the test of time and still remains meaningful. While it is true that much that was created in the past has been tried in the balance, found wanting, and discarded, leaving only the best of past ages, this answer does not help in assessing modern works. Here are certain over-all criteria you can apply.

**Sincerity.** Are the artist's intentions perfectly honest, or is he striving for effect either by sentimentality (affected emotion) or sensation (excited feeling)? Subjects like human love and motherhood are fraught with danger. There can be sentiment without sentimentality. Murillo's paintings of the "Virgin and Child" are slightly sentimental; those of Raphael never are. Madame LeBrun's portrait of herself and her daughter is sentimental in pose while Chardin's "The Blessing" and Daumier's "The Laundress" accomplish the same purpose without sentimentality. Rodin's "The Kiss" is a well-integrated piece of sculpture, but it is sentimental. Chagall is in such ecstasy of love for his wife that he soars into the air when he presents his "Birthday Gift." We get the point without his being sentimental. Bernini's "Ecstasy of Saint Theresa" is sensational; Michelangelo's "Pietà" is not.

**Universality.** Does the work of art have only momentary value, or does it embody universal truths which are permanent? Rubens' "Garden of Venus" and Debussy's "Afternoon of a Faun" have great charm, but nothing which lifts them beyond the appeal of the moment. On the other hand, Millet's painting "Man with the Hoe," and Edwin Markham's poem of the same name speak for the downtrodden toiler of every age, and Delacroix' painting of "Liberty Leading the People" is not just a scene from the French Revolution; it speaks of man's universal yearning for freedom. Always look for the universal truth hidden in the particular work.

Be alert also for violations of fundamental truth. W. H. Auden's poem "Musée des Beaux Arts" and Brueghel's painting "The Fall of Icarus," on which it is based, say that people are unconcerned with the sufferings of others. This may seem true when we read of injured people lying on the street unattended because the passers-by are afraid of involvement. We remember Jesus' parable of the two who "passed by on the other side," while the third, the Good Samaritan, stopped to assist the victim. Most of us are so self-engrossed that we do not always see opportunities to help others, but we are not callous, and the fact remains that there are probably more Good Samaritans in the world today than ever before. We often read newspaper and magazine stories of individuals who endanger their own lives to save others and who give generously to victims of wars and disasters. Hemingway's short story "The Killers" is the story of a Good Samaritan. William Blake's "Little Black Boy" is a charming poem, but its sentimentality does not quite ring true. In the last line the black boy says that when he and the white boy reach heaven, [I shall] *"be like him,* and he will then love me." Is white a better color than black?

**Magnitude.** There are a few masterpieces which transcend all others in scope and monumentality. Don't think that you must plumb their depths at your first contact. Scholars have spent a lifetime studying Dante's *Divine Comedy,* Goethe's *Faust,* Michelangelo's frescoes in the Sistine Chapel, Bach's *Saint Matthew Passion.* Get what you can and return to them later, for they are well worth the effort.

**Craftsmanship.** Does the artist understand his craft and is his workmanship sound? Has he gone beyond the limits of taste? These questions arise chiefly in judging modern works. Of course, good taste and poor taste are as difficult to define as is a work of art. We have to rely on a consensus of opinion among thinking people. Most would probably agree that a side of raw beef dripping with blood and hanging on a nail is a poor subject for a painting, and that pages and pages of profanity make poor reading matter. We are living in a very prolific period, prolific because there is a very wide interest in and demand for the arts. It is impossible to foresee what direction our civilization will take; therefore, it is impossible to know what art is significant for the future and what is ephemeral. All we can do is to try to understand what is going on, see how it reflects our period, and reserve our final judgment on its worth.

# Chapter 3 / The Greeks

As we consider the diversity and complexity of the modern world, it is only natural to ask: "Where did it all begin?" To answer that question, we must go back to a small town on the western edge of the settled world about five hundred years before the birth of Christ—Athens. It was the Athenians who for the first time in history discovered how to achieve happiness by using their minds. Their time of glory was brief, only a couple of hundred years, but what they accomplished has had more influence on Western civilization than the achievement of any group of people before or since.

Their story must be pieced together from broken fragments. Indeed, it is a miracle that anything has survived, because Athens lies in a major earthquake zone. Greek sculpture has been painstakingly put together from broken pieces, or else we know it from a Roman copy. Yet enough of the buildings remains to give an idea of the perfection of proportion. There were portrait and landscape painters, but not one painting has survived except for the designs on vases and jars. Aeschylus wrote ninety tragedies of which only seven are extant. Works of the other two tragedians, Sophocles and Euripides, survive in similarly small proportions; comedy fares a little better. There are about a dozen extant examples of Greek music, some fragmentary.

## Historical Background

The Golden Age did not spring into being overnight, as in mythology, Athena sprang fully armed from the forehead of Zeus. Great art never matures and comes to full fruition quickly. About four hundred years before the Golden Age, Homer wrote the greatest epics ever penned and showed that he already was aware of the difference between tragedy and comedy. Sappho was a celebrated lyrical poetess of the sixth century B.C. Here is her "Noonday Rest," almost as concentrated as a Japanese *haiku*.

*The Lullaby of waters cool*
*Through apple boughs is softly blown,*

*And, shaken from the rippling leaves,*
*Sleep dropeth down.*[1]

That is a small lyric gem: simple language, perfect form, exquisite melody, profound feeling for beauty.

Since the Greeks believed in a sound mind in a sound body, they cultivated their play as systematically as their wars or their politics. They invented all kinds of games and trials of skill in music and poetry as well as in wrestling and running. For over a thousand years, from 776 B.C. to A.D. 393, athletic contests of every description were held at Olympia in connection with religious festivals. They became known as the Olympic games. If two city-states happened to be fighting a war, a truce was declared and weapons were laid aside so that everyone could attend the games and watch the "glorious-limbed youth," as Pindar called them. Some of the Olympic victors were celebrated in statues like "The Discus Thrower," "The Charioteer," "The Wrestling Boys," and "The Dancing Flute Players." They were awarded laurel wreaths and honor equal to that of the bravest warrior. The cold and austere poet Pindar (whose poetry is difficult to read and more difficult to translate) to celebrate these heroes composed "Victory Odes," in which instead of praising the technique and strategy of the winner, he praises the boy's parents and hopes that in the future he will bring honor to Greece. When the games were discontinued the spirit of competitive play died out in the world until almost modern times. The Olympic games were revived on an international level in 1896 and have continued since every four years, except during the World Wars.

Since such high-spirited people could not exist under the heel of a tyrant, the Athenians invented the idea of freedom in a democratic society. To be sure, the large slave population had no part in their democracy, but they must not be judged too severely on this account. It was many hundreds of years before morality reached the point where slavery could not be tolerated. Has the whole world reached that point even today?

For most Greeks, a daily trip to some temple to offer sacrifice to a god was common practice, but they didn't take it very seriously. They never went to a priest for advice or guidance, although they did consult an oracle or soothsayer to know whether the time was propitious for an important project. The fact that

---

[1] C. D. Warner, ed., *Library of the World's Best Literature,* Vol. XXXII (New York: J. A. Hill Company, 1902).

Socrates took no part in religious practices was one reason why he incurred enemies. The words said to have been inscribed in the shrine at Delphi were "Know thyself" and "Nothing in excess."

In fact, the Greeks were intellectuals with a passion for using their minds. Our word *school* comes from the Greek word for *leisure*. They thought that if a man had leisure he would use it in thinking and finding out about the world. They called their healers *physicians*, which meant those versed in the ways of nature. Our scientific method is founded on this concept. "Man the measure of all things" became the Athenian motto.

Both the state and religion as a rule left the Athenian free to think and say what he pleased. Socrates was probably the only man in Athens to suffer death for his opinions. Ideas were even more important to young people than their beloved games. There is a story of how they stopped practicing and crowded around Socrates to ask questions whenever he appeared in their gymnasium.

Although intellectuals, the Greeks were not effeminate but hard fighters. In the lengthy wars with the Persians, they succeeded in defeating the Persian forces under Cyrus the Great, Darius I, and Xerxes. The first great Greek victory was the Battle of Marathon in 490 B.C. The Greeks lost the Battle of Thermopylae, supposedly because of a traitor in the Spartan army, which was defending the pass. However, the Greeks won the ensuing naval battle in the Bay of Salamis. A young Athenian soldier on one of the ships later dramatized in a famous Greek tragedy the scene he witnessed that day. He was Aeschylus and his play, called *The Persians,* is the only Greek tragedy based on a contemporary event.

## Archaic Art

Since the Greeks believed in "man the measure of all things," it was logical that their artists should be primarily concerned with the representation of the human figure. They started where the Egyptians left off. If you have seen reliefs on Egyptian tombs, you will remember that they depict the human form in the easiest and most characteristic pose. The head is always seen in profile, the torso strictly frontal, and the feet again in profile. The Egyptians did not experiment; they depicted people in this way because people had always been shown in this way.

But in Athens, from the eighth to the sixth century and extending into the early fifth century B.C., the so-called Archaic period, occurred the most astonishing revolution in the whole history of art. Artists began to use their eyes and to take nature as a model. They studied the anatomy of bones and muscles and what effect these would have on representation; they discovered that every part of the body does not have to be shown, that a foot or hand is often concealed behind the torso; they also discovered foreshortening. It is difficult to imagine how radical was the first artist to show the foot in frontal position by five little circles for the ends of the toes. It would no doubt be easier to trace this progress if Greek paintings had survived, but you can see the results in the vase paintings of this period.

The free-standing figures of the Archaic period are usually young athletic males (*kouroi*), such as were winners in athletic games, and young women (*kore*, plural *korai*), fully clothed with long crimped locks of hair and with the corners of the mouth turned up in a stereotyped smile so that they would look more "lifelike." Very recently, a beautiful bronze kouros was dug up in the harbor of Piraeus where he had lain for two thousand years after the Roman ship which was taking him away sank in the harbor.

**Polyclitus.** Because the Athenians were great mathematicians, they worked out the ideal mathematical proportions for the various parts of the body: that the height of a man should be seven times the height of the head, and so on. Polyclitus in the early fifth century B.C. demonstrated this mathematical canon in a sort of pattern figure called the "Doryphoros" or "Spear-Bearer." Notice that the weight, which rests on the right leg, shows these muscles more taut than those in the left leg, which are relaxed. Similarly, the right arm is relaxed while the left grasps the spear. The contour of the skull is revealed by the close-cropped ringlets of hair. The upper eyelids overlap the lower at the outer edges; the left leg is foreshortened. The figure is perfectly poised. All these things are the result of close observation of nature. Polyclitus wrote a book called *The Canon* which sets forth the mathematical proportions of the body.

**Myron.** At about the same time (460 B.C.), the sculptor Myron was working out the canon of movement. This was easier to depict in relief sculpture because the forms were attached to the background. For figures in the round, bronze, which is stronger and lighter than marble, was better adapted to show movement. Examine the bronze figure of Zeus (or Poseidon) found at Artemision. It shows the legs and arms extended in position to hurl a spear. Marble would be too brittle to use for such a figure. Notice in Myron's bronze "Discobolos" ("Discus Thrower") how convincingly he has shown the bones of the rib cage and the muscles of the left leg, while representing the face in perfect repose. When the Romans copied this figure in marble, they added a heavy block of marble behind the figure to support it. The sculptors of the Golden Age had all this knowledge behind them when they began to decorate the temples of the Acropolis.

**The Temple.** The Greek temple was also developed in the Archaic period. It was in the form of a small rectangular wooden box covered with a flat roof. The temple contained the statue of the god or goddess to whom it was dedicated and usually a small altar with a priest in charge. The worshipers remained outside.

When this structure was translated into stone, the Greeks conceived the idea of masking the monotony of blank walls with an open porch all the way around, supported on columns. By applying mathematics to the alternating solids and spaces, that is, the relative dimensions of height, width, and thickness of columns, they achieved the rhythm and harmony of their architecture. By the fifth century B.C., architects were using a low, gabled roof which left at either end of the temple a triangular pediment suited to sculptural decoration.

The three basic orders of columns, differing not only in the decoration of the capitals, but also in their relative height and thickness, correspond rather closely to the ideals of the fifth, fourth, and third centuries B.C.

The *Doric order* is plain, short, and thick. It expresses strength and nobility. Since the Greeks knew nothing about vaulting, there are no arches. The columns therefore had to be placed rather close together to support the entire weight of the stone entablature as well as the slight thrust of the gabled roof. The fluted triglyphs in the entablature are the remains of the ends of the old wooden roof joists. The spaces between them, called *metopes*, offer another opportunity for sculptural figures.

The *Ionic order* is more slender and graceful, with its capital imitating the softness of a cushion. It represents the naturalness and tender sentiment of the fourth century B.C. At the same time it is less self-assured; the disastrous outcome of the Peloponnesian War had robbed the Athenians of their confidence. Since it was no longer necessary to indicate the ends of the roof joists, a continuous frieze of sculptured figures takes the place of triglyph and metope.

The *Corinthian order* is the highest, most slender, and most decorative of the three. It uses Oriental decorative elements like the acanthus leaves at the top of the column. Such elements are purely decorative and have no relationship to structural necessity whatsoever. They came into Athens as a result of Alexander's conquests. This order, then, displays the exaggerated sentiment and emotional extravagance of the Hellenistic period.

## Sculpture and Architecture of the Golden Age

Greece was divided into many small, autonomous city-states, each self-contained, self-supporting, and proudly self-sufficient. Although from time to time they combined against a common enemy such as Persia, they never established a permanent confederation. Sparta and Athens especially were diametrically opposed in their way of life and their dominant interests. The Spartans cultivated discipline in order to produce fighters; the Athenians cultivated intelligence in order to produce thinkers.

The Persian Wars ended in 479 B.C. The Athenians were jubilant: the gods had brought them victory and a testimonial of gratitude was due. Pericles entered public life in 470 B.C., and by his oratorical power and statesmanship began to build toward Athenian supremacy. His decisive move was the transfer of the spoils of war and the taxes obtained from the Naval Federation from the shrine of Delos to the Acropolis in Athens. The League was a league no longer, but an Athenian Empire nakedly revealed. These were the circumstances which produced the Golden Age of Greece. Within fifty years were built all the architectural splendors which have made Athens the art capital of the world.

Since the Athenians were intellectuals, we must approach their art intellectually; there are no trivia to capture the emotions. The finest of the buildings were those on the Acropolis, a hill formerly used as a fortress. Some sixty marble steps led to a covered entrance hall, the Propylaea, consisting of noble colonnades and porticoes. Beyond these, the visitor emerged on the level top of the hill and was at once surrounded by statues and temples. Directly ahead was the colossal bronze statue of Athena the Defender whose spear tip, glittering in the sun, guided the mariner far out at sea. To the right was the small temple of the Athena Nike (built c. 421 B.C., restored 1935–1940) and beyond rose the two largest buildings, the Parthenon and the Erechtheum. All the buildings and statues were of white Pantelic marble, put together without mortar. However, the polychroming of statues in the triangular pediments, the friezes, and the metopes tended to alleviate the whiteness of the marble.

Now that you have your bearings on the Acropolis, let us examine the Parthenon, said to be the most nearly perfect building in the world. It is of no great size, only about one hundred feet by two hundred fifty feet, the Doric columns supporting the low pediment about thirty-four feet in height. The chief architect, Iktinus, was wise enough not to make the building mathematically exact. There is a very slight parabolic curve in the columns which gives the impression that they are yielding a little under the weight they support. The entablatures and stylobates are not exactly level, but curve upward in the middle. Again, the columns are not exactly the same distance apart, and they are tilted slightly backward. One cannot detect with the naked eye these deviations from mathematical exactness. In fact, the allowances compensate for the beholder's imperfect vision. One only feels that the temple has elasticity and a buoyancy which might give it wings to take off into the air. Young architectural students go there with measuring lines and levels to measure and argue about it.

Phidias, as chief sculptor, at least designed and supervised all the figures of the Parthenon, which are the highest expression of the Greek spirit. The gods are conceived as heroic men and women, impersonal and supermundane. Gravity and grace combine in a perfection of harmony which no artist has ever surpassed. This is what the artists of the Renaissance and again of the eighteenth century meant by "returning to the classic ideal." But they could only approximate it.

SCHOOL OF PHIDAIS: *Athena Lemnia*. Bologna, Museo Civico (Alinari—Art Reference Bureau)

The eastern pediment represents the birth of Athena. It contains the figure of Mount Olympus, the three Fates on one side of the central figure; Persephone, Demeter, and Artemis on the other side. Perfect balance and rhythmic flow lead the eye up to the central figure. The western pediment represents the dispute between Athena and Poseidon for the sponsorship of the city. The frieze which goes all the way around at the top of the wall under the colonnade represents in low relief the Panathenaic procession held every four years in honor of the goddess. It contains three hundred and fifty human figures and two hundred horses and sacrificial animals all interrelated and integrated into a sweeping rhythmic pattern. The ninety-two metopes depict mythological incidents.

No original sculpture by Phidias exists, but there is in Bologna, Italy, a marble head copied from a bronze statue by Phidias called the "Athena Lemnia." The original bronze stood on the Acropolis. If you study this head, you can better visualize the missing heads on the pediment figures. The "Athena Lemnia" (see p. 31) illustrates perfectly the fifth-century ideal of beauty. The face is not cold or austere, but rather reserved and impersonal. The cheeks are soft and delicately modeled, the nose straight and well proportioned, the chin firm, the lips full and sensual. But she holds herself aloof from the passing throng.

It remains to speak of the interior of the Parthenon. A large part of it was walled in and contained the state treasury. In Aristophanes' comedy *Lysistrata*, the women barricade the Acropolis to keep the men from access to this treasury. The near end of the temple was the private apartment or boudoir of Athena. It contained an enormous statue of the goddess done by Phidias himself in gold and ivory. No trace of it remains.

The Parthenon probably existed more or less intact until 1687 when it exploded while the Turks were using it as a powder magazine. In 1801, Lord Elgin, a British diplomat, obtained permission from the Turkish government (then in control of Greece) to gather up all the broken pieces of the sculptures and take them to England to be put together. Later, England paid for them. The "Elgin Marbles" are now in the British Museum.

## The Fourth-Century Ideal of Beauty

Toward the end of the fifth century B.C., artists had become fully aware of their mastery and ordinary people had become more art-conscious. They demanded less of the ideal and impersonal, and more of the natural and graceful.

**Praxiteles.** Praxiteles, pupil of Phidias, was now the chief sculptor. We know that the statue of Hermes holding the infant Dionysus was done by him (see p. 33). Notice that the figure of Hermes is not erect, but assumes a graceful *S* curve (hereafter always known as the curve of Praxiteles). Note also the suggestion of a teasing smile on Hermes' face. Scholars believe he once held a bunch of grapes just beyond the baby's reach. There is still no violent emotion expressed, but Hermes is certainly less like a god and more like a human father. Praxiteles was the first sculptor who dared to portray the feminine body nude. To him or his school is attributed the "Venus dei Medici," now in the Uffizi in Florence. All the later Aphrodites derive from him, including the "Venus de Milo," as does also the "Apollo Belvedere," now in the Vatican. It is a Roman copy of the "Venus de Milo" which is in the Louvre.

**The Erechtheum.** In the fourth century B.C. were built on the Acropolis the Erechtheum Temple with its porch held up on the heads of the caryatids and also the small temple to Athena Nike. On the balustrade of this little temple is the graceful figure of Nike untying her sandal. The Erechtheum (begun in 421 B.C.) is considered the finest extant example of the Ionic order. It has an irregular plan because it is really three small temples in one. It was dedicated to Erechtheus, a mythological king who supposedly invented the four-wheel chariot, and also dedicated to Poseidon and Athena. Some scholars say that it was never completed because it would have encroached on the territory of another god. The temple contained an old and ugly wooden statue of Athena which Pericles

PRAXITELES: *Hermes with Infant Dionysus.* Museum, Olympia, Greece. (Alinari—Art Reference Bureau)

wanted to move elsewhere, but the Athenians would not hear of it.

**Lysippus.** You may have noticed that so far the Greek artists seem to have avoided strong feeling. Near the end of the fourth century B.C. came the sculptor Lysippus, whose faces not only look more animated but also express personality. His head of Alexander the Great might be called a modern portrait. Of course we have no photograph of Alexander, but we can say that the restless conqueror of Asia, somewhat overconfident of his role in world history, may well have looked like this.

## Greek Music

Two subjects required of every Greek schoolboy were mathematics and music. The word *music* had two meanings. First was the mathematics of music: the laws governing vibrations of tones and their application in the seven scales used in Greek music. We commonly use only two scales, major and minor, but the Greeks formed a new scale or tonal system on every degree of our diatonic scale. While this sounds complicated, in reality it was not, because the Greek scales did not serve as foundations for harmony as ours do, but merely determined the upper and lower limits of the melody. The Greeks had no harmony in the modern sense. When they used the word *harmony* they meant *melody,* and when they wanted to express the idea of two tones heard simultaneously, they used the word *symphony*. They considered the octave and the fifth and fourth degrees of the scale consonances, the third and sixth dissonances. These concepts, taken over by medieval musical theorists, influenced the development of polyphony for hundreds of years.

The other meaning of *music* was music and poetry. While music may have existed without poetry, poetry did not exist without music. Word and tone, poem and melody, were created simultaneously. The melody supported and vivified the poetic text through close union with the melodic and rhythmic nuances of the language. Our basic two-, three-, and four-beat measure came from the iambic, trochaic, anapaestic, and dactylic meters of Greek poetry.

As a rule, Greek singing was accompanied by an instrument. The seven-stringed lyre, because of its restrained tone, accompanied lyric poetry and was the instrument of the pure Apollonian cult whose seat was at Delos, later Delphi. According to myth, Apollo himself was supposed to have played the lyre. The larger and more sonorous cithara was preferred by professional players. The shrill and penetrating aulos, sounding something like a double oboe, seemed, to the Greeks at least, more stirring and passionate. Hence it was the instrument of the cult of Dionysus, god of wine and fertility. His festival in early spring was the occasion when the competitive tragedies and comedies were given. The theater of Dionysus is located on the southern slope of the Acropolis. It does not seem very large, but at one time it was said to seat eighteen thousand people.

The highest form of choric poetry was the *dithyramb*, consisting of *strophe* (turn), *antistrophe* (counter turn), and *epode* (aftersong). As the chorus of only twelve singers chanted the words, they executed slow, rhythmic steps, bringing out the

Greek Chorus in Performance of Euripides' *Medea*. Chorus Appeals to the Gods to Divert the Tragedy. Edith Wynn Matheson and Charles Rann Kennedy School of Drama, Millbrook, N.Y., *c.* 1922.

meaning of the words by gestures and attitudes. Greek tragedy grew out of the dithyramb. The form of the dithyramb might be designated by the letters A A B. This form is found in many medieval folk songs, and was a favorite with the Meistersinger and minnesingers of Germany. This is one indication of how Greek ideas found their way into Western art.

In drama, Sophocles did not make extensive use of the chorus because he was not a musician; his main interest was in the plot, but Aeschylus was primarily a musician. If you read his *Agamemnon* you will see that most of it is sung. The idea is that when man is so deeply stirred by emotion that he becomes inarticulate, then music takes over to express his passion. The simplest function of the chorus was to separate the episodes. But choruses in Greek drama do much more. They may warn the main characters of impending disaster, express the comments of the audience on the action, remind the actors of what has already happened, or reinforce the tragic situation. Every Greek citizen was supposed to be able to take his part in the chorus.

The Greek doctrine of the *ethos* was also important. According to this doctrine, held by Plato, Aristotle, and the other Greek philosophers, certain tonal successions were capable of calling forth definite emotions. The Dorian scale, for instance, was believed to evoke poise, temperance, and simplicity. In Plato's system music is the most important of the arts because it is part of the harmony of the cosmos. Hence, music was thought to have an ethical value, especially in the training of youth. Modern science has rediscovered the therapeutic value of music, and industry is now using music to calm nerves and speed production.

Not one Greek dithyramb has survived. You may hear two pieces of genuine Greek music. The older is the "Epitaph of Seikelos," found engraved on a *stele* (tombstone) in Tralles, Asia Minor, and dating from the first century A.D. The second is a "Hymn to Apollo" by Mesomedes of Crete, dating from the second century A.D.

## Greek Literature

The lyrical poetess Sappho, who lived on the island of Lesbos, and Pindar, author of the Victory Odes, have already been mentioned (see pp. 25–26). There were also orators and historians who do not particularly concern us in our survey of the arts. The greatest Greek literary legacy consists of the dramas of four men: Aeschylus, Sophocles, Euripides, and Aristophanes. Probably their best dramas have been preserved, and they are still very much alive today because they are based on flaws in human character which are the same in every generation. The plays are frequently given today, sometimes in their original form and sometimes modernized. The same stories occur again and again in different forms. The audience knew the stories by heart, and so their concern was for the artistic value of the poetry and the presentation. This situation was quite different from that which prevails among theater audiences today.

In the spring of the year occurred the great festival in honor of Dionysus, god of fertility and wine. A great procession occupied the first day; the competition between ten dithyrambic choruses occurred on the second day; on the third, five comic poets each produced a play. The last three days were given over to three tragic poets, previously selected, each of whom presented four plays: a trilogy of three tragedies usually on the same general theme, and a mock-heroic "satyr play" as a relief. The name of the winning tragedian, the titles of his plays, and the names of the protagonists were carved on stone.

Normally in the fifth century B.C., there were three actors in a tragedy (although each might take more than one part) and fifteen singers in the chorus. The Theater of Dionysus, where the competitions were held, was on the southern slope of the

Acropolis and was uncovered. Since it would have been impossible for an audience of eighteen thousand to see changes in facial expression, the actors, all men, wore masks which served somewhat as a megaphone does in voice projection. Very simple painted panels, probably first used by Sophocles, were the only scenery. If a god intervened miraculously in the course of the play, he was lowered by a crane on the roof above the proscenium. This was called "the god of the machine," later in Latin, *deus ex machina.* The audience probably became as excited as we are at a football game, but even the most avid of modern fans would hardly relish four football games in one day.

**Aeschylus.** Aeschylus (*c.* 525–456 B.C.) was a musician and a fighter. He probably took part in the Battle of Salamis which closed the Persian Wars. Hence he was living and writing at the time of Athens' greatest exaltation, which is mirrored in his mind and spirit. He threw off the shackles of the old choral dithyramb, added another actor, and reduced the chorus to fifteen. He wrote some ninety plays of which seven tragedies remain. The one called *The Persians,* as noted previously, is the only extant Greek tragedy based on a contemporary event.

Aeschylus' affirmation of the will to live in the face of death is the underlying theme of his plays. He presents suffering and death in such a way that it exalts rather than depresses us. Great spirits face suffering not with passive resignation but with exaltation. This is the essence of tragedy. Antigone, about to defy her uncle, an act which she knows means death, cries "Courage! The power will be mine and the means to act." Clytemnestra, having killed her husband, flings wide the palace doors and proclaims her deed. Prometheus, chained to the rock for disobedience to Zeus, is still unconquered. When the herald advises him to submit, he says: "Seek to persuade the sea wave not to break. You will persuade me no more easily."

From the pen of Aeschylus we have the Agamemnon trilogy complete. In *Agamemnon,* when Agamemnon returns after the Trojan War, his wife and her lover put him to death. In *The Libation Bearers,* Agamemnon's daughter Electra and her brother Orestes slay their mother Clytemnestra and her lover. In *The Eumenides* Orestes is delivered from the avenging Furies and reconciled to his homeland through the mercy of the goddess Athena. The Greeks were inclined to believe that the gods were jealous of man's happiness and prosperity. Aeschylus tosses the gods to one side and gropes toward monotheism. Then he faces the old problem: How can a just God allow the innocent to suffer? He solves the problem by saying that it is the curse of sin which brings suffering, and God is not responsible, but man gains wisdom through pain and error. If you read the Oresteia trilogy you will see how these ideas are worked out.

**Sophocles.** Sophocles (*c.* 496–406 B.C.) at fifteen was a singer and leader of the chorus. He wrote 123 plays, of which seven remain. In the two decades which had elapsed between the writing of Aeschylus and of Sophocles, the spirit of Athens had changed completely. She had grown powerful, imperial, and tyrannical. Before Sophocles died Sparta was at her gates. With that sixth sense which great poets always possess, he knew what was coming but was powerless to prevent it. His melancholy led him to turn to his own inner spirit where he felt free and honorable. He had the warmth of human sympathy and a sure sense of what made good theater. Many people enjoy his plays best of the Greek dramas. This is why we have chosen *Oedipus Tyrannus* for special study. But first a careful reading of Aristotle's *Poetics* is a good preparation for an analysis of this play.

*Aristotle's Definition of Tragedy.* If you compare the dates of the three great tragedians and the dates of Aristotle (384–322 B.C.), you will see that theory followed practice; it did not precede it. The laws of good tragedy were worked out by trial and error for some one hundred years before Aristotle came along and summarized them.

Aristotle said that a tragedy is an imitation of an action (life situation) which is serious, complete, and of considerable magnitude, and it is couched in poetic language. It should be dramatic, not narrative, with incidents arousing pity and fear, "wherewith to accomplish a catharsis of such emotions." It should be long enough to show a character passing gradually from happiness to misery. It should represent one complete action with the incidents so closely integrated that nothing can be deleted without destroying the unity of the whole.

In Aristotle's view, the incidents which arouse pity and fear are best when they occur unexpectedly, but in consequence of one another. A good plot involves *peripety* (reversal), which is a change from one state of affairs to its opposite, and *discovery*, a change from ignorance to knowledge. Pity is aroused by undeserved suffering, and we fear lest the same misfortune happen to us. The change from happiness to misery should be in consequence of some great error which causes the character to commit the tragic deed. The effect of the tragedy should be to purify the emotions of the observer. These are his main ideas.

Aristotle does not mention unity of place, but this third unity can be assumed. Since there was no change of scenery in a

Greek play, all the action had to take place in one spot. Anything which happened elsewhere (for instance, Jocasta's suicide) was told by another character. These three unities, time, place, and action, became a kind of dogma for future dramatists, especially in eighteenth-century France.

It will be helpful to remember these Greek words: *nemesis*— just punishment for wrongdoing; *hubris*—pride, the tragic flaw; *catharsis*—a purging of the emotions; *aulos*—double-reed instrument; *lyre, cithara*—harp; *tragic irony*—statement or situation that means to the character something in contrast to what is discovered to be true; *Oedipus*—swollen foot; *logos*—word.

*Oedipus Tyrannus.* There is no English equivalent for the Greek word *Tyrannus*. It is usually translated *king* or *rex*. Oedipus was king, surely, because he was the son of King Laius, but the word means more than that. *Tyrant* is inaccurate because he did not attain power ruthlessly. *Tyrannus* means the man who had overcome all obstacles by his own intelligence and was master of his own destiny. It was what the Greeks meant by "man the measure of all things," which was implied in Oedipus' answer to the riddle of the Sphinx. It is similar to what wᵉ mean by a self-made man.

The entire action of the play is built on reversal. Oedipus changes from the liberator of men to the most accursed of men. This reversal represents the movement of the play. His first question "Who killed Laius?" turns into "Who am I?" His intelligence spurs on the search even while he himself is the object of the search. This is an example of *tragic irony*, and there are many other instances of it in the play. When Oedipus curses the murderer of Laius, he is really cursing himself. Jocasta hopes the oracles were wrong, but could they possibly be wrong when the play itself was part of a religious observance? Hence the validity of the performance itself depends on the denouement of the play. Analyze the entire play in the light of Aristotle's requirements for tragedy. At the end the *Tyrannus* is completely overthrown. You may say that this fate is not deserved. But Oedipus is not completely innocent; his tragic flaw is pride.

Oedipus has thought that he possessed knowledge, certainty, but he does not. Because he is human, man never does. In Sophocles' next play, *Oedipus at Colonus*, Oedipus gradually comes to learn this limitation; then he becomes godlike.

The play deals with fundamental problems that have concerned men throughout the ages. Who am I? Am I responsible for a wrong which I have committed unwittingly? Can suffering for wrong be avoided? Is there any hope for one who has committed a great wrong? How can I love my enemies? These are the questions which give the play its universality and the stamp of greatness.

**Euripides.** Euripides (*c.* 485–407 B.C.) was the last of the great Greek tragedians and the most modern. He was poet of the world's grief, but not necessarily the most tragic. He knew pain better than exaltation; he was attuned to the suffering of an individual because he realized that individual's inherent worth. His spirit was critical, subversive, destructive—the same spirit we find in T. S. Eliot, but Eliot does not seem to have the pity of Euripides for those who suffer. Euripides, writing during the Peloponnesian War, had first-hand knowledge of distress. His purpose was to show in his plays the hideousness of cruelty and passion, and the piteousness of suffering, thereby to move men to compassion. The heroines of both *Electra* and *Medea* are driven by a passion for revenge: directed in Electra against her mother, in Medea against her husband. This lust for revenge becomes their sole reason for existence, and makes them inhuman. We shall take up Euripides' *Hippolytus* in the chapter on the eighteenth century (see p. 194) in order to compare it with Racine's *Phèdre*.

**Aristophanes.** Perhaps as an antidote for tragedy, the Greeks enjoyed their comedy, which is mad, rollicking, full of vitality and energy, often bawdy. It is not the pie-throwing variety, however, but usually satire directed at some phase of their life, or against some person whom everyone knew. Edith Hamilton likened it to Gilbert and Sullivan operettas.

The master of Greek comedy was Aristophanes (*c.* 450–385 B.C.), who wrote some forty comedies of which we have eleven. In these plays there were three actors and a chorus of twenty-four singers which divided the action by song and dance. Halfway through the performance the chorus delivered the opinions of the author on subjects often not connected with the play. Some modern producers think it necessary to expurgate the four-letter words, but the Greeks were in the habit of calling a spade a spade, and most of the audience consisted of men.

*The Wasps* is a satire on the Athenian love of law courts. The defendant is a dog accused of stealing cheese. *The Birds* criticizes Athens by comparing it with the Utopia built by the birds in the clouds. *The Frogs* shows Aeschylus, Sophocles, and Euripides contending in the underworld for dramatic supremacy, with Dionysus as judge. *The Clouds* is a satire on the Sophists and Socrates. Perhaps most entertaining for a modern audience is *Lysistrata*, a satire on the folly of the Peloponnesian War. In this play the women barricade the entrance to the Acropolis so that the men cannot reach the treasury to get money to pay the soldiers. The tongue-lashing between women and men is riotous. Aristophanes pictured life as coarse and vulgar, but never foul and rotten. He used every known device for provoking laughter: parody, burlesque, farce, apt quotations, and unexpected turns. And yet, embedded in the nonsense are choral songs beautiful enough to qualify Aristophanes as one of the finest Greek lyrical poets.

## Greek Philosophy

You will note that the great philosophers come at the end of the "Golden Age" and the beginning of the fourth century B.C. The fifth century B.C. was an age of *doing:* building, decorating, providing plays to entertain the *doers*. The fourth century B.C. was an age of contemplation; there was time then in which to think.

**Socrates.** Socrates (*c.* 470–399 B.C.) was one of the greatest teachers of all time, and he wrote nothing. As soon as he appeared a group of young men would gather about him. He would sit down under a tree, and perhaps someone would ask: "Socrates, which is more important, love or friendship?" The teacher would immediately counter with: "What do you mean by love?" "What do you mean by friendship?" The class had started, and several hours later when Socrates stood up to go, he had still not answered their questions, but he had given them much to think about and material whereby they could come to their own conclusions.

This is great teaching, and the Athenians loved it. They still loved it several centuries later when St. Paul appeared among them. He said in Acts 17:21: "Now all the Athenians and the strangers sojourning there spent their time in nothing else, but either to tell or to hear some new thing."

Socrates was put to death in 399 B.C., accused of "corrupting youth." The truth of the matter was, however, that he was on the wrong side of the political fence. He might have defended himself, or run away, but he was seventy years old and chose to die, a teacher to the end. Read Plato's account of his last conversation with his friends and of his death in the Dialogue called *Phaedo.*

**Plato.** Plato (*c.* 428–347 B.C.) was an aristocrat, a soldier, an athlete, and a musician. His meeting with Socrates proved to be the turning point in his life. He became a philosopher and a passionate lover of wisdom. The *Dialogues* purport to be the actual words of Socrates, but the organization of each one seems to indicate that they are Plato's application and extension of the master's teaching.

Socrates' death filled Plato with bitter scorn of democracy and hatred of the mob. He devoted his life to the finding of a system of government in which the state would be ruled by the wisest and best men. The results of his search are embodied in *The Republic*, Plato's most important legacy. It not only tells how the "philosopher kings" should be chosen and educated to rule, but also gives Plato's ideas on theology, ethics, psychology, politics, and art. Ideas which we think of as being very "modern" are also included: communism and socialism, birth control and eugenics, psychoanalysis and the therapeutic value of music. Einstein's theory of relativity is Platonic because it stresses faith based on a mathematical solution rather than the evidence of the senses. St. John based his doctrine of the Incarnation on Plato when he said, "In the beginning was the Word." *Logos* is Plato's "Divine Idea."

Strangely enough, Plato's system was virtually put into practice for a thousand years. The medieval Church ruled the greatest oligarchy the world has ever known. There were three classes of people: workers, soldiers, and clergy. The clergy monopolized the opportunities of culture and came to power not by suffrage, but by their training in ecclesiastical studies and administration. Separated from family responsibilities, the clergy lived lives of simplicity and meditation. Their *quadrivium* (arithmetic, geometry, astronomy, and music) was modeled on Plato's curriculum. It worked just so long as the economy was agricultural, but when industry and commerce developed, the power of the Church began to crumble. This was the flaw in Plato's Utopia: it was static and made no provision for change. If the guardians have political but not economic power, how can they enforce their rule? They might conceivably be inflexible, hostile to invention, jealous of change. Essentially, however, Plato was right; we need to be governed by our wisest men.

**Aristotle.** Aristotle (384–322 B.C.) was born in Macedonia, the son of the King's physician. He went to Athens to study at Plato's Academy, but the two geniuses did not get along very well. He was recalled home to become the tutor of the young Alexander. In two years' time, Alexander was on the throne and soon off on his world conquests, and Aristotle went back to Athens, where he started a school.

Plato and Aristotle were diametrically opposed. Plato was interested in ideas. Aristotle was interested in things, and so he became the world's first scientist. Alexander gave him large sums of money to further his scientific inquiry: the first example of the financing of science by public wealth. At one time, as many as a thousand men were gathering specimens of flora and fauna for him. He established the world's first zoological garden.

One should not blame Aristotle for going astray in some of his conclusions. He had no watch, no thermometer, no telescope, no barometer, no microscope. All he had was a ruler and a compass. The application of mathematics to physics was unknown to him; his astronomy is childish romance, his biology absurd. The Greeks disdained manual labor, and their slaves had no opportunity to learn. The invention of tools and industry did not come until later. However, in spite of Aristotle' errors and absurdities, his data became the *Encyclopaedia Britannica* for two thousand years. He created a new science, logic, which is explained in his *Organon*. This treatise is an elaborate set of formulae which govern right reasoning. These are the basis of all scientific inquiry as well as the tools of debating. The key to his method resides in the syllogism, which consists of major premise, minor premise, and conclusion. If the premises are correct and the conclusion follows from them, the conclusion is irrefutable. For instance:

All art is creative—major premise
Sculpture is an art—minor premise
Therefore sculpture is creative—conclusion

If all art is creative, every example of art must be creative ("All *A* is *B*" means that each *A* is *B*). However, if the premises are incorrect or if the conclusion does not follow from them, the conclusion may be ridiculous. For instance:

All cows eat grass—major premise
This man eats grass—minor premise
Therefore this man is a cow—conclusion

If all cows are grass-eating animals it does not necessarily follow that all grass-eating animals are cows ("All *A* is *B*" does not mean that all *B* is *A*).

**Greek Philosophy in the Medieval Period.** Aristotle's terminology was destined to provide the vehicle of philosophic thought for almost a thousand years. The *Organon* was translated by the Roman philosopher Boethius at the end of the fifth century A.D. and became the basis of Scholastic philosophy. Theoretically, the Church Fathers banned Plato and Aristotle because they were pagans. But they couldn't stop free inquiry, and besides, the best way to arouse interest in a book is to ban it. There is considerable evidence that these Greek works were translated, copied, and studied by medieval monks. In the fourth century A.D. St. Augustine combined Plato's idealism with Aristotle's organization. His City of God is Platonic. In the sixth century A.D., St. Benedict founded the Monte Cassino Library, which included Plato and Aristotle. In the ninth century, John Scotus Erigena interpreted Christian theology in Neoplatonic terms. In the tenth century there was a Neoplatonic school at Chartres.

Aristotle's treatises passed from Byzantium to the Moslem peoples of the East (Saracens), who carried them to western Europe by way of Spain. These Saracens, firmly entrenched in southern Spain, established a very fine university in Cordova. Averroës, an important philosopher in Cordova, made Aristotle pre-eminent in his work. Averroës demonstrated the superiority of reason and philosophy over knowledge founded on faith alone. In the twelfth century, Abelard made Aristotle's logic the basis of his teaching at the University of Paris. He was attacked as a heretic, condemned by a church council, and forced to stop teaching.

In 1231, Pope Gregory IX became alarmed and appointed a commission to expurgate Aristotle, but twenty-nine years later Aristotle was taught in every Christian school. Why the sudden change? Thomas Aquinas, the "Angelic Doctor," had made *reason* a legitimate partner of *faith* in his *Summa Theologica*, which has endured to this day as the official Roman Catholic philosophy. Indeed, so firmly was Aristotle's earth-centered universe embedded in church dogma that it became a great handicap to scientists like Galileo and Copernicus and their heliocentric (sun-centered) theory.

It is not necessary to remember all these facts. They are inserted because many people have been taught that Plato and Aristotle were "lost" during the medieval period, and had to wait until the Renaissance to be "reborn."

**Realism versus Nominalism.** Plato and Aristotle were on opposite sides in the debate over *universals*. A universal is any general concept: goodness, justice, beauty. Plato maintained that these universals had objective existence, in fact were more lasting and substantial than individual objects or people. Men come and go, but *Man* goes on forever. This is Platonic *realism*. Aristotle, as a scientist, stressed the individual man or object, and his followers called themselves *nominalists*. They held that all that exists outside us is a world of specific objects, and that "universals" are merely names or terms. Friederich Schlegel, nineteenth-century German philosopher, said, "Every man is born either a Platonist or an Aristotelian." You see, Plato loved ideas, abstract concepts; Aristotle loved things, concrete realities. Now you can decide for yourself whether you are a Platonist or an Aristotelian.

## The Hellenistic Period

To understand the empire of Alexander the Great (356–323 B.C.) we must make an excursion into the history of the period. The Peloponnesian War (431–404 B.C.), in which Athens and Sparta had fought to the death for supremacy in Greece, exhausted Athens both politically and creatively. As often happens in history, fresh, vigorous blood infused the tired social fabric from barbarian sources—in this case from the little kingdom of Macedon far to the north. The Macedonians were part Greek and part Oriental. Their king, Philip, was ambitious and unscrupulous, but deeply imbedded in his nature was an ardent respect for the culture of his Hellenic neighbors. When Athens lay prostrate at his feet, he spared her because of his admiration for her intellectual greatness. Small wonder then that he sent to Athens for Aristotle to be the tutor of his twelve-year-old son Alexander. Since early boyhood Alexander was conscious of

SCHOOL OF PERGAMUM: *Dying Gaul.* Capotiline, Rome. (Alinari—Art Reference Bureau)

a mission in life, and his study with Aristotle gave him a real love for organization and knowledge for its own sake. Alexander was only twenty when he ascended his father's throne, and soon thereafter he was off on what might be called the greatest cultural conquest in history.

**Art.** Town life had always been the essence of Greek civilization. Hence after making a conquest, Alexander established a town if one was not there already. The most flourishing cultural centers were Alexandria in Egypt, Antioch in Syria, and Pergamum in Asia Minor. These rich cities demanded luxurious and ornamental art and a sensational style. If you examine the altar of Zeus in Pergamum, which depicts a battle between gods and giants, you will notice that everything is in violent upheaval with the figures spilling out on the very steps of the altar. From Pergamum also comes the "Dying Gaul" (see p. 45), a Roman copy of a third-century B.C. bronze. The old warrior with his hard, dry skin, matted hair, and gaping wound represents the epitome of anguished defeat, but it is anguish of spirit rather than physical pain which the sculptor seeks to express.

At certain periods of art history, people have judged the "Laocoön Group" to be one of the finest examples of Greek sculpture. In mythology Laocoön was a Trojan priest who tried to warn his compatriots against accepting the Trojan horse. The gods, seeing their plans frustrated, sent two serpents from the sea to kill Laocoön and his two sons. The sculpture, which depicts their deaths, is an impressive group, certainly, and one's sympathy is aroused for the innocent victims, but great art seems to demand some restraint. Even the "Winged Victory," placed so strategically in the Louvre, is very dramatic. The Golden Age of Greece was gone.

**Philosophy.** In Alexander's empire, the little city-states of Greece became insignificant. People lost their bearings, and the result was the first "Age of Anxiety." Other philosophies lived briefly, but did not satisfy. The Epicureans were opportunistic; the Stoics were cold; the Cynics were the "beatniks" of their day; the Skeptics were sure of nothing. Then Neoplatonism was born and furnished Christian revelation with a structure of ideas. "In the beginning was the Word."

**Cosmopolitanism.** Hellenistic culture did not extend beyond the towns of Alexander's conquests, but the Greek language took permanent root. This explains why the Jews of Alexandria adopted Greek for their Septuagint version of the Old Testament and why most of the New Testament books were written in Greek. Jesus and his disciples were probably familiar with a colloquial form of the Greek language. The fact that there were Hellenizing Jews in Jerusalem, of whom Stephen the martyr may have been one, helped St. Paul spread his message. As Hellenism lost its creative impulse, it gained a universal outlook. Alexander created a cosmopolitan spirit based on intellectual ideas and cultural standards.

Ptolemy I (*c.* 367–283 B.C.) and his successors in Egypt made Alexandria with its university and fine library the greatest intellectual center in the world. The export of papyrus from Alexandria was forbidden; the scribes of Pergamum therefore invented parchment, a more durable and flexible material for manuscripts.

## The Roman Conquest

In Athens, philosophy and debate lingered on after the city's political and economic decay. While Alexander's successors were squabbling over the division of his empire, Rome had been completing her conquest of the Italian peninsula. After defeating Hannibal and gaining Carthage, the Romans took another thirty years to subdue Macedon; then it was the turn of the Greeks to be conquered.

In A.D. 146 Greece was made subject to the Roman governor of Macedon, although Athens and Sparta were allowed to retain their autonomy. Corinth, however, for an act of "discourtesy" was practically destroyed, and the victorious Roman consul sent home a shipful of priceless artistic treasures to grace his "triumph."

For a hundred years well-to-do Roman parents had sent their sons to the University of Athens. By the middle of the second century A.D. Greek ideas had permeated Roman society, and they were soon to permeate the Christian Church as far as its systematic organization of belief was concerned. There was a striking difference, however: whereas self-realization had been the gospel of Aristotle, self-sacrifice was the gospel of Christianity.

# Chapter 4 / The Romans and the Early Medieval Period

We shall spend very little time on the Romans, because they were not an artistic people. Their great contribution to the future was in the fields of law and engineering. Some time between 1000 B.C., and 753 B.C., there was a small Italic tribe of farmers and tradesmen, living in a tiny village on the banks of the Tiber. The village, located in what was later the Roman Forum, was somewhat protected by the surrounding seven hills. It is not known where these people came from. According to legend, Rome was founded by Romulus and Remus, twin brothers descended from Venus and Mars. From 753 to 509 B.C. the Romans were subjects of the Etruscans, whose civilization was superior to theirs in industry, commerce, and the arts. But the Etruscans lacked the very qualities which promoted the destiny of Rome: tenacity, patience, and ability to organize. Pushed from the north by Celtic peoples from central Europe and from the south by the now organized Romans, the Etruscans gave up town after town until by 260 B.C. the Romans were in control of the whole of Tuscany in central Italy. The system of Roman roads was begun, and the first steps were taken to build up the Empire which was to control the known world around the Mediterranean and to build a civilization many elements of which survived into the medieval period.

## Roman Civilization

In every town they subjugated, in every colony they established, the Romans at once set up a system of law and order which would govern the people with justice. These procedures became standardized and formed the basis for all subsequent legal procedure in Western civilization.

The Romans had the insight to take from their subjugated peoples devices and accomplishments which they could adapt to their own purposes. From the Etruscans they took the round arch and the groined vault. These structures gave them the ability to hold up large volumes of space both horizontally and vertically. With the round arch, they were able to build the aqueducts which still carry a plentiful supply of water from the

Apennine Mountains into Rome. The Colosseum, the Roman arena, consisted of four tiers of round arches placed one above the other. The Pantheon, temple of the gods, was built to accommodate a large congregation. The building is round, extended on one side by a rectangular box against which is placed a porch held up by Corinthian columns which are surmounted by a stubby Greek pediment. The roof over the circular portion is a dome derived from Oriental architecture. There are no windows in the building; the only light enters through a hole in the center of the dome. Quite impressive from within, the building on the outside seems like a conflicting hodge-podge of lines and styles. It certainly lacks the symmetry and proportion of the Parthenon.

When the Romans conquered a Greek town, they despoiled it of all the art treasures they could carry away and even took the artists themselves to work for them in adorning their homes with sculpture and *objets d'art*. They preferred the emotional style of the late Hellenistic period to the idealistic figures of the Golden Age. Wealthy Romans wanted to perpetuate themselves with their own statues to adorn public buildings or their graves. So great was the demand that the sculptors made a supply of standard torsos. Then all they had to do was to sculpture the client's head and attach it to the torso. The Romans even appropriated Greek gods and added them to their own roster.

We would not be able to appraise the luxury and magnificence of the wealthy Roman's villa had it not been for the devastating eruption of Mount Vesuvius in A.D. 79. The towns of Pompeii and Herculaneum were summer resorts of the wealthy, whose villas were pleasure houses in every sense of the word. Careful excavation reveals not only the plan of these homes but also the sculpture, fountains, and even wall paintings which adorned them. The walls are divided into panels on which scenes of domestic life are painted. Each panel is "framed" with a border of black on which small figures of nymphs, satyrs, and goat-drawn chariots carrying beautiful women are depicted. They are in earth colors, a good deal of Pazzuoli red, and a lovely shade of green-blue. These paintings are sensual in the extreme, some so licentious that women are not allowed to see them today. It is easy to understand why this pagan art was anathema to the early Christians. In fact, it was partly to get away from the remains of this pagan culture that Emperor Constantine moved the Christian capital to Byzantium.

The Romans were not very musical, though they employed Greek slave musicians to play the lyre during their banquets.

You can see Roman women performing on the lyre in some of their wall paintings, and music was a part of their educational system, but it probably lacked a high degree of merit. Because they were not intellectual enough to appreciate the subtleties of Greek tragedy, the Romans' drama degenerated into dance pantomimes. They did, however, perfect the long, straight tubular trumpet and the drum for military purposes. These instruments continued to be used throughout the Middle Ages.

The literature of the Romans is much better than their fine arts or music. Some of it is derived from Greek sources. However, because of the universality of Latin during the Middle Ages and Renaissance, Western authors were more likely to obtain their source material from Roman than from Greek writers. Unless we become Latin scholars, this is our chief interest in these men, most of whom wrote in the first century B.C. or the first century A.D.

**Virgil.** By all odds, the greatest Roman poet was Virgil. His aim was to compose a work of art about the Roman hero Aeneas which would compare in magnitude with the Homeric epics and which would glorify Roman ideals. In other words, he wanted to be the Homer of his country. He employed the same verse form which Homer had used, the dactylic hexameter.

The *Aeneid* tells about the wanderings of Aeneas after the fall of Troy. It follows rather closely the wanderings of Homer's Ulysses, including an account of a descent into Hades. Aeneas was the legendary ancestor of the rulers of Rome and of the founders of the city. Perhaps the most interesting episode of the *Aeneid* occurs in Book Four. An unfavorable wind drives Aeneas' ship to Carthage, whose beautiful queen, Dido, falls in love with him. But the gods will that he must reach Italy, and so he bids her farewell and leaves. Dido, broken-hearted, takes her own life. This story is the basis of an English opera called *Dido and Aeneas* by the seventeenth-century composer Henry Purcell. It has recently been revived, and according to most critics is the best opera composed by an Englishman. Read Book Four of the *Aeneid* in a good prose translation. Virgil was no soldier, and his battle scenes are inferior to those of Homer; yet the *Aeneid* is a great poem. Dante admired Virgil so much that he made Virgil, symbol of human wisdom, his guide through the Inferno and Purgatorio of the *Divine Comedy*.

**Horace.** Horace, friend of Virgil, is probably the most read and quoted Roman poet. He was brilliant and witty, and a close observer of life. His *Odes* and *Epodes* are his best work.

**Catullus.** Catullus wrote lyric poems primarily about his love affair with a famous Roman beauty. These poems have been set to music by a twentieth-century German composer, Carl Orff; his setting is called *Catulli Carmina.*

**Ovid.** Ovid wrote the *Ars Amatoria* ("Art of Love"). In A.D. 8 the Emperor Augustus banished him to Costanza on the west coast of the Black Sea and also banned his poems from public libraries. At this time the Emperor was trying to reform Roman morals. Ovid speaks of an "error," which may refer to his involvement with Augustus' licentious daughter Julia. At any rate, the banishment broke his spirit, and he died ten years later. Ovid's poetry strongly influenced French Provençal poetry, *The Romance of the Rose,* and the literature of courtly love. In his *Metamorphoses* he retells some old myths in a new and interesting manner. Among them are the stories of Pyramus and Thisbe, Narcissus, and Orpheus and Eurydice. This last has probably been the basis of more operas than any other story. The greatest is by the eighteenth-century German, Christoph Willibald Gluck.

**Playwrights.** The Romans couldn't appreciate sophisticated, satiric comedies like those of Aristophanes. They chose instead to imitate the later Greek "comedy of manners" of Menander and Apollodorus. The *Pot of Gold* by Plautus is the basis of Molière's comedy *The Miser.* Terence borrowed plots and characters from the Greeks and added a thin coating of Roman veneer. In a similar way Seneca retold in Latin the tragedies of Aeschylus, Sophocles, and Euripides.

**Plutarch.** After the Augustan Age came Plutarch, the first good biographer. His *Parallel Lives of Illustrious Greeks and Romans* was Shakespeare's source book for the characters and stories in his Roman plays.

**Epictetus.** The first-century philosopher Epictetus was born in Phrygia, and as a boy he was a slave in a Roman household. Later freed, he was banished from Rome by the Emperor Domitian and lived in Nicopolis, where he taught philosophy. His pupil Arrian wrote down his *Discourses* which contain his Stoic philosophy of acceptance and endurance. Because of some remarkable coincidences in language with the New Testament Epistles, it is thought that he may have been exposed to the preaching of Epaphras, a follower of St. Paul.[1]

---

[1] *The Interpreter's Bible* (New York: The Abingdon Press, 1955), XI, 134.

## The Early Medieval Period

During the whole medieval period of almost a thousand years, there was a record of continual struggle and fighting. But the period was never "dark" if we mean by *dark* a time when the urge to create and the will to change one's environment cease—as the old Hebrew lament puts it: "When desire shall fail and the spirit returns to dust." It has been aptly said that the only thing dark about the "Dark Ages" was the early historians who didn't know much about them. The period is tremendously vital and dynamic.

In 313 Constantine the Great issued an edict of toleration, an act which paved the way for the Emperor Theodosius I to make Christianity the Roman state religion about 365. In 330 Constantine moved his capital from Rome to Byzantium and renamed the city Constantinople.

**The Barbarians.** The barbaric invasions which started in the fourth and fifth centuries and spread gradually over the whole of southern Europe were destructive, of course, but in the long run their effect was salutary because they infused the tired social fabric with new blood and energy. It may be well to note that every time a civilization becomes overcultivated, it is revitalized from folk or "barbarian" sources. This has happened again and again right down to our own day.

*Celts.* In the Capitoline Museum in Rome, there is a Roman copy of a late Greek bronze sculpture called "The Dying Gaul" (see p. 45). Who were the "Gauls"? They were the Celts, roving bands of tall, blond warriors who swept across northern Europe from the Black Sea to the Atlantic for perhaps a thousand years before the birth of Christ. Modern archeologists have only recently begun to trace their history and evaluate their rich culture. They remain in the twilight-zone of history because while they had a fund of oral literature, they appear never to have written down their legends.[1]

The Greek historian Herodotus said, in the fifth century B.C., that the source of the Danube lies in Celtic country and that you would encounter Celts if you sailed beyond the Strait of Gibraltar. Alexander the Great encountered them in Bulgaria in 335 B.C., and Julius Caesar fought them in Gaul (France) in 58 B.C. In 425 B.C., four tribes invaded northern Italy and sacked Rome; in 280 B.C., three tribes invaded Asia Minor and gave their

---

[1] Some modern scholars believe that the Irish may have reached North America long before the Vikings.

name to the province of Galatia. While they extended their conquests over a wide area, they never seem to have united into any kind of confederacy. Pushed by the Greeks and Romans from the south and by the Teutonic peoples from the north, they seem to have made their last stand in Scotland, Ireland, and Wales. Remains of Celtic bronze and gold workmanship were unearthed in 1953 and 1954 in Switzerland, Burgundy, Denmark, and England. These show that besides fighting, the Celts lavished skill on worldly luxuries. But of greatest interest to us is the influence of their language and literature. The few Celtic words which appear in classical writing are strikingly similar to the languages now known as Gaelic and Welsh. Furthermore, their way of life, religious practices, and beliefs are found in the stories of ancient Ireland. St. Patrick, who had gone to Ireland as a Christian missionary, in A.D. 438 met with the Celtic poets, or scholar-magicians, and recorded the rhythmic texts known as *The Great Tradition*. You may read the mythological tales, stories of fighting and of romance, and the heroic tales. So our first group of "barbarians" has considerably enriched the literature of the British Isles as well as the English language.

*The Goths, Franks, and Lombards.* The fourth-century invaders, unlike the Celts, were of Teutonic origin. They were nomads with no indigenous culture, a fact which made them easier to assimilate and Christianize. The Goths were the most gifted. The Visigoths (West Goths) settled in Spain, the Ostrogoths (East Goths) in Italy and Byzantium. The Franks in Gaul and the Lombards in northern Italy had absorbed Oriental traditions from Greek monks and Syrian merchants. Their beautiful cloisonné work in gold led directly to Byzantine mosaics and stained-glass windows. It is amazing how quickly the assimilation of the barbarians took place. We have probably not done as well assimilating our American Indians and Negroes. The first invasion was in 361; and in 493, Theodoric the Ostrogoth became King of Italy. In 799, Charlemagne, himself a Frank whose wife was a Lombard princess, put Pope Leo III back on his papal throne and as a reward for this service was made the first Holy Roman Emperor.

**The Early Church.** From humble beginnings, the Church gradually rose to a position of power and authority. When pagan Rome died, the Church took over its organization and many of its ceremonies. The Roman Senate, for instance, became the Church Curia. Although Constantine's Edict of Milan (A.D. 313), granting religious toleration, was largely a political move, it had far-reaching religious consequences. Constantine saw clearly that if the Empire had one Emperor, one law, and one citizenship for all free men, it should also have one religion. He moved slowly, however. He simply gave Christianity the support of the government so that gradually it became the state religion.

Under imperial favor, the Church grew by leaps and bounds. The Eastern churches were the strongest, but they were torn by schisms and "heretical" sects. Constantine's transfer of the capital to Byzantium left the Bishop of Rome the most conspicuous man in the ancient capital. At first each bishop exercised autonomy in his see, but through the work of two strong Roman bishops, Innocent I (402–417) and Leo I (440–461), the universal jurisdiction of the Roman bishop (the Papacy) was established. It was due to the weakness of Pope Leo III and his need for temporal support that the "Holy Roman Emperor" was established in 800.

*Architecture.* The first great need of the early church was for a building large enough for communal worship. In the Roman basilica, the Christians found a structure which they adapted to their purpose. It was a large rectangular hall, covered with a gabled wooden roof, with narrower, lower aisles on the longer sides, divided from the main hall by rows of columns connected by round arches. At the far end was a semicircular dais (later a half-dome) which became the apse for the high altar. The Romans had used such buildings for covered markets and public law courts. An open atrium in front of the entrance contained a fountain for baptism and ceremonial cleansing. At first, the basilica was simply utilitarian with no decoration whatsoever, the greatest disadvantage being a vulnerability to fire. The basilica is the style of church architecture indigenous to Italy, and even today you can see many beautiful basilican churches there. Saint Apollinare in Classe, built in 530, still stands in Ravenna. Saint Paul Outside the Walls, in Rome, dates from the fourth century but was completely rebuilt after a fire in 1823.

*Painting.* After many disputes a new art developed. Sculptured figures were not allowed because of the Biblical injunction against "graven images." The realistic style of Roman wall painting was too sensual and too pagan. What was needed was a style of painting that was didactic but not aesthetic. Pope Gregory at the end of the sixth century finally settled the argument, saying, "Painting can do for the illiterate what writing does for those who can read."

In time, a sort of canon of representation grew up which all the artists followed. Here are a few of the "rules." Drapery should not reveal the structure of the body beneath it; deity, the

Virgin, and the Apostles should be crowned with halos; saints should be represented with their distinguishing symbol: St. Catherine with the wheel on which she was martyred, St. Lucia with the sword through her neck, St. Mark with the lion, St. Luke with the ox, St. Barbara with the tower in which she was imprisoned for her faith. You can see that after hundreds of years of such didactic painting the laws of realistic representation were forgotten, and had to be discovered anew at the beginning of the Renaissance.

*Theology.* The new religious faith also required a new philosophy of history—the indestructibility of the spiritual life. The Church was not only indestructible; it was omnipresent in the lives of the people. All the arts were in the service of the Church. The ideals of Plato and Aristotle helped lay the foundations for the new philosophy (see p. 43), and the monastic orders kept it alive and extended it to realms undreamed of by the Greek philosophers. This life was only a stepping stone to eternity; God had placed a man where He wanted him to be, whether serf, noble, artisan, or scholar. It was therefore futile, even wrong, to try to better a man's earthly condition beyond offering him a little cheer at Christmas time. The names of the architects and sculptors of the great cathedrals are unknown. They worked for God and not for personal glory.

**The Byzantine Empire.** Constantinople (formerly Byzantium, today Istanbul) is considered the greatest art center of the early medieval period. Constantine left Rome because it was a hotbed of conspiracy and intrigue. The little town of Byzantium on its rocky peninsula jutting out between the Sea of Marmora and the Black Sea had a good climate and a fine harbor, and it was a focus of trade between the Orient and Europe. To Byzantium came ships from the East bearing spices, ivory, amber, pearls and precious stones, porcelain, taffeta, and damask. From the North came cargoes of wheat, furs, gold, and slaves. Constantine built his city well and decorated it with works of art filched from the entire classical world, including the four bronze horses which now gallop above the portal of St. Mark's Cathedral in Venice, the bronze triple pillar from Delphi, and the Caledonian boar. He built the Senate House, the Great Palace with its porphyry pavilion for the Empress, and the vast Hippodrome which could seat forty thousand people, and on the highest plateau, the Church of the Holy Wisdom, Hagia Sophia, probably the most sumptuous church ever built. A triple line of walls protected the city on the land side. In 330 the city was dedicated and the Byzantine Empire began; it was an empire that fused the political legacy of Rome, the cultural legacy of Greece, and the dynamics of the Christian faith.

The height of the Byzantine Empire was the reign of Justinian and Theodora in the sixth century. At this time the empire extended to all the lands bordering the Mediterranean and its islands. Justinian, who was a stern and ruthless upholder of the orthodox Christian faith, considered that he had divine as well as imperial sanction. He rebuilt the church of Hagia Sophia, and he recodified Roman law in what is known as the Justinian Code. After he conquered Italy, Ravenna became the capital of the West, the seat of the Byzantine exarch, or viceroy. The Empress Theodora, the daughter of a bearkeeper in the circus, was elevated to the throne with Justinian in 527 and became a power in the government. As a lover of pomp and glory, she was responsible for the Oriental magnificence of the court. Ambitious, unscrupulous, and cruel, she was a powerful friend and a dangerous enemy. Much of her time was spent in Ravenna, where she could keep her finger on the political situation. She elevated her favorite Vigilius to the Papal throne and found time to build or decorate three churches in Ravenna with mosaics finer than those in Byzantium. These mosaics are worthy of considerable study. The figures are types, hallowed by age-old tradition, with a solemn splendor in spite of their rigidity. Other churches which have superb Byzantine mosaics are Monreale Cathedral in Sicily, the tiny Cathedral in Torcello outside Venice, one recently restored on the top of Mount Sinai, and St. Mark's Cathedral in Venice, in pure Byzantine style, begun in 1063.

In architecture, the Byzantine church combines the Christian basilica with the domed octagon or rotunda. Justinian is reported to have said of his rebuilt Hagia Sophia, "Solomon, I have surpassed thee." The dome is the important feature because it had symbolic as well as architectural meaning. (The Persian kings held court under the dome of a tent; Castor and Pollux, intermediaries between heaven and earth, wore dome-shaped helmets; Hagia Sophia's dome was so light it looked as though suspended from heaven.) The dome symbolized transcendent authority and the coming of the Kingdom of God. It is the fusion of Oriental and Hellenistic features which keeps Byzantine art from being lifeless.

The end of the story is soon told. A city as rich as Byzantium is not safe even behind walls. In the seventh century, after the death of Mohammed, the Moslems, fired with religious zeal, invaded the Empire, which gradually shrank to the shores of Hellas. In the thirteenth century, the Fourth Crusaders, led by

Baldwin of Flanders, sacked Constantinople.[1] It was rebuilt, but fell finally to the Ottoman Turks in 1453. The beautiful mosaics were covered with whitewash and paint and inscriptions from the Koran were substituted. The overlay was a blessing in disguise because in this way the mosaics have been preserved. It was not until the twentieth century that the paint was carefully removed to reveal the glowing mosaics beneath.

One more point must be made before we leave Byzantium. In the seventh century, and again in the ninth, religious "puritans" succeeded in having images (*icons*) forbidden. Incidentally, this is the origin of our word *iconoclast* (literally, "image-breaker"). Artists thus thrown out of work fanned out over western Europe. Some of them in the ninth century found a refuge at the court of Otto I, Emperor of Germany. If you look carefully at Carolingian and Ottonian sculpture, and even at the later Romanesque sculpture, you will see undoubted Byzantine stylisms. Some Byzantine churchmen went as far as Ireland. This country, far removed from the turmoil in Europe proper, was a repository of learning and a Christianizing influence in Iceland, Germany, and the North. Scholarship is only recently assessing the enormous contribution of the Irish monks to philosophy, art, and music.

**Charlemagne.** Of the three great conquerors of Europe— Caesar, Charlemagne, and Napoleon—it is undoubtedly Charlemagne who has had the most lasting effect. Had he not been crowned Holy Roman Emperor (on Christmas Day in 800), subsequent history would have been very different.

Possessed of great energy and strength, an excellent horseman and swimmer, Charlemagne is remembered today rather for making his court a mecca for scholars and artists. He helped merge the barbaric tribes of the North with the civilization of the South in the name of the Christian faith, and he turned back the Saracenic hordes who were threatening to overrun Europe. By defeating the Lombards, he united under his banner lands we know today as West Germany, France, the Low Countries, and the northern half of Italy. It was an incident in his campaign against the Saracens in Spain that inspired the great epic poem of the twelfth century, *The Song of Roland*.

Charlemagne never returned to Rome after his coronation. He established his capital at the old Frankish town of Aachen, where he built a magnificent palace and a church based on the architecture of San Vitale in Ravenna and adorned it with

---

[1] The nineteenth-century French Romantic painter Eugène Delacroix made a colorful painting of this scene (see p. 240).

murals, mosaics, and sculptured reliefs. Although all trace of these has perished, we do have ivories, metalwork, and illuminated manuscripts of the period, with decorations based on the classical tradition and the rich cultural symbols of Celtic and Germanic peoples.

.To satisfy his own intellectual curiosity, and to further his reforms, Charlemagne gathered about him the greatest minds of Europe—theologians and scholars—as instructors in his academy. From Aachen this search for knowledge was taken up in every monastery school in western Europe, and it culminated in the Scholasticism of the twelfth and thirteenth centuries. The barbarian and classical art forms were gradually united until they found a home in the glories of Romanesque art.

The very letters which you are reading in this book have shapes derived from Carolingian manuscripts, mistakenly called Roman because Charlemagne collected and copied the texts of many classical Latin authors. It was his aim to establish a second Augustan age among the semibarbaric tribes of the North.

We know from contemporary writers that Carolingian churches were profusely decorated with mosaics, murals, and relief sculptures, but of these almost nothing has survived. We can, however, understand the qualities of the art by examining illuminated manuscripts and objects fashioned from ivory and gold.

The first example is a picture, "St. Matthew Writing his Gospel." Taken from the Gospel Book of Charlemagne, probably found in his tomb, it dates from about 800, but except for the large golden halo behind the evangelist's head, it might be mistaken for a fully integrated Roman portrait of the first century A.D. Matthew is seated on a stool before a lectern on which his gospel rests. He is wrapped in a conventional Roman toga with sandals on his feet. His mien is calm and studious. The frame is decorated with an acanthus leaf pattern.

A detail from the Grandval Bible of the School of Tours dates from several decades later (see p. 59). It represents Moses and Joshua addressing the Israelites in the Temple. Actually it is a Roman interior, the roof supported by Corinthean pillars separated by round arches. The colorful robes are Oriental and short, showing striped skirts below them. Joshua is dressed in a Roman soldier's uniform under his robe and he holds aside the curtain as though he were ready to dash out and do battle, if necessary. Moses has the scroll of the Ten Commandments under one arm, and his right hand points to the group. The pointed finger was the conventional medieval symbol of a man talking. The most interesting feature is the reaction registered on the

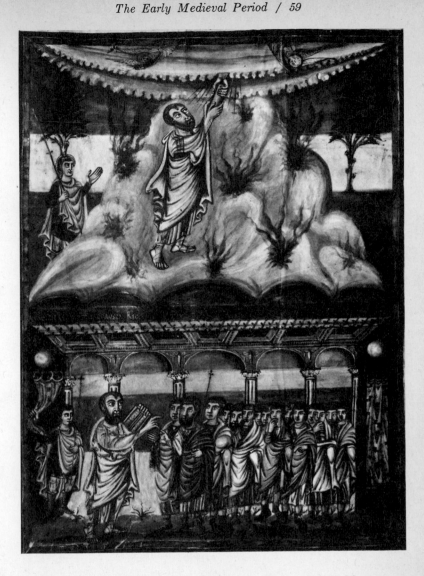

GRANDVAL BIBLE: *Moses and Israelites in the Temple.* British Museum, London. (Copyright, British Museum)

faces in the group: acceptance, surprise, concern, disbelief, suspicion.

One more illustration of Carolingian workmanship is the gold and jeweled cover of the Lindau Gospels, probably from the

*Madonna of Essen.* Cathedral Crypt, Essen, Germany. (Marburg —Art Reference Bureau)

School of St. Denis, about 870. The semiprecious stones are not set directly into the gold, but are raised on little claw feet so that light can penetrate under the stones, giving them greater brilliance. The crucified Christ shows no sign of pain or death; he seems to stand rather than hang. The small angels who are a part of the design may be expressing sorrow. If you take a magnifying glass and examine the filigree work around the cross and between the jewels, you will see elements of Celtic-Germanic design.

When this Gospel was made, Charlemagne was dead and his two grandsons were fighting over his empire. Too weak to sustain his sovereignty, they allowed the empire once more to become a prey to Moslems, Slavs, and Vikings. It was at this time that the Scandinavians became entrenched in Normandy. They adopted Christianity and Carolingian civilization and became so powerful that one of them, William the Conqueror, could invade England, win the Battle of Hastings (1066), and become king.

**The Ottonian Period.** In the meanwhile, in Germany, the Saxon kings became strong and gradually took over the imperial traditions of Charlemagne. The most important of them, Otto I, in 962 became Holy Roman Emperor, a position which remained a German prerogative up until the end of the Napoleonic campaign in 1806. In the second half of the tenth century Germany was the strongest nation in Europe, politically and artistically. We find many Byzantine traits in Ottonian art not only because there were Byzantine artists working at the court, but also because Otto II married a Byzantine princess. However, Ottonian sculpture is more monumental in size and more expressively realistic, traits which have characterized German art ever since.

As illustrations of Ottonian workmanship let us examine two sumptuous expressions of the goldsmith's art. The "Golden Madonna and Child of Essen Cathedral" (see p. 60), dating from about the end of the tenth century, is thirty inches high. The Madonna sits as rigidly as a Byzantine queen, her blue enameled eyes fixed on the ornate apple (symbol of redemption from Eve's sin), which she holds out for the Child to see. Her robes fall in stylized folds, ornamented at the neck with a brooch which once held a relic. The Child looks like a little old man in his ornate jeweled halo. The gold filigree on the Madonna's crown and the halo, apple, and book under the Child's arm all show traces of Celtic designs. The gold was inlaid and hammered over a carved wooden core. As one looks at this resplendent statue in the dim cloister, one cannot help wondering about the identity of the artist who wrought with such love and zeal.

More monumental but less personal is the three by four-and-a-half foot gold antependium (altar screen) given to Basel Cathedral by Henry II, grandnephew of Otto I. It was presented in 1019 as a token of thanks to St. Benedict, who had miraculously cured the king of an infirmity. Five figures stand rigidly in semicircular niches: Christ in the center flanked by the angels Michael, Gabriel, and Raphael with Benedict on the left end, and the donor and his wife kneeling at Christ's feet. Behind all the figures are jeweled halos. The faces show no emotion, but the drapery is softer and begins to reveal the form of the body beneath it. The ornamental designs in the background and borders are again Celtic or Germanic leaf forms with animals.

# Chapter 5 / The High Middle Ages

Before we proceed to a discussion of the great Romanesque and Gothic art styles and of medieval music and literary master-pieces, we must understand the historical conditions that emerged in the later Middle Ages.

First, practically all the intellectual and artistic activity throughout the medieval period was associated with the monastery. Some artists worked for princes, to be sure, but since their castles were frequently destroyed by fire or war, this secular art has largely disappeared.

Second, a monastery complex was like a small town, housing, besides the monks and the "regular clergy," hundreds of workmen of all kinds, poor boys and orphans taken in by the monks, and travelers on pilgrimage who received hospitality without charge. Since every priest was required to say Mass once a day, monastery churches needed many altars. Because the church served the monastic community, rather than outsiders, there was often an apse at both east and west ends of the nave, while the entrances to the church led from the cloisters or other parts of the monastery complex.

Third, this was the period of veneration of relics and pilgrimages to shrines. The whole cult of martyrs represented a renewal of the passion and resurrection of Christ. As time went on, relics of the saints came to assume more importance than the emulation of their lives. Bodies were dug up, dismembered, divided, fought over, and stolen. No price was too high to pay for a relic, either real or spurious. All Christendom, it seemed, took up the pilgrim's staff and set out on foot to visit the most sacred shrines—Santiago de Compostella in Spain (the tomb of St. James), Rome (tomb of St. Peter), and of course Jerusalem, the holy city. A lesser shrine was the tomb of Thomas à Becket in Canterbury. The largest monasteries with the finest churches and the most "authentic" relics lay along these pilgrimage routes.

Fourth, these churches took many years to build, sometimes more than a century. When the original architect died and another was appointed, he often changed the plans to suit a more modern style. You will frequently see Romanesque and Gothic stylisms happily wedded in the same church. This has happened in our own day to the Cathedral of St. John the Divine in New York. You can see Byzantine, Romanesque, and Gothic elements there now, and the church isn't nearly finished. Often, too, fires and wars have necessitated reconstruction. In the case of Mont-Saint-Michel, part of the church fell into the ocean. Only four arches of the original eleventh-century church remain in the nave. From outside the whole church looks Gothic.

Consider how much art of the eleventh and twelfth centuries came into being as a result of these circumstances: hundreds of churches of cathedral size so costly that they left France well-nigh bankrupt for three hundred years, golden altarpieces and reliquaries either to propitiate the saint or as a thank-offering for miraculous services rendered, the *chanson de geste* ("song of deeds") sung by the minstrels on all the battlefields from Hastings to Byzantium, and finally Chaucer's *Canterbury Tales*.

## Monasticism

The mind of antiquity regarded the practice of contemplation as more estimable than the active virtues. Asceticism and monasticism are to be found in the religions of India and among Jews, Greeks, and Egyptians. Some early Christians, seeing the world as hopelessly evil, sought not to reform it but to abandon it completely. Christian monasticism began about A.D. 250 among the Coptic Christians in Egypt; it emphasized work, prayer, and Bible-reading. By the end of the fourth century monasticism had been introduced into the West, where the exhortations and examples of Jerome, Ambrose, and Augustine had brought it much favor.

There was opportunity in a monastery complex for monks of many aptitudes: scholarly enterprise and preaching, missionary endeavor and teaching, social work among the poor and needy, the copying and illuminating of books, and the humbler work of building and farming. The primary occupations continued to be Bible-reading, prayer, and contemplation.

The rapid assimilation and Christianization of the barbarian tribes from the North is in large part attributable to the monastic orders. The Benedictine order, founded by St. Benedict on Monte Cassino in 529, had the finest library in Europe. Its monks set forth to convert England and Germany to Christianity. In 563, the Irish monk St. Columba arrived in his coracle on the tiny island of Iona, off the western coast of Scotland, to convert the warring Scottish tribes. There he built a monastery which became a haven of refuge for sages in search of wisdom, for kings in search of advice, consecration, and confession, as well as for needy common people. Today, beautifully restored, it serves as a retreat for religious folk of all faiths. The Cistercians, a French branch of the Benedictines, were sometimes known as Trappist monks. The Franciscan order, dedicated to poverty, obedience, and celibacy, was founded by St. Francis of Assisi in 1209. Francis trudged, barefoot, through the hill towns of Italy, singing hymns and preaching repentance. Almost like a pantheist, he preached to birds and called stones, trees, and celestial bodies his "brothers." It is said that when his robe caught fire, he refused to put the fire out because the fire was his "Brother." It is very moving to hear his "Hymn to the Creatures" sung in half a dozen different tongues at his grave in the Church of Assisi. The Dominican order, founded by St. Dominic, in thirteenth-century Spain, is called the "Order of Preaching Friars." Fra Angelico, Thomas Aquinas, and Savonarola belonged to this order.

Most of the early Church Fathers came not from Italy but from those centers of Greek learning which had been established by Alexander's conquests. St. Augustine was Bishop of Hippo in North Africa. In 412, while Rome was still smoking from Alaric's sack, Augustine began his *City of God* to remind Christians that there is a heavenly city, embracing the faithful in all lands, which cannot be destroyed.

## The University

Cathedral and monastic schools flourished in the eleventh and twelfth centuries, and out of these grew the first universities. The number of teachers was multiplying, and they gathered about them students from all lands. Because of the variety of languages, classes were conducted in Latin, and because the classrooms were unheated, students and teachers wore the academic robes and hoods now worn for formal convocations and commencements. Since many students were extremely poor, they aroused the concern of benefactors like Robert de Sorbon (1207–1274), who provided a home and special teachers for them under the guidance of "fellows" of the house. The University of Paris is still called the Sorbonne today.

The university consisted of four faculties (courses). The first (like our undergraduate) taught the *trivium* (grammar, rhetoric, and logic) and the *quadrivium* (astronomy, arithmetic, geometry, and music). It conferred the bachelor's degree, which was similar in a profession to completion of apprenticeship in a guild. The three higher faculties of theology, canon law, and medicine conferred the master's or doctor's degree and the privilege of teaching in the university. Paris and Oxford were famed for theology, Bologna for church and civil law, Salerno for medicine. Teaching was by lecture and *constant debate,* which tended to make the student master of his knowledge.

## Scholasticism

The general practice of debate gave rise to the philosophical-religious movement of Scholasticism which marked the highest intellectual achievement of the Middle Ages.

**The Influence of Plato and Aristotle.** The theology of Christianity had never been far from Platonism or Neoplatonism, a philosophy which combined Greek and Oriental elements, holding that the world is an emanation from one Divine Being. Many of St. Paul's writings are Platonic, as are those of the Gospel of John. When Paul wrote (II Corinthians 4:18): "For the things that are seen are temporal, but the things that are not seen are eternal," he was emphasizing Plato's "universals" as opposed to Aristotle's concrete objects. Whenever St. Augustine thought of God philosophically, he borrowed terms from Neoplatonism. Christian Neoplatonists believed in one transcendent God whose followers sought by mystical means to attain a union with him. God is simple, absolute Being as distinguished from all created things which are manifold and variable. Augustine's three Persons of the Trinity are "of one and the same substance, and they work indivisibly." Many other great churchmen, including Bonaventura, friend and colleague of Thomas Aquinas at the University of Paris, were Neoplatonists.

We have already indicated that Aristotle was known throughout the medieval period, possibly in fragmentary and garbled translations. Now in the thirteenth century the whole of Aristotle's extant works were recovered. They met with much hostility from the churchmen because Aristotle emphasized the evidence of the senses rather than divine revelation. However, Aristotle's philosophy was taught by a growing number of followers of the Arabian philosopher Averroës, and Thomas Aquinas was called to Paris to combat Averroism.

**Thomas Aquinas.** Thomas Aquinas (*c.* 1225–1274) was born in southern Italy, but his mother was a Norman, connected with the German imperial house of Hohenstaufen. It was against the wishes of his parents that Thomas entered the Dominican order in 1243. His superiors sent him to Cologne to study with Albertus Magnus, who had a remarkable knowledge of science, Aristotle, and the Arabian scholars. Throughout his lifetime of teaching Thomas found time to write his *Summa Theologiae*, the source of Roman Catholic philosophy today. He was a simple, deeply religious, prayerful man whose work is marked by a clarity, logic, and breadth that place him among the few great teachers of the Church.

According to Aquinas, the aim of theological investigation is to give knowledge of God and of man's origin and destiny. Such knowledge comes partly by reason (natural theology), but this is inadequate. It must be augmented by God's supernatural gifts (gifts of Grace), added to nature in such a way that they do not destroy nature, but rather bring it to perfection. Since God is the author of both faith and natural law, the light of faith does not destroy the natural light of knowledge which is inborn in us. Faith is a kind of knowledge. It gives assent to revealed truth because it has been spoken by God, but it requires the determinative action of the will. This is the origin of the "leap of faith" taught today by the Christian existentialists. Therefore, there can be no conflict between philosophy and theology because both are from God.

God is the first cause, pure activity; He is also the most real and perfect of existences. God needs nothing, and therefore the creation of the world is an expression of the divine love which He bestows upon his creatures. Sin makes it impossible for man to please God. Man's restoration is possible only through the free and unmerited Grace of God whereby man's nature is changed, his sins forgiven, and the power to practice the three Christian virtues (faith, hope, and charity) infused. The work of Christ was the wisest and most efficient method for forgiving man's sins. The Church is one, wherever it is represented, in heaven, on earth, or in purgatory. When one member suffers, all suffer; when one does well, all share in his good work.

You can see that in Aquinas' reconciliation of faith and reason, he always lifts faith above reason, but he does not lower reason. His faith and his philosophy grow into an organic unity because they both spring from the same divine source. When you read Dante's *Divine Comedy*, you will see how his philosophy and his theology are echoed there.

We have mentioned only a few of the main ideas from the *Summa*, but perhaps enough to show that its structure is just as rational, just as logical, just as clear as the structure of that other great achievement of the thirteenth century, the Gothic cathedral. As Henry Adams says, "The method was the same for both, and the result was an art marked by singular unity, which endured and served its purpose until man changed his attitude toward the universe. St. Thomas' church was the most expressive that man has made, and the great Gothic cathedrals were its most complete expression." [1] Just so at long last did Thomas Aquinas reconcile Plato, Aristotle, and Christian theology.

## Romanesque Art

There is no better way to get the "feel" of the Romanesque and Gothic periods than to read Henry Adams' *Mont-Saint-Michel and Chartres*. Adams was an historian, but the book is not technical; it was written for young people. The American architect Ralph Adams Cram was responsible for having it published in 1913. It has had wide popularity and is available in several reprint editions.

The term *Romanesque* has created much confusion. The early historians of medieval art called Romanesque anything that was not-yet-Gothic because, being round-arched, solid, and heavy, these churches looked rather like the ancient Roman style of building. Its spirit is not happy enough to suit the Italian temperament or frivolous enough to suit the French, but it does seem to belong to the heavy, sturdy, reliable Germans. Some scholars think that it started at Hildesheim in 940 or at Limbourg-on-the-Hardt around 1025. We had best not become involved in scholarly disputes, and just say that Romanesque architecture belongs to the Church Militant and the monastery, and is ideally suited to prayer and contemplation. (Henry Adams said that it is a man's church and that no woman has any business there.) The period from 1050 to 1200 saw the beginning of an urban middle class of craftsmen and merchants. Hence the international trade patterns, the urban quality, and the military strength did resemble ancient imperial times.

**Churches.** Romanesque churches sprang up like mushrooms all over Europe at about the same time and had no uniform stylistic pattern. In general, a heavy, barrel-vaulted (like a half cylinder) stone roof replaced the flat or gabled wooden roof of the old basilica. A transept between choir and nave gave the building the form of a Latin cross with a tower over the groin-vaulted crossing. The enormous weight of the stone roof rested on huge piers between the nave and side aisles, but some of the lateral thrust was transferred to the side walls, which must also be heavy and well-nigh windowless.

---

[1] Henry Adams, *Mont-Saint-Michel and Chartres* (Boston: Houghton Mifflin Company, 1933), p. 376.

Romanesque architecture in England is called Norman, and the churches, such as Durham Cathedral, are very large and impressive. The German architects specialized in towers and an extra rectangular addition on the west which they called a "westwork." Sometimes they built two transepts to give opportunity for additional altars. Important reliquaries were generally in the crypt below the high altar or below the crossing.

If you study the interior and exterior of Morienval, you will have an idea of a German Romanesque church. The façade of St. Trophime is a good illustration of Romanesque sculpture. In the tympanum above the entrance you see Christ surrounded by St. Mark, the lion; St. Matthew, the winged angel; St. Luke, the ox; St. John, the eagle. These derive from the vision of the Old Testament prophet Ezekiel, who saw the throne of the Lord carried by these four creatures. On the lintel below, the twelve seated figures are the Apostles; left of them, lost souls being dragged off to Hell; right of them, the blessed who are destined for Heaven. Below are the rigid figures of the saints, each holding his emblem, each ready to intercede in Heaven for the faithful. Thus the sermon preached on the outside of the church was probably more understandable than the sermon preached within.

**Sculpture.** Most sightseers would not care to spend a great deal of time examining Romanesque sculpture, but there is one church in the small Burgundian town of Autun which amply repays the visitor. Here in the church of St. Lazare (St. Lazarus or Ladre) worked one of the greatest geniuses in the whole history of art, Gislebertus by name. We know very little about Gislebertus except that he had probably worked at the Abbey of Cluny not far away and that he carved the sculpture of St. Lazare both on the outside portals and the capitals of the piers within the church during the years between 1120 and 1140 while the church was being built. The story of the rediscovery of his sculpture reads like fiction.

The church itself is not pure Romanesque. The tall, pointed spire above the crossing was added in the fifteenth century, and the twin towers on the west portal were added in the nineteenth century. In the eighteenth century, the so-called Classic period, when popular taste was for the sublime, idealistic beauty of the Greeks, people were ashamed of the earthy, realistic, "barbaric" art of the Middle Ages. After chiseling away the head of Christ which protruded on one of the archivolts above the main portal, they covered the tympanum with smooth plaster. This, of course, as in the case of Hagia Sophia's mosaics, preserved the sculpture from further mutilation. The head of Christ came to rest in a small museum in Autun, while other pieces of sculpture, including that of Eve tempting Adam with the apple, which had graced the north portal, were used by the townspeople in the foundations of their houses. At this time also the apse was "modernized" with a coating of marble.

In 1837, the plaster over the tympanum began to crack and peel, and a priest discovered the sculptured "Last Judgment" scene with the carved words, *Gislebertus Hoc Fecit* ("Gislebertus made this") just below the feet of Christ. Restoration was begun in 1858, and the marble was removed from the apse in 1939, but not until 1948 did the choirmaster connect the head in the Autun museum with the missing head of Christ in the tympanum. Searchers are still trying to find missing pieces.

The hundreds of figures which make up the phenomenal wealth of St. Lazare's sculpture are the output of one mature personality in concept, planning, and execution. The figures all show the naïve simplicity usual in medieval sculpture, but they have an extraordinary subtlety of expression, drapery which reveals rather than conceals the form beneath it, and a freedom of movement completely at variance with the crowded grouping of other Romanesque sculptures. But most amazing is the psychological depiction of character which the sculptor has shown on the faces and in the attitudes of his figures. Nothing like this was known in Flanders until the fifteenth century. These are the qualities which led French Minister of Culture André Malraux to call Gislebertus the "Cézanne of the Middle Ages." Indeed, he must have been admired and beloved by his contemporaries to have been allowed to sign his work.

The tall figure of Christ, standing with arms outstretched, dominates the tympanum, while above him angels blow the trumpets of doom. The Virgin is on his right, two angelic figures, possibly Elias and Enoch, are on his left. The dead arise, some with the insignia of pilgrims and Crusaders; children implore an angel to let them into Paradise, while fear and remorse animate the faces of the damned. A miser writhes in a serpent's coil; a lustful woman's breasts are bitten by snakes; another woman is impaled on a fork by a demon. Some little demons try to tip the scales in order to keep a worthy soul from St. Michael. While powerfully dramatic, the technique has been kept subservient to the sculptor's vision of a world where good is triumphant over evil.

Some of the small scenes on the capitals are touching in their simplicity and psychological penetration. God looks like a stern but loving father as he confronts his errant son with the words,

"Where is now thy brother Abel?" In the "Adoration of the Magi," the Christ Child reaches for a gift while Joseph looks distinctly puzzled. Perhaps the most striking scene is the "Flight into Egypt," where the donkey, usually portrayed as meek and stupid, here looks both intelligent and proud of his burden. Scenes like the "Hanging of Judas" and "Simon Magus" are warnings to potential wrongdoers. Many figures show that they were originally polychromed, which would have made them easier to see in remote niches. Even a twentieth-century visitor is impressed with the fact that Gislebertus must have thoroughly enjoyed his work.

In the twelfth century, women were demanding the right to be heard. And since the French women wanted decoration, after eight hundred years sculpture, still didactic, was used to decorate the façade of the Romanesque church. Then the Norman architects began to try out a new method of lessening the weight of the roof. With a good strong "rib" horizontally extended between the piers, and two diagonal crossed ribs, the triangular spaces between could be of lighter material. Examine a picture of Durham Cathedral in England to see how this rib-vaulting looks. It was a revolutionary discovery and the one which made Gothic architecture possible. Even so, the delicate balance between thrust and counterthrust was so precarious that it could only be accomplished by strict geometrical planning. This mathematics was analogous to the laws of the universe controlled by Divine Reason. The light which could now flood the church through the stained-glass windows was analogous to the Light Divine, the mystic revelation of the Spirit of God. Thus reasoned the churchmen and architects.

## Gothic Art

The Gothic was an achievement of the architects of the Île-de-France in Paris.[1] It was so completely new and different that the Italians, unable to comprehend, called it "Gothic," meaning barbaric. It was not barbaric, just the result of good French logic. If the pillars were strong enough to support the ribs of the vaulting, then the whole building could be tied together by a stone skeleton and the massive walls would be superfluous because every thrust would be offset by a counterthrust. Furthermore, the pointed arch was better than the round arch because the

---

[1] The Ile-de-France is the province surrounding Paris and extending some forty miles out from the city. It was considered an "island" because it was bounded by rivers, the Seine, the Marne, and the Oise.

horizontal thrust was less. Flying buttresses outside the church would take care of the horizontal pressure. The walls could now be opened by fenestration to let in the light. Each new church demanded a vault higher than the last one until the end came at Beauvais, whose vault, finished in 1272, was 156 feet, 9 inches high. Badly supported by a too isolated framework, it collapsed after twelve years. If you don't read anything else in Adams' book, do read what he says about the enormous cost of these cathedrals, and how the townspeople assisted in their construction. Be able to recognize at least Notre Dame de Paris and Chartres.

**The Influence of Women.** If the Romanesque was a man's church, the Gothic appealed to women, especially French noblewomen with their taste for refinement and luxury. Perhaps for the first time in history, woman had come into her own as the arbiter of taste and the ruler of her husband's affairs. Her intelligence ruled the household, the economy, and often the politics while her husband was away fighting, sometimes even when he was at home. There is a story that Duke William (the Norman, later William I of England), furious at having his bastardy thrown in his face by the Duchess Matilda, dragged her with her hair tied to his horse's tail as far as Vaucelles. When his rage abated he was sorry and gave her money to build a convent, the Abbey-aux-Dames. Eleanor of Aquitaine ruled her husband Henry II of England and her son, the refined but cruel Richard the Lion-hearted. Henry imprisoned Eleanor for twelve years, but in the end she got what she wanted. Louis IX (St. Louis) was brought up exclusively by his mother, Blanche of Castile. If you are still not convinced of woman's superiority, read the literature of the period. Long after these great queens were gone, Chaucer has the Wife of Bath say:

> *My Liege Lady! generally, quoth he,*
> *Women desiren to have the soveraintee.*

They not only desired it, but they got it. There is even a contemporary drawing of Aristotle being driven by a woman.

It was during this period, too, that the worship of the Virgin Mary became so universal in Europe. Almost every Gothic cathedral was dedicated to her, and many are the charming stories of her miracles. The French peasant women could not understand the arguments of the theologians, but they could understand Mary who was both Queen and Mother. In the Gothic church, her worshipers gave her what they believed she wanted: light, space, and color.

**Cathedral Art.** Gothic churches are filled with illuminated manuscripts, rich tapestries, and sculptured figures, but their greatest glory is in the stained-glass windows. The twelfth-century glass is considered the best; after this time the art gradually deteriorated and the method was lost. Modern experts in glass are relearning it today; perhaps the best is to be found in the Cathedral of St. John the Divine in New York. How do you judge good stained glass? The radiating power of blue is the key. Blue is the light which has value only by opposition. This blue was not made of sapphires because they lose their brilliance when ground. The material was probably cobalt which would be more expensive today than sapphires. Why? There should be no perspective in a stained-glass window because the window is a part of the wall. With this as a standard, judge the stained-glass windows in your town.

If you compare the manuscript illustrations and the sculpture of the Romanesque period with those of the Gothic period, such as the figures on the north porch of Chartres and the Prodigal Son window of Chartres, you will notice that a change is taking place. The Gothic figures are more lifelike, and once again there is a human body under the drapery. The art is still didactic with all the old symbolism, but the figures express more individuality and even real emotion. The artist has at last looked at nature, and he has begun to study how he can make his figures look convincing. This is as far as the thirteenth century could go.

## Medieval Music

The early Church needed not only a philosophy and a building, but also a ritual or form of worship. This required music. Many Christian chants have been traced to early Hebrew sources. Since there were Christian churches established by St. Paul in Asia Minor, Syria, and North Africa, some early chants show Oriental influence.

You remember that St. Mark says in his story of the Last Supper that, "when they had sung a hymn they went out." This was undoubtedly a chanted psalm which the Apostles had learned in the synagogue. There is also a "Hymn of Jesus" found in the Apocrypha which is definitely Hellenic. Organized in the form of a litany between Jesus and the disciples, it was apparently meant to be danced like a Greek dithyramb. This need not surprise us when we remember that there are many references to religious dancing in the Old Testament as well as in Oriental and Greek sources.

The early Christians probably did very little singing in the catacombs for fear of detection. As soon as basilican worship started and a liturgy was needed, Rome seems to have taken the lead because of its organizational ability. The Church Fathers had much trouble with heretical sects who sang propaganda songs and even songs from secular pantomimes. The Church disapproved of all instruments except the psaltery.

At first, every Christian community had its own ritual, but gradually the Roman form became universal except for parts of Spain which still use the Mozarabic, Milan which uses the Ambrosian, and the Eastern Orthodox Church whose ritual stems from Byzantium. The most important service was the Mass or Eucharist, which was essentially dramatic and was sung by the officiating priest with responses by the congregation. Just when "congregational" singing gave way to that of trained singers we do not know, but probably quite early. Tradition says that the Roman *Schola Cantorum* (school of singing) was founded as early as the fourth century. Every missionary monk established a similar school connected with the monastery that he built, thereby spreading the traditional manner of singing throughout Europe. Possibly the more elaborate settings of the Psalms, the Gradual, Alleluia, Introit, and Offertory were sung by trained singers, while the Kyrie, Gloria, and Sanctus were sung by the congregation.

**Gregorian Chant.** Two names stand out in the early period. In the fourth century St. Ambrose, Bishop of Milan, introduced Eastern chants into the West, organized the liturgy, and established four scales (based on those of the Greeks) to be used in singing. At the end of the sixth century, Pope Gregory I made a reorganization and codification of all the chants used for the entire church year. Tradition says that this *Antiphonale Missarum* was chained to the high altar in St. Peter's Basilica. Oddly enough, the man who gave his name to *Gregorian plain chant* was not a musician or a composer, but he was a great organizer and raised the Papacy to a prestige it had not known before. Gregorian chant is the oldest form of music still in regular use today. These chants are not only very beautiful, when well performed, but they are conducive to the real spirit of worship. They are the musical equivalent of Romanesque architecture.

You should hear as many of these chants as possible. Modern ears are so bombarded with chromatic harmony and dissonance that it takes a while to get used to the utter simplicity of Gregorian chant. The melodies are diatonic and flow smoothly within the octave of the chosen scale, without wide leaps. The rhythm follows the natural speech-rhythm of the Latin words, and there is no harmony or accompaniment of any kind. The only decoration is the little melismatic passages which emphasize important words like *Alleluiah*. (A *melisma* consists of many notes sung to a single syllable.) The scale chosen depended on the mood of the chant. The first and second scales were contemplative, the third and fourth ecstatic, the fifth and sixth buoyant and uplifting, the seventh solemn, the eighth serene. Medieval theorists developed a system of notation called *neumes*, little hooks placed above the word to indicate the direction of the melody. Guido of Arezzo, a monk of the eleventh century, put the neumes on lines to indicate fixed pitch. Out of this practice grew our modern musical notation.

Since for five hundred years the neumes did not indicate fixed pitch, there was much leeway in their interpretation. With repeated copying there were inevitable mistakes, and later centuries did not hesitate to change the chants deliberately according to the taste of the period. Even in the twelfth century, St. Bernard, church philosopher and mystic, wrote: "Take the *Antiphonale* of Rheims and compare it with that of Amiens, or Beauvais, or Soissons. If, beginning with the first page, you find any similarity, render homage unto God." About 1850, the Benedictine scholars of the Abbey of Solesmes in southern France undertook to collate and compare all existing copies of the Gregorian *Antiphonale*, to find the oldest, and to study manuscripts which had to do with their early method of execution. The result of this research, which took fifty years, was the so-called Solesmes version which was made official by Pope Pius X in 1903. Recordings of the chants by the monks of Solesmes are available.

The oldest version, still five hundred years after Gregory, was found in the monastery library of St. Gall, in Switzerland. The monastery had been founded in the seventh century by St. Gall, an Irish monk. In 790, acceding to repeated requests of Charlemagne, the Pope dispatched two singers with copies of the *Antiphonale*. One monk fell ill upon reaching St. Gall and remained there as head of the music school. It was the author's privilege to examine this oldest existing copy of the *Antiphonale*. The book is about seven inches by eleven inches in size, bound in carved ivory. The writing is as clean and clear as though the scribe had just finished it. The library, decorated in the Baroque style, is probably the most beautiful library in existence. Also in the library are some of the *sequences* of Notker Balbulus, a ninth-century theorist, and some early tropes by Tuotilo of the tenth century. A *sequence* was a text fitted to an elaborate melismatic passage in the chants; a *trope* was very similar but made a comment on the meaning of the chant. Sequences and tropes are important because out of them grew the liturgical drama and later the Miracle and Mystery plays. And out of these eventually grew opera and oratorio.

We are fortunate in having a recording of a twelfth-century liturgical drama, *The Play of Daniel,* composed for a Christmas Eve service by the students of Beauvais Cathedral school. It was taken from a manuscript in the British Museum, and presented by the *Pro Musica Society* of New York in the *Cloisters* in 1958. The Latin words, the music, and the instrumentation are absolutely authentic.

**Polyphony.** There was another medieval development, which was more important than Gregorian chant to the future of music. This was *polyphony,* or many-voiced music. Plain chant was an Eastern art, and although the Church forced it on them, the peoples north and west of the Alps did not find it congenial to their musical taste. Scholars are still arguing about who started polyphony and when and where. Although it began at least as early as the eighth century, it approached an artistic creation in the thirteenth.

The first records of actual music for more than one voice are English, but writers as early as the seventh century mention the practice as being common in Ireland and among the Danes in Iceland where it seems to have been a children's game similar to our "Three Blind Mice." The celebrated English *rota* "Sumer is Icumen In" must be mentioned here. It is attributed to a monk of Reading Abbey, John of Fornsete, and dates from about the middle of the thirteenth century. In the form of an endless double canon for six voices, it was probably intended as a fun song, and it can be performed by students in the classroom with a minimum of outside preparation. It is difficult to believe that a composition so perfect in workmanship could have been an isolated phenomenon.

The first serious compositions for two voices date from eleventh-century England, where the name *organum* was applied to them. In its most primitive form, organum consisted of a Gregorian chant with another part moving in parallel motion of fourths or fifths above or below the chant. But in written composition the organal part consisted of a *decorated* passage of predominantly fourths, fifths, and octaves (the Greek perfect intervals) which might move in any direction, and was sung by a solo singer. The first artistic compositions of this type come from the twelfth-century school of Notre Dame in Paris, where they are called Gothic motets. The first significant composer is

Leoninus, who advanced the work already done by the monks of Limoges. He was active while the Cathedral of Notre Dame, begun in 1163, was being built.

In the motets of Leoninus, the Gregorian chant consisted of long-held notes while the organal voice wove garlands of notes (melismas) against them.

**Perotinus.** The portion of the Notre Dame Cathedral intended for the choir was completed about twenty years after building began. The first great new musician in service there was Perotinus (died c. 1200). In his style (called *discantus* or *déchant*) both plain chant and organal voice moved more or less at the same *pace,* but often in contrary motion. In proceeding from consonance to consonance in contrary motion, the "dissonant" intervals (sixths, thirds, even seconds and sevenths) were heard, but were treated "with circumspection." Perotinus composed some motets for three and even four parts, a practice which did not become normal for another two hundred years. He also was governed by the standardized rhythmic modes—short rhythmic patterns which were repeated often enough to unify the work, but not for long at a stretch. Remember, his work antedates the "Summer Canon" (see p. 75). Perotinus also wrote another type called *conductus,* which was more metrical and often not based on a Gregorian chant. The words might even be secular. The *conductus* was probably first used in 1140 in the *Play of Daniel,* where it was used to accompany the exits and entrances of characters. The motets of Leoninus and Perotinus are not in any sense "primitive." They are musical works of massive breadth and lofty grandeur, worthy of the mighty Gothic cathedrals in which they were sung.

**Drinking Songs.** By this time you are probably convinced that medieval man was sober, concerned with nothing but his soul's salvation. Not a bit of it. He was robust and he liked his fun raw, even lewd. The Feast of the Ass, stemming vaguely from the flight of the Holy Family into Egypt, was his most celebrated holiday of the year, a time of raucous practical joking. Students in the universities especially were guilty of profaning the sacred services. The song of the Virgin, *Verbum bonum et suave,* became a drinking song, *Vinum bonum et suave. Ave Virgo Benedicta* ("Hail, Blessed Virgin") became *Alba limpha maledicta* ("Cursed Clear Drinking Water"). Even the Mass became *Missa de potatoribus* ("Mass of Drinkers").

**Troubadours and Trouvères.** If you have read Henry Adams' *Mont-Saint-Michel and Chartres* (see p. 67), you will remember his lively account of how Taillefer, William the Norman's *jongleur*, sang the *Song of Roland* at the Battle of Hastings and was ennobled by his master for his part in the fray. The *jongleurs* (actors, singers, and tricksters) were sometimes "ghost" composers who set to music the chivalric poetry of their noble masters, the troubadours, trouvères, and minnesingers. The *troubadours* hailed from Provence and wrote in the *langue d'oc*, the dialect spoken in southern France. The *trouvères* were their northern French imitators who wrote in the *langue d'oil*, which later grew into modern French. These verses celebrate the ideal of courtly love: worship of the chosen lady from afar until such time as she would deign to grant a "boon" in return for service rendered. Without doubt, many of the noble poets composed their own music, but the jongleur did the singing. We have the words of some 2,600 troubadour poems, but only 264 melodies survive. We have 4,000 trouvère poems and some 1,400 melodies.

Gustave Reese believes that these love songs do not always reflect genuine chivalrous devotion, but were inspired by the imagination to entertain a courtly society and win recognition. They are frequently artificial and formal in their treatment of love. Besides love songs, there were dance songs which were more strongly rhythmic, the pastoral in which a knight woos a shepherdess more or less discreetly, spinning songs in which a girl moans for an absent lover, and the so-called *alba*, or dawn song. In this type, "the singer is the vigilant friend of two lovers in whose behalf he stands watch and announces the break of day." [1]

The finest poet and composer of the troubadours was Bernart de Ventadorn, who apparently started out as a kitchen scullion. The most important trouvères were Thibaut de Navarre, Chrétien de Troyes, and Adam de la Halle, composer of the charming pastoral *Le Jeu de Robin et Marion,* sometimes considered the first comic opera.

As to musical characteristics, these songs tend to be rhythmic (following the meters of the poetry) and diatonic (following the simple scale patterns and keeping well within the octave range). Their form is quite strict, built on repetition and contrast, and their tonality nearer to our major and minor scales. The French *estampie* (stamping song) is among the earliest known examples of purely instrumental music.

**Minnesingers.** The songs of the German *minnesingers*

---

[1] Gustave Reese, *Music in the Middle Ages* (New York: W. W. Norton & Company, 1940), pp. 213–214.

(*Minne* means chivalrous love) developed somewhat later than those of the French, and were obviously influenced by them. The German songs are more idealistic than the French and often express sincere feeling. We know these poet-singers well because they are all pictured in the so-called *Manesse Manuscript* now in Heidelberg University Library, a modern reprint of which is available in color. Walther von der Vogelweide, Tannhäuser, and Wolfram von Eschenbach actually participated in the song contest at the Wartburg Castle in 1207. This is the source of Wagner's opera *Tannhäuser*. One of Wolfram's epics, *Parzival*, inspired the last of Wagner's music dramas. The story of Tristan was a favorite theme with both the trouvères and the minne-singers. We have Gottfried von Strassburg's version of this story, but it is probably based on an earlier version by Chrétien de Troyes which is lost. Walther's "Palestine Song" seems to indicate that he went on the Crusade of 1228. Musically, the minne-songs are similar to those of the French except that the Germans prefer the A A B, or bar form. These songs may not sound like modern "popular" music, but the sentiments expressed are quite similar.

## Medieval Literature

*This is the way to al good aventure;*
*Be glad, thow redere, and thy sorwe of caste;*
*Al open am I :passe in, and speed thee faste.*
                    *Chaucer*, Parlement of Foules

Everyone likes a good story. As some cold winter night you pick up a book, turn on your television, or dash off to see the latest movie, your medieval ancestors sent for the professional storyteller. If the host was affluent, there was probably a bard "in residence." If not, the court was dependent on the less professional itinerant tale-teller. What matter if the story had been told a dozen times before in the same hall? That merely served to tax the ingenuity of the teller to refurbish the old tale or invent new details. He always brought his harp or psaltery along, but don't think for one minute that he accompanied himself by strumming chords as a modern guitarist would do. It was still many hundreds of years before the birth of what we know as harmony. He simply punctuated his sentences with a few plucked notes, and perhaps played a little tune between episodes.

**Beowulf.** The heroic epics began to appear with the beginning of the vernacular languages in the eighth century. The oldest is the Anglo-Saxon epic *Beowulf*, which tells how this hero of the Geats (Swedes) rescued the Danish court from the monster Grendel and after ruling his country wisely for fifty years, died fighting a fire-breathing dragon. Certain barbaric elements go back at least as early as the sixth century, but since it was written down in England by a Christian monk, it also shows the Christian aristocracy of an eighth-century Anglo-Saxon court.

**Northern Epics.** The heroic epics of the North: the *Eddas* of Iceland, the *Volsunga Saga* of the Scandinavian countries, and the *Nibelungenlied* of Germany all deal with similar material, but the threads of the stories are so intertwined and tangled that it is well-nigh impossible to find a coherent pattern. They have to do with the ambitions and rivalries between the Volsungs (descendants of the gods), the mortals, and the dwarfish Nibelungs. Their main interest for us is probably Wagner's use of the material in his four music dramas of the *Ring Cycle,* although Wagner changed the stories to suit his purpose. The *Volsunga Saga,* a prose account, goes back to the fifth century but was not written down in a completely unified form until the thirteenth century. It is a tragedy based on strong elemental emotions. The Middle High German Nibelungenlied is a thirteenth-century poetic version.

**British and French Epics.** The epics of Britain and France were tales of Aeneas and Alexander the Great ("Matter of Rome and Greece"), tales of Charlemagne and his Paladins ("Matter of France"), and tales of King Arthur and his knights ("Matter of Britain"). According to legend, Arthur was a Breton who, after the Romans left, restored order in Britain and for a time held off the Anglo-Saxon invaders. The Italians, having no epic hero of their own, appropriated the French Roland (Orlando). The Spanish hero is the Cid, who in the eleventh century fought on both sides in the struggle between Christianity and Islam.

The *Song of Roland,* the greatest of the French *chansons de geste* (songs of deeds), dates from the early twelfth century, according to the Oxford manuscript we possess. But there were undoubtedly earlier versions. With its theme of unswerving devotion to duty, it was probably sung as inspiration to knights going into every battle of the eleventh and twelfth centuries, and it was sung also on the Crusades. We have already mentioned how Taillefer chanted it during the Battle of Hastings. The story has some basis in history. In 778, Charlemagne went into Spain to secure his frontiers by alliance. He went home for Christmas, leaving his rear guard under the command of his general, Roland, to defend the Pass of Roncevalles. The Basque mountaineers (not the Saracens) descended upon the Christians and killed all of them, including Roland. In the poem, Roland is Charlemagne's nephew, and this skirmish becomes a major catastrophe. Roland's men are ambushed by the Saracens and defeated because Roland fails to blow his horn to summon Charlemagne. Read the inspiring death scene in which Roland disposes of his sword and extends his gloves to God's representative in token of fealty.[1]

**Romances.** By the mid-twelfth century the tales had become less concerned with heroic exploits and more concerned with courtly love. This concept, foreign to the notions of most Americans, needs some explanation, for which we are indebted to *The Allegory of Love* by C. S. Lewis.[2] It put love in the center of the literary stage, a position which it has never relinquished.

Courtly love, or *courtesie*, was a product of the Provençal troubadours in the eleventh century. They passed it on to the Neoplatonic School of Chartres and the northern trouvères, especially those at the court of Eleanor of Aquitaine and her daughter, Marie, Countess of Champagne, who were the high priestesses of the cult. It was Marie's chaplain Andreas Capellanus who wrote the Rules of Courtly Love, part of which you may read in the *Medieval Reader*.[3]

Eleanor of Aquitaine was by all odds the most important woman of the twelfth century. Her first husband was Louis VII of France, with whom she went to the Holy Land on crusade and to whom she bore two daughters, one of whom was Marie. Eleanor was both intelligent and dynamic, and a great marriage prize because of her large land holdings in eastern France.

Louis was too lethargic and religious to suit her. The marriage was annulled on grounds of consanguinity, and she married his enemy, Henry II (Plantagenet) of England. She appears in the movie *Becket*, but her part was played down because it would have interfered with the theme of fundamental conflict between Henry and Becket. She bore Henry eight children, two of whom were Richard the Lion-Hearted and John, of Magna Carta fame.

Eleanor tried to rule both husbands and children, and they would have come off better if they had always followed her advice. After one family quarrel with Henry, she ran away to her

---

[1] This passage is quoted in Henry Adams' *Mont-Saint-Michel and Chartres,* Chapter 2.

[2] C. S. Lewis, *The Allegory of Love* (New York: Oxford University Press, 1936).

[3] James Bruce Ross and Mary Martin McLaughlin, eds. (New York: Viking Press, 1955), p. 115.

own court at Poitiers, taking her children with her. At that time, marriages were often arranged for political reasons when children were three or four years old, and the prospective wives were given over to the groom's mother to be brought up. Hence there was a crowd of little "hoodlums" at Poitiers who needed training in courtly etiquette and refinement. Eleanor sent for her oldest daughter, Marie, who by this time was a widow with a son and daughter of her own, to come to Poitiers to train the youngsters. Eleanor's barons and vassals were a crude lot, who often appeared in her presence in hunting garb, dirty, and smelling of animals.

The "court," instituted to train children and vassals in courtly etiquette, had much to do with the freeing of woman from the position of inferiority which had been imposed upon her for hundreds of years. Andreas' "rules," derived partly from Ovid's *Art of Loving* and from the traditions of King Arthur's court, were actually the work of Marie and her mother.

The idea behind *courtesie* is the power of love to call forth all knightly and courtly excellence. Hence it can be freely bestowed by the lady only upon the knight who merits this reward. Such love is characterized by *Humility* before the beloved, that is, willingness to accept in silence her jibes, unreasonableness, and foibles; *Courtesy* in the performance of every service she requires; *Adultery,* the reward of faithful service; and the *Religion of Love,* the worship at her shrine. The relationship between the knight and his chosen lady was analogous to that between the feudal lord and his vassal. Such love could not exist within the marriage relationship, which was the result of a bargain with the lady's father. Her duty to her husband, therefore, resulted from necessity, not free choice. The lady was allowed free choice in the acceptance or rejection of a lover, but she was not to abuse her power to satisfy her own whims. The knight on his part was required to be truthful, modest, religious, clean of speech, hospitable, and generous toward his adversaries. He also had to be courageous in battle, and while devoted to one lady, ready to succor any lady in distress. The worship of the Virgin was a sort of sublimation of courtly love, and when you read Dante's *Divine Comedy* you will see the complete spiritualization of such love.

*Chrétien de Troyes.* The trouvère Chrétien de Troyes is probably the greatest French poet of chivalric love, and, significantly, his creative sphere was the court of Marie de Champagne. If you read his *Lancelot,* you will see how the theory of courtly love is worked out. You can understand that the knightly hero might often be involved in psychological conflicts between two duties, between reason and duty, or between duty and love. When such occur in his poems, Chrétien, along with later poets, slips into allegory, which is the objectivization of inner states.

Chrétien's other great poem is *Perceval,* whose theme is not primarily that of courtly love, but rather of Perceval's development from boorish naïveté to knightly courtesy and then to spiritual humiliation. His troubles come as a result of following his advisors too literally. The advice which his mother gives him before he leaves home is much like Polonius' advice to Laertes in *Hamlet.* His other counselor, an aged knight, tells him that loquaciousness is a sin; hence he fails to ask the meaning of the Grail and the dripping lance. Had he done so, he might have cured the wasting Fisher King.

Chrétien did not finish the tale. He breaks off following Perceval's meeting with an ancient hermit who is about to celebrate Mass on the morning of Good Friday. The hermit, actually his uncle, tells him that it was sin, his failure to perform his religious obligations, which had prevented his asking the strategic questions and had caused his fifteen years of suffering. Perceval confesses, receives absolution, and partakes of the sacraments.[1] We assume that Chrétien intended to have his hero return and with his regenerated spear, cure the Fisher King. Two later poets, as well as Wagner, finish the story in this manner. These poets may have taken the idea of the "pure fool" from Jesus' injunction to become as innocent as children.

Although Chrétien apparently took his story from a single French prose account, it had probably been sung by Welsh and Irish minstrels for at least three hundred years previously. An eminent twentieth-century medieval scholar, Jessie L. Weston, traced the Holy Grail and the Eucharist legends back to the earliest days of the Christian era. She showed how the archetypal events and symbols: the Waste Land, the Fisher King, the Grail, the Bleeding Lance, and the Perilous Chapel go back to the Eastern mystery cults of nature, rituals performed by the adherents of Adonis, Mithra, and Attis. Miss Weston's book is both fascinating and provocative. It inspired T. S. Eliot to write his poem "The Waste Land." [2]

---

[1] Chrétien de Troyes, *Perceval or the Story of the Grail* in Roger Sherman Loomis, ed., *Medieval Romances* (New York: Random House, Modern Library, 1957).
[2] Jessie L. Weston, *From Ritual to Romance* (Garden City, N.Y.: Doubleday, Anchor Books, 1957).

*Gottfried von Strassburg.* The greatest German chivalric romance is Gottfried von Strassburg's *Tristan and Isolt*. The Germans emphasized the Religion of Love; without *Minne* (romantic love) there is no honor, and in *Minne* grief becomes bliss. Love is spiritualized until it resembles the union of the soul with Christ. In the poem the Love grotto where the lovers live in the wilderness is the temple of the Love Goddess, Minne. It is interesting to note that it resembles a Romanesque church in which, according to August Closs, the rounded vault of the trees represents single-heartedness; the breadth, love's boundless power; the height, noble-mindedness; the white wall, purity; the floor, constancy; the three windows, kindness, humility, and good breeding; and the light, honor.[1] Wagner's greatest music drama is based on this poem.

Evidently there was no greater assurance of successful marriage in medieval times than there is today. Often the bride's mother concocted a love potion which would keep the bride and groom faithful for life, or until the effect of the potion wore off. In the long, rambling love story of *Tristan and Isolt,* the flask containing the love potion is carelessly left lying about, and its contents consumed by the right girl and the wrong man. Tristan is bringing back the Irish Princess Isolt to be the bride of his uncle Mark when the fatal accident occurs. Isolt marries Mark and for the rest of their lives she and Tristan suffer for their guilty love in passionate stolen embraces and anguished partings. Gottfried sublimates their love, which, though leading to sin and grief, is higher than both. Although Gottfried did not finish his poem, two later minnesingers as well as Wagner concluded the tale with the death of both lovers.

*Aucassin and Nicolette.* *Aucassin and Nicolette* is an isolated gem of the thirteenth century, a *chante-fable* (song-story) by an unknown author. It exists in but one manuscript, published in facsimile at Oxford in 1896. It has been republished and translated many times; Andrew Lang's translation is probably the best because it retains the sweetness and whimsicality of the story.

It is in alternating short sections of prose narrative and verse, obviously intended to be sung and perhaps acted for a courtly audience of adolescents. Although the manuscript dates from about twenty-five years after Eleanor of Aquitaine set up her

---

[1] August Closs, *Medusa's Mirror: Studies in German Literature* (Chester Springs, Pa.: Dufour Editions, 1957).

"Court" at Poitiers in 1170, it is tempting to imagine its performance there. If an earlier manuscript existed, this is just possible. Its long popular appeal is evidenced by the fact that it was given dramatically before Louis XVI and Marie Antoinette in 1779, and recently in the King-Coit Children's Theatre in New York.

The poetic sections are similar to our trochaic tetrameter (four feet of long-short syllables), ending with a shorter two-foot line. The music consists of only three different musical phrases in the form of a *laisse*, which means that the first two phrases were repeated on alternate lines, the third being used for the last, short line of the stanza.[1]

Aucassin is the young son of the Count of Beaucaire, as gentle and courteous as a knight should be. Nicolette, the foster daughter of the Viscount who is one of the Count's liege men, is as sweet and fair as any noble lady. Although she is unaware of the fact, she is the daughter of the King of Carthage, stolen by the Saracens in infancy and sold to the Viscount. He has made a Christian of her and brought her up carefully. The two young people have fallen in love, and are as passionately devoted as any two teen-agers. When Aucassin tells his father that he wants to marry Nicolette the Count says that he will obtain for his son any princess in France, but a slave girl is not in Auccasin's class. If he persists in this foolish notion he will never reach Heaven. Aucassin replies that he does not wish to go to Heaven, which is peopled only by old priests, beggars, and cripples. He prefers to go to Hell, the abode of valiant knights, harpers, and jongleurs. Who has not heard such extravagant arguments from teen-age lovers? Although his father's enemies are even now at the gates, Aucassin refuses to fight unless he can have Nicolette. The father eventually promises the two one kiss, whereupon Aucassin fights more valiantly than any other knight.

Nicolette, meantime, has been locked up in a high tower from which she escapes by letting down bed sheets, and, terrified by lions (a bit of poetic licence), wild boars, and wolves, seeks Aucassin in the forest. Reunited, the lovers make their way to the seacoast as they merrily sing of their love. Their happiness is short-lived. They are seized by the Saracens, and each is put on a different ship. Nicolette is taken to Carthage, where she finds her real father, who promptly tries to marry her off to a rich Paynim. She dyes her skin, buys a lute, and escapes to the coast

---

[1] Theodore Gérold, *Histoire de la Musique des Origines a la Fin du XIVe Siècle* (Paris: Librairie Renouard, 1936), p. 262.

in the disguise of a minstrel. You see, Nicolette, unlike Chaucer's Criseyde, is both smart and resourceful. Aucassin, like most of these romantic heroes, is doughty enough but not very bright. It is the girl who makes all the decisions; the boy just "goes along."

Eventually the lovers get back to Beaucaire to find that both fathers have conveniently died. Aucassin has still refused to marry any maiden but his "fair, sweet sister." Nicolette reveals herself to her foster mother who "let wash and bathe her, and there rested she eight full days." When her beauty has returned, Aucassin is brought and the lovers are reunited. With its gentle wit and delicate absurdity, the story is a parody on courtly love. You may read the first part of the tale in Henry Adams' book. The entire tale is in *Medieval Romances.*

*The Romance of the Rose.* It has been aptly said that whoso would understand the Middle Ages should read three books: Dante's *Divine Comedy,* Chaucer's *Canterbury Tales,* and the *Roman de la Rose* (*Romance of the Rose*). *The Romance of the Rose* is the work of two French poets. The first, Guillaume de Lorris, who wrote in the early thirteenth century, composed 4,000 lines but left the work unfinished. About fifty years later, Jean de Meung added another 18,000 lines and completely changed the tone of the poem.

The poem is written in the form of a dream allegory describing a lover's pursuit of his ideal. The poet is concerned with what the lovers think and feel during the course of the pursuit. The lover himself is the storyteller. Wandering beside the River of Life, he comes upon a walled garden (Courtly Life). On the wall he sees the images of those excluded from the garden: Avarice, Envy, Poverty, Age, Sadness, and Prudery. At the gate the portress, Idleness, bids him enter. He wanders around, closely followed by the god of Love. Suddenly he sees a beautiful Rose and desires it. This Rose is not the lady, but the Lady's Love. As he reaches to pluck the Rose, he is struck by five arrows. He yields to the god of Love, does homage, and becomes Love's man. He cannot pluck the Rose because there is a thorny hedge about it. The Lady's friendliness, Bialacoil, is his ally, but he also encounters Danger, Evil Tongue, Shame, Fear, and Jealousy. These are other traits of the Lady herself. Reason appears and tries to persuade the Dreamer to give up the chase, but he renounces this good sense. Venus, representing natural passion, now enters the picture. Innocence is carried away and the lover kisses the Rose. Immediately, Jealousy, Shame, and Evil Tongue descend and put Bialacoil in prison. This means that the Lady's modesty, her fears, and her "danger" co-operate with the gossips of the court and the horror of her relatives to temporarily stifle her friendliness. Here de Lorris' part of the poem ends. You see that it is a love story of considerable subtlety and truth. We shall see how Chaucer's Criseyde is derived not from Boccaccio but from Guillaume de Lorris.

In Jean de Meung's portion of the poem, the allegory breaks down completely. Meung presents Reason as a rival mistress seeking the Dreamer's love. He goes off into many philosophical digressions which spoil the unity of the poem. He concludes that Hell, sin, and courtly love are only appearances, a curtain which veils eternity from mortal eyes. This eternity is the walled garden which the Dreamer has been seeking to enter. Here Meung anticipates Dante. The *Romance of the Rose*, translated, paraphrased, and answered, influenced almost every writer of romance for the next three hundred years.

**Chaucer.** Chaucer learned the courtly concept of love from the *Romance of the Rose*. He presents the literal story, rather than the allegorical conception of it, in his masterpiece *Troilus and Criseyde*. Whether you read it from a fourteenth- or a twentieth-century point of view, it remains an intriguing love story. Watch for parallelisms with the *Romance of the Rose*. Pandarus is, of course, *Frend*, whose early aim is to produce Bialacoil in Criseyde. In this he succeeds, but *Daunger* is aroused and, later, her greatest enemy, *Fear*. What Criseyde lacked was some of the imagination, ingenuity, and pluck which Nicolette had in abundance. As for Troilus, like most of the heroes in these chivalric tales, he shows very little spirit. He weeps copiously instead of pursuing his ladylove, and when the psychological moment arrives, he "swoons" and has to be pushed into her arms. Chaucer is very gentle toward Criseyde. When Shakespeare told the story later he was much more severe. Our expression "as false as Cressida" comes from Shakespeare.

Unlike other women of the period, such as Eleanor of Aquitaine and Nicolette, Criseyde is a timid creature. She needs someone to take care of her, and yet she is afraid of love entanglements because of her equivocal position in Troy, which her father has deserted for the enemy camp. Pandarus is by all odds the most interesting character. He is sophisticated and urbane, but also interested in young love.

This story has been called the earliest psychological love story of English fiction. Its setting is during the Trojan War, although Homer barely mentions Troilus as a son of King Priam of Troy. A twelfth-century French poet, Benoit de St. Maure, is said to have invented the love story. It was translated into Latin, then became the subject of a long narrative poem by Boccaccio, called *Il Filostrato*. Chaucer took only the bare plot from Boccaccio, but the entire pattern of the story from *The Romance of the Rose*.

In *Troilus and Criseyde*, Chaucer is humorous, witty, and cynical, but he is sympathetic to human frailty. He puts the gods of antiquity and the Christian saints on an equal footing, sometimes appealing to both in the same stanza. At the end he seems to disparage the seriousness of passion.

Most readers know Chaucer best by *The Canterbury Tales*, a group of stories, mostly in verse, told by pilgrims on their way to Canterbury Cathedral, the shrine of Thomas à Becket. At the suggestion of the Innkeeper, who acts as host to the party, each of the thirty pilgrims agrees to tell four stories, two while going to the shrine and two on the way back. Chaucer thus intended one hundred and twenty stories, of which twenty were completed, two left incomplete, and two deliberately interrupted by the group. The pilgrims represent a cross section of fourteenth-century English society, and the greatness of the work lies in Chaucer's ability to clothe each character with real flesh and blood.

In the General Prologue, Chaucer with few words characterizes each pilgrim: the Miller with the wart on his nose; the emaciated Pardoner, who never has had and never will have, a beard; the Clerk of Oxford, who would rather own Aristotle's books than fine robes; the Wife of Bath, who has had five husbands already and has ruled them all. The pilgrims come from all classes of society: rich and poor, wise and ignorant, religious and irreligious, generous and niggardly, officials of the manor and merchants of the town.

As we travel along with them we get to know them better for they quarrel and interrupt each other, or tell a story which will confound a too pretentious traveler. This device, together with the portrayal of the Host as a kind of moderator and Chaucer himself as observer, knits the whole thing together in a tight, literary structure. The tales the pilgrims tell cover the whole range of literary forms of the period: the Knight's tale is a chivalric romance; the Prioress tells a medieval legend; the Nun's Priest tells an animal fable; the Pardoner's tale is a medieval morality. After preaching a sermon against drunkenness, greed, and gambling, he reveals himself as a vicious man whose besetting sin is avarice. Perhaps the best characterization is that of the Wife of Bath. Seemingly immoral, she proceeds to tell a moral tale of

King Arthur whose theme is that true nobility comes by grace and not by age or birth or wealth. The Franklin tells a Breton lai, a tale of magic whose theme is that generosity in one inspires generosity in others.

The strength of the work rests on its total artistic merit. Chaucer's wit, humor, and tolerant humanity rise even above his psychological realism. Chaucer writes in Middle English, which is not difficult to read when one gets used to it. The real flavor of the period is caught by reading the stories in Chaucer's own dialect which is more readily comprehensible once you have hurdled the difference in spelling.

**Dante.** When a twentieth-century American poet (John Ciardi) spends many years making an American-English translation of a fourteenth-century allegory, and then in ten years sells one million copies of it, we are bound to conclude that the work has relevance today. Dante's *Divina Commedia* (*Divine Comedy*) has become a best seller. Why is this? It may be because most thinking people today are profoundly disturbed by the erosion of values in our mechanistic civilization, and are floundering around in search of the eternal verities of beauty and truth as a stabilizing force in their lives. Dante "has framed all the parts of his enormous perception within a total relationship of values and within a total dramatization of reality." [1] By the power of his personal genius and by the power of his metaphoric language we can translate his particular conceptions into endless revelations of universal truth. *The Divine Comedy* is not light reading. Dante requires us to discipline ourselves by strict attention, but we are rewarded by a feeling of personal achievement and by the expanding power of our perception. First, we must know a little about the historic Dante.

Dante was born in 1265 in Florence of a good but not wealthy family. It was a time when the Church was disputing its historic power with the rising mercantile class. There were two political parties, the Guelfs who favored the Church, and the Ghibellines who supported the Emperor. You will remember that this factionalism was the cause of the dissension between the families of Romeo and Juliet. Dante was loyal to the Church, but he did not believe that the Pope should have temporal power. The showdown came when Dante was a member of the governing council of Florence. His property was confiscated and he was exiled. He never returned to his beloved Florence.

---

[1] John Ciardi, "The Relevance of Dante," *Saturday Review*, May 15, 1965.

We also need to know something about his personal affairs. He was married to Gemma Donati and had several children. He was apparently loyal to his family, because his sons jeopardized their own safety to take to their father in exile the first five cantos of the *Commedia*, which he had left behind. He lived mostly at the villas of various friends, and when he had completed parts of the manuscript, he sent them to a noble friend, Con Grande. At the time of his death the last thirteen cantos were missing. Dante's son Jacopo is said to have had a dream in which his father led him to the room where he died and placed his hand upon the wall. Jacopo got up and found Dante's disciple, Piero Guardino, and together they went to the room. Behind a matting they found a hole and the missing cantos.

Now to Beatrice. She also came of a good family, and she was married at an early age to Simone dei Bardi. (Both Dante and Beatrice were probably pledged to their respective mates in early childhood.) In an earlier work called *La Vita Nuova* (*The New Life*) Dante tells about meeting Beatrice. Dante was a genius with what modern psychologists would call extrasensory perception. When he was nine years old and Beatrice was eight, he saw her for the first time, in a scarlet dress. It was a case of love at first sight, a love which remained with him all his life. Nine years later, at the ninth hour, he saw her again in a white robe, and she smiled on him so ineffably that he was transported with joy. He had a vision of her in the arms of Love, who forced her to eat Dante's heart and then bore her heavenward. Another vision prophesied her death. She died on the ninth day of the ninth month in 1290, "Wherein the perfect number ten was completed nine times." After these experiences, Dante decided to write no more until she became for him the idealization of spiritual beauty which would lead him from human to Divine Love. In a last vision, she told him that when the relationship becomes utterly spiritual, death can make no difference. He must teach the world that Love is the center of spiritual gravity in the universe. Dante wrote in *La Vita Nuova* (*The New Life*), which is his autobiographical account of his devotion to Beatrice: "Wherefore, if it be His pleasure through whom is the Life of all things, that my life continue a few years, it is my hope that I shall write concerning her what hath not before been written of any woman. After the which, may it seem good unto Him who is the Master of Grace, that my spirit should go hence to behold the glory of its lady: to whit, of that Blessed Beatrice who now gazes continually on His countenance, who is blessed through all eternity.

Glory to God!"[1] The *Commedia* is the fulfillment of this promise.

The poem is divided into three large sections, Inferno (Hell), Purgatorio (Purgatory), and Paradiso (Heaven). Each is pictured as a series of concentric circles. At the beginning, when Dante is "lost" in the wood, he meets Virgil, human reason, who offers to guide him through Hell and Purgatory. (Since Virgil is a pagan, he cannot enter the realm of Heaven.) In the second circle of Hell, Dante encounters the souls of Paolo and Francesca and hears the sad story of their adulterous love. Down through ever narrower circles he meets souls condemned by ever blacker sins until in the lowest circle he finds the archtraitors Judas, Brutus, and Cassius. At the very center is Lucifer, traitor to God himself, frozen solid in ice.

On Easter Day Dante and Virgil emerge from Hell and behold before them the Mountain of Purgatory. In concentric circles of Purgatory are the souls of those repentant ones who are being disciplined for Heaven by learning humility to overcome pride, zeal to cast out sloth, liberality to replace avarice, and chastity to burn out lust. On top of the mountain is the Earthly Paradise where dwell all the great souls who died before the coming of Christ. The poet has now reached that state of purification in which he is free to follow his soul's prompting, knowing that no source of evil remains within it. Here Virgil leaves Dante, who grieves for the loss of his mentor until he beholds Beatrice in the midst of a throng of angels. She sternly rebukes him for departing from the ideals of his youth, and, weeping, he confesses his sins.

Beatrice, Revelation, herself conducts the poet up through the circles of Heaven and it is in this section that Dante's pictorial language becomes most sublime. But we are also interested in the change in his attitude toward Beatrice. When he first meets her, the old earthly attraction is uppermost, but gradually he changes until his heart is so filled with heavenly love that he forgets her utterly and she smiles. This smile reflects the joy of Infinite Love. In the highest circle Beatrice takes her place beside the Virgin Mary and Saint Bernard stands beside Dante. Then he beholds the Empyrean where God himself abides.

Dante is the epitome of the spirit of self-sacrifice, high courage, persistent hope. He urges that we shake ourselves free of

---

[1] Dante Alighieri, *La Vita Nuova,* Ch. 7; trans. Dante Gabriel Rossetti (1861).

lethargy and set love in order by self-discipline. Love and righteousness can and will, by God's help, prevail.

I challenge you to read the *Inferno*. Having gone so far, you will read the rest of *The Divine Comedy*. There is something here to stimulate every interest. If you like mathematics, you can study the poem for symbolism of numbers. For instance, there are three poems in one, with a dynamic motion from three to one (unity), then to ten and one hundred, symbols of perfection. Dante uses *terza rima*, a three-line stanza of eleven-syllable lines. In the exact center is one fourteen-syllable line which is like the keystone of an arch. Virgil has been pointing down; from now on he points up. If you are interested in painting, you can study it for the symbolism of color. If your interest is astronomy and geography, here is the whole Ptolemaic system spelled out for you. If architecture is your interest, you can study the poem's architectural symmetry. As a historian, you can study Dante's judgment of the great historical and mythological figures who lived before his time. If you like music and pageantry, the poem is full of it. Everybody sang and danced in the thirteenth century. In the Earthly Paradise and Starry Heaven there are masques, processions, tableaux. And if you are religious you can study it for Church theology and doctrine. Above all, it is transcendent poetry, yours to appropriate for a living aesthetic experience.

# Chapter 6 / The Renaissance

*Ladies and gay lovers young,*
*Long live Bacchus, live Desire!*
*Dance and play, let songs be sung,*
*Let sweet love your bosoms fire.*[1]

This little quatrain, taken from one of Lorenzo de Medici's *Carnival Songs*, might be considered a sort of theme song for the Renaissance. You notice that the accent is on enjoying this life rather than preparing for the next one.

What was the Renaissance? You have probably learned that it was a rebirth of interest in the classics, but, as in most generalizations, that is only part of the truth. Plato and Aristotle and some of the Roman writers were very much alive in the Middle Ages. In fact they were influential in shaping the doctrines of the Church, as well as furnishing the material for endless philosophical debates and scholastic interpretations. If the Greek tragedies and comedies were anathema to medieval asceticism, and very few of the scholars knew Greek at all, at least people were acquainted with the Homeric stories. It is true that Roman ruins were torn apart and the material used to build Christian churches, but some Hellenistic sculpture survived. The medieval musicians had played around with Greek scales and made quite erroneous guesses about Greek musical practice.

Then what *was* the Renaissance? It was primarily a gradual shift in attitude, interest, and concern about the next world to an awakened interest in and concern for this world. Many factors contributed to this changed emphasis. First, the enormous power and wealth of the Church had led to abuses which caused a certain loss of prestige. Second, the Crusaders had found in some Hellenistic cities like Alexandria a standard of culture superior to that of most European cities. Third, explorers like Marco Polo and Vasco da Gama had brought back tales of Oriental luxuries that whetted the appetite of wealthy Europeans.

---

[1] J. A. Symonds, *Renaissance in Italy* (New York: Random House, Modern Library, 1935), II, 94.

Fourth, the new trade routes by sea and land were actually bringing back Oriental treasures in quantity. Fifth, cities were growing in size at the termini of such trade routes. Cities needing tradesmen and merchants found them in serfs who were ready and willing to leave the feudal estates and to run off to a city where they would be paid for their work. Sixth, there was a change from an economy based on land to an economy based on money. Seventh, the new aristocracy of wealth sought an identification with the ancient Roman world.

Renaissance zest for life precluded any danger of boredom, and it spread to old, young, rich, poor, educated, and uneducated. The *uomo universale,* especially the artist, engaged in a bewildering number of activities. The same man was often painter, sculptor, architect, goldsmith, and poet. He read music, sang and played, wrote sonnets to his lady or patron, composed court pageants, designing the scenery and costumes, and also directed the show. He built fortifications in time of war, and was sent on diplomatic missions in which he acted as the state department, bureau of espionage, and liaison officer. Or he purchased manuscripts and dug up Roman ruins. Of course, he had many assistants and apprentices working under him, but in the light of these manifold activities it is small wonder that so few masterpieces were actually finished by the hand of the master. (Leonardo da Vinci especially was prone to accept commissions and often part payment for projects which he never finished.)

## The Early Renaissance

No one date can ever be found to mark the beginning of a stylistic epoch. The factors outlined above produced an excitement which stimulated the artists toward new discoveries in each field. No doubt the reappraisal of Giotto's work and the experiments of the Flemish polyphonists helped to stir fresh thinking in painting and music. Artists in all fields realized that great technical questions remained to be solved, and they set out to solve these problems with exuberance and energy. The literary men began to study Roman stylisms so that they might use them in their own creations. The sculptors became interested in the structure of the human body and tried to establish laws governing its representation. The painters began to formulate the laws of linear and aerial perspective and the mathematics of space. Then the musicians began to study the laws of the vibration of sound and to reassess tonal relationships. They were all stimulated by an enormous demand for their creations and an awareness of their own dignity and importance.

The Church remained the greatest patron of the arts, but the courts of the great merchant princes created a whole new market. Just as some modern industrialists collect works of art and amass libraries which they later open to the public in museums, the Renaissance merchant princes had the wealth and leisure to cultivate the arts: to collect books and to hire painters, sculptors, architects, and musicians to gratify their desire for sumptuous living. Their intent was not to impress their rivals but to become, each one, an *uomo universale,* "universal man," trained in body, mind, and spirit for his exalted position as head of a great family, a *Humanist* whose life, based on classical models, should be a work of art and a reflection of the divine. Not that these men were perfect; the courts were often torn by intrigue, rivalry, and dissension, but at least their purpose was sound. Even the Humanistic leaders did not aim to resuscitate the classical past, but through a study of that past they tried to find guiding principles for a new cultural life of their own outside the religious sphere. Musical historian Dr. Paul Henry Lang calls Humanism "the awakening of Italian national consciousness to an independent leadership of European culture." [1] But it did not stop with Italy. Slowly but inexorably, the Humanistic spirit spread across the Alps to invade the Low Countries, France, England, and later America. Each ethnic group reacted differently, and we must take into consideration the different cultural patterns encountered.

For reference, here are the most important of the Italian princely families:

The Medici family in Florence
The Este family in Ferrara
The Sforza family in Milan
The Scala family in Vicenza
The Carrara family in Padua
The Gonzaga family in Mantua
The Montefeltro family in Urbino

**Vittorino's School.** These courts also provided schools where the children were trained to become *uomini universali.* One famous school began in Mantua in 1423 under the direction of Vittorino da Feltre, an inspired Humanist. Out of his school came the future enlightened princes of the courts of Mantua, Urbino, Ferrara, and Milan. So great was his reputation that

---

[1] Paul Henry Lang, *Music in Western Civilization* (New York: W. W. Norton & Company, 1949), p. 170.

when he knelt at the feet of Pope Eugenius IX, the Pope exclaimed: "How great a soul is lodged in this little body! Had my position allowed it, it is I who would have liked to rise as he came in." Vittorino was given a fine villa on the outskirts of Mantua for his school, and his first act was to strip it of every luxury. When the scholars arrived they were "spoiled brats," dressed in costly silks, scented and pomaded. Vittorino quickly changed this situation. He summoned former pupils from Venice so that there would be a competent teacher in every branch of learning. His object was to train the mind and body according to the Platonic doctrine, with Christianity inculcated to train the heart. There were all kinds of sports, including Alpine climbing in summer. Following the Roman educator Quintilian, Vittorino taught his pupils Greek and Latin, philosophy and history, mathematics, music, and dancing. In choice of literature his motto was "Begin with the best." First they studied Virgil, Homer, Cicero, and Demosthenes. When they had mastered these, they went on to Lucan, Ovid, Xenophon, and Herodotus. They studied the Greek tragedies, Pindar, and parts of Aristophanes. Their mathematics included geometry and astronomy. They learned to sing and play the lute and lyre.

At first Vittorino seems to have had in his school only the children of noble families, but later he enrolled children from the lower classes, for such education was not to be restricted to any one class. The teacher required the same mental effort from all regardless of social position. Renaissance Italy made woman the equal of man, and in her important position as head of the household, she needed the same education as her husband. After the emperor Sigismund had visited the Mantuan court, he wrote to a friend how Cecilia Gonzaga, aged ten, had written for him in Greek and Latin "with so much elegance as to put me to shame."

One famous product of the school was Guidobaldo da Montefeltro, Duke of Urbino, who married Elisabetta Gonzaga. Their court at Urbino attracted the best artists and scholars of Italy; among them was Baldassare Castiglione, who described life there in his book, *The Courtier,* and Ludovico Gonzaga, Duke of Mantua. Ludovico brought the architects Brunelleschi and Alberti to his court; he summoned the painter Mantegna to decorate his palace, and the poet Poliziano to compose and produce his pageants. Piero della Francesca painted Ludovico's portrait, and also that of his wife, Battista Sforza, a well-educated little Humanist, of such wisdom that she acted as her husband's regent when he was away. Married at fourteen, she had six daughters, one of them the mother of Vittoria Colonna, the great Florentine beauty.

**Guarino's School.** Vittorino's school was not the only one in Renaissance Italy. Niccolò d'Este brought Guarino da Verona to teach at Ferrara. This school produced Isabella d'Este, an excellent Humanist, who patronized Leonardo da Vinci (see p. 109), Ariosto (see p. 107), and Castiglione (see p. 117), and enjoyed the homage of many great men. Perhaps the most outstanding woman Humanist was Vittoria Colonna (1490–1574), poet and friend of the aged Michelangelo (see p. 111), who derived deep comfort from her sympathy and understanding.

**Sculpture.** The great achievements in sculpture and architecture of the Middle Ages had been made in the North. Now in the fifteenth century Italy took the lead and held it for the next two hundred years. Even in the thirteenth century, Niccolò Pisano and his son Giovanni showed some traces of classical influence in the pulpits of the Cathedrals of Pisa and Sienna. The panels exhibit the customary Gothic overcrowding, but some of the figures look as though they might have been copied from Roman tombs which are still in the cemetery at Pisa. Their work, however, cannot be called Renaissance.

Parenthetically, many of the stories about Renaissance artists are taken from *Lives of the Most Eminent Painters, Sculptors, and Architects*, by Giorgio Vasari (d. 1574), probably the first art historian. His short biographies are very interesting, but not always reliable.

*Ghiberti.* In 1401 occurred the famous competition to determine who should be the sculptor of the bronze doors for the north side of the Baptistry at Florence. The trial subject was the Sacrifice of Isaac, and the shape of the panel was purposely difficult: a quatrafoil with triangles between the foils. The two chief contestants were Filippo Brunelleschi (1377–1446) and Lorenzo Ghiberti (1378–1455). The latter won the contest and since we are fortunate enough to have both designs, you may examine them to see whether you agree with the judges' decision. Brunelleschi was not a good loser. He sold his farm and went off to Rome to study Roman buildings, taking Donatello (c. 1386–1466) with him.

Ghiberti made these north doors to match those on the opposite side which had been sculpted in the previous century by Andrea Pisano. The north doors depict twenty-eight scenes from the life of Christ, each in a geometrical frame. They were finished in 1423 in a style close to Gothic, but with a limited number of figures in each panel.

Ghiberti's greatest fame rests on the east doors which face the

Cathedral. Each door has only five panels, and this larger panel size enabled the sculptor to show more detail and more perspective. Because of the thickness of the bronze, he could use very high relief, which adds to the sense of depth. The figures are idealized, but very dramatic and vigorous. Michelangelo called them the "Gates of Paradise," and they have been so named ever since. When you see them recently burnished, it is easy to believe that Ghiberti had been trained as a goldsmith.

*Donatello.* The best Florentine sculptor of this period was Donatello (*c.* 1386–1466). His figures are utterly natural and yet idealized, poised and yet full of vigor. All trace of rigidity is gone. His bronze "David" was made to stand in the open, not in the customary niche. There are two other "Davids," one by Verrocchio and one by Michelangelo. Compare them and decide which you prefer and which you think closest to the Biblical hero. Donatello's equestrian statue of the soldier Gattamelata shows complete harmony of form, action, and thought. The bust of the "Child Jesus" and the "Singing Choir" in the Cathedral of Florence are lyrical and tender.

*Verrocchio.* Andrea del Verrocchio (1435–1488) was a similar master of anatomy and realistic form. His figures have such assurance that they seem slightly bombastic. It was in Verrocchio's studio that the youthful Leonardo da Vinci got his start.

**Architecture.** The first major innovation of Renaissance architects was in getting rid of the Gothic influence, which had never found a congenial home in Italy.

*Brunelleschi.* When Brunelleschi came back to Florence after his exhaustive study of Roman buildings, he immediately entered a competition for the dome of the Cathedral of Santa Maria del Fiore. This vast church had been begun in the thirteenth century and in 1420 was finished except for the dome. The base was 140 feet across and octagonal in shape, causing a tough engineering problem. Brunelleschi presented a design but not his plans for construction, because he said some one else might utilize his ideas. (This attitude is quite different from the anonymity of medieval architects.) The judges, with many misgivings, finally gave Brunelleschi the contract. His solution was to build two concentric, octagonal domes, joined at the corners by ribs and held together by great oaken beams fastened by iron clamps. The structure was finished in 1436 and the lantern added later. This dome and the beautiful lacy *campanile*, or bell tower, of Giotto are the most familiar features of the Florentine skyline. In two other churches, San Lorenzo and Santo Spirito, Brunelleschi went back to the indigenous style of the early basilica, adorned with classical, decorative features and Corinthian columns.

**Alberti.** The Renaissance merchant princes required city palaces spacious enough for gracious living and for holding their libraries and art treasures. Leon Battista Alberti (1404–1472) was the most typical architect in this type of construction, and his Rucellai Palace in Florence is a good example of it. Alberti was a real *uomo universale*, proficient in everything. He had studied a recently discovered book on Roman architecture by Vitruvius. Its ideas provided norms for the classical revival. The palaces are huge rectangular granite structures, generally three stories in height surmounted by a flat roof with a deep overhanging cornice. The first story of rough or rusticated blocks has small barred windows, showing the need for protection from outside disturbances. Rooms on this floor were used for storing provisions and transacting business. The rough stones of the first story become smooth with beveled joints in the second, and perfectly plain in the third. The stringcourses that separate the stories emphasize the horizontal which was so carefully avoided by Gothic builders. Windows on the upper floors are sometimes surmounted by a round arch with columns or pilasters, and sometimes by a triagular pediment. A large entrance leads from the street into a spacious open court surrounded by columns and arches which support the living quarters on the upper two floors. Sculptured figures adorn the court. Alberti's work is typical of Renaissance architecture in general.

**Painting.** Renaissance painting is generally considered to have started with Giotto about the beginning of the fourteenth century. During the next two hundred years experiments were made that resulted in technical advances and the development of perspective.

**Giotto.** John Canaday, modern art critic and historian, believes that the most decisive day in the history of Western painting was in 1306 when Giotto di Bondone completed his series of thirty-eight frescoes on the walls of the Arena Chapel in Padua. Soft and glowing even today, they depict scenes in the lives of Joachim and Anne, the Virgin, and Christ. It was Giotto's interpretation of Biblical scenes that lifted painting to its preeminent position in Italian Renaissance life. He abandoned the old technical formulas for drawing and made each scene an intense, dramatic moment within an organization that was completely unified and coherent. If you look carefully, you will find mistakes in perspective, but you must remember that Giotto had no classical models to guide him as the architects and sculptors had. Analyze as many of these frescoes as possible, especially the

GIOTTO DI BONDONI: *Lamentation*. Arena Chapel, Padua. (Alinari—Art Reference Bureau)

"Flight into Egypt" and the "Lamentation" (see above). "Giotto changed painting from an art of symbols to an art of passion."[1] He was rewarded in his lifetime by money, fame, and political position. He was a close friend of Dante, and he probably painted the lovely fresco of "St. Francis Blessing the Birds" in the Church of Assisi. Perhaps it was because of Giotto's great reputation that no painter arose to challenge him for the next fifty years.

*Fifteenth-Century Painters.* All the painters of the fifteenth century were concerned with technical problems: how to represent three-dimensional reality on a two-dimensional surface. This involved perspective, foreshortening, unity, thought in posture and facial expression, arrangement of individuals in a crowd, and effects of light, shade, and color. All these problems

[1] John Canaday, "Giotto and Duccio," *Horizon Magazine of the Arts,* Summer, 1965, p. 92.

were mastered largely by Florentine painters from Masaccio (1401–1428) to Botticelli (1444–1510). The architect Brunelleschi was the first to work out mathematically the rules of linear perspective, and the painter Masaccio was the first to put them into practice.

MASACCIO. We know little about Masaccio except that he died when only twenty-seven years old, without finishing the series of frescoes on the walls of the Brancacci Chapel in Florence. If you study just two of these paintings, "The Expulsion of Adam and Eve" and "The Tribute Money," you will see that his figures have bone, muscle, and flesh and that the single source of light molds the bodies and the draperies. Vasari summed up Masaccio when he wrote: "He recognized that painting is nought but the imitation of things as they are."

FRA ANGELICO. Masaccio's achievement becomes more startling when "The Tribute Money" is compared with Fra Angelico's "Lamentation." Fra Angelico (1387–1455) was a Dominican monk who decorated every cell of his monastery of San Marco with a religious picture. Gentle and sweet, he was the last survivor in art of the medieval, mystic point of view. Like the composer Bach, two hundred years later, he knew about the "modern" innovations but turned his back on them. He deliberately chose to paint in an outmoded style. His Annunciations are never sentimental but spiritual and devotional. There is a gorgeous angel with rainbow wings at the top of the stairs leading to the monks' cells. Vasari says that when he painted a crucifix, tears streamed from his eyes. "Except ye become as a little child . . ." certainly applies to Fra Angelico.

PIERO. Piero della Francesca (*c.* 1420–1492) filled his pictures with light and air by the silvery tones in the coloring. There is a great deal of tension and energy expressed in his figures, but little manifestation of emotion or feeling in the faces. The great modern art critic Bernard Berenson believed that this is an asset in a painting because it leaves the beholder undisturbed in his concentration. Piero solved the problem of space for Raphael and the problem of chiaroscuro for Leonardo da Vinci. You should study his excellent portraits of the Duke of Urbino and his wife, Battista Sforza.[1]

---

[1] Dr. Eugenio Battisti, professor of art history at the Pennsylvania State University, has recently explored the documents found in the home of Piero della Francesca in the small town of Borgo San Sepolcro, Italy. The documents include designs for the streets, architecture, and fortifications of the town: probably the first instance of organized town-planning in history.

FRA FILIPPO LIPPI: *Madonna and Child with Two Angels*. Uffizi, Florence. (Alinari—Art Reference Bureau)

LIPPI. Fra Filippo Lippi (1406–1469) also painted superb portraits. His Virgins are natural Florentine girls, charming but always perfectly poised. At the same time, in his well-known "Madonna and Child with Angels" (see p. 101) in the Uffizi, Lippi indulges in sly humor in the little angel who is holding up the Christ Child. Don't fail to read Browning's poem "Fra Lippo Lippi," an account of how the painter monk lets himself down from the Medici palace by a ladder made of sheets in order to enjoy a night "on the town" and then is caught by a watchman. The episode is imaginary, of course, but not impossible because Lippi did elope with a nun and may have married her after their vows were rescinded.[1]

BOTTICELLI. Sandro Botticelli (1447–1510) was a pupil of Lippi. He started realistically, like his teacher, but became increasingly idealistic and abstract. His best-known paintings, "Spring" and "Birth of Venus" (see p. 103), are both based on pagan subjects. Botticelli is a poetic painter, blending charm of story with charm of line and color. At the same time, he is melancholy, a feeling which you sense even in the goddess of love; there is a foreshadowing of death in the gray flesh and wan flowers. In late life, he fell under the influence of the religious reformer Savonarola and burned some of his earlier paintings.

**Music.** The most important concept which the Renaissance has bequeathed to us is the optimistic faith in man's ability to create enduring works of beauty. In no field of activity is this buoyant faith more evident than in music. Not every *uomo universale* could paint a picture or build a church, but he could make music. Participation, not passive listening, was the key to enjoyment. Music held everyone under its spell: kings, courtiers, popes, monks, nuns, courtesans, merchants, tradesmen, laborers, and on down to the humblest peasant.

The French and Flemish composers maintained the leadership in this kind of "art music" throughout the Renaissance. When their creativity had culminated in artistic masterpieces, their services were sought in every court of Europe to teach the new style. Polyphony did not exactly suit the more lyric Italian temperament, but the Italians were so innately musical that they mastered polyphonic complexities and in the High Renaissance

---

[1] According to Vasari, Lippi did not marry Lucrezia, but she refused to leave him. She bore him a son, also named Filippo, who was only ten years old when his father died. He became an excellent portrait painter and was called Filippino Lippi to distinguish him from his father.

SANDRO BOTTICELLI: *Birth of Venus.* Uffizi, Florence. (Alinari—Art Reference Bureau)

period produced some glorious music. The melodic and rhythmic freedom of the interweaving voices became stimulating entertainment for small groups of singers and instrumentalists as they sat around a table with their part books in front of them. In the fifteenth century, there was an increasing trend toward secular forms and also toward greater simplicity and lyricism which came from English, Italian, and minstrel influences.

The lute was the favorite household instrument of the entire Renaissance because its tone was soft and intimate. Since there was as yet no difference between an instrumental and a vocal style, these polyphonic songs could be performed by any combination of voices and instruments that happened to be available.

*Machaut.* The development of polyphony has already been traced from its rather haphazard beginnings perhaps in England, through the Gothic motets of Leoninus and Perotinus (see p. 76). The next great composer was Guillaume de Machaut (*c.* 1300–1377), musician, poet, priest, and the much-traveled diplomatic agent to King John of Bohemia, brother-in-law of Charles IV of France. The French compared his poetry to that of the contemporary Petrarch and the younger Chaucer. (The idea that proficiency in one art implied proficiency in other arts was new in the Renaissance.) He set many of his own love poems to a sophisticated type of music which marks him as an innovator. This worldly prelate composed more secular works than sacred, but is remembered chiefly for his *Mass of Notre Dame,* the first completely integrated polyphonic four-part mass. *Integrated* means that the same melodic and rhythmic material runs through all six sections of the mass. This unifying principle anticipates not only the masters of the High Renaissance, but also Bach, Beethoven, in fact all composers of extended works right down to modern times. When he called his work *ars nova,* "new art," he spoke more truly than he knew. There is a tradition that this mass was used at the coronation of Charles V in 1364.

*Dufay.* In the latter fifteenth century, there began a wholesale exodus to Italy of Flemish musicians attracted by liturgic display in Rome, the natural warmth of popular Italian music, and the splendor of Renaissance life at the courts.

Guillaume Dufay (*c.* 1400–1474) left his home in Burgundy to become the youngest singer in the Papal Choir. He accompanied Pope Eugenius IV to Pisa and Florence and later was at the courts of Savoy and Paris. He was thus well acquainted with all European musical styles. His style reconciles French with Italian and English elements. In religious music he often builds on a secular instead of a Gregorian *cantus firmus.* His secular songs, rather plaintive and melancholy, give a perfect picture of the poem and its meaning.

*Isaac.* Heinrich Isaac (*c.* 1450–1517) left Flanders for the court of Lorenzo de' Medici about 1480 when Florence was at the height of its Renaissance grandeur. He learned to compose graceful music in the Italian style. Later he entered the service of Emperor Maximilian I at his court in Innsbruck. It was Maximilian's custom to take all his musicians, including his choir, along with him wherever he went, even to war. When the Emperor moved his court to Vienna, Isaac composed the expressive lament, "Innsbruck, I Must Leave Thee," a song still sung in Germany today to express sorrow at leaving one's home.

*Landino.* The Italian *ars nova* of the fourteenth century is best exemplified by Francesco Landino (d. 1397), who in fact composed more than a third of all the extant Italian music of the period. He was organist of San Lorenzo in Florence and was blind since childhood (probably from smallpox). He played every instrument known to his period and is usually pictured in the manuscripts playing a small portative organ held in his arm. A great friend of Petrarch, he wrote much poetry and was awarded a laurel crown for a poem in Venice in 1364. His compositions fall into three types, all secular: madrigals (real art songs), *ballate* (rhythmic dance songs), and *cacce* (programmatic fun songs). While all these types are polyphonic and show as great artistry as those of Machaut, Landino's style shows a greater emphasis on the soprano part, greater interest in thirds and sixths (the lush intervals), a strong trend toward our major and minor tonalities, and a preference for the A B B A form. Landino set only one *caccia.* It is a fishing song and here is part of the text:

> *Thus thoughtful, as love guides me*
> *along the green coast slowly,*
> *I hear: "Lift that rock!"*
> *"Look at the crawfish, look! Look at the fish!*
> *Catch him, catch him."*
> *"This is marvelous!"*
> *Isabella began with screams:*
> *"Oh, Oh!" "What's the matter? What's the Matter?"*
> *"I've been bit in the toe!"*
> *Meanwhile I came to the amorous crowd,*
> *Where I found charming ladies and lovers*
> *Who drew me to them with beautiful countenances.*[1]

**Literature.** Italy produced no great literary masterpieces during the Renaissance. The reason is that all the literary men were trying to find in the works of antiquity literary canons which would ensure excellence in structure and style. Sometimes their work shows creativeness and sometimes only imitation of classical models. At least their efforts produced the Petrarchan sonnet, the short story, the pastoral romance, and the romantic epic, which, if not great, provided the raw material upon which future French, English, Spanish, and German writers built. It is sometimes said that the Italian writers had a Freudian obsession with sex, but most of them were attached to one of the courts and they wrote to entertain their frivolous courtly clientele.

The voracious Renaissance appetite for songs of all kinds— from the ribald *villanelli* and carnival songs, through the poetic love songs sent to a fair lady, the madrigals, the *ballate,* on up the scale to the sacred street songs (*laudi spirituali*)—all de- manded literary texts. Since everyone who made any claim to education tossed off poetry as a matter of course, composers had

---

[1] Quoted in "Francesco Landino and His Music," by Leonard Ellinwood, *Musical Quarterly,* April, 1936. Reprinted by permission of G. Schirmer, Inc., copyright owner.

plenty of material to draw from. That so little of it is great poetry is understandable, but it is better than the insipid inanities of most modern "popular" songs. The prevailing sentiment then as now was exquisite and voluptuous melancholy.

*Petrarch.* One of the most popular lyricists was Francesco Petrarch (1304–1374). Petrarch's father was a noble Florentine who was driven into exile at the same time as Dante. He took his family to Avignon, France, because the Papal court was there during the "Babylonian captivity" when the papacy moved from Rome. Like Boccaccio, Petrarch was in love with a young married woman, who appears as Laura in his poetry. Petrarch was a real Humanist, intensely interested in the classics. He expressed his love and torment in highly polished, intellectual poems which, while they show careful workmanship, do not always seem sincere. Petrarch's most polished lyrics are in the sonnet form: fourteen lines long with the rhyme scheme abba, abba, cde, cde. The first eight lines present the theme (problem, doubt, or question) ; the last six lines answer the question, resolve the problem, and drive home the point by an abstract comment. This balanced structure and parallelism between form and content made the Petrarchan sonnet the most popular form during the Renaissance and gave it lasting validity even into our own day. It was a favorite with Ronsard and the *Pléiade* in France, and with John Milton and Elizabeth Barrett Browning in England. After Laura died, Petrarch went on a number of diplomatic missions, then went back to Italy, where he became a close friend of Boccaccio. In later life he seems to have been torn between a desire for worldly fame and religious devotion. He was honored by most of the brilliant courts of Europe and imitated by later poets.

*Boccaccio.* Giovanni Boccaccio (1313–1375) also was passionately devoted to classical literature. He was born in Paris of an Italian father and a French mother. He learned the game of courtly love at the dissolute Spanish court in Naples. He too fell in love with a married woman. When she jilted him for another, he went to Florence and wrote for Lorenzo's court. Boccaccio reacted differently from Petrarch to his love experience. He became cynical toward women. In *Il Filostrato* ("The Man Conquered by Love"), Criseyde is the incarnation of falseness. Chaucer took the bare outline of this plot for his *Troilus and Criseyde* (see p. 87), but he is more gentle toward the heroine.

Boccaccio's fame rests on the short stories in *The Decameron;* but very few of these have real literary merit, and some are only anecdotes. *Decameron* comes from the Greek and means "ten days." According to the "Frame Tale" (Introduction), which is similar to that of the Prologue in Chaucer's *Canterbury Tales,* a group of young Florentine nobles, seven women and three men, escape from the plague-ridden city during the Black Death of 1348, taking refuge in their country estates. To while away the time, each agrees to tell a story on each of the ten days. A different person presides each day and chooses a theme for the next day's stories. To give the work verisimilitude, Boccaccio begins with a vivid description of the plague in the city, and also describes rural scenes as the group journeys from one villa to another. The tales told on the Tenth Day are most like what we have been led to expect of a good short story. With Boccaccio, love is a stimulating pastime, and man is just a human beast. In his glorification of physical love, he struck at the root of romantic sentimentality. He was a true Epicurean, believing that man's end was to enjoy life. His style is a straightforward, rapid narration with vigorous dialogue. He preferred incongruous and ironic situations, and was scathing in his satire on corrupt churchmen.

*Romantic Epics.* Storytelling was popular entertainment at Renaissance courts just as it had been in the Middle Ages. To satisfy this demand Luigi Pulci (1432–1484) created the romantic epic tale based on the French hero, Roland. Called *Il Morgante Maggiore* ("The Greater Morgante"), it is a mixture of ridiculous events written in the style of low comedy. Next came the epic of Boiardo (1434–1494), *Orlando Innamorato* ("Roland in Love"), which tells about the hero's infatuation with a bewitching Saracen princess. The love affair is woven through a bewildering tapestry of battles, magic, pursuit, and fantasy with all sorts of digressions involving King Arthur's knights and Charlemagne. Like *The Decameron,* it is both earthy and vigorous.

Next to elaborate the Roland narrative was Ariosto (1474–1533). His work, called *Orlando Furioso* ("Mad Roland"), continues Boiardo's story. Every line of the poetry is polished like a jewel, but there is little internal unity. In the poem Roland has gone mad because of love and another character makes a trip to the moon to recover his lost senses. Sometimes the story is purely romantic, sometimes patriotic, or moral, or allegorical. In the midst of all this it advises using gunpowder to drive out the Turks. The poem shows Renaissance interest in every aspect of life without penetrating below the surface of any one of them. Ariosto's poem was the principal model for Spenser's *Faerie Queene.*

The last Renaissance poet to deal with the Roland material was Torquato Tasso (1544–1595), who lived when the Inquisition was in force. He wrote *Gerusalemme Liberata* ("Jerusalem Liberated") at the court of the Duke of Ferrara. A story of the First Crusade, it attempts to achieve the unity of action which the other epics lacked. After recounting many love entanglements between Crusaders and pagan sorceresses, the story ends with the Crusaders kneeling before the Holy Sepulchre and offering thanks to God. Tasso had the ability to make vivid word pictures, and his love scenes are idyllic rather than impassioned. Canto II tells the story of Tancred's battle with the pagan maid Clorinda. He kills her, but dying, she asks for Christian baptism. This is the subject of Monteverdi's late madrigal using the *stile concitato* ("agitated style") (see p. 169).

## The High Renaissance

For well-nigh two hundred years the creative geniuses of the early Renaissance had been seeking in the classical world artistic canons which would revive that ancient period. What they achieved was an entirely new style. Their efforts reached a culminating synthesis in the opening years of the sixteenth century which we term the High Renaissance.

In the meantime social and political conditions had changed. Whereas the early Renaissance princes had been energetic bourgeois merchants, their descendants, with inherited power and wealth, wanted only to enjoy the leisure that was the status symbol of their social position. The courts became centers of patronage for artists who celebrated the glory of and provided the entertainment for their masters. What was demanded was an art that was aristocratic and exalted. Rome was also an important center of patronage. Because the Popes had great wealth and ambitions to rebuild the city on a grand scale, increasingly the greatest artists were called to Rome to execute commissions.

The technical problems like perspective, counterpoint, and versification, which had occupied so much of the attention of the earlier masters, had by the beginning of the sixteenth century been solved, and the solutions were passed on to the geniuses of the High Renaissance. This inheritance is analogous to Cosimo de Medici's wealth being passed on to Lorenzo the Magnificent. Neither artists nor patrons had to worry about these problems any longer. But by the same token High Renaissance masters lost some of the freshness and charming naïveté which had been hallmarks of early struggles. What the High Renaissance sought was an *ideal harmony of free parts*. Any detail, no matter how attractive, which did not contribute to this ideal harmony had to be discarded as irrelevant.

A reference to music may illustrate this principle. In early Renaissance polyphony a composer often added another voice part to someone else's composition. Similarly, if a work was written for six voices, and only four performers were present, two of the parts could be left out without damage. But in the High Renaissance, and even more in the Baroque period which followed, parts could not be added or subtracted without destroying the architectonic balance of the whole. This fact is very important.

**Painting.** In sixteenth-century paintings there are fewer figures, and they express abstract qualities rather than individualized emotion. Portraits idealize the subject and minimize his imperfections; all bits of local color are eliminated. Landscape is reduced to a minimum so that the meaning of the painting can be grasped at once, even from a distance. If a subject calls for many figures, they tend to be placed in separate planes parallel to the front edge of the frame.

*Leonardo da Vinci.* These stylisms are clearly revealed in the work of Leonardo da Vinci (1452–1519). Leonardo spent thirty years in Florence, twenty years in Milan, and nineteen years wandering, eventually coming to rest in a chateau near Paris, given to him by Francis I. Even as a child he liked to design and construct models of beautiful objects, and his father took him to the workshop of Verrocchio, then the most famous artist in Florence. Verrocchio was a painter, sculptor, worker in metals, and designer of fine household and religious objects. He happened to be working on a Baptism scene for the Vallombrosia monastery, and Leonardo was allowed to finish an angel in the left-hand corner. When Verrocchio came back to look, he turned away stunned, so bright and animated was the little angel. The pupil had already surpassed the master. From Verrocchio he learned to paint all beautiful objects, but he was unsatisfied. Characteristically, he plunged into a study of nature systematically, especially to help solve two supreme problems: the smiling of women and the effect of falling water.

In 1483 Leonardo wrote Ludovico Sforza in Milan, offering to sell him strange secrets in the art of war. Ludovico invited him to come to model a colossal statue of Francesco, first Duke of Milan. Leonardo appeared at the court as a harp player. He had designed his silver harp in the shape of a horse's skull. With his musical ability he became a skillful designer of court pageants.

Just as Leonardo had plunged into the study of natural phenomena, he plunged into a study of human personality and how to portray it. But there were facets of human personality which eluded him and this may be the enigma in the smile of the "Mona Lisa." There seems to be a hidden sadness in the faces he paints.

Following the sudden death of Ludovico's wife Beatrice, Leonardo began to paint the "Last Supper" (see below) on the wall of the refectory of Santa Maria delle Grazie, the convent which had been Beatrice's favorite oratory. The walls were damp; yet Leonardo used oil paint which allowed slower work, changes, and afterthoughts. No medium could have been less durable. Within fifty years it had fallen into decay. This was the first of many vicissitudes of fortune, or rather misfortune, suffered by this painting. During the Napoleonic wars a hole was cut through the lower part of the painting so that horses could be stabled in the room. Leonardo presents the subject not in the medieval mystical sense, but as a leave-taking among friends. The painter is interested in the psychological reaction of each disciple to Christ's words, "One of you shall betray me." You should study this painting for its structural organization. The architecture of the painting repeats exactly the architecture of the room, so that it makes the room look twice as large as it is. Study the perspective and the symmetrical grouping of the disciples on each side of Christ. Notice where the lines converge and the fact that all the figures are in one horizontal plane.

The year after Leonardo finished this painting, 1499, the French army entered Milan and Ludovico was driven into exile.

LEONARDO DA VINCI: *Last Supper*. Santa Maria delle Grazie, Milan. (Alinari—Art Reference Bureau)

Leonardo spent time briefly in Mantua, Venice, and Florence, where he painted the "Mona Lisa" and the "Virgin and Child with St. Anne." Eventually he went to the court of Francis I of France, who had long sought him, taking the "Mona Lisa" with him. That is why this painting is in the Louvre today. Tradition says that he died in the arms of Francis.

Leonardo was a genius in whatever he undertook, and his insatiable curiosity led him to investigate too many subjects. His notebooks reveal detailed drawings of plants, animals, the human embryo, hydraulic machines, military fortifications and engines of war, canals, flying machines, atmospheric disturbances, cloud formations, the physical properties of sound. This diversity of interests and duties (he had to design ingenious scenic effects for court pageants and then direct the performances) accounts for the fact that so few paintings were finished. He often accepted commissions and sometimes part payment for works which were never begun. Leonardo discovered the technique of *sfumato* ("smokey"), which means a blurring of the edges of figures as if they were disappearing in shadow. It takes away the rigidity of the figures and makes them look more lifelike.

*Raphael.* Raphael (1483–1520) was the most poetic and idealistic of the High Renaissance giants. He and the eighteenth-century composer Mozart might be said to represent the pure Apollonian cult. When Raphael came to Florence from Perugia at twenty-one, he stood in awe before the works of Leonardo and Michelangelo. It took him four years to assimilate their discoveries; then he was called to Rome to decorate the rooms of the Vatican. Raphael's greatest contribution is in space composition. This is the art of getting the utmost tactile values and movement out of figures and masses in action. In his paintings the figures have room to move about. Test this spatiality in his "School of Athens." The actual shape of the wall is echoed in the painted vaults of the picture, and through these arches the groups of figures are unified in articulated space. It is the perfect solution of the problem of how to decorate a wall without destroying its actual space-defining function.

Raphael is probably best known for his paintings of the Madonna and Child (see p. 112). Most of these are arranged in pyramidal grouping with only very simple background or none at all. Mother and Child are not simply natural and human as in Lippi, but they are idealized to represent universal motherhood and childhood.

*Michelangelo.* The last of the Florentine titans is Michelangelo (1475–1564). If Raphael and Mozart represent the

RAPHAEL SANZIO: *Sistine Madonna*. Gallery, Dresden. (Alinari—Art Reference Bureau)

Apollonian ideal, Michelangelo and Beethoven represent the Dionysiac cult of vehemence and power. Michelangelo lived to be eighty-nine years old, and his life spans three stylistic periods— High Renaissance, Mannerism, and early Baroque. Since he was first a sculptor, then painter, then architect, all three periods can be studied in the work of this one man. He was primarily interested in the nude human figure, and his figures are larger than life-size. His painting of the "Holy Family" in the Uffizi and to a certain extent the figures on the Sistine Chapel ceiling are in the calm, poised style of the High Renaissance.

The Sistine ceiling covers seven hundred square yards and contains more than three hundred figures representing Biblical Stories of the Creation through the Flood. Everything is nebulous until the Creation of Adam (see p. 113). He lies like a young Greek god (the model is said to have been a torso of Hercules in the Vatican), muscles fully developed, but listless until he should be touched by the finger of the Creator. Perhaps if we had only the figure of Adam to look at day after day, life would be meaningful and sweet and whole. These figures reveal Michelangelo's skill in depicting the human body in every conceivable position and from every angle.

MICHELANGELO BUONARROTI: *Creation of Man.* Sistine Chapel, Rome. (Alinari—Art Reference Bureau)

*Venetian Painters.* There was a parallel development in painting that was going on in Venice during this period. The point of departure for Venetian art was the Byzantine style, strongly infused with Oriental elements. Venice, protected by its lagoons, and relatively safe from attack, was also the focus of the trade routes from the Orient. Its wealthy and independent citizens were well able to indulge their love of Oriental luxuries. Venice produced no ascetic mystics like St. Francis and Fra Angelico, no intellectual giants like Leonardo and Michelangelo. It was a city of commerce, banking, and pleasure. And after the sun has burned away the mist from the surrounding water, it still is a city of sparkling light and color. No wonder then that Venetian artists thought of their work in terms of decoration, and surely the most decorative element is color.

BELLINI AND GIORGIONE. The earliest Venetian master was Giovanni Bellini (*c.* 1430–1516), who was the first painter to attempt harmony through the use of color. Then came Giorgione (1478–1511), who might be called the inventor of Italian *genre* painting. A genre painting is an easily movable picture which presents a moment of actual life, refined and idealized. There is still great mystery surrounding Giorgione. Nobody knows for certain which paintings are his, and which were done by his assistants. There may be two or as many as seventy. There is also mystery in what he was trying to represent in "The Open Air Concert" (see below), and especially in "The Tempest." Since no two people agree, your guess is as good as another's. At any rate, the landscape is just as important as the people, and everything is suffused with a golden, sensuous light. You will be interested to compare his "Sleeping Venus" with Botticelli's "Birth of Venus."

TITIAN. Titian (1477–1576), pupil of Giorgione, lived sixty-five years after his master died. He never attained the poetic vision of Giorgione; his nude figures are more earthbound and do not seem quite so much an integral part of the landscape. His interests are all-embracing: pagan subjects, Christian mysteries, the delights of love, the mystery of death, the beauty of nature. Titian shares with Raphael the highest position in Renaissance portraiture. In his portrait of Pope Paul III, he did not idealize his subject. The instantaneous impression reveals the complete personality.

GIORGIONE: *The Open Air Concert*. Louvre, Paris. (Alinari—Art Reference Bureau)

**Sculpture and Architecture.** Michelangelo made his first reputation as a sculptor and always called himself a sculptor. In fact, Pope Julius II persuaded him to do the Sistine frescoes against his will. Two pieces of sculpture best represent his High Renaissance style: his "David" and the "Pietà" in St. Peter's. He was so interested in the adult male figure that he seems to have forgotten that he was portraying David as a very young lad. Almost as an afterthought, he made the hands and feet unusually large as a concession to David's adolescence. The "Pietà" is the expression of a calm and controlled grief, idealized both in the figure of the Virgin and in that of Christ.

The buildings of the High Renaissance, characterized by the grandeur and monumentality of Roman architecture, are to be found chiefly in Rome. Bramante (1444-1514) was the greatest architect, although few of his buildings survive. The best example is the graceful, small chapel called the "Tempietto."

In 1505, Pope Julius II commissioned Michelangelo to build a magnificent tomb for him in the old basilica of Constantine (St. Peter's). With Michelangelo's penchant for size, it soon became apparent that the church would not hold the tomb. The Pope commissioned Bramante to pull the old basilica down, and to design a grandiose pontifical city and an enlarged St. Peter's. Bramante designed the church in the form of a Greek cross with a dome over the crossing where the tomb would stand. But Bramante and his associates died before the plan was carried out. Inferior architects changed the plans again, but finally in 1546 Michelangelo was appointed director of construction. He started the enormous dome and the choir. A free-standing portico would have provided a monumental entrance without cutting off the view of the dome from the front. But Michelangelo died, and his followers, Carlo Moderna and Bernini, again changed the design. They made it again a Latin cross with a huge façade and Doric colonnades enclosing the vast piazza in front. The result is that Moderna's façade dwarfs the dome behind it, and Bernini's colonnade distracts attention from the church itself. The real irony is that poor Julius II, who started all the reconstruction is not even buried there. "Sic transit gloria mundi."

The interior of St. Peter's is disappointing, too, for it seems to be smaller than its actual size. The Corinthian pilasters are so thick, and barrel vaulting covers so much of the nave that it is impossible to see the dome until one stands directly under it. There is nothing to make one aware of the size and monumentality which are in fact there.

The Italian garden is another achievement of the High Renaissance. When you visit Rome, don't fail to see the beautiful gardens surrounding the Villa d'Este at Tivoli. Laid out in a formal pattern of hedges, trees, statues, and fountains, these gardens became the inspiration for palace gardens everywhere in Europe from Versailles to Potsdam to St. Petersburg.

**Music.** The calm, ethereal beauty of the pure *a cappella* style of polyphony in the High Renaissance is the crowning achievement of some six hundred years of effort by countless musicians in England, France, the Low Countries, and Italy. This is the only real *a cappella* period in history. The Franco-Flemish technique still held sway, but the spirit had become Italianized. The increasing importance of the text resulted from the ideals of the Humanists and the efforts of the Church to make the words intelligible to the worshipers. The two chief forms of church music, the motet and the mass, show sections of imitative polyphony alternating with sections of *homophony:* that is, blocks of chords in which all the voices sing the same text *at the same time.* The invention of music printing in Venice in 1501 enormously facilitated the spread of new ideas and techniques throughout Europe.

The Franco-Flemish composers were still the leaders. To Josquin Desprès (1450–1521), expression was more important than the subtleties of counterpoint. In the more than three hundred masses and motets by Philippe da Monte (1521–1603), Franco-Flemish style became internationalized. But the real musical *uomo universale* was Orlandus Lassus (1532–1594). He was born at Mons in Burgundian country and started his career as a choirboy in his native town. His fine voice was recognized by Fernando Gonzaga (Viceroy of Sicily and general of the Netherlands armies of Emperor Charles V), who spirited him off to Sicily and Milan. He directed the choir in the Lateran Church in Rome. Later he lived in France, then the Low Countries, perhaps England, and finally in Munich. What is important is not the extent of his travels, but that he assimilated the temperamental differences of all these countries and combined them with his own consummate mastery of the technique of composition. As a result, he wrote equally well the love-sick Italian madrigal, the delicate and dancing French *chanson,* and the robust German *lied.* Indeed his range extended from the little vulgar Italian *villanella* to the most spiritual mass and motet.

Throughout the Renaissance, there had been virtuosi on the lute, organ, or keyboard who had won great fame on their chosen instrument. In the early sixteenth century, when choral music became emancipated from its dependence on instruments, instrumental composers found that they could get along very well without voices. The Spanish lutanist Don Luis Milan (*c.* 1500–after 1561) composed very artistic dance music, and the Italian lutanist Francesco da Milano (1490–1566) composed all kinds of contrapuntal fantasies.

**Literature.** Two prose works of the High Renaissance should be known to every educated person who is interested in government and the arts. They are *Il Principe* (*The Prince*) by Machiavelli and *Il Cortegiano* (*The Courtier*) by Castiglione. These two documents adequately sum up the entire Italian literary Renaissance.

*Machiavelli.* Niccolò Machiavelli (1469–1527) came of an honorable but poor Florentine family. He served the Republic of Florence in a judicial capacity and journeyed to the court of France and Rome when Caesar Borgia was nearly at the end of his nefarious career. He was also sent on other diplomatic missions without great success. When *The Prince* was published in 1513, Florence had been through twenty years of political turmoil; Machiavelli had languished for a time in prison; Savonarola had been burned; and Lorenzo de Medici had been brought back to power. We must read *The Prince* against this political background. Machiavelli saw civilization as a development to be achieved in the future and not by imitating an old pattern. He maintained that a people bound by law is superior to a prince, and he looked to peace as the object of war.

In *The Prince*, Machiavelli described what often happens in a democratic form of government in words that might apply today. He says democracy soon "runs into that kind of license which inflicts injury upon public as well as private interests." He sees each individual consulting his own passions, committing a thousand acts of injustice. He believes that a wise and benevolent prince, governing under good laws, by the consent of the governed, with a strong military force, establishes the best kind of government. But he qualifies his statement by saying that a prince, unbound by law, is far worse than a people's government.

*Castiglione.* The background of Castiglione's *The Courtier* is quite different from that of *The Prince*. Castiglione lived at the court of Urbino in the closing years of Guidobaldo da Montefeltro at the turn of the sixteenth century. He was a close friend of Raphael and a collector of works of art. The Urbino court was the best governed and most enlightened of all the Renaissance courts, because it was the product of Vittorino da Feltre's teaching (see p. 95).

In form *The Courtier* echoes *The Orator* of Cicero. Castiglione sets out to depict the perfect courtier as Cicero had depicted the perfect orator. The author puts as first requirements noble birth and the profession of arms. But the courtier is not wedded to his cuirass, as is witnessed by the biting answer of the lady to the soldier who would not dance or listen to music. She suggests that he get himself well-greased and put away with his armor in a cupboard until needed, so that he might not rust more than he had. In the perfect courtier, goodness precedes letters, which are the second ornament of the mind.

In the Platonic climax of the work, goodness is equated with beauty, for from Castiglione to Rousseau in the eighteenth century the arts dominated the civilization of Europe. Therefore the perfect courtier is the one who draws, paints, plays instruments, and writes poetry. Here at last the medieval knightly symbols of the purse and the sword have been replaced by the interests of a refined gentleman. And what a transformation of the medieval concept of marriage! Castiglione says that marriage is the proper goal of love, that other kinds of love bring only remorse. He says further that the lady of the palace should share the cultural interests of her husband and that "the tributes to her as a softening and civilizing influence should ring with a lyric intensity."

### Effects of the Italian Renaissance on the West

Western Europe and England were slow to feel the effects of the Renaissance for a number of reasons. France was busy for a hundred years trying to expel the English from French soil. When peace came in 1453 at the end of the Hundred Years' War (also the date of the destruction of Constantinople by the Turks), internal conditions were so deplorable that it took France fifty years to recover. Spain experienced a rebirth of medieval religious mysticism as a result of the Jesuit Counter Reformation, while many of her ablest men were swallowed up in the American jungles. After the partition of Burgundy in 1477, the Low Countries were involved in the political ambitions of the Hapsburgs. Germany was completely dislocated by the Protestant Reformation and after that by the Thirty Years' War (1618–1648). In the fifteenth century England was fighting the futile Wars of the Roses. Almost the only art to go merrily along despite these conflagrations was music.

Another reason for the tardiness of the Renaissance in the West was that the Gothic spirit with all of its manifestations (great churches, Mariolatry, Scholasticism, heroic tales, courtly love, etc.) was very strong and the stronger the stylistic impulse, the harder it is to break. As has been said before, to the Italians the Gothic was incomprehensible. Except for isolated individuals, Spain, Germany, and the Low Countries jumped over the Renaissance and landed in either Mannerism or the Baroque. Therefore they lacked the classic calm which might have tempered Baroque excesses.

**France and Burgundy.** The court of the dukes of Burgundy at Dijon was a mecca for artists, musicians, and poets. The duchy of Burgundy had been given by King John II of France to his son, Philip, about mid-fourteenth century. Each succeeding duke added to the dominions until by mid-fifteenth century the duchy comprised most of eastern France, the Low Countries, and territory on up to the North Sea. When Charles the Bold was killed in battle in 1477, he left his only daughter, Mary, as heiress. She married Archduke Maximilian of Austria, soon to become Emperor Maximilian I. After Mary died in 1482, Burgundy was divided between the French crown (Louis XI) and the Emperor. That is how the Hapsburgs came to control the Low Countries. Dufay, important in the developing of polyphonic music (see p. 104), has already been mentioned as being at the Burgundian Court. Machaut, composer of the fourteenth-century *ars nova,* was connected with Burgundy through his nephew, the poet Deschamps. Machaut himself was a good lyric poet, skilled in such poetic forms as the ballade, virelai, and rondeau. Even Chaucer imitated Machaut.

But it is the painters at the Burgundian Court who are of primary interest. Remember that the whole tone of the court was now French and medieval, and it remained medieval throughout the fifteenth century. The painters themselves came from Germany, Flanders, Holland, and France, but they show the same characteristics: clean lines, brilliant and hard color, a love of minute detail, and symbolism. These traits with the exception of symbolism persisted in Flemish and Dutch painting for the next three hundred years. Much scholarly work on the early Flemish painters remains to be done. Some of them are nameless, and it is not clear how they obtained their bright, hard color. Their methods were secret, strictly regulated by the guilds. They probably used a quick-drying oil paint mixed with natural resin as a binder. The wood panel was covered with a thin white coat, possibly of lime and glue, and the color applied in a series of superimposed glazes, each rubbed down and polished. The original white layer shines through the color like light. Their love of dazzling color might have come from the highly perfected art of the illuminated manuscripts of the fourteenth and fifteenth centuries. If so, then the original white layer would have approximated the white parchment of the book.

Each one of these early Flemish artists had something to contribute to the evolution of representational art, and they prepared the way for the great flowering of Flemish and Dutch art in the seventeenth century.

Study and compare the *Book of Hours of the Duc de Berry* by the famous Limbourg brothers and the Merode altarpiece, completed around 1426 by a Flemish painter, whose identity has been the subject of controversy. He is usually called the Master of Flémalle.[1]

An unsolved problem is how these artists learned perspective, probably not from Italy. As you know, Italian painters directed all lines toward a vanishing point on the horizon. Robert L. Delevoy of the Institute of Art and Archeology, Brussels, thinks that the Burgundians used an imaginary vertical line through the center of the picture toward which pairs of lines on all levels would converge. He cites the central panel of the Ghent altarpiece.[2]

Before the Battle of Agincourt (see p. 133) Paris, Bruges (Brugge), and Dijon had been the wealthiest centers of art and manuscript illumination. About 1420 Duke Philip the Good moved his court to Bruges and allied himself with England. As the princely courts, weakened by constant warfare and intrigue, declined in prestige and power, the artists accepted commissions from the wealthy middle-class merchants, bankers, and shipowners in this cosmopolitan commercial city. Visiting Italians bought Flemish paintings which they took back to Italy. The sculptor Claus Sluter (active *c.* 1380–1405) who was at Philip's court did a famous statue of Moses which can be compared with Michelangelo's. Paintings became more bourgeois than princely. The Virgin, for instance, was depicted not as a queen or chatelaine, but as a wealthy middle-class *Hausfrau*, surrounded by all the possessions dear to such a woman's heart.

*The Merode Altarpiece.* It is obvious that the painters loved to reproduce the shapes and textures of things which they copied

---

[1] Modern scholars generally agree that the name of this painter was Robert Campin.

[2] Robert L. Delevoy, *Early Flemish Painting* (New York: McGraw-Hill Book Company, 1963), p. 9.

directly. If these things had symbolic significance, so much the better. It is worth while discussing the Merode altarpiece because it is typical of Flemish workmanship at this time, and also because it has found a permanent home in the Cloisters, a New York museum of medieval art.

The painting is a triptych with a central panel depicting the Annunciation by the Angel Gabriel to Mary, who is seated on the footrest of a settee. The panel on the right shows Joseph working at his carpenter's bench, boring holes in a block of wood. Through the windows we see the buildings, streets, and people of Bruges in minute detail. In the panel on the left we see the donor (the man who commissioned the altarpiece and gave it to the church) and his fiancée peeping around the door of a walled garden. The first thing that probably strikes us is that the perspective is wrong. We are not sure where our eye level is supposed to be. The painter is trying to give three-dimensional reality to the scene, and at the same time to treat it as a decorated flat surface in medieval fashion. Instead of coming from a single source, light floods the entire room so that each object can be illuminated symbolically.

Probably every object was meant to have symbolic meaning. The lily in the jug represents the chastity of Mary; its yellow center, Christ in her womb. The candlestick also is Mary because it holds the candle, Christ's body. Its flame, divinity, has just gone out because Christ will assume human form. The cleanliness of Mary is represented by the cloth which protects her missal and by the white towel hanging on the rack. The polished vessel also symbolizes Mary because she is the "vessel most clean"; the seven rays of light streaming from a circular window are the seven gifts of the Holy Spirit. In one of the rays is Christ bearing his cross.

The mousetrap on Joseph's table is derived from St. Augustine, who said that Christ's human form fooled the devil as bait fools mice; the Crucifixion was the trap which caught the devil. Joseph is constructing spite blocks, bristling with nails, which the people believed were hung around Christ's waist to torment him on the way to Calvary. In the left panel, the door is hope, the lock is charity, and the key is the "desire of God" according to a mystical writer, St. Bridget of Sweden. The rosebush symbolizes Christ's martyrdom and Mary's love. The violets and daisies stand for Mary's humility, the forget-me-nots for the color of her eyes. St. Bernard, the holy abbot of Clairvaux, said that Christ wished to be conceived "of a flower in the time of flowers." The walled garden comes from the Song of Solomon, "A garden enclosed is my sister." [1] We certainly need no further proof that fifteenth-century Flanders was still medieval in thinking.

*Van Eyck.* After studying the symbolism in the Merode altarpiece, you will be able to identify some of the same symbols in Jan Van Eyck's double wedding portrait of "Giovanni Arnolfini and Giovanna Cenani." We are here witnessing a wedding ceremony. The discarded slippers refer to the Biblical injunction to remove the shoes, "because the place whereon thou standest is holy ground." The dog symbolizes fidelity; the fruit recalls the Garden of Eden, the mirror, purity. St. Margaret, whose figure is carved on the chair, is the patron saint of childbirth. To make the portrait fully legal, the painter has signed his name and the date, 1434, on the back wall.[2] Can you tell from the perspective and lighting that this is a later painting than the Merode altarpiece?

Only about five years separate the Merode altarpiece from the more famous Ghent altarpiece, a truly "modern" work. Jan Van Eyck (*c.* 1385–1441) went far beyond the Master of Flémalle in depicting observable reality. Completed in 1432 for a chapel in the Cathedral of St. Bavon, the altarpiece has suffered many vicissitudes but was restored intact to Ghent in 1945. In the form of a polyptych, it has twenty panels (twelve on the inside and eight on the outside of the wings) on the general theme of Christ's sacrificial death. The central panel, "The Adoration of the Lamb," shows clearly that Van Eyck had mastered perspective because it leads the eye far back to a Gothic city in the distance. He also had mastered the use of oil instead of egg (as in tempera) as a medium, which permitted him to model the figures in light and shadow. The two end panels of Adam and Eve reveal a new appreciation of the human form and show clearly that they were painted from living models. The normal appearance as the basis of expression was more interesting to Van Eyck than idealistic modifications or symbolic meanings.

*Van der Weyden.* At about the same time another innovator, Rogier Van der Weyden (1399–1464), was painting his "Descent

---

[1] Symbolism of the Merode altarpiece given by John Canaday in "Flowering of Flemish Art," *Horizon Magazine*, VIII, no. 1; his source: Erwin Panofsky, *Early Netherlandish Painting* (Cambridge, Mass.: Harvard University Press, 1954).

[2] Symbolism in *Arnolfini and Wife* given by John Canaday in Metropolitan Seminars of Art, Vol. I. His source: Erwin Panofsky, *Early Netherlandish Painting, op. cit.*

ROGIER VAN DER WEYDEN: *Descent from the Cross*. Prado, Madrid.
(Anderson—Art Reference Bureau)

from the Cross" (see above). He declared that his primary interest was in depicting emotion, and this concentration led him to reject the conventional Calvary landscape and to crowd his ten figures on a shallow stage against a gold screen. If one studies the design of Rogier's painting, one sees that the figures are united by the flow of line across the group just as their anguish ties them together emotionally. What the artist has done here is to shift the emphasis from the outer appearance to the psychological revelation of the inner life. So great was the painting's impact that it found its way all over Europe in the form of reproductions, and it still exerts a powerful appeal to the serious art student today.

*Christus.* "The Legend of Sts. Eligius and Godeberta" by Petrus Christus (c. 1395–1472) is essentially a genre picture in that it records an important episode in the lives of three people. Godeberta, having confided to the saint her desire to enter the religious life rather than wed the nobleman her parents have selected, receives from Eligius a ring wedding her to Christ while the nobleman looks on in dismay. The story was appropriate since the painting was commissioned by the jewelers of Antwerp.

*David.* Flemish art owes the first dense, thick landscapes to Gerard David (*c.* 1460–1523). In his "Rest on the Flight into Egypt," the landscape is no longer a frame or a background but an environment for human action.

*Villon.* It seems logical to consider the poet François Villon of Paris after the Burgundian painters because he was their contemporary and also medieval in style. Scholars have gleaned details of his life from a perusal of Paris police records. He was born in 1431, the year that Joan of Arc was burned at the stake. His father died when he was very young, and his mother was very poor. François was brought up and educated at the University of Paris by a churchman whose name he assumed. He was in and out of jail for the most outrageous pranks, or in exile for robbery and murder. One episode is recounted by Robert Louis Stevenson in his short story "Lodging for a Night." Villon always assumed that he would die on the gallows and quite possibly he did. Nobody knows where, when, or how he died. But in six years he turned out a body of poetry unexcelled at the time in his own country or perhaps that of any other.

His verses have only one subject—himself and his attitude toward those around him. He was absolutely fearless and absolutely straight. He played pranks for fun; he stole to avoid starvation. In his poems he speaks about his little attic room where the ink froze in his inkwell. He is preoccupied with death and the hereafter. He writes wills and legacies leaving good thoughts to his friends, and bad wishes to his enemies. It is not the subject matter but the internal quality of his poetic feeling and expression which distinguish his poetry. His approach is direct and he never minces words. His integrity and his pride controlled actions and poetry. He often resembles Cyrano de Bergerac in Rostand's drama (see p. 345). He believed himself the equal of any man, priest, or king, and acknowledged no superior. One line: "But where are the snows of yesteryears?" has become a proverb. You should know the "Ballade of the Ladies of Bygone Times." "Ballade for Fat Margot," and his "Epitaph for Himself."

**Germany.** "Behold, how great a matter a little fire kindleth." How could Michelangelo know when he designed an enormous tomb for Pope Julius II, or this Pope when he commissioned Bramante to tear down the old basilica of Constantine and build a grandiose pontifical city and an enlarged St. Peter's to accommodate the tomb that they were lighting the spark which would touch off the Protestant Reformation in Germany? Despite the fact that every church in Christendom was pouring money into the papal treasury in the form of taxes (not to mention the Church's income from the Papal States), this building project required enormous sums of money in addition to what was needed to run such a vast bureaucracy. To acquire this money the Popes resorted to a method known as the "sale" of indulgences. This meant that if he made a voluntary contribution to the Church, part of a sinner's penance would be remitted and his stay in Purgatory shortened.

From the eleventh century on there had been many conscientious churchmen who had seen the necessity of reform within the Church. There were two types of clergy: the "regular" clergy (monks and priests who had had theological training), and "secular" clergy (appointees of the feudal lords or kings). The secular clergy in general held the highest and most lucrative positions. Feudal lords gave such positions to their relatives (nepotism), or awarded them to the highest bidder (simony). In France two groups of reformers, the Waldensians and the Albigensians, criticized the worldliness of the Church and abrogated its authority. Their members were hunted down, tried by the Inquisition (the Church court), and condemned as heretics. In the twelfth century, St. Bernard constantly attacked the worldliness of the regular and the secular clergy. The scandal of the "Great Schism" (1378–1417) was the result of an altercation among three different popes, each claiming to be the legitimate heir of St. Peter. Following this came a series of notorious Renaissance popes, some from the dissolute Borgia family, who lived in luxury, kept mistresses, and in general desecrated the high office. By the beginning of the sixteenth century, dissatisfaction with the Church was so widespread that only a drastic reform could have prevented an explosion.

*Luther and the Reformation.* Martin Luther (1483–1546) was an Augustinian monk whose parents had been poor peasants. He was an earnest student at the University of Erfurt, received an excellent Humanistic training, and earned the bachelor's and master's degrees there. An inner compulsion led him, against his father's wishes, to enter a monastery. After three more years of study he was ordained a priest and began to lecture in philosophy at Erfurt and Wittenberg. Sent on a mission to Rome, he was aghast at the corruption he saw there. Although held in high esteem and awarded a doctorate in theology, he was still not satisfied. He could not believe that the Pope had the power to shorten a man's stay in Purgatory. Thus he came to the belief that no one could forgive sins save God, and if this were true no intermediary was necessary. Man was justified by his faith, a doctrine which made every man his own priest.

When a Dominican monk, Tetzel by name, came into Saxony to sell indulgences, Luther tacked a statement of these beliefs to his church door in Wittenberg. Luther did not set out to establish a new church. He was loyal to the Catholic Church, but wanted to cleanse it of impurities. When in 1521 the Holy Roman Emperor Charles V called him to an assembly at Worms and bade him recant, he spoke these words: "Here I stand. I can do no other, God help me." He was excommunicated by the Pope, and when a price was put on his head, he went into voluntary imprisonment in the Wartburg castle high on the hilltop above the sleepy little town of Eisenach, whose cobblestones were to echo to the childish tread of Johann Sebastian Bach a hundred and fifty years later. This is the same Wartburg castle where in 1207 the minnesingers had held their song contest which is celebrated in Wagner's opera *Tannhäuser*. When you visit this historic town you can climb the hill to the castle by the same path which the pilgrims took on their way to Rome, the same path used in the thirteenth century by St. Elizabeth, who, against her husband's orders, was carrying a loaf of bread to a poor villager. According to legend, when her husband encountered her on the path and bade her open her cloak, out flew the dove of the Holy Spirit. You will visit the hall of the minnesingers and the little *Stube* (room) where Luther lodged and where he translated the Bible into German. The castle also contains an excellent collection of medieval armor. But don't take a conducted tour; go alone so that you can actually feel a part of history.

Luther wrote three pamphlets which were widely disseminated and won support from nobles and princes anxious to be free from the exhaustive taxation, which was ultimately passed along to the peasants. Most of Germany with the exception of the larger towns was still living under the feudal system, but there was enough mercantile economy so that the nobles needed money at home. Meanwhile the state of the peasants worsened, and they were even denied their ancient hunting and fishing rights. They revolted in 1524–1525, and Luther did nothing to help them. When reminded of his belief in the equality of all believers before God, he said that this did not apply to secular matters.

Eventually Luther and his followers formed a new church with a German liturgy, although for a long time Luther considered himself a Catholic. When Charles V finished his war against Francis I of France and turned to stamp out the Protestants, it was too late. But the Peasant Revolt had made Luther conservative, and he leaned heavily on the power of princes. He argued that since all political authority was instituted by God, the secular government possessed the right to manage ecclesiastical affairs. This theory meant that Lutheran churches would become state churches, and the religion of the head of the state would determine the religion of his subjects. Thus did Luther in late life abrogate his most fundamental doctrine (the priesthood of believers). State religion became the provision of the Peace of Augsburg in 1555, and medieval institutions in Germany took a longer lease on life. North Germany remained Protestant; and South Germany remained Catholic, and Salzburg, Austria, became the "Rome of the North." The date 1546, the year before Luther died, marked the beginning of the Council of Trent, which reformed the Catholic Church.

*Erasmus.* A Dutchman, Desiderius Erasmus of Rotterdam (c. 1466–1536), is considered by many scholars the greatest Humanist of the entire Renaissance. He was a friend of Luther's but refused to join the Protestant cause and hoped that the conflict between Luther and the Catholic Church could be settled by arbitration. He believed that true worship lay not in ceremonies but in imitation of Christ's life. His Greek New Testament was the first printed edition of the Greek text, and by profound study of ancient manuscripts he exposed inaccuracies in the Latin Vulgate, on which theological discussions had been based for a thousand years. He also made a Latin translation of the New Testament, on which Luther based his German translation. He lectured at Cambridge and dedicated his *In Praise of Folly* to Sir Thomas More, author of *Utopia*. Holbein painted Erasmus' portrait, and Dürer made an engraving of him. Charles Reade's novel *The Cloister and the Hearth* tells the love story of Erasmus' parents.

*Music.* There was never any question about the role of music in the Lutheran church. Luther himself was a good musician, played several instruments, and had a well-trained tenor voice. While the organists of Zurich and Bern had to stand by and watch their magnificent instruments hacked to pieces by the Calvinists (and the same thing happened among the Puritans in England), Luther and his friend Johann Walter went to work immediately on a congregational songbook in German for the Lutheran churches. The Germans loved to sing and had a rich fund of folk songs, many of which had been published in the so-called *Lochheimer Liederbuch* around 1455. A number of these were given sacred texts taken from the Psalms, but Luther did not disdain to use Latin hymns and even Gregorian melodies. These beautiful old *chorales,* as they are called, furnished the pattern for later Protestant hymns. At least two chorales are definitely from Luther's own hand: "A Mighty Fortress Is Our God" and "Out of the Depths I Cry unto Thee." But his conception was not limited to congregational singing; from the very beginning he probably encouraged trained choirs. We possess the beginning of a German mass by Luther, also a setting of the Lord's Prayer in the style of the Flemish polyphonists. It soon became customary after the sermon every Sunday for the choir to sing an entire cantata, or a complete mass based on a German tune. This practice laid the foundation for the rich literature of cantatas and oratorios by German composers in the next century, especially the larger sacred works of Schütz and Bach, which rivaled the music of the Catholic Church (see p. 147).

The German towns encouraged musical performance, and provided excellent musical training in the schools. The Germans particularly liked brass music and perfected these instruments. Every town had its *Stadtpfeifer* (municipal band) which "blew down" music from the tower of the city hall on market days. Divine Providence must have prompted these solid German burghers to provide such good musical training, because without this background it would be difficult to account for the tremendous flowering of German music in the seventeenth, eighteenth, and nineteenth centuries.

*Art.* The Reformation had a strong repercussion on German art, which was completely overwhelmed by the religious upheaval just when the young Humanistic movement was trying its wings. The Germans loved nature and life, but not having any classical tradition behind them, they lacked a refined sense of form, proportion, and organic structure. Like Flemish painting, their art shows an overabundance of detail, but they lacked the Flemish ability to integrate it. Without the classical spirit of moderation and equilibrium they let themselves be carried away by violently emotional and almost terrifyingly dramatic representions of the Passion.

DÜRER. The one artist who achieved a synthesis of the Renaissance spirit of control and the Reformation spirit of passion was Albrecht Dürer (1471–1528). In Dürer's woodcuts and engravings, German genius and fantasy found adequate expression. As a staunch Protestant and friend of Erasmus, Dürer was concerned with the will of God and with man's place in the hierarchy of nature and the world of the spirit.

Like Leonardo, to whom he is often compared, Dürer was a profound student of anatomy, mathematics, botany, zoology, and engineering. But above all he was interested in man, his thinking and aspirations, and in how to reveal them in art. Dürer made his home in Nuremberg, but he traveled extensively, first to the Low Countries, where he studied the medieval art of the Flemish masters, and then in 1494 to Venice. How could he know

ALBRECHT DURER: *Self-Portrait*. Prado, Madrid. (Anderson—Art Reference Bureau)

when he made that first trip to Italy, that he was crossing not only the Alps, but the dividing line between the medieval age of faith and the modern world of power? When he returned he set the course for the Renaissance in the North.

The self-portrait reproduced in this book (see p. 129) was painted when the artist was twenty-seven and already a master of some international fame. It shows him superbly delineated, impeccably dressed, and slightly arrogant, not just a German craftsman, but an *uomo universale* who was at ease with and the equal of courtiers. His panels of "The Four Apostles" are superb in color and characterization.

However, it is not painting but woodcut and engraving on which Dürer's greatest fame rests. His woodcuts illustrating the Apocalypse are so fantastic they would probably be called surrealistic today. Perhaps his best-known engraving is "Knight, Death and the Devil," built on the old theme of life as a journey through tortuous places where man is beset by dangers and temptations. Every rock, tree, and beast is a potential peril, but the stalwart knight on his noble horse reduces Death with his pitiful nag to the role of beggar, while the Devil, following along behind, is no more fearsome than a Halloween mask. Courageous man, says the artist, will reach his eternal home high on the hilltop. The temptations of man are only spooks and phantoms.

GRÜNEWALD. The only German painter comparable to Dürer in ability and power is the artist of Aschaffenburg generally known as Mathias Grünewald, according to a seventeenth-century writer. (It is believed that this writer made an error and that his real name was Mathis Gothardt Nithardt.) Grünewald's greatest masterpiece is the triptych Isenheim altarpiece, now in Colmar. Its three wings depict the birth of Christ, his crucifixion and resurrection, and two legends about the life of St. Anthony. Grünewald was completely medieval and used all the symbolic canons, and yet the pictures are almost unbearably realistic. The twentieth-century German composer Paul Hindemith wrote a tone poem called *Mathis der Maler* ("Matthew the Painter"). Hindemith was attracted to the subject because of the curious analogy between St. Anthony, tempted to forsake Christ for worldly allurements; Grünewald, tempted to join the Peasants' Revolt of 1524; and Hindemith, tempted to forsake his principles and join the Nazis. All three men resisted their temptations. Grünewald, more expressionistic in the modern sense than Dürer, possibly appeals more to the modern taste.

CRANACH. Lucas Cranach (1472–1553) began as a most promising painter. When the Venetian Giorgione was discovering the painterly possibilities of landscape, Cranach was intrigued by the ancient forests of Germany. In a painting dated 1504, he represents the Holy Family on the flight to Egypt, resting near a spring in a wooded region. A host of little angels gathers about, offering berries, water in a shell, and entertainment with pipes and flutes. The painting has sincerity, simplicity, and lyric charm.

Then, alas, Cranach made a trip to Italy, and either lacked the capacity, or did not stay long enough, to assimilate what he saw. He came back with a few classical trappings and became a slick and fashionable court painter in Saxony. His "Judgment of Paris" is amusing. Paris is a heavy-set, bearded German, clothed in medieval armor, who would look more natural presenting a stein of beer than an apple. The three coy goddesses are unanatomical nudes clothed in a hat or a string of beads which make them look less than idealized.

HOLBEIN. A German painter of international fame was Hans Holbein the Younger (1497–1543), who came from Augsburg, a rich merchant city that maintained close trade relations with Italy. Holbein adopted the aesthetics of the Venetian school, especially of Bellini and Titian, but his careful attention to detail reveals his Northern heritage. When the Reformation began, he went to England, carrying with him a letter of recommendation from Erasmus to Sir Thomas More, author of *Utopia*. He became court painter to Henry VIII and made portraits of the king and each of his six wives. It is said that Henry would send Holbein to paint a marital prospect, and from the portrait would decide whether he wanted to marry the lady. At least once it was the lady who did the deciding: Christina of Denmark concluded that he was a poor risk as a husband. In Holbein's earlier portraits such as that of George Gisze (1532), he characterized the subject by the intimate details surrounding him, but as his art progressed, he omitted these German mannerisms and concentrated on the personality and character of the sitter. This development is apparent in the portrait of Christina of Denmark. His portraits of Henry VIII and Anne of Cleves show his ability to paint the rich jewels and clothing of the period.

France. In 1500, King Louis XII descended on Italy to claim the Duchy of Milan. He stayed twelve years and immersed himself in Italian art, but the real French Renaissance begins with the accession in 1515 of Francis I, who brought Leonardo, Cellini, and Andrea del Sarto to his court.

*The Pléiade.* The French poets and musicians joined forces

to create a new poetry based on Petrarchan forms and expressing Platonic love. The group called themselves the *Pléiade*.
The greatest poet among them was Pierre Ronsard (1524–1585).
The importance of their poetry rested upon its intimate connection with the music, and poetry determined the form and the
style of the French Renaissance *chanson*. Perhaps the greatest
composers were Clement Janequin (*c.* 1485–1550) and Claude le
Jeune (1528–1601). Under the influence of the Pleiades, Charles
IX established the Academy of Poetry and Music, whose aim
was to purify and ennoble the French language. Marguerite de
Navarre, sister of Francis I, wrote meditative poetry; she was
probably the most gifted woman of the entire period.

*Rabelais.* As a physician, monk, scholar, educator, Humanist,
François Rabelais (*c.* 1495–1553) is only historically interesting, but he remains one of the greatest of humorists and satirists.
His mottoes were: "All men desire to know," and "Laughter is
a proper function of man." He created two books which depict
the adventures of two enormous giants, *Gargantua* and *Pantagruel*, adventures which are thrown together without unity or
coherence and which are by turns boisterous, irreverent, realistic,
funny, vulgar, and meaningful. Rabelais represents the typical
French rationalist's desire to explore every facet of life with
tolerance and sympathy. Read especially Chapter Nineteen of
*Gargantua*, which tells of Gargantua's education.

**England.** The Renaissance ushered in England's Golden Age
of music and literature. The period may be dated roughly from
the accession of Henry VIII in 1509 to the death of Elizabeth I
in 1603. At last the country was at peace. The nobles were well
educated and able to travel in France and Italy, where they
soaked up Renaissance achievements. They bought Italian art,
rebuilt their mansions in the Renaissance style, and landscaped
them by formal gardens in the Italian manner. The middle class
of tradesmen and merchants lived in comfortable Tudor houses
with leisure enough to enjoy songs, poetry, and the theater. The
lower classes were not so well off, but they were used to living
from hand to mouth. When Henry VIII met Francis I of France,
their costumes were so rich that the place was called "Field of
the Cloth of Gold." Elizabeth I was rich, happy, comfortable,
and relatively secure. A new patriotic sentiment was in the air,
and the Queen was proud of her new Empire and new learning.
This was just the right atmosphere to foster the arts.

*Poets and Playwrights.* Sir Philip Sidney (1554–1586) wrote
his pastoral *Arcadia* and penned sonnets to Penelope Devereaux.
Sidney knew Greek, Latin, Italian, French, and Spanish. His

friend Edmund Spenser (1552–1599) was a gifted poet and had a fine classical education. He labored for twenty years on the *Faerie Queene*, in which he tried to combine elements of Homer, Virgil, Ariosto, and Tasso. Christopher Marlowe (1564–1593) wrote popular plays in blank verse (*Dr. Faustus* and *Tamburlaine the Great* are the best-known). Ben Jonson (1573–1637) wrote comedies and satires, among them *Volpone* and *The Alchemist*. In this period, too, Shakespeare (1564–1616) wrote his sonnets, early comedies (including *Midsummer Night's Dream, Merchant of Venice, As You Like It,* and *Twelfth Night*) and most of his historical plays.

MUSIC. Someone has said that England in this period resembled a nest of singing birds, an apt simile except that these birds also played instruments. England had always been in the forefront of musical development. Before the Battle of Agincourt (1415), when Henry V's miserable, starved little army was facing a French army several times its size, the King's chaplain said that the priests chanted the *Miserere* "vociferously." When the English had won the battle somebody composed a polyphonic motet right on the field, and it was sung by King and soldiers. This is the "Agincourt Song," *Deo Gracias Anglia,* which we still possess. Henry V was called King David by his subjects, and his Tudor successors were likewise musical.

Henry VIII supported a small army of seventy-nine musicians at his court constantly, with more added for special occasions. He had sent to Hungary for his drums, and had so many brasses that it took six men just to keep them cleaned and polished. His daughter Elizabeth spent over 1,500 pounds a year on her musical household, and for every penny spent, probably got a shilling's worth of value. Nests of cornets and sackbutts strengthened the organ in her chapel; seventy-eight flutes and fifes led her processions. Elizabeth may have liked them because they didn't cost much. She had fifteen hunting horns to lead the chase; trumpets and kettle drums led the cavalry into battle. She used shawms and bombards in processions and delighted in the big double bass bombard which was nine feet, eight inches long and required an extra man to hold it up. Henry had left her seventy-six recorders, which were a nuisance because they had to be kept in tune for a guest who preferred to play on a particular one. There were also chests of viols in four sizes which had to be tuned every day and two pairs of long virginals with double keyboard, although *she* preferred to play on her little spinet. There were harpsichords of English make and clavicembalos from Italy. Elizabeth invariably commanded twelve trumpets and a pair of kettle drums to play in the dining hall, first because she liked them, and also because they provided opportunities for conversational misunderstandings. Her library of part books must be kept in good order; there was no telling when some guest might call for "Sellinger's Round" or "My Lady Carey's Dump." You could hear these tunes any day on the street played with pipe and tabor, but Elizabeth's guests liked them, too. She was always glad when the guests gathered around a table and the part books were passed out. Music obviated dangerous political discussions. Lutes of all sizes were necessary for solo song and love making, but Elizabeth didn't care for that recent Italian instrument called a violin. She provided scarlet and gold vestments for the singers in her Royal Chapel. They were trained to sing the latest motets and great services composed by the organist.

If you think this is an exaggerated picture, just take any one of Shakespeare's comedies and list the allusions to music: actual songs sung and played, puns on musical devices and reading music. Shakespeare would not have used these allusions so freely if his audience had not understood them. His own estimate of the power of music may be judged from these lines:

> *The man who hath no music in himself,*
> *Nor is not moved with concord of sweet sounds,*
> *Is fit for treasons, strategems and spoils;*
> *The motions of his spirit are dull as night,*
> *And his affections dark as Erebus.*
> *Let no such man be trusted.*
> *(Merchant of Venice,* V, 1, 83–88)

The noblest and most devotional church music was composed by William Byrd (1542–1623). Thomas Morley (1557–1603) composed beautiful madrigals. Orlando Gibbons (1583–1625) composed all kinds of keyboard music, and there are dozens more Elizabethan composers. In 1603 was published a collection of twenty-nine madrigals, called *The Triumphs of Oriana*, each by a different composer and all ending with the words: "Then sang the shepherds and nymphs of Diana: long live fair Oriana!" The last two madrigals were changed to "In Heaven lies Oriana." Thus was celebrated a queen who had become a wrinkled old lady with false red hair, her face painted and patched, and her person decorated like a Christmas tree.

### The End of the Renaissance

Any stylistic period is difficult to date. Frederick B. Artz has given these significant closing dates for the Renaissance: in Italy with the sack of Rome in 1527 and the fall of the Florentine Republic in 1530; in Spain when the dour Philip II replaced his father Charles V in 1556; in France with the St. Bartholomew massacre of 1572; in England with the death of Elizabeth in 1603; in Germany with the outbreak of the Thirty Years' War in 1618.[1] It was truly a magnificent era.

---

[1] Frederick B. Artz, *From the Renaissance to Romanticism* (Chicago: University of Chicago Press, 1962), p. 10.

# Chapter 7 / The Age of Mannerism

In every aspect of life the law of change is inexorable; the *status quo* can never be preserved. No matter how well a house is swept and garnished today, it is bound to deteriorate by tomorrow. This law operates in private affairs, in business, in international relations, and it operates also in the field of the arts. The arts had reached a very lofty stage by the end of the High Renaissance, and this level could not be maintained. Some creative artists tried to backtrack and start over in a style that had been successful previously, but the conditions which had precipitated the first successes were no longer valid. The result was empty formalism or frank imitation.

For a long time the term *Mannerist* was applied to painters who took details from earlier artists and combined them to form new or different or complicated results. This is the real meaning of the word *eclectic*. In its origin Mannerist was a derogatory term that implied a kind of tasteless perversion. But the meaning of the term has changed in modern criticism to characterize artists who were experimenting to find new ways to make art meaningful in the context of the prevailing conditions. The period of Mannerism lasted from about 1530 to 1616.

## Historical Background

In 1475 when Lorenzo de Medici composed the lines which stand at the beginning of the chapter on the Renaissance, Italy was free, flourishing, and expanding in all directions. In 1527 the sack of Rome by Emperor Charles V spelled the "final pricking of the bubble of imperial greatness of the Romans." The patriotic urge which had started and sustained the Renaissance ceased abruptly. Italy, caught in a vise between Bourbons (France) and Hapsburgs (Spain and the Holy Roman Emperor), was politically enslaved.

The country was still divided into eleven independent city states. Three of these (Venice, Genoa, and Lucca) were republics; four (Mantua, Tuscany, Parma, and Urbino) were still ruled by the descendants of the vigorous merchant princes, but these descendants, weakened by inherited power and luxury, tried to compensate for their lack of stamina by a rule of political expediency, oppression, and display of power. The Popes competed with the secular princes in costly display and maintained their authority through the religious orders and the Holy Inquisition. The Este family was gone and Farrara was a papal fief. Spanish rule in south Italy was absolute, with Naples the seat of a brilliant court life. There was a craze for rank among the Italian nobility who flocked around the Spanish viceroy; the bourgeois population was oppressed by taxation to furnish court amusement and to keep the mob quiet with spectacles and processions. Coronations, royal weddings, and wars were pretexts for increased taxation. The burial of a princess was delayed for weeks because it was claimed that her coffin bore arms to which she was not entitled. Only the dukes of Savoy showed efficiency and energy, and from the soil of Savoy would spring up, some three hundred years later, the seeds of Italian unification.

In Germany the Peace of Augsburg (1555) was designed to settle the religious conflict, but it only stirred up more trouble. Many German princes declared their lands Lutheran, but they refused to join forces with the Calvinists to form a solid front with which to oppose the Holy Roman Emperors, who were all Catholic. Bohemia was largely Protestant; Austria and Hungary had large Protestant minorities. This situation was intolerable to the Jesuits and to many Catholic princes, especially Maximilian, Duke of Bavaria, who was head of the Catholic League. France, although Catholic, sided with the Protestants because she saw an opportunity to weaken both Spanish and Austrian branches of the Hapsburg family, her traditional enemy. You can see that in the ensuing Thirty Years' War (1618–1648) religious and political issues were hopelessly confused. The mercenary troops on both sides ravaged the country and despoiled the peasants so that German civilization was set back for a century afterward.

There is a very entertaining contemporary picaresque novel of the Thirty Years' War by Johann Jacob von Grimmelshausen called *Simplicius Simplicissimus*. The young lad who is the hero, the Simplest of the Simple, has been brought up in the forest where he learned nothing about the ways of the world. But he is not stupid, and quickly learns the meaning of expediency. He changes sides several times during the war, depending on which side offers the better chance for pilfering and horse-stealing and the richer food for his stomach.

France was fighting Spain and the Emperor abroad and the Huguenots at home. Henry II (1547–1559) started the familiar pattern of being ruled by his mistress, Diane de Poitiers (her portrait painted by François Clouet is called "Diana Bathing"). When Henry was killed, his wife Catherine de Medici became regent for her sons. They both died violently without heirs, and thus the Valois line ended. At this time (1572) occurred the St. Bartholomew Massacre when so many Huguenots were killed. Next on the throne was Henry IV (1589–1610) a Bourbon and a Huguenot. When the Catholics, backed by Spain, threatened to displace him, he decided to abjure his Protestanism ("Paris is worth a Mass").

The Low Countries were seething under Spanish rule. When Emperor Charles V abdicated in 1556, his Spanish and Dutch possessions were inherited by his son Philip II of Spain, a staunch and bigoted Catholic. Philip was engaged in so many wars that he promptly increased his taxation of the wealthy Dutch provinces and sent in succession two prominent nobles, the Duke of Alva and the Duke of Parma, with Spanish soldiery to force the people to return to Catholicism. The southern, Catholic provinces remained under Spanish rule, but the Hollanders, all Protestants, united under William of Orange and declared their independence in 1579. With some help from Queen Elizabeth, the Republic defeated all Spanish efforts to destroy it, but it was not formally recognized until the Peace of Westphalia in 1648.

Spain was practically untouched by the Renaissance. The kingdoms of Aragon and Castile had been united by the marriage of Ferdinand and Isabella, who in 1479 embarked on a program of nationalism and expansion that made Spain for a century the mightiest power in Europe. The capture of Granada from the Moors in 1492 and the expulsion of the Jews in the same year were a part of that program. During the sixteenth century most able-bodied Spaniards were either fighting Protestants on foreign soil or trying to administer their colonies in the New World with Indian (slave) labor. The discovery of gold and silver mines turned the colonists from agriculture to a mining economy. Spain soon found herself gripped by inflation and in debt to all the banking houses of Europe. The effect of the influx of bullion was a rise in all commodity prices—about 400 per cent in the course of the sixteenth century. Wages lagged behind prices, and there was a general contempt for manual labor. This situation is reflected in literature.

Culturally Spain was medieval throughout the sixteenth century. The grandees and churchmen were reading chivalric romances when the High Renaissance in Italy was in full swing. *The Amadis of Gaul*, by Ordonez de Montalvo, based on Arthurian legends, came out in 1508 and ran to twenty-three volumes. It is said that even St. Theresa and the Grand Inquisitor were addicted to chivalric stories.

The sixteenth century in England was a period of strong government and growth. The Tudor monarchs knew how to rule by managing Parliament rather than by opposing it. Henry VII (1485–1509) was penny-pinching, but he left a full treasury to his extravagant son, Henry VIII (1509–1547). This Henry strengthened the country internationally, and after his conflicts with the Pope left England with a nationalized Protestant church. Elizabeth I (1558–1603) was a great diplomat and managed to avoid "entangling alliances" by not marrying. She was popular with Parliament and the middle classes, and was not above helping the Protestants in the Netherlands to free themselves from Spain. The defeat of the Spanish Armada in 1588, partly the result of good luck, as the English fleet was able to take advantage of a storm, encouraged English nationalism and seafaring enterprises. .

This picture changed completely when James I (1603–1625), the first Stuart king, came to the throne. The sunlight departed from England and left the most dismal of London fogs. James believed in the divine right of kings and tried to impose his will on Parliament and the English Church. He deposed judges who would not give verdicts in his favor and by oppressing the Puritans, drove many of them out of the country, eventually to America.

All this does not make a pretty picture, but it is the climate in which Michelangelo painted his "Last Judgment," Cervantes wrote his *Don Quixote,* and Shakespeare wrote his great tragedies. Don't misunderstand. Shakespeare did not write *Macbeth* and *King Lear because* James I was on the throne, nor did Michelangelo paint the "Last Judgment" *because* Pope Leo X was weak. But all great artists are hypersensitive individuals who unconsciously absorb the spirit of their era. This is the reason for the dissertation on the history and politics of the Age of Mannerism.

> *Astonishment's the poet's aim and aid;*
> *Who cannot startle best had stick to trade.*[1]

These two lines taken from a translation of Marino's (1569–1625) pastoral poem *Adone* might be considered the motto of the

---

[1] Jefferson Butler Fletcher, *Literature of the Italian Renaissance* (New York: The Macmillan Company, 1934), p. 323.

Age of Mannerism. Two other pastorals were written at this time: *Aminta* by Tasso (1544–1595) and *Il Pastor Fido* ("The Faithful Shepherd") by Guarini (1537–1612). Pastoral literature always arises when a courtly society has become overcultivated and weary of endless intrigue. To such people the life of farmers and shepherds looks alluring. First let us see how Marino's motto is borne out in the fine arts of the period.

## Mannerism in Fine Arts

These are the most important painters of the Mannerist period:

| | |
|---|---|
| Tintoretto (1518–1594) | Venice |
| El Greco (1541–1614) | A Greek, born in Crete; lived in Toledo, Spain. |
| Correggio (1494–1534) | Parma |
| Bronzino (1502–1572) | Florence |
| Veronese (1528–1588) | Venice |
| Brueghel (*c.* 1525–1569) | Antwerp and Brussels |

In Michaelangelo's "Last Judgment" the figures writhe and twist to show they are souls in torment. The sculptured figures precariously perched on the Medici tombs are colossal, the poses are awkward, the muscles under great strain. In El Greco's "Burial of the Count of Orgaz" and Veronese's "Marriage at

TINTORETTO: *Last Supper*. San Giorgio Maggiore, Venice. (Alinari—Art Reference Bureau)

Cana" classic repose is gone, all is in violent turmoil, and the canvases are overcrowded. 'In "Slaughter of the Innocents" by Tintoretto, classic structure (in which the pictured scene is a self-contained unit always leading the eye back to the center of interest) is no more; there is no center of interest and many of the figures are cut in two by the edges of the frame. The organization of a painting, instead of being in one plane or a series of horizontal planes as in Raphael's "School of Athens," is projected diagonally as in Tintoretto's "Last Supper" (see p. 140) and the observer is pulled violently back into the picture.

**Tintoretto.** Tintoretto's paintings, especially, are conceived in color and light. In his "Feeding of the Five Thousand" the light, which often comes from several directions at once, swallows up the figures irrationally. Notice that the figures of Christ and the little boy with the basket, the dominant actors in the story, are in darkness while the light falls on subsidiary figures. All Tintoretto's paintings are dynamic and powerful; he himself was called "The Thunderbolt." He often chose weird, unusual subjects like the legend of St. Mark, patron saint of Venice, who was thought to have been Bishop of Alexandria. After St. Mark's Cathedral was built, the Venetians wanted to find and bring back the saint's body for veneration. The setting of one picture is the catacombs of Alexandria where the Venetians are searching for the body, but are not sure they have found the right one. In another painting the body is being hoisted onto a camel in the midst of a storm.

**El Greco, Correggio, Bronzino, and Veronese.** In El Greco's paintings the drapery, often sharp and jagged, has a life of its own and seems to move. See especially his "Christ at Gethsemane" (p. 142) and "Assumption of the Virgin." He shows the tendency to use thin elongated bodies and small heads. Correggio's Madonnas are sentimental and bathed in irrational light. Bronzino's portraits, such as that of Marie de Medici when about ten years old, have stiff, unyielding figures and staring eyes. Veronese enjoyed *trompe l'oeil* ("fool the eye") tricks. The summer villa of the Barbaro family outside Venice has been called a masterpiece of illusion. Veronese covered the walls with frescoes which look like classic architectural panels filled with mythological figures. The dining room has painted picture windows opening onto painted garden scenes. The members of the family are also painted in, peeping through doors, looking out of windows, or leaning over painted balconies. Veronese even painted himself in hunting garb coming through a door, and his mistress rising to greet him.

**Brueghel.** Pieter Brueghel, who lived and worked in Antwerp and Brussels, painted scenes from peasant life because it was less covered up with the veneer of respectability than that of the gentlefolk. He pointed out the evils of society often brutally, as in the "Parable of the Blind Leading the Blind" and the "Fall of Icarus" (see p. 143).

"The Parable of the Blind Leading the Blind" depicts in a quiet Flemish countryside five blind men following each other by sticks and hands as they move diagonally across the canvas toward a ditch. The first man has already fallen in; the second man is about to fall. The artist is castigating society for allowing such unfortunates to roam around unprotected. In "The Fall of Icarus" the mythical boy has already fallen into the sea and only his legs are visible. There are many people nearby, but they are all busy and utterly oblivious to the tragedy. A splendid ship is sailing toward the city in the distance; a peasant is fishing; another is ploughing his field; a herdsman is gazing at

EL GRECO: *Christ at Gethsemane.* The Toledo Museum of Art, Toledo, Ohio. (Gift of Edward Drummond Libbey)

PIETER BRUEGEL THE ELDER: *Fall of Icarus*. Museum, Brussels. (Marburg—Art Reference Bureau)

the sky while his sheep are grazing. The artist is saying that people are so preoccupied with their own concerns that they are callous to the suffering of others. In the twentieth century W. H. Auden used this painting as the subject of his poem "Musée des Beaux Arts" (see p. 351).

**Cellini.** Benvenuto Cellini (1500–1571) was a Florentine master craftsman in bronze and gold. He was always trying experiments which his contemporaries said couldn't be carried out. He lived in France for five years at the court of Francis I and introduced Manneristic ideas to France. He led a wild life in Florence and gives an intriguing account of it in his *Autobiography*. Read the part about casting "Perseus and the Medusa" in the *Renaissance Reader*.

**Palladio.** The great master of domestic architecture was Palladio (1508–1580) of Vicenza. He built many villas for the wealthy in and around Vicenza and Venice; of these the Villa Rotonda is justly famous. It is in the form of a cube with an identical pedimented portico on each of the four sides and a dome over the center. It is pure classic, unspoiled by excessive decoration. Palladio also designed the Villa Maser, which Veronese painted, and a theater of illusion (the Teatro Olympico) in Vicenza. Palladian style mansions were very popular in France, England, and America (especially in Virginia).

**Churches.** The unrest and anxiety of the Mannerist period are mirrored in the Roman Catholic Church. Great sections of Europe had been lost to the Protestants; in spite of many reform measures within the Catholic Church, some instigated even before the Reformation, the people were not flocking back to the fold. Then help came from an unexpected source—Spain. Ignatius Loyola (1491–1556) wrote his *Spiritual Exercises* and organized the Society of Jesus (later called Jesuits) to educate Catholics and spread the faith. During the Renaissance Savonarola had tried to accomplish the same ends in Florence, where he preached and organized the burning of worldly books and art treasures in the Piazza Signoria, but the Renaissance spirit was too strong and he had been burned at the stake. Now the situation was different, and as a result of Jesuit piety, the people came back to the Church. Because of this ascetic impulse Mannerist churches are quite plain. Vignola (1507–1573) built the Gesu (Jesuit) church in Rome on the plan of the old Roman basilica with just a wide nave and small side chapels around it. Also in the ascetic style are the Church of St. Francis in Assisi and the Cathedral of Salzburg, Austria, not completed until 1628. (We shall see how this taste for ascetic simplicity is reversed in the Baroque period.)

## Mannerism in Music

Music during the Manneristic period shows few of the peculiarities and even artificialities which have been noted in the field of the fine arts. The Italians at last had had enough of the complicated Flemish polyphony. It was, however, ideally suited to the new spirit of devotion and spirituality which pervaded the Church as a result of the Counter Reformation.

**Palestrina, Victoria, and Lassus.** The masses and motets of the Italian Palestrina (*c.* 1525–1594) and his Spanish friend Victoria (*c.* 1540–1611), in their ardent passion and dramatic expressiveness, represent the ideal music of the Catholic faith.

Musicians often link Lassus and Palestrina because they were contemporary (both died in 1594), and both composed the purest of *a cappella* church music. Stylistically they are similar—in their mixture of polyphony and homophony and their use of the old church scales but with an increased feeling for major and minor tonality. However the *spirit* behind them is completely different. Lassus remained the true man of the Renaissance, the hearty Fleming at home in every musical form of the period. Palestrina and the younger Victoria were Jesuit-inspired, writing nothing but church music—mystical, tenuous, visionary, and of a lofty purity. It is their mood of excessive awe and sublimity that links them with the Mannerist period.

**Marenzio.** The composer who completed this development was Marenzio (*c.* 1560–1599). In his music all the resources of polyphony and homophony are made to serve the poetic text. In order to paint in music the dramatic word pictures of the text he deliberately turned his back on the old church scales in favor of modern tonality. So doing, Marenzio became the first "modern" composer.

**Zarlino and the Development of Harmony.** Before the resources of modern harmony, based on the interrelationship of keys, could be fully exploited, a battle that had been going on throughout the sixteenth century had to be resolved. This was whether to tune a keyboard instrument by mathematics or by ear. If the classical Greek influence had been less strong, it would probably have been settled sooner. The ear tuning, or equal temperament as it came to be called, was finally established by Zarlino, a Venetian theorist, in 1558. But long before Zarlino's treatise the simple folk of Italy had enjoyed solo songs accompanied by simple chords. We know this from the books of *frottole, villanelle,* and *laudi spirituali* which were published between 1504 and 1514. Zarlino calls the four-voice setting the normal one, and he likens the four voices to the four elements. The bass is earth, which is the foundation of the harmony. The tenor is water, the alto air, and the soprano is fire which is "the most important part because of its ornamental and elegant cantilena, proceeding in such a manner that it nourishes and feeds the souls of those who listen." [1]

This was as radical an innovation for music as Galileo's sun-centered universe had been for astronomy. At last Greek and medieval musical theory was discarded. Again, do not misunderstand. Counterpoint did not die with the birth of harmony. Counterpoint is as valid today as it has been in every age, but after Zarlino it was based on the laws of harmony.

**Opera and Oratorio.** One of the first practical applications of Zarlino's ideas was in the opera and oratorio which were born in the same year, 1600. There had been throughout the fifteenth and sixteenth centuries societies called "academies" where groups of artistic dilletantes gathered to discuss art and enjoy a social good time. One of these, called "Camerata," met in the home of Count Bardi in Florence, and some of their names should sound

---

[1] Hugo Riemann, *Geschichte der Musiktheorie* (Berlin: Max Hesses Verlag, 1920), p. 423.

familiar: Tasso, Marino, Galilei (father of the astronomer), and two singers, Peri and Caccini. The whole group wanted to bring poetry and music closer together by giving the text to a solo voice against a simple chordal accompaniment realized at the keyboard from a single bass part called *basso continuo*. If the harmony was doubtful, figures below the bass line could designate the chords to be used.

All these men firmly believed that the ancient Greeks and Romans had sung on the stage the entire tragedy. Thus opera was really the result of a Renaissance ideal, but the form it took was something completely new. The result of the first experiment was *Dafne*, which was nothing more than a dramatized pastoral play with music. The next and first really complete opera was *Euridice*. Rinuccini wrote the text in 1600 for the marriage of Henry IV and Maria de' Medici, the little girl whom Bronzino had painted. As with the Greeks, the chorus sang comments on the story, but the soloists intoned their lines *on the same pitch* until the meaning of the text warranted a change. It is to be feared that the little bride fell asleep.

The Roman musical stage was closer than opera to the old sacred mystery plays. It was encouraged by the Jesuits, who saw in it an opportunity for religious education. The Latin oratorios were performed in church, but those in the vernacular were performed in an oratory or prayer meeting. They were similar in style to the opera, but were performed without acting, scenery, or costumes. The instigator in Rome was Filippo de Neri (1515–1595), a very saintly priest, and the first composer of oratorio was Emilio de Cavalieri (*c.* 1550–1602). In 1600 Cavalieri presented his dramatic composition *The Representation of Mind and Body*. Since this work was acted, it was a religious drama rather than a real oratorio. Its characters were allegorical figures called Time, Life, World, Pleasure, Intellect, etc.

While opera and oratorio developed in the interest of greater simplicity, a parallel development in Venice resulted in greater complexity. This was the so-called *concerted style* which found its way into the cantatas and Passions of Schütz and Bach, and eventually into the eighteenth-century concertos and symphonies.

**Church Music.** When in 1527 the Flemish composer Adrian Willaert reached Venice to become Master of Music in St. Mark's Cathedral, there were already two organs installed in the church. Since the echo was a favorite Renaissance device, it was only natural to use one organ to echo the other. The next step was to use two choirs with the organs to answer each other antiphonally.

From a purely pictorial effect the echo became a necessary adjunct to the musical syntax, so that each theme came to be repeated, each motif doubled, until the whole took on the sharp light-shadow play of contemporary architecture and painting. There is something moving, dynamic, exciting, about the subtle play of light and shadow as we find it in the concertos for orchestra and the triple and quadruple choirs heard in Venice by the end of the century. In the churches were built small galleries, or swallow's nests, where singers and players were stationed, so that music could be heard from every quarter. Just as the ceilings were painted to simulate the open sky, in order that the minds of the worshipers could be transported to heaven, so by means of multiple choirs earthly singers were joined with the heavenly cohorts.

These facilities were built into St. Peter's Cathedral in Rome, where Orazio Benevoli learned the technique. The style reached the ultimate in the fifty-three-part mass which he composed for the dedication of the Salzburg Cathedral in 1628. This belongs to the monumental Baroque style, but its mention here indicates what is coming.

The polychoral style of writing, founded by Willaert and cultivated by his successors, reached a high state of development under Giovanni Gabrieli (1557–1612). He liked the opposition of unequal sound bodies: high opposed to low, instruments opposed to voices. Chromatic harmony, the mixture of different timbres, give his *Sacred Symphonies* both brilliance and depth, splendor and churchly power. His famous *Sonata Pian e Forte* is the first composition in which dynamic markings (loud and soft) are written in the score. This work is purely instrumental: the first choir consists of a cornet and three trombones, the second choir of a violin and three trombones. It is amazing how the tone of the violin cuts through the brasses. In transmitting polychoral writing to instruments, Gabrieli laid the foundation for the modern orchestra.

Gabrieli was a fine teacher; his two most famous pupils were Heinrich Schütz of Dresden and Jan Pieters Sweelinck of Amsterdam. Schütz took the Venetian double choir style back to Germany, and Sweelinck became the teacher of a great line of north German organists which led to Bach.

## Mannerism in Literature

The same tendencies to seek the different, the unusual, and the startling which have been noted in the fine arts and music are also apparent in the literature of this period. Creative artists felt insecure, and insecurity made them self-conscious. So they began to gather in little groups like the *Camerata* in Florence and the Neri group in Rome to discuss aims and procedures. It would never have occurred to Brunelleschi to call a meeting of the architects of Florence to discuss his plans for the dome of the Cathedral; on the contrary, he tried to keep his plans secret. Renaissance artists had a job to do—to build a church, decorate a palace, compose a mass for a particular service, or a poem in praise of a patron, and they did the job probably with relish but without chattering about it. Now in the Manneristic period began the endless talk about art, first among the artists themselves, later among self-constituted authorities called "Art Critics." This does not apply to the greatest creative artists. There is no record that Shakespeare discussed a new play with his fellow actors. Certainly Bach had no time for discourse. With twenty children to support and four choirs to prepare for services every Sunday, he probably never thought of what future generations would say of his fame as a composer.

In the second half of the sixteenth century there started a vogue to prettify language by means of literary "conceits": prolonged metaphors, obscure allusions, plays on words, and fanciful decorations. This style appears in its most exaggerated form in the Italian poet Marino, author of *Adone,* and is thus called *Marinism* in Italy. In Spain it is called *Gongorism* after the poet Gongora; in England *Euphuism* (from John Lyly's *Euphues*), as exemplified by Lyly and John Donne; in France the style is called *Préciosité* (preciousness). The French king, Henry IV, felt that French manners and language needed to be refined, and so his Queen, Maria de' Medici invited Marino to Paris. At this time a number of great ladies opened salons, gatherings of society people and artists, to discuss literary and artistic matters. They discarded vulgar words and cultivated an affected manner of speech which was echoed in the verses of Voiture and the novels of Mlle. de Scudery. To make these refinements official, so to speak, the Minister of State, Cardinal Richelieu, founded the French Academy in 1635.

**Montaigne.** The greatest French writer of the period was Michel de Montaigne (1533–1592). Montaigne originated the *essay,* a short piece of prose expounding the author's ideas on some particular subject. He called them *Essais* because he wanted to *essay* or test his character in the many circumstances of life. Though his essays are personal observations, they have the universality of all great literature. He was serious, skeptical of human nature, but never satiric or cynical. Many of his ideas are as pertinent today as they were in sixteenth-century France. All extreme and dogmatic opinions offended him; he was the implacable enemy of cocksureness. "Education," he says, "should enable us to understand men and things as they are, and to live a more harmonious life." He stressed not the accumulation of knowledge, as did Rabelais, but the importance of acquiring judgment. His ninety-four essays deal with such diverse subjects as leisure, friendship, cannibals, women, solitude, prayer, books. This type of personal essay had great influence on Bacon, Addison, Emerson, and Thoreau and especially on the free thinkers of the eighteenth century, Voltaire and the *Encyclopédists*.

**Cervantes.** When Cervantes (1547–1616) brought out *Don Quixote* (Part I in 1605 and Part II in 1615), chivalry had begun to lose its savor. Cervantes' masterpiece finished it. *Don Quixote* is one of the greatest pieces of literature of all time.

The story begins as a burlesque on the exaggerated deeds of chivalric heroes. The Don says that he is going to do far greater works than all the chivalric knights put together, and the book is concerned with his attempts to make good that boast. He is a lesser nobleman, ugly in looks, who has gone out of his mind from reading chivalric romances. He dresses in full armor, and on a dyspeptic nag rides forth to right wrong and rescue damsels in distress. His squire is Sancho Panza, a big-bellied farmer, and his lady, Dulcinea, is a buxom farm girl. In Part I his many adventures are all disastrous. He fights a giant who turns out to be a windmill, and a hostile army which is a flock of sheep. Part II, written ten years later, shows that Cervantes has matured and his purpose deepened. The Don's mission has developed into a serious search for the real behind the appearance. We admire him even in his folly and respect him more than we do the realists who constantly frustrate his high-minded efforts. The idealistic dreamer becomes the real accomplisher, and Sancho, symbol of rationalism, is a talker. Cervantes brings out the paradox that those who are considered wise are often foolish and morally inferior, while the man who only wants to do right is considered mad.

**Shakespeare.** It is next to impossible to pigeonhole Shakespeare (1564–1616). Like the Bible, he is all things to all men. His early plays and sonnets show the harmony, balance, and idealized love of life of the Renaissance. Sometimes he reveals the power and triumphant force of the Baroque. In the last great tragedies we find the unresolved inner tensions and the morbid preoccupation with death which characterize the Age of Mannerism. In the ninteenth century the Romanticists idolized Shakespeare as the "Great Romantic."

*King Lear* is the most cosmic, the most elemental, of the tragedies. In setting it defies the stage although the motion pictures might be able to portray it with wide lens and color. The storm scene in Act III may well be the most consummate piece of writing in all literature. The aged Lear, gigantic in his faults, suffers their consequences as do the heroes in Greek tragedy and commands enormous pity. The structure of the play is built up in two parallel plots: that of Lear and his daughters, and that of Gloucester and his sons. Among Shakespeare's sources for the Lear plot was Spenser's *Faerie Queene,* and for the Gloucester plot was Sidney's *Arcadia.* But it was his own genius which intertwined them inextricably. The storm becomes an actor in the play just as the drapery in El Greco's paintings and the light in those of Tintoretto become mobile.

Lear is an old man, but he is not senile; his troubles come from errors in judgment—"a tragic flaw" such as Aristotle prescribed in his rules for tragedy. By the close of scene one the fundamental conflict is apparent: between those who equate success in terms of personal advantage and those who love, without thought of success.

The King's pride takes the form of self-will. He wants the privileges of kingship without its obligations, and he mistakenly thinks that love can be measured by words and land. He misunderstands Cordelia because, in an excess of integrity, she tells him the truth, although he lacks the imagination to understand her meaning. He misunderstands the two eldest daughters because he fails to see that they are scheming for power. Their misinterpretation of his "need" robs him of his followers who are his only status symbol. Finally denied a home with either of them, Lear is left to weather the forces of nature.

The subplot, instead of offering comic relief, echoes and supports the main plot. Gloucester fails to understand his two sons: Edgar, who really loves his father, and Edmund, who has a real grudge because he has suffered under the appellation of "bastard" all his life. Hence both Lear and Gloucester are deceived by their scheming children because of their failure to understand the available evidence. During the ensuing complications, Gloucester loses his sight and Lear loses his reason.

In the climactic storm scene, amid the tongue-lashing of the Fool, the pretended madness of Edgar, and his own mental anguish, Lear begins to recover his imagination. Somewhat later, when the blind Gloucester is led to an imaginary precipice where he expects to take his own life, he begins to recover his "insight" as to the true worth of his sons. After Lear's recovery he emerges as a new man, purified by suffering and happy in his brief reunion with Cordelia.

The absurdity of the grasping nature of the two eldest daughters is shown dramatically when both of them try to get Edmund. This passion is their nearest approach to love, and it destroys both of them, coldly and violently.

The greatness of the play depends on a form of irony called *paradox,* a statement which is contrary to reason and yet true. First, Gloucester is physically blinded at the moment when he begins to achieve spiritual insight; that is, it is the blind who really see. Second, Lear strips himself, Cordelia, and Kent of possessions and tries to imitate Edgar's nakedness, but it is the naked who have the warmth of spiritual love. Third, there is more insight in the Fool's raving, in Edgar's pretended madness, and in Lear's real madness than there is in the coldly "sane" people like Regan and Goneril. Fourth, in tragedy there is death and yet victory: he who loses his life often finds it.

One can find in *King Lear* manifestations of the change from the medieval outlook on life to the modern. The idea that bastardy implies base character and the idea of the Fool as a privileged character are medieval concepts which still persist in the play. But we see the formerly strong parental authority begin to weaken. The Renaissance held that there was a universal order in nature which had moral as well as physical manifestations. The storm symbolizes this disintegrating moral universe. The old medieval concept of loyalty, as represented by Kent, Cordelia, and eventually Gloucester, is opposed to the modern idea of loyalty only to one's own advantage, as represented by Regan, Goneril, and Edmund. That is, get what you want no matter how you get it, or as Edmund says: "Thou, Nature, art my goddess." Shakespeare seems to be saying that moral values will endure even though they may be temporarily obscured, and that man can recover his lost moral insight through suffering. This play marks the end of the Age of Mannerism.

# Chapter 8 / The Baroque Period

When Mannerism had run its course, there arose a new generation which, tired of Jesuit austerity, sought to express the triumphant Church in terms of a new style that we call the Baroque. This style reached its height in Rome between 1630 and 1670, then left Rome to appear in northern Italy, Spain, and Portugal and later (in the eighteenth century) in Austria, the Catholic portions of Switzerland, and South Germany, where it reached its most exuberant form and was mixed with the Rococo style (see p. 195) emanating from the dissolute court of Louis XV of France. By 1715 (the end of the reign of Louis XIV) Classicism was in full swing, Paris had become the art capital of the world, and Rome had gone back to its natural classical tradition. All this is very confusing, but the events of history never occur in such a way as to make life easy for future students.

The terms *Gothic, Mannerist,* and *Baroque,* were all first used in a derogatory sense, illustrating the natural human impulse to make fun of something one does not understand. Scholars are still not certain of the etymology of the term *Baroque.* The Italian word *baroco* is a philosophical term meaning "contradictory" or "paradoxical"; the Portugese word *barocco* means a crooked round pearl; another Italian word *parucca* means periwig or false hair.

## Historical Background

The Baroque period lasted from about 1600 to 1750. The heavy hand of the Jesuits rested on all of Italy and Spain and extended into other parts of Europe which had remained loyal to Catholicism. This control was implemented by the Holy Office or Inquisition, an ecclesiastical court before whom persons with ideas considered dangerous to the faith were tried for heresy. The new exuberant vigor of militant Catholicism filled the arts with its spirit, putting to flight the uncertainty and unrest of Mannerism. Great awe-inspiring churches were erected, and all the arts combined to lift the faithful into the world of the triumphant Church. Festivals were celebrated by richly decked clergy under the colossal vaults decorated with sunbursts, cupids, angels overladen with gold, and statues and pictures. Priests officiated before scintillating altars with priceless vessels, to the accompaniment of impressive and resonant music of multiple choirs, organs, and orchestras. There were elaborate processions with flags, candles, and torches, triumphal carriages and floats, with marchers singing, trumpets blaring, bells ringing, and cannon booming. Churchmen and students, guilds and corporations, princes and populace united to demonstrate their allegiance to the regenerated Church. To lose himself by a crescendo of passion until the senses were completely overwhelmed in ecstasy was for the Baroque man the strongest compulsion of life, and not one but all of the arts contributed to it.

The organ replaced the lute as king of instruments. With its many-colored fullness of register, its overpowering *fortissimo,* the fantasy and endlessness of its mixtures, it could speak with a thousand tongues. An eyewitness to the dedication of the Salzburg Cathedral, for which Benevoli composed his fifty-three part mass, has left this colorful description of the service:

> *The interior of the church is conceived as a section of the universe. Every bit of melody is carried by angel voices to every corner of the room, and awakens echoes and reverberations from all directions, from the heights and from the depths. Emerging incessantly from every corner, the voices answer each other, interweave, are repeated in ever farther and farthest echoes. Then all at once all twelve choirs burst forth in unison: "Una sancta Catholica Ecclesia" ("One holy Catholic Church").* [1]

Only two of the choirs were singers—sixteen voices all told. The others were players: twelve strings, six woodwinds, fifteen brasses, two organs, two sets of drums, and *continuo* (probably a clavecin).

The same passionate exuberance found its way into secular courtly entertainments. In 1469 (early Renaissance) Lorenzo de' Medici, in describing the festivities celebrating his betrothal, says that he exercised restraint in the number of courses at the banquet in order to give the citizens an example of moderation "which must not be forgotten at weddings." In 1661 Cosimo III de' Medici married Marguerite de' Orleans.

---

[1] Oscar Hagen, *Art Epochs and Their Leaders* (New York: Charles Scribner's Sons, 1927), p. 183.

*The expense of the wedding perceptibly increased the burden of taxation on the luckless Tuscans. The Medici sent the bride jewels, including a pearl necklace valued at 150,000 crowns. The galley which brought her from Marseilles to Italy cost 50,000 crowns. At Leghorn she was met by twenty coaches, her own being drawn by twenty horses. The streets of Florence, which had been repaved for the occasion, were hung with the best tapestries and pictures, and she was welcomed by salvos of artillery and bursting rockets, followed by fireworks. The Cathedral had been fitted with a sham baroque front for the ceremony, embellished with the deeds of the Royal House of France, but it was blown down by an outraged wind, while the beautiful simplicity of the interior had its nakedness hidden under costly hangings, and every possible elaboration of decoration in the best Jesuit style.*

*The Princess was borne in a costly white litter, even the white mules being shod with silver. At a magnificent banquet, served on gold plate, the napkins of the finest Flemish linen were folded so as to represent France, Tuscany, and the royal bridegroom. There were two great court entertainments for the occasion. The first was "The World in Festival," which represented a terrific battle, Europe and America against Asia and Africa, which ended by Jove coming down to earth in a cloud and compelling peace.*

*Around the amphitheatre, which had been rebuilt to accommodate 20,000 spectators, were a number of pyramids covered with lights, which turned night into day. The culminating point was a ballet on horseback in which all the young nobles participated. Prince Cosimo's valour in the battle was equaled by the grace of his riding in the ballet. The other was the opera,* Hercules in Thebes, *with the usual elaborately staged interludes, given in the theatre of the Pergola before an audience of nobles only. Many young nobles sang in the chorus. Among the singers were not only some famous castrates, but also some of the best soloists, including Adriana Baroni herself. This opera cost the Grand Duke 96,440 Tuscan lire.*[1]

In descriptions like this one can almost smell the acrid fumes of revolution nearly two hundred years in the future.

---

[1] Lacy Collison Morley, *Italy after the Renaissance* (London: Routledge & Kegan Paul Ltd., 1930). Reprinted by permission of the publisher.

Such lavish exhibitions were a characteristic of Italian Baroque. They were not found in western Europe, where temporal power tended to be consolidated around a few absolute monarchs. Following the Thirty Years' War, Germany was too poor to build lavishly; hence the Baroque in Germany was delayed until the eighteenth century. Then the country fairly exploded in monumental Baroque and Rococo churches.

During the Puritan Commonwealth in England (1649–1660), the theaters were closed, but it is a mistake to assume that the Puritans were hostile to music. Cromwell was very fond of it and Milton (1608–1674), the greatest literary representative of Puritanism, was the son of a professional musician and as devoted to music as was Shakespeare. When cathedral choirs were disbanded and organs destroyed, it was because of hatred for the pomp-loving "popish" High Church. Cromwell apparently tried to prevent the actual destruction of organs and choir books. The suppression of church music may have promoted the performance of secular music (although not on the Sabbath). With the return of the Stuarts, the theaters were opened and England witnessed a period of gayety and looseness in excess of that which had preceded the Puritans.

Although Galileo (1564–1642) had been forced by the Inquisition to give up his theses, René Descartes (1596–1650), the French philosopher and mathematician, in his book *Discours de la Méthode (An Essay on Method)*, proposed the substitution of reason for authority. "Think it through," he said in effect, "instead of appealing to Aristotle or any other established authority." This clearly indicates that the inflexible attitude of the Church on doctrine was beginning to weaken at least in France, and it points to the approaching Age of Enlightenment.

## Baroque Architecture and Sculpture

We have already seen the Baroque style anticipated in the massive dome and façade planned by Michelangelo for St. Peter's in Rome (see p. 115). After Michelangelo's death, Carlo Moderna finished the dome according to his specifications, but changed the plan of the nave and façade. Bernini added the imposing semicircular Doric arcade.

In the ground plan of Baroque churches, the circle gave way to the oval or series of ovals, which seem less finite and more suggestive of movement in space. No one who enters a Baroque church can understand the elements of its structure because the whole thing seems to rock and roll. Space seems hollowed out by the sculptor, walls molded as if they were clay. Façades often feature two concave curves at each side and a convex curve in the center. Everywhere arches and pediments are broken, columns twisted.

To such undulating spatial designs, Baroque sculptors and decorators applied every conceivable type of ornamentation: saints, angels, cherubs, animals in carved stone or painted wood, metal sunbursts overlaid with gold, all held together by stucco garlands of flowers, leaves, shells, scrolls in seeming confusion. *Trompe l'oeil* effects were obtained by hidden windows in the vaults which cast unexpected beams of light on important figures. The observer's first reaction is: "I don't like it. How can I worship in a church that looks like an overdecorated wedding cake?" Nothing is symmetrical, and yet there is a unity of spatial effects which is both satisfying and undeniably exciting.

**Italy.** The popes and cardinals of the seventeenth century were enthusiastic patrons, eager to leave behind them magnificent churches, palaces, and tombs. The men they hired were not Romans; Gianlorenzo Bernini came from Naples, Francesco Borromini came from the lake district of north Italy. Working together, they constructed the Barbarini Palace, which has the breadth and freedom of Palladian homes. It has two short wings jutting forward and an open façade of columns which seems to invite the public to enter. Bernini's first masterpiece of Baroque decoration was the bronze *baldacchino* (canopy) directly under Michelangelo's dome in the center of St. Peter's. It is nearly one hundred feet high and has four gigantic twisted black marble columns surmounted by an ornate crown. Its unrestrained grandeur, wild extravagance, and luxury of detail would probably have been distasteful to Michelangelo.

Bernini was a very great sculptor. Much of the beauty of Rome today comes from the ubiquitous fountains which he decorated with sculptured figures. But perhaps his greatest triumph of illusion was the chapel of St. Teresa in the church of Santa Maria della Vittoria. The chapel is faced with dark marble, and in the middle of the wall in front of the entrance is the altar of the saint. It is flanked by heavy columns and pilasters supporting a broken pediment. In the center, where one would expect to find a painting, is a niche containing the sculptured figure of St. Teresa, reclining diagonally on a cloud, swooning in voluptuous ecstasy as the angel is about to pierce her heart with the arrow of the Divine Presence (see p. 157). Beams of gold (gilt metal shafts) cover the back wall of the niche, while a concealed window high up behind the entablature throws a magical golden light upon the figures. The illusion of reality is almost over-

GIOVANNI LORENZO BERNINI: *Ecstasy of St. Theresa*. Santa Maria della Vittoria, Rome. (Alinari—Art Reference Bureau)

powering. Examine as many of Bernini's sculptured figures as you can find, and notice especially how the drapery in the St. Teresa group and also in the "Death of Lodovica Albertoni" becomes an actor in the emotional drama.

**Spain.** The mystical, emotional temperament of the Spanish people provided an ideal soil for Baroque extravagance. Remember that Spain was the home of St. Theresa, St. John of the Cross, and Loyola. As fast as the Moors were driven out of a city, architects began to build elaborate churches. One, the Cathedral of Toledo, has been called the richest church in Christendom. Begun in 1227 and built over a period of five hundred years, it comprises a primer of stylistic periods. The gilded larchwood screen, ninety feet high, stands in the groin-vaulted apse behind the high altar. It is the work of Flemish and Burgundian artists of the sixteenth century, who painted it with twenty-one Biblical scenes. In Spanish churches the choir is not in the apse but in a separate enclosure in the middle of the church. The Toledo choir stalls were handsomely carved by a German sculptor and a Spanish sculptor of the sixteenth century.

But the crowning glory of the church is the so-called "Trasparente," an eighty-five-foot-high tabernacle to hold the Eucharist. This Baroque–Rococo extravaganza is the work of Narciso Tome in the early eighteenth century. The double columns and upward curving cornices together with the relief scenes on the panels below give the illusion of great depth. Angels cover all structural details and lead our eyes up to where the Last Supper is enacted by figures of polychromatic marble. Still higher up the Virgin soars to heaven to join the angels painted on the vault, where a hidden dormer window floods the whole scene with a golden light.

In the late seventeenth century when Spanish missionaries were converting the Indians of Mexico and Central America to Christianity, they sent for Spanish sculptors to teach the Indians how to carve in wood and stone to decorate their churches. The Indians were such apt pupils and so naturally artistic that they were soon surpassing their teachers. You can still see their exquisite workmanship in the cathedrals of Mexico City, Taxco, and Tepotzotlan, although in some churches the gold leaf which originally encrusted the carved wood has long since been scraped off to pay revolutionary soldiers. In the eighteenth century, some of these Indians came to Spain and influenced the plateresque (from gold plate) and Churrigueresque (from José Churriguera (1650–1725) styles which are the height of fantasy. Similarly, the influence of the East Indies is found in Portugal.

**Germany and Switzerland.** Southern Germany and Switzerland in the eighteenth century were almost as fond of ornament for ornament's sake as was Spain. But the decorative motifs are lighter in weight because they stem from the French Rococo style. Between 1700 and 1780, two hundred churches were built in this region, and sculptors and craftsmen were kept moving from one job to another. These churches were conceived as "sacred theaters" in which the worshipers participated in the religious drama unfolding around them. All kinds of *trompe l'oeil* tricks made the masonry dissolve in ecstatic visions. Two of the finest artists were Johann Balthasar Neumann and Johann Fischer von Erlach. Outstanding churches are the Benedictine churches at Zwiefalten and St. Gall in Switzerland and the pilgrimage church of Vierzehnheiligen in Franconia.

The same tendency to model space and volume, the same three-dimensional curve, and the same lavish decoration are found in the palaces of bishops and princes. Good examples are the castle at Bruchsal, the Amalienburg in Munich, and the Zwinger in Dresden. The Residence Theatre in Munich, where Mozart concerts are held every summer, glows like a little gold jewel box. Mozart festivals are also given in the Emperor's Hall of the Palace in Wurzburg. These buildings represent the high-water mark of the Baroque and, its successor, the Rococo styles. They were soon to be cast aside by the "enlightened" thinkers of the Classic period who called them "vain trumperies," just as they cast aside Johann Sebastian Bach and called him "Old Periwig."

## Baroque Painting

*If you get simple beauty and naught else,*
*You get about the best thing God invents.*

These words which Browning put into the mouth of Filippo Lippi represent the aesthetic creed of some three hundred years of Italian painting. Baroque art was in dynamic contrast to it.

**Caravaggio.** Caravaggio (*c.* 1565–1610) was "fed up" with beautiful females, whether Venus or the Virgin, beautiful male figures, whether Adam or Hercules, and said: "Let's get back to nature." He was equally weary of the staring eyes, elongated figures, and thunder clouds of the Mannerists. Caravaggio was not a very great painter, but he was a very important painter because he forced subsequent Baroque artists, and even the nineteenth-century French artist Corbet, to take a big, strong dose of realism.

Caravaggio read the Bible stories very carefully and found that the men whom Jesus chose as his disciples were unlettered workers, and so he chose the humblest peasant types he could find in Rome as his models. He was commissioned to paint St. Matthew writing his Gospel in the presence of an angel. When the picture was submitted, there was an ungainly, bald old man so illiterate that the angel, with a look of anguished concern on her face, was forced to lean over and guide the hand which was trying to write. Rome was shocked; the picture was rejected, and Caravaggio had to try again. The second picture is not much different, but at least the old man has a halo. To be afraid of ugliness seemed to this painter a contemptible weakness; all he wanted was truth. Light and shadow, he found, do not make a body look soft and graceful, but rather harsh and awkward. His uncompromising sincerity was the tonic that painting needed.

**Rubens.** The first great painter to come in contact with Caravaggio's work was the Fleming Peter Paul Rubens (1577–1640). In 1600, Rubens went to Italy, where he kept his eyes and ears open but took no part in the heated discussions. After all, he was the inheritor of the traditions of the van Eycks, van der Weyden, and Brueghel—artists who had sought to paint faithfully everything the eye could see, without bothering about aesthetic creeds. In 1608, he returned to Antwerp, the master of all the techniques of the painter's craft. He could paint huge canvases, crowded with figures, and yet keep the spatial organization natural and clear. He could paint the portrait of his little daughter and bring out the utter simplicity and candor of childhood.

No other artist had ever been so successful as Rubens. Sometimes he had as many as twenty assistants, and he ran his huge studio in Antwerp almost on an assembly-line basis. The more important the commission, the more of the master's own hand went into the painting. His private life was fortunate, too. He was happily married twice, the second time to Helena Fourment, a young girl of sixteen. If you learn to recognize his wives you will see them repeated sometimes a half-dozen times in the same painting.

He accepted commissions from the rulers of Flanders, from Louis XIII of France, and from Louis' shrewd mother, Maria de Medici, for whom he painted huge canvases, which are now in the Louvre, telling the story of her life. He painted for Philip III of Spain and Charles I of England, who conferred knighthood upon him after an important mission in the cause of peace which he had carried out during a period he spent in the diplomatic service.

The energy of life pervades all his forms, which spiral diagonally through space even beyond the limits of the frame. This dynamic movement is typically Baroque. Everything is bathed in a fluid, mellow light, with colors clear and transparent. Some people criticize him for painting too many "fat women," but they were the result of an exuberant joy of life which saved him from

PETER PAUL RUBENS: *Helena Fourment and Her Two Children*. Louvre, Paris. (Alinari—Art Reference Bureau)

becoming just a virtuoso decorator of palace walls. His output was enormous; and in almost every first-rate museum today you will see his canvases, as alive and glowing as the day when they were finished.

**Frans Hals.** While Rubens was making money, plenty of

it, in Catholic Antwerp largely for a Catholic clientele, the artists of Protestant Holland were not faring so well. The demand for elaborate altar-paintings for churches was cut off, and the artists had to concentrate on branches of painting to which there were no religious objections. This meant portraiture and landscape. Again, since there were no patrons who were willing to employ an artist full time, a painter was forced to depend on his own reputation to lure wealthy burghers or guilds into having a picture painted. If he lacked these opportunities, he either had to peddle his pictures himself or pay an enormous commission to a dealer to sell them for him.

For these reasons the first master painter of free Holland, Frans Hals (1580–1666), led a precarious existence. He had moved to Haarlem from the Catholic South because he was a Protestant. He frequently owed money to his baker or shoemaker, and he was dependent on charity during his old age. While Rubens, Van Dyck, and Velasquez were forced to idealize their wealthy subjects, Frans Hals gives us a fleeting impression, and invariably a happy impression, of his sitter. His portraits are almost like candid-camera shots. "Pieter van der Broeke" is obviously a wealthy burgher, but other portraits depict humble people: "The Jester," the "Witch of Haarlem," "Merry Lute Player," and "La Bohemienne." We must not be fooled, however, by what looks like careless impressions. Each is the result of a carefully thought-out effect.

**Rembrandt.** Rembrandt van Ryn (1606–1669) of Amsterdam had a personality very different from that of Rubens and Hals. He was an introvert who never once doubted his own genius, a stubborn Dutchman who refused to compromise his own artistic integrity for any patron no matter how wealthy. Having become eminently successful, he was commissioned to paint group portraits of civic societies and guilds. But gradually he became more and more engrossed with effects of strong light and shadow, and with realism. An important civic leader was not likely to be pleased when only the tip of his nose appeared in a group painting.

Rembrandt liked to indulge his luxurious taste by living in a fine home surrounded by expensive objects of art. But when his wealthy clientele withdrew, he painted humble people and religious scenes. His lot would have been far worse had he not had two devoted wives who loved him and took care of him. He died in poverty. One wonders what he would say today if he knew that the Metropolitan Museum of Art paid over two million dol-

REMBRANDT VAN RIJN : *Aristotle Contemplating the Bust of Homer.*
Metropolitan Museum of Art, New York. (The Metropolitan Museum of Art, purchased with special funds and gifts of friends of the Museum, 1961)

lars for his painting of "Aristotle Contemplating the Bust of Homer" (see above). But let us not forget that money cannot evaluate a work of art.

With Rembrandt truth and sincerity were more important than harmony and beauty. His portraits of himself and others reveal human beings with their tragic failings and sufferings with no hint of pose, vanity, or sentimentality. His drawings and etchings of Biblical scenes tell in a few meaningful lines just how the characters felt in a given situation. In his paintings, such as "Supper at Emmaus" strong spots of light illuminate the essential elements of character or story while everything else is swallowed up in shadow. He became more and more engrossed with effects of chiaroscuro as he grew older.

**Other Dutch Artists.** Jacob van Ruisdael (*c.* 1628–1682) applied Rembrandt's ideas of chiaroscuro to landscape. He was the first to see the artistic possibilities of pure landscape without figures or a story element. He loved the weatherbeaten trees on the wooded dunes near Haarlem, dark storm clouds, ruined castles, and rushing brooks. Although not a great master, he was important because he anticipated the landscape painters of the eighteenth and nineteenth centuries.

Following Rembrandt came a group of painters generally referred to as the Dutch Little Masters. For inspiration they went back to the homely peasant scenes of Peter Brueghel. These artists painted genre pictures, candid-camera shots of ordinary Dutch life. To appreciate them one must realize that much of Holland is water; houses therefore are tight together and light can enter the rooms only from front and back, never from the sides. In most of their paintings light enters from a single window, illuminating people engaged in ordinary domestic duties. Jan Steen (1626–1679) liked to paint ribald scenes of peasant merrymaking, such as "Eve of St. Nicholas"; Nicolas Maes (1632–1693), more serious and contemplative, liked old people spinning, reading, or dozing by an open window.

**Vermeer.** The most accomplished of the "Little Masters" was Jan Vermeer of Delft (1632–1675). Vermeer was a master craftsman and a perfectionist. Although his output was small, and his paintings rarely more than fifteen by eighteen inches, each is polished like a gem. This fact makes them well worth careful analysis by the student. A very well-known painting is called "The Studio" or "Artist in His Studio" (see p. 165). It shows Vermeer himself, with his back to the observer, busily engaged in painting a young lady obviously dressed in a costume representing some allegorical figure. There are many "props" in the painting: two chairs, a table with a cloth draped over it, a curtain pulled back, a map, a chandelier, and an easel. Although everything looks perfectly natural, each object has been carefully placed to bring out the unity and symmetry of the whole. If you don't believe this, try shifting things about, in your imagination and see how the spatial organization is upset. Note also how adept is the artist in painting textures: the oak beams of the ceiling, the brass of the chandelier, the stiff silk of the costume, the nap of the heavy curtain, the tiles of the floor.

**Van Dyck.** The greatest of Rubens' students was Anthony

JAN VERMEER: *The Artist in His Studio*. Kunsthistorisches Museum, Vienna.

Van Dyck (1599–1641). He had all the skill of his master in rendering people and textures, and even more suavity and elegance. After working in Genoa and Rome, he became court painter for Charles I of England. He suited that dissolute court perfectly because he painted the King, the courtiers, and the great ladies not as they really were, but as they liked to think they were: noble, dignified, and cultured. So he was lionized, overburdened with commissions, and even knighted by the king.

According to Gladys Schmitt's fictionalized life of Rembrandt,[1] Van Dyck visited Rembrandt in Amsterdam and tried to get Rembrandt to adopt his own elegant style, but the great master preferred hunger to insincerity. There is no doubt that Van Dyck established a precedent in flattering his subjects, but nonetheless his portraits show masterful technique.

**Velásquez.** A position similar to that of Van Dyck at the Court of Charles I was held by a Spanish painter at the Court of Philip IV. This was Diego Velásquez (1599–1660). Velásquez admired Caravaggio's work, and before he became court painter, he turned out similar pictures of humble people like "The Water Seller of Seville" and "Man With a Wine Glass." He went to Italy twice to study the old masters but did not remain long. The most famous of his court paintings is "The Maids of Honor" (see p. 167). If you study this painting carefully, you will discover something quite new. The artist himself is facing us in the picture, busily painting a portrait of the king and queen. Although we do not see them, we see their reflections in a mirror on the back wall. The little princess, with her maids of honor, her dwarf, and her dog, has come into the studio to see what is going on. It all looks natural and lifelike, but if you examine details, such as the hair of the princess and the ribbons and braid of the fashionable costumes, you will see that Velásquez has not really painted these details, but with a few deft strokes of his brush has merely suggested them. Your own imagination has supplied the details. This is the essence of the impressionistic technique which was to be developed by Monet and Renoir and others two hundred years later. Velásquez created a world of more subtle visual harmonies than the real one he set out to paint. His paintings do not reproduce well in prints; you must go to the Prado gallery in Madrid to see them.

## Baroque Music

We have seen that in the Age of Mannerism music did not develop the extremes and artificialities which were characteristic of it in the fine arts and literature. The only thing extreme about the first operas and oratorios was that they were extremely dull, but at least they gave Baroque composers a new type of simple, declamatory, and intelligible melody which could develop into a dramatic and expressive art form. Regardless of how dry and dull they may sound to us, they were received with enthusiasm.

---

[1] *Rembrandt* (New York: Random House, 1961); reprinted by Dell.

DIEGO VELASQUEZ: *Maids of Honor*. Prado, Madrid. (Anderson—Art Reference Bureau)

It is amazing how fast the new style spread. As early as 1608 Agazzari, composer and theorist wrote: "At last the right way has been found to express the words, so that singing is exactly like speaking." [1] And by 1640, Pietro della Valle, another theorist, wrote:

*Madrigals are not much cultivated any more; people would rather hear rote songs accompanied by an instrument in the*

---

[1] Otto Kinkeldey, *Orgel und Klavier in der Musik des 16ten Jahrhunderts* (Leipzig: Breitkopf und Härtel, 1910), p. 220.

*hand of the singer. The sight of four or five people sitting around a table with part books in their hands smacks of students and the classroom.*[1]

Thus in place of the pure Renaissance joy in experiencing and expressing life in all its fullness came the desire to startle, to live dramatically. In place of group activity came the individual singer. In place of ideal classic restraint and poise came the desire to overwhelm the senses through passion. Virtuosity was valued for its own sake; theater and concert became supreme; and all life became theatrical. On the heels of the public theater came the prima donna, the impressario, the conductor, the press agent, the claque, the box-office returns: indeed, all the "improvements'" of modern music.

**Italian Opera.** A sumptuous private opera house built in Rome by the Barbarini brothers, wealthy patrons of art, opened in 1632, while the first public opera house opened in Venice in 1637. Two years later there were three. By the end of the century every parish in Venice had its own opera theater and there was hardly a wealthy court or city in Europe which did not boast an Italian composer putting on Italian opera.

Opera, then, became the most characteristic form of the musical Baroque because it satisfied the taste for luxury and extravagant display. The characters became types, the happy ending mandatory, and the melodies were overloaded with ornaments to show off the skill of the virtuoso singer. Because the vocal acrobatics required of the virtuosi were beyond the province of women, it became the practice to employ eunuchs for the female parts. These singers combined the range and flexibility of boys with the vocal power of grown men. Men with conventional voices gradually dropped out of the operatic picture. Added to this abnormal situation was the increasing need for mechanical equipment to show gods descending from Olympus, whirlwinds, and disappearing acts. All of these artificialities would have caused the complete extinction of opera for good and all except for two facts: the natural Italian love of beautiful melody and the ability of her best composers to write beautiful melodies for the human voice. This is what is meant by *bel canto*. When the Roman and Venetian vitality was exhausted, Neopolitan opera arose to revitalize the form.

By the middle of the seventeenth century, Italy had become

---

[1] A. Solerti, *L'Origini del Melodrama* (Torino: Vicenzo Bonz, 1903), p. 171.

"opera-mad." One reason that there is no conventional Italian literature during this period may be that the poets were all writing libretti for operas, and realizing a good income from their sale, at least until the printing presses became so overburdened that they stopped printing them. Incidentally, the world's largest collection of early opera scores and libretti are in the archives of the Library of Congress in Washington. Many of the libretti are covered with wax drippings because people liked to follow the libretto by the light of a candle during performances.

*Monteverdi.* But let us go back to Mantua in 1607 to hear the first really modern opera: *Orfeo* by Claudio Monteverdi (1567–1643). One would almost think from the number of opera composers who used the old myth of Orpheus and Eurydice that they knew no other story, but you remember that the Greek tragedians used the same story many times. According to legend, Orpheus was such a skilled musician that he could even move inanimate objects by his playing. When his wife Eurydice died, he was so heartbroken that he vowed he would invade the Underworld and either bring her back or remain with her among the dead. He so charmed Pluto, king of the Underworld, by his playing that she was released on condition that Orpheus would not look back until they reached the earth. On the very last step he turned around and Eurydice vanished.

Since the Duke of Mantua, Vincenzo Gonzaga, regularly employed seventy musicians, instrumentalists, and virtuoso singers, at his court, the composer had everything to work with. Of course the story was well-known, and Monteverdi's great success was not due to the libretto, but rather to the extraordinary variety and rich, vital warmth with which he clothed the ancient myth. He not only used the new recitative style, but drew on the rich heritage of polyphonic art in his choruses. He used instruments not simply as background accompaniment but for psychological characterization. There are also fourteen purely instrumental interludes which set the mood of the coming scene.

Monteverdi's *Orfeo* has been recorded, and it would be well worth your while to hear it in its entirety.

The most dramatic moments are reserved for recitative in which the composer forces us to follow the changing moods of the hero. For instance, when the messenger informs Orfeo of Euridice's death, he cries out a single syllable, then "Thou art dead," he whispers, scarcely realizing its significance. The tones rise as he rebels against Fate and vows to bring her back to the light. Doubt assails him. If he fails he will remain with her among the dead, and he bids farewell to earth and sun. The tones, low on "earth," rise chromatically on "heaven," still higher on "sun," then drop abruptly on the last "farewell." This is the first illustration of that type of melodic building for passionate expression which Monteverdi perfected in his next opera, *Arianna,* and which was copied by every dramatic composer for the next hundred years. The first modern opera had been achieved.

In his later operas, Monteverdi never again went back to the rich instrumental palette of *Orfeo*. Why? It would be easy from our vantage point of three hundred years later to endow the composer with prophetic vision and to make him aware of the need to build up the orchestra on a sound string basis before attempting any more coloristic tricks. But a plausible explanation is that his later operas were composed for a public opera house dependent on box-office returns and not on the unlimited extravagance of a ducal court.

*Carissimi.* Giovanni Carissimi (1604–1674) occupies the same position in the field of oratorio that Monteverdi represents in the field of opera. His libretti were written in Latin by Jesuits. They are real oratorios in the modern sense with recitatives, solo songs, and monodic choruses of expressive dramatic power. (It is well known that Handel, when pressed for time, appropriated whole scenes from Carissimi.) He was choir master at St. Appolinare in Rome for forty-six years, but much of his work was destroyed along with the archives of this Jesuit church. We do have a recording of the climactic episode in *The Judgment of Solomon,* in which this wise king settled the claims of two women to the same child. Notice the psychological characterization of the three people involved as brought out in the music.

*Opera Buffa.* At about the same time Italian comic opera, *opera buffa,* was born in Rome. Its immediate progenitors were the comic interludes given between the acts of serious operas, which satisfied the Italian love of intrigue and ridiculous situations. The first full-length opera buffa, performed in the Barbarini theater in 1637, was composed by Mazzocchi (d. 1646), choir master at St. Peter's, with libretto by Cardinal Rospigliosi, who later became Pope Clement IX. While papal envoy in Madrid, this worthy prelate had come in contact with Calderón's plays, and he was accused of being more interested in opera than in Church affairs. By 1653 the style of the buffoon comedy with its rapid burlesque dialogue had become fixed.

*Scarlatti.* Allesandro Scarlatti (1659–1725) of Naples was the originator of modern Italian opera. He composed more than a hundred operas, and about a hundred and fifty oratorios. He had original musical ideas, sound craftsmanship, and ability to

write beautiful melodies based on the simple A B A form called
the *da capo aria*. He established the form of the operatic overture
and reinstated polyphony in the choruses. Without the achievements of Scarlatti, the oratorios of Handel and the Italian operas
of Mozart would be inconceivable.

**French Opera.** Out of the rollicking Renaissance chanson
grew the court ballet (*ballet de cour*), an institution financed by
the state, in which the King and his courtiers often participated.
It was composed of songs, recitatives, choruses, and dances,
loosely strung together. In 1647, Mazarin, Richelieu's successor
in the post of prime minister and also Italian by birth, brought
an Italian opera troupe to Paris to put on three Italian operas.
The people loved them, but the Church and the politicians ob-
jected. After twenty years, two Frenchmen (one Robert Cambert,
a second-rate composer; the other, Pierre Perrin, an adventurer
who frequently spent time in jail) tried opera again. Once more
the public responded with alacrity. Molière, writer of popular
comedies, bought out the other two. He surrounded some of his
popular comedies like *Le Bourgeois Gentilhomme* (*Bourgeois
Gentleman*) and *Le Malade Imaginaire* (*The Imaginary Invalid*)
with music. If Molière had continued, he probably would have
created a French opera buffa. But another Italian, Jean Baptiste
Lully (1632–1687), came along and superseded Molière. By this
time, Louis XIV was on the throne, and in 1661 the King made
Lully his "superintendent" of music, and after Molière's death,
director of the *Academie Royal de Musique*, the Paris Opera
House.

Lully had the diplomatic finesse of a courtier and the business
methods of a real-estate agent. In addition, he was a great artist
and musician. He created the form and language of the French
lyric tragedy based on the inner laws of the French language.
The French classical dramas of Racine became his model for
expressive declamation. He established the form of the French
overture (slow introduction, fugal section, stately close), enlarged the orchestra, and introduced ballet because it appealed
to French taste. His reputation and glory were so great that
Italian, German, and English musicians came to study with him.

**English Opera.** In 1689 Henry Purcell (1658–1695) produced the only truly great opera in English musical history, *Dido
and Aeneas*. It is short, but the tragedy is well sustained to the
bitter end when Aeneas sails away and Dido kills herself. Nahum
Tate, the "honest dull man" who had the audacity to change
Shakespeare's *King Lear*, at least proved in the libretto of Purcell's opera that he had dramatic ability. (There is a superb

recording of this little opera with Kirsten Flagstad in the title role.) Purcell died young, however, and there was no other composer to continue the tradition.

Ordinary Englishmen liked the raucous ballads of Elizabethan times, and they welcomed *The Beggar's Opera,* which was produced in 1728. This ballad opera, a clever satire on Italian grand opera, consists of simple, popular songs and dances interspersed with racy dialogue. The libretto was written by the satiric poet John Gay, and the music was arranged by Pepusch, an Anglicized Prussian. The little piece helped to cause the downfall of Italian opera in England, and incidentally hastened Handel's bankruptcy. Its influence extends right down to Gershwin's *Porgy and Bess* in our own day.

**The Decline of Opera.** Why did opera, so popular in the seventeenth and eighteenth centuries, degenerate so quickly into the cult of the virtuoso singer with his vocal acrobatics? Of the hundreds of Italian operas written and performed during this period, why are they so seldom given today?

First, the recitative style was adapted to dramatic expression, but they had no drama to express. For libretti they used the old Graeco-Roman myths or tales of bucolic shepherds and shepherdesses based on the pastorals of Tasso, Guarini, or Marino. The only good librettist was the Austrian court poet Metastasio (1698–1782), whose services were in such demand that a single one of his libretti was used forty times. Second, as noted earlier (see p. 168), vocal gymnastics replaced conventional singing. Third, opera is an artificial hybrid, a compound of drama and music, and unless people are willing to accept its artificiality as a first premise they cannot enjoy it. To most Anglo-Saxon minds it still remains an alien form. Handel with all his ability could not sell opera to the rank and file of Englishmen. The English essayist Joseph Addison brings this out succinctly in this quotation taken from *The Spectator,* 1712.

*There is no question but our great-grandchildren will be very curious to know the reason why their forefathers used to sit together like an audience of foreigners in their own country, to hear whole plays acted before them in a tongue they didn't understand. There is nothing that has more startled our English audience than the Italian recitativo at its first entrance upon the stage. People were wonderfully surprised to hear generals singing the word of command, and ladies delivering messages in music. Our countrymen could not forbear laughing when they heard a lover chanting out a billet* doux, *and even the superscription of a letter set to a tune.*[1]

**German Church Music.** While every court in Germany had
its Italian composer putting on Italian operas, the poor people
had nothing but the church to satisfy their longing for music. It
is pathetic to read of their attempts to collect money to rebuild
the churches and organs which had been destroyed by the Thirty
Years' War. They often started amateur singing societies where
they might learn the elaborate music that they craved in the
church services.

Since all this Protestant church music was based on the Lutheran chorale which is in strophic, closed form (i.e., hymn form),
German composers took as their point of departure the concerted style of Gabrieli. Their first outstanding composer was
Michael Praetorius (Latin form of Schultz). He tried all forms
of music, even French dances. He composed thousands of settings
of the chorale tunes, from simple two-part songs to monumental
works for quadruple choirs of instruments and voices. He shows
his German temperament in his preference for heavy bass and a
great deal of brass. He also wrote a musical treatise called
*Syntagma Musicum,* our most important source of information for
this period. In Chapter III of his treatise, he says:

> *Octaves can be tolerated in all the voices when one part
> is sung and the rest played. It doesn't sound bad when the
> leader is singing to have cornets, fiddles, flutes, trombones
> and bassoons double the vocal parts both above and below.
> It gives a sumptuous harmony to have a trombone, bassoon,
> and contrabassoon play the bass part as written, while a bass
> trombone, contrabassoon or great double bassoon and great
> string bass should, just as in the organ, double the bass an
> octave below, as is the custom in Italian concertos.*

Then he adds "if these instruments are available," as though
this staggering bass were a secret ambition, seldom realized.[2]

Heinrich Schütz (1585–1672), one of the outstanding creative
geniuses in all music, studied with Gabrieli in Venice from 1609
until Gabrieli died in 1612. On his return to Germany he became
court composer to the Elector of Saxony, a position he held for
fifty-five years, until his death. He put all the Baroque Italian

---

[1] *The Spectator,* Essay 18.
[2] Michael Praetorius, Syntagma Musicum III. *Gesammtausgabe der Musi-
kalischen Werke* (Leipzig: C. F. Kant Nachfolger, 1916. Reprinted by
Georg Kallmeyer: Berlin, 1927).

techniques (recitative, aria, polyphony, concerted style, instruments) in the service of the Protestant Church. For instance, he took the parables of Jesus, such as the story of the rich man and Lazarus, and dramatized them in music. His cantatas, oratorios, and Passions lead directly to those of Bach. All this fine music has been neglected in the United States although it is constantly performed in Germany.

**Instrumental Music.** One more thread must be woven into the loom of Baroque music in order to make the tapestry complete. This is the increasing independence of instrumental music, especially that of the organ. The organ is an old instrument, originally imported into Europe from the Orient and used since the time of Charlemagne. If you examine the pictures in medieval illuminated manuscripts, you will see small portative organs being carried in processions.

The principle of organ construction is simple. Each stop controls a set of pipes whose material, wood or metal, has a certain timbre. The beauty of organ tone depends on the quality of material used in the pipes and the quality of workmanship in their construction and tuning, a delicate procedure called "voicing" which requires a sensitive ear and a skillful hand. No two organs sound alike, because the builder must adapt the tone to the acoustical properties of the room for which it is designed.

Organ-building has been, and still is, a craft, like that of making stained-glass windows. During the Renaissance and Baroque periods, the craft was often passed down from generation to generation in the same family, such as the Compenius family in North Germany. The tone of these old organs has never been surpassed and rarely equaled. (E. Power Biggs, one of America's finest modern organists, recently made a tour of northern Europe and recorded seventeenth- and eighteenth-century organ compositions on the very instruments the composers used.)

You are probably thinking: "What, no improvement in three hundred years?" Yes, much improvement in mechanics. For hundreds of years builders struggled with the problem of how to maintain a *constant* supply of air in the pipes. Today an electric motor has solved that problem. Another problem was how to get an instantaneous response from a pipe when a key was depressed. In old organs a series of wooden levers, called trackers, extended from the keyboard to the valve which opened the pipe. The trackers had to turn many corners to get around other pipes and at each corner was a small hinge. Hence the response was slow, and the physical exertion on the part of the player was great. Today a small electromagnet makes instantaneous contact at each joint; the response is immediate while no physical exertion is necessary. In some of Biggs's recordings you can distinctly hear the clatter of the trackers, and there is one recording which sounds startlingly out of tune because the organ was tuned by the old mathematical method instead of by equal temperament.

The composer who drew organ art "out of the kindergarten" was Girolamo Frescobaldi (1583–1643), for thirty years organist at St. Peter's in Rome. His fame as an improviser at the keyboard was so great that often ten thousand people crowded the church to hear him play. The old *ricercare* and *canzona*, derived from choral music, assumed under his hand a typically instrumental character. In Renaissance polyphony such as the motet or madrigal, every line of poetry was worked out with different music. The text was the unifying force. As soon as composers realized that in purely instrumental polyphony a unifying force was needed, they built the entire composition on *one* theme, and the fugue was born. A fugue has a psychological impact on the hearer. The theme enters in one voice after another without break until it builds to a mighty climax at the end in the same way that Baroque architecture leads the emotions of the worshiper up to heaven. Frescobaldi never went quite the whole way. His *Capriccio sopra un Soggetto* ("Capriccio on One Subject") shows that he had worked out the principle of thematic unity, but the composition is not a fugue. Three monothematic fugues often attributed to him are actually the work of Muzio Clementi in the next century. What his audiences loved to hear were the free forms, the fantasias, toccatas, and capriccios which demonstrated the player's virtuosity just like that of the popular opera singers.

The man who finally achieved the monothematic fugue was Jan Pieters Sweelinck (1562–1621) of Amsterdam, a student of Gabrieli (who had so many pupils that he was called "the Maker of German Organists"). One of Gabrieli's other pupils was a teacher of Johann Reinken (1623–1672), who had also studied in Rome with Frescobaldi. Reinken was organist at Lübeck in Germany. When he was ready to retire, he wanted to provide for his unmarried daughter, and so he said that the organist who took his job must also marry his daughter. Dietrich Buxtehude (1637–1707) won both the job and the girl, and Bach *walked* from Arnstadt to Lübeck to hear Buxtehude play and stayed so long that he was severely reprimanded by the consistory of his church.

We have seen that the Mannerists in the Venetian school enjoyed the opposition of unequal bodies of sound in their concertos. Concerto literature became more prominent as instruments became more mechanically perfect. The viol family dropped out in favor of the violin family, which includes the modern viola, violoncello, and double bass. The recorder family was reduced to the transverse flute and the clarinet; the shawms were reduced to oboe and bassoon, while horns and trombones took the middle and bass registers, displacing the other instruments which Praetorius mentioned in the quoted passage (see p. 173). At the beginning of the eighteenth century, the solo sonata, trio sonata, and concerto grosso became individualized. Last to gain its freedom was the harpsichord, main support of the basso continuo.

The great Cremona masters of violin manufacture, Stradivarius, Amati, and Guarneri, were all working around the turn of the eighteenth century. Naturally there were composers like Archangelo Corelli (1653–1713) who composed violin sonatas and violin concertos for these beautiful instruments. Corelli's compositions were organized in several movements, unified by key relationship and generally used as an opening movement the more highly integrated French overture perfected by Lully or the Italian overture perfected by Scarlatti. Under Antonio Vivaldi (1680–1743), the solo violin became the dominant instrument, and the other instruments began to display the sonority of the modern symphony orchestra.

At last, every thread in the Baroque sound tapestry is in place. If you have followed the development closely, you will see that every technique, every device, every achievement leads inexorably to the two great masters who synthesize and finish the entire Baroque period: Johann Sebastian Bach and George Frederick Handel.

Both these giants of the late Baroque were born in the same year, Bach (1685–1750) at Eisenach in Thuringia, Handel (1685–1759) at Halle, not very far away. Both came from middle-class parents; Handel's father was a barber-surgeon. The two men were diametrically different. Bach was an introvert, a lover of home, church, and family who never traveled far; Handel was an extrovert and a cosmopolitan. Bach was married twice and had twenty children; Handel never married. Bach composed for the glory of God and because it was his job; Handel composed music for the whole world to enjoy. The two men never met.

*Bach.* In Thuringia the name *Bach* was synonymous with musician. There were more than fifty members of this amazing family who were professionals: organists, choir directors, town players, and dancing masters. If one resigned or died, his place was immediately taken by brother, son, cousin, or uncle. The greatest of the tribe was Johann Sebastian. Orphaned at an early age, he was introduced to music by an older brother who procured for him a scholarship in St. Michael's School in Lüneburg. He often sat up all night copying scores by candlelight. He knew what was being composed everywhere in Europe, but he deliberately turned his back on operatic style and composed in the polyphonic style of a hundred years before him, taking as his points of departure Gabrieli, Frescobaldi, and Schütz. His compositions were not appreciated until a hundred years after his death, when Mendelssohn discovered the score of his *St. Matthew Passion* and performed it. Then at long last he was given his due reward. Although Bach wrote no operas, he used operatic devices —recitative, arias, ensembles—especially in the Passions. The *St. Matthew Passion* is dramatic enough to be considered religious opera.

Bach held five positions during his lifetime. The first two were church organ posts, at Arnstadt and Mühlhausen. The third was as court organist at Weimar. Here he came into contact with Italian instrumental music, especially that of Vivaldi. In 1717 he became court conductor to the Prince of Anhalt-Cöthen. Since he had an eighteen-piece orchestra at his disposal, he composed chamber music and concertos and part of the *Well-Tempered Clavier*. In 1722, he became cantor at the Thomasschule in Leipzig, the position he held for the rest of his life. Out of the fifty-four boys to whom he taught singing and Latin, he had to provide the music for four different churches every Sunday. These services were four hours long, and it was customary for the choir to sing a complete cantata after the sermon. Bach had to compose the cantatas, then teach the boys to sing them and also to play the instrumental accompaniment. A few of the students were good musicians, but most were mediocre and some so inept they could sing nothing but the tune. Bach and his family lived in the dormitory which was cold. The food was bad and the boys dirty, coarse, and unruly. Because Bach was too much wrapped up in music to be a good disciplinarian, the rector disapproved of him and his music. Under these conditions he lived and composed for twenty-eight years.

Bach was very devout. His thinking was always in terms of the organ and the church service. Sometimes when death is mentioned in one of the cantatas there is a suppressed excitement in the music as if he just couldn't wait to join his Creator. Some of his works, like the *Passions*, the *B Minor Mass*, and *The Art of the Fugue*, are monumental, but one of his simple little chorale preludes is just as much an artistic gem. Musicians have spent a lifetime studying his music. Take one short composition—a chorus or aria from one of the cantatas if you like choral music, part of a *Brandenburg Concerto* if you prefer orchestra, one of the fugues if you like organ, or part of the *Well-Tempered Clavier* if you like piano—and play it again and again until it has a chance to sink into your soul.

*Handel.* Whereas Bach tended to be reactionary, Handel was progressive. There are many foreshadowings of the new Classic style in his music.

Handel's father was not at all happy about the career of musician, but on the advice of a nobleman, finally consented to let the boy study clavier and organ. When Handel was eighteen, following his father's death, he went to Hamburg which was considered the most musical city of Germany. There he came into contact with Italian opera and composed several operas himself, with German texts. After studying with Italian opera composers in Rome, Florence, and Naples, he became court composer for the Elector of Hanover. A leave of absence permitted him to go to London in 1712 to put on Italian operas for the English court.

Feted and lionized by the courtiers, Handel forgot to go back to Hanover. Suddenly, Queen Anne died and Prince George, Elector of Hanover, became George I of England. It was to reinstate himself in the good graces of the King that Handel composed the famous *Water Music.*

Handel's operas were successful with the court, but the rank and file of English people could not tolerate the absurdities of Italian opera. Handel was not a good businessman; he had trouble with rival singers, and eventually went into bankruptcy. To pull himself out of the financial doldrums, he turned to oratorio, a much cheaper form because it involved no scenery, costumes, or acting.

Handel's oratorios are more than mighty Baroque edifices; they reveal the self-confident spirit of the English people reaching out toward world-conquering power. In other words, the Children of Israel in his Biblical narratives are really the English people themselves. You cannot help feeling this when you hear one of the great choruses in the *Messiah.* The Baroque period in music ended in a blaze of glory.

### Baroque Literature

The Baroque in literature, as in art and music, was complex, expressive and forceful. New forms were developed in fiction, drama, and poetry.

**The Picaresque Tale.** It seems strange that the Golden Age in Spanish art and literature began after 1588 when Spain's political power began to collapse. The wealth which had not been dissipated in war was in the hands of the royal court, a few privileged grandees, and the Church. As you know, the working class, Jews and Moors, had been expelled; the nobility wouldn't work, and many of the ordinary citizenry preferred to pick up what they could by chicanery. Virtually the entire country was starving. This is the background of the picaresque stories. They all picture the impossible-to-dampen cheerfulness emanating from the little victories of the weak over the proud, and the grim determination to make the best of life as it is against overwhelming odds. These stories are the precursors of Fielding's *Tom Jones* and Dickens' *Oliver Twist*.

The picaresque story is not a true novel because it is not organized around a central plot, but rather a series of adventures in the life of its hero. The true picaresque hero is a young peasant lad who lives by his wits, chiefly by getting the better of the law, the Church, and the nobility. He has to open his way through a veritable hell peopled by double-dealers, sycophants, and cold calculators—in short, through a macabre world conceivable only in a time of utter corruption.

*Quevedo.*  Francisco de Quevedo (1580–1643), the best writer of the picaresque tale, has been called the Spanish Swift. Quevedo's prose is a mixture of the vulgar jargon of the gutter with the refined euphuisms and exaggerated punning then in fashion. In his best-known story, *Historia y Vida del Buscon* ("The Life and Adventures of Don Pablo the Sharper"), he traces sardonically the "education" of his hero and the valet-companion who acts as narrator of the tale. If you enjoy modern beatnik literature, you will like it.

*Lazarillo de Tormes.*  A better, anonymous picaresque tale is *Lazarillo de Tormes*. The author is thought by some to have been a pupil of the Dutch Humanist Erasmus. The characters are more sharply drawn, and although the hero is completely amoral, he shows more wit and ingenuity in conquering his difficulties. The story also gives a better picture of all classes of people in Spain at this time. In the tale hunger has become a literary theme, replacing the idealized love of the chivalric romances and the feats of arms of the heroic epics. And for the first time in literary history a puny little rogue without social prestige or moral character has become a dramatic personage.

Lazarillo leaves home so that there will be one less mouth for his mother to feed. His first master is a blind man who will not share his food. Lazarillo manages to achieve his self-destruction by a trick. The second master is a niggardly priest who keeps the Holy Bread locked up in a chest for his own use. When the hero's clever expedients are discovered, he is almost beaten to death and dismissed. The next episode is the best. In it his master is a nobleman who, without a penny to his name or a bite to eat, preserves all the airs, graces, and ceremonies of his noble rank. When the bailiff comes to collect the rent, the "nobleman" has disappeared. This episode is followed by the clever trick of a seller of indulgences in fooling the credulous church people. The tale ends with Lazarillo becoming a "respectable" town crier.

*Lesage.* Perhaps the best picaresque novel, *Gil Blas* was written in the next century by a Frenchman, René Lesage (1668–1747), who had traveled in Spain and was well versed in Spanish picaresque stories. In fact, the characterization, setting, organization, and moral tone of the novel are so similar to their Spanish prototypes that Lesage was accused of plagiarism. The hero, Gil Blas, a likable rascal, while seeking his fortune from town to town, encounters an assortment of characters—dishonest, ignoble, or amoral—who confide their experiences to him. The author, like Molière, is really satirizing French people of all classes and French social conditions. The tale formed the basis of several French comic operas. We have already mentioned a comparable German picaresque tale by Grimmelshausen (see p. 137).

**Drama.** Contrasting with the sordid reality of the picaresque tale is the glamorous world of the Spanish theater with its colorful costumes, grandiloquent gesturing, make-believe, and tinsel. The Spanish people love the theater almost as much as their bullfights. Theaters of seventeenth-century Spain were similar to those of Elizabethan days: courtyards of inns and taverns, close to the common people. The plays presented were not subject to rules; tragedy was mixed with comedy, real with imaginary. Emphasizing action, they are sheer entertainment like our musical comedies of today or the *commedia dell' arte* of the Italians.

*Lope.* The most dynamic dramatist was Lope de Vega (1562–1635), a prolific and versatile genius who in fifty years turned out more than two thousand plays. It is understandable that not all show literary merit. One of the best is *Fuente Ovejuna* ("The Sheep Well"), in which the peasant hero rouses the villages to stand against their oppressive feudal landlords. The peasants are finally delivered through the intervention of King Ferdinand.

*The Don Juan Story.* Another type of drama was the cloak-and-sword play represented by Tirso de Molina, who contributed the character of Don Juan to world literature. Molina did not invent the Don. He was a legendary character of folk song and folk tale, as was Till Eulenspiegel in Germany. You remember that romantic love appeared among the eleventh-century troubadours. Courtly love professed chastity and at the same time glorified adultery. The troubadours saw clearly that desire, not fulfillment, is the most attractive stimulus to love. The Don is a sneering rather than a weeping Troilus. Once on the stage, he never left it, and we can follow his metamorphoses through every literary period right down to Shaw's *Man and Superman* (1903), and even into our own day. Now he is dead. Why? Modern literature lacks the characteristic dash of heroics, the gay defiance and wit which are the Don's proper sphere. He is as out of place today as a cloak and sword at a cocktail party.

Probably the best Don Juan is in Mozart's opera, *Don Giovanni*, where the music not only characterizes the Don with consummate skill, but in a magnificent denouement takes him to hell. In the opera, Don Juan's servant sings to one of the women: [1]

> *Little lady, this is the catalogue*
> *Of the beauties my master has loved:*
> *In Italy six hundred forty, in Germany two hundred*
> *    thirty-one,*
> *A hundred in France, in Turkey ninety-one,*
> *But in Spain already one thousand and three.*
> *Amongst these are peasant girls,*
> *Chambermaids, townswomen;*
> *There are countesses, baronesses,*
> *Marchionesses, princesses,*
> *And there are women of every degree,*
> *Every shape, every age. Repent? No!*

Tirso called his play *The Trickster of Seville*. We must understand that the Spanish have always had an exaggerated sense of honor. Every insult to a woman must be avenged. When a girl is seduced, her father, brothers, husband, or fiancé rush to avenge her honor no matter how co-operative she has been. If her seducer will not marry her, she has but one course: to enter a nunnery. Knowing this, wouldn't you think the girls would hesitate? Not a bit of it; they rush for the gallant and handsome gentleman. In the course of three acts, Don Juan seduces four women: two of them highborn and two of them peasants. His technique shows no great imagination. He wins the noble ladies by impersonating their true suitors, and the peasant girls by promising marriage.

---

[1] Leporello's aria in Act I. Libretto by Lorenzo da Ponte. Reprinted by permission of G. Schirmer, Inc., copyright owner.

He has not even affection for these women. Love is a game; he hangs his conquests to his belt as Indians hung scalps there. He says: [1]

> *I'm called the Trickster; and my greatest pleasure*
> *Is to trick women, leaving them dishonored.*

He usually plans his getaway before beginning his conquest:

> *Why for her love I'm almost dying*
> *I'll have her now, then scamper flying.*

Generally, he cleverly evades pursuit, but in the course of one escape, he kills Dona Anna's father, who as the King's favorite courtier is given a costly tomb and statue in the church. In the final scene, the statue comes to life and drags the Don to hell.

You see, Don Juan is in rebellion not only against convention and the Church but also against woman herself and romantic love. What he enjoys is the risk involved and the freedom to toss his life away if he chooses. He sees in death a gesture of defiance against human limitations and against God himslf. Again and again his servant warns him: "What you have done you pay for." But he is willing to pay the price, even of hell-fire. This is an act of rebellion against God, similar to that of Faust and of Prometheus.

When the statue first calls upon him, he rationalizes his fear:

> *If I am not afraid of noble bodies*
> *With all their powers, alive with wits and reason—*
> *To fear dead bodies is a stupid thing.*

But his humor, his courage, his pride never desert him.

> *Oh, to Hell with all that nonsense*
> *Which only fools and madmen take to heart.*
> *That day alone's unlucky, cursed, and foul,*
> *When I run out of money. Other days—*
> *All other days—are revelry and laughter.*

There are just two lines of repentance.

> *Then let me send for a confessor quickly,*
> *So to absolve my soul before I die.*

---

[1] Angel Flores, ed., *Masterpieces of the Spanish Golden Age* (New York: Holt, Rinehart & Winston, 1960). This and following quotations reprinted by permission of Eric Bentley, copyright owner.

As Angel Flores aptly remarks: "This gesture is about as convincing as a moralistic ending tacked onto a Hollywood movie to appease the Legion of Decency."

Molière (see p. 192), whose real name was Jean Baptiste Poquelin (1622–1673), was the great French satiric dramatist of Louis XIV's reign. He wrote his version called *Don Juan, ou le Festin de Pierre* ("Don Juan, or the Statue's Feast") just thirty-five years after Tirso de Molina's play. Molière's comedies poked fun at human foibles and contemporary institutions, but did so without malice. As a result, his plays were popular with the King and court almost up to the time of Molière's death. It is interesting to compare the two versions of the Don Juan story.

In Molière's version, a few seductions have been removed; two vengeful brothers have been added; and the servant has been given a better part. There is a duped creditor, typical of this playwright, and two peasant girls being wooed simultaneously, one on either side of the Don. The hero is more amusing, more French, and more of a hypocrite. He has actually married one of his women, Dona Elvira, daughter of the King's favorite soldier, and he justifies his desertion of her with a dazzling show of Jesuit reasoning.

"I carried you off from the seclusion of a convent . . . and these are things which God does not forgive. . . ." This is the typical French libertine speaking: "I cannot refuse love to what I find lovable, and so . . . if I had ten thousand hearts I would freely bestow every one of them. . . ."

He tells his father that he is going to repent and seek absolution; then, when his servant censures him for playing the hypocrite, he says: "Hypocrisy is a fashionable vice, and all vices pass for virtues once they become fashionable." After the Statue has left him, he tries to rationalize the supernatural appearance by explaining that it might have been a "trick of light," or a "momentary giddiness." The play ends without any repentance.

This tendency to rationalize, that is, to find a reasonable excuse for doing what one wants to do, or believing what one wants to believe, is typical of eighteenth-century thinking. Don Juan talks nobly about his fear of getting himself "into the bad books of Heaven," but we know that he doesn't really care about Heaven or Hell or God or man. Sganarelle, his servant, tries to argue that there is something wonderful in man that cannot be explained by reason, but the Don replies: "I think we have gone astray in the course of discussion." His statement that goodness is only expediency reminds us of Edmund's speech in *King Lear:* "Thou, Nature, art my goddess." But Sganarelle is quite logical when he says: "Without law men live like animals, which all goes to prove that you'll be damned to all eternity." [1] This is the old recourse to morality as a determinant of conduct as opposed to the Don's reasoning that man should be loyal only to his own interests. Molière's principal target is the absurdity of man, but the mistakes he portrays are flaws in a fundamentally stable order; hence his characters are both eighteenth-century individuals and universal types. Instead of developing a complex plot as Shakespeare did in his comedies, Molière built his play around a single comic or incongruous idea, such as hypocrisy, avarice, middle-class pretensions, or medical ineptitude. His belief in the right of every individual to develop his nature under the guidance of reason is the cardinal principle of the French Enlightenment.

*Calderón.* One more Spanish dramatist must be mentioned: Don Pedro Calderón de la Barca (1600–1681), who is probably the most interesting and worthy of study from a modern point of view. Calderón's plays are often allegorical and philosophical. *El Gran Teatro del Mundo* ("The Great Theater of the World") is an allegory like *Everyman*, seeming to say that life is only a preparation for eternity. It might be considered medieval, but the deep pathos and poetic language make it worthy of nine-teenth-century Romanticism.

**Poetry: Milton.** England produced one great Baroque giant and one epic poem of colossal scope: *Paradise Lost* by John Milton (1608–1674). It is unfortunate that Milton spent the years of middle age, which should have been the most productive, in writing political and religious tracts. But he was a serious thinker and sincere in believing that England was justified in ridding herself of the unbridled license of the Stuart court. The fact remains that his best writing was done after the Restoration. *Paradise Lost* was published in 1667.

Milton's avowed purpose in writing his colossal epic was "to justify the ways of God to men." The theme of the poem, the meaning of evil in a universe created by a benevolent God, has perplexed thoughtful people of every age even down to the present. The poet plunges "into the middle of things" by presenting Satan's decision to wreak vengeance upon God by tempting God's creation Man to sin. In a flashback Milton shows how Satan and his cohorts had been hurled out of Heaven because they aspired to equality with God. Then follows the story of the creation of

---

[1] Molière, *Five Plays,* translated by John Wood (Baltimore: Penguin Books, Inc., 1960).

the world and man. The poem continues with Satan's entry into the serpent, the temptation, and the fall of Adam and Eve. In the last book, the Archangel Michael leads the grieving Adam and Eve out of the garden, but comforts them with the promise that from the seed of Eve would come Christ to make atonement for their sins.

This is epic poetry of a lofty grandeur; the cadences roll forth like some great Baroque organ. All his life Milton had pondered the problems of freedom, knowledge, free will, and sin. Now near the end of his life and blind, he reaches his solution: since man has been given free will, he must accept the moral responsibility for his deeds. Both Satan and man have fallen because of pride, but man can atone through repentance and faith. The titanic figure of Satan, at first so alluring, almost deludes us into believing that he, and not all humanity, is the protagonist. Milton fully grasped the need for a unifying theme, and never once do details of image or story obscure the development of his theme. All these are characteristic of the monumental Baroque style.

But there are other traits in the poem that do not seem to fit this picture. Milton emphasizes man's need for order and restraint, the need to discipline his unruly passions and emotions. Then there are the many allusions to the classical writers, and the constant emphasis on the sin of *hubris* (pride). These traits foreshadow the dawning Classical Age. Thus Milton, and the same may be said of his great contemporary Handel, sums up the Age of the Baroque and ushers in the Classic.

# Chapter 9 / The Classic Period

Before going on into the new stylistic period, it seems desirable to make a brief recapitulation of areas of cultural leadership which have been surveyed up to this point. In the fifth and fourth centuries B.C., Athens was the seat of a cultural activity hitherto unknown in world history. After Alexander's conquests, this culture passed to Oriental cities which he founded, chiefly Alexandria, and from there it was transmitted to Rome and Byzantium. Through the Christian missionaries it found its way into western Europe and the British Isles. Here it sought a refuge in the monastery schools which developed into the universities of the late medieval period.

In the twelfth and thirteenth centuries, what is now France achieved pre-eminence in architecture and sculpture; the Low Countries excelled in music and somewhat later in painting. Achievements in literature were quite evenly divided between Italy and France. During the Renaissance, Italian cities—chiefly Florence and Venice—were the leaders in fine arts; the Flemish carried their musical culture to Italy, Spain, and Germany, while England began to assert her hegemony in the field of literature. In the High Renaissance of the sixteenth century, Italy was supreme in fine arts and music, England in literature and music (the Tudor period). In the seventeenth century, Italian Baroque architecture and decoration found their way into Spain and southern Germany; Spain enjoyed her Golden Age of literature; and Germany began her long march to pre-eminence in the field of music. In the Classic period we shall see how France became dominant in fine arts and literature, and Germany in music.

By now it should be abundantly clear that history does not develop with an eye to future historians or students. In old-fashioned history books, with their emphasis on wars, battles, kings, popes, emperors, etc., chronology took care of the matter without great difficulty. But now that history is primarily concerned with the impact of man's thinking on life, manners, arts, economy, and politics, the fabric of history becomes increasingly complex, and dates are of less importance. This is particularly true of the last half of the seventeenth century and all of the eighteenth.

Although the Baroque was a fairly homogenous style that affected all of Europe, it never gained much of a foothold in France, because there the political absolutism of the monarch took the place of the religious absolutism of the Church. The Baroque, which was still in the service of the Church, was eminently suited to the grandeur of Louis XIV, the "Sun King," whose wishes set the French pace, and whose tastes set the style. His palace at Versailles, in size and magnificence out of all proportion to need and monetary resources, was a major contributing factor to the French Revolution. But the ceremony and etiquette which the King imposed on the whole courtly establishment, extending even to the gardens of Versailles, were not Baroque but Classic.

Historians often use the terms *Classic* and *Neoclassic* indiscriminately. In this book we shall use *Classic* to refer to its earlier manifestations in the visual arts and drama of the late seventeenth century when the monumental Baroque was in full force. We shall use *Neoclassic* to refer to the complete flowering of the style in the eighteenth century. The more one studies the periodicity of styles the more one is convinced that stylistic changes are due to physiological-psychological determinants more than to outside influences such as the Church or the French Academy. Man seems to have in his physical make-up a desire for order and balance, but he also likes to throw overboard these restraints and allow his imagination and emotion to soar as evidenced in the dynamic-explosive Baroque style. Having had enough of this, he goes back to poise and order again.

The term "Classic" needs further clarification. Used to differentiate "long-haired" music from the "popular" brand, the term is meaningless. Again, people refer to "classics" when they mean literary works which have stood the test of time and are commonly considered great, like *The Divine Comedy, Don Quixote,* and *David Copperfield*. In academic parlance "the classics" refer to the legacy of Greece and Rome, and the ideals that we believe guided the ancients. In the historical sense, then, Classicism is closely bound up with a revival of interest in Greek art and the spirit which inspired it.

What were these qualities of the Greek spirit? They were measure and discipline, simplicity and clearness, formal beauty, calm and complete self-control. How were these ideals carried out? Art must be restrained; it must show mastery of material and perfect workmanship. Art must be impersonal, dealing with human types rather than with individuals. Painting must use clean formal lines in closed form. Sculptors and architects must follow Greek norms. Music must use decorous, formal patterns. Drama must follow the unities of time, place, and action, and must be devoid of overdecorative or sordid elements. These rules were strictly enforced by the French Academy. Is it any wonder that creative artists found their individuality so completely stifled that only the very greatest were able to maintain their artistic integrity?

The French Academy was neither a building nor a school, but a group of men appointed by the Crown, somewhat similar to the United States Supreme Court. This group had to pass judgment on every work of art before it could be exhibited, on every literary work before it could be published. The men were supposed to be professionals who had already established themselves, that is, whose works had been accepted. Richelieu established the Academy of Letters in 1635 to formulate the rules of French syntax and to rid the language of vulgarity. The Academy of Painting and Sculpture was established in 1648, the Academy of Architecture in 1671.

The trouble with any such Academy is that it tends to be reactionary, which means that it seeks to perpetuate its own sacrosanct style to the detriment of originality and change. To win a seat on the Academy was a great honor and often meant a professor's chair in the College of France, an office of dignity and pecuniary value under government. In the case of an accepted writer, it meant that the work would be read all over the world because of the universality of the French language. Therefore an artist was often faced with a dilemma: to create in the accepted tradition or to be progressive. In our government, arts were generally neglected until John F. Kennedy entered the White House. When he began to talk about government sponsorship of the arts, a great cry went up in the United States that such a program would tend to curb individuality. Thus the issue is still alive today.

## Historical Background

In its early phase, Classicism came as a reaction against the exuberance of the Baroque. People were tired of ecstasy and passion. In a sense it was a return to Renaissance ideals, but Renaissance artists were never so restricted. From 1661 to 1715 Baroque and Classicism traveled along together; from 1715 to 1774 Rococo appeared as a sort of dying gasp of the Baroque; and from 1774 to 1793 with Neoclassicism at its height the new Romantic style was lifting its head above the artistic horizon. To assist you in keeping your bearings amid these conflicting changes, we have invented a purely fictitious "Drama of Three Kings."

> *Act I. Louis XIV—1643–1715.*
> *The scene is the new palace at Versailles.*
> *The time is about 1700.*

The magnificent Sun King, emulated by every princeling in Europe, parades down the full two hundred and forty feet of the Hall of Mirrors, admiring the crystal chandeliers, and seeing himself repeated endlessly in the mirrors which line the walls. His Queen, Maria Theresa, daughter of Philip IV of Spain, is on his arm, and they are followed by bewigged and bejeweled courtiers and ministers of state. The great gilded royal coach is waiting to take them to the city to see one of those amusing comedies by Molière, with incidental music by the court composer, Lully. *Bourgeois Gentilhomme*, it is called. It will be accompanied by the King's own band, *Les Vingtquartre Violins du Roi* ("King's Twenty-four Violins"), Louis' pride and joy. As the coach passes the new façade of the Louvre, the King turns to admire the stately grandeur of the colonnade. Yes, his reign will be remembered for its fine buildings, but the colonnade proved too costly.

> *Act II. Louis XV—1715–1774.*
> *The scene is again Versailles; the King's bedchamber.*
> *The time is 1762.*

The King opens his eyes as a courtier draws apart the heavy damask draperies. The new Gobelin tapestries on the walls sway in the warm breeze. Louis looks up, admiring the Rococo cupids, flowers, and shells painted on the ceiling. What must he do today? Have a fitting of his white satin and gold lace shepherd costume for the *Fête Champêtre* this evening in the garden of the Trianon. Then he'll visit Mme. de Pompadour. No, she's dead, Mme. du Barry in her boudoir. Must ask her about a new tax. Same old story: no money. He'd like to hear about something besides an empty treasury. Peasants troublesome again. Bah, boors! Louis is weak but not stupid. "After us the deluge," he says aloud, "but only after us."

> *Act III. Louis XVI—1774–1793.*
> *Again Versailles; the audience chamber.*
> *The time is July, 1789.*

The King sits dozing in his high-backed throne chair while the endless debate of the Estates-General goes on. He has had to sit here for six weeks now. He will sign anything, within reason, just so long as all these people go home and let him go back to tinkering with his locks. But things seem to be improving. That fellow, Voltaire, with his absurd novel *Candide,* and Rousseau with his nature books, they have been dead eleven years, their books burned. They should have been exiled before they began to write. Diderot's gone, too. Twenty volumes! Who would read twenty volumes? Certainly not Louis. Write, write, write, and talk, talk, talk. While Louis dozes, a grim, silent woman in a wineshop on the Rue St. Antoine goes on with her knitting.[1]

## Early French Classicism

The French are by nature rationalists, and the Baroque style was not calculated to appeal to the rational mind. France had had no real Renaissance; at the time of the Italian Renaissance she had been occupied with more mundane matters such as driving the English back to their island.

**Fine Arts.** Throughout the seventeenth century there were many artists who flocked to Rome to get away from the stultifying effect of the Academy and to study the remains of classical antiquity and the works of the Italian Renaissance masters. They were all "bitten by the mirage of antiquity." They left Charles Le Brun (1619–1690) behind them to exercise dictatorship over the arts, and to provide Louis XIV with the pompous background he so much desired. It was Le Brun who created the ceiling of the famous Hall of Mirrors.

*Poussin and Lorrain.* The two best-known French expatriate artists were Nicolas Poussin (1594–1665) and Claude Lorrain (1600–1682). Both men were primarily interested in landscape —not nature in the raw, but nature in which each tree, bush, path, and building was methodically organized in space according to the artist's predetermined design, carried out with idealism and classic restraint. When figures are included, they, too, become a part of the design, or else they are so small we feel their only purpose is to give a title to the painting.

Poussin's innate love of nature prevented an overdose of rationalism. He said that he tried to reduce the infinite complexity of the world to an intellectual unity, and to humanize nature by associating it with some moral theme: religious as in "Matthew and the Angel," historical as in "Burial of Phocion," philosophical as in "Shepherds in Arcady," mythological as in "Polyphemus," poetic as in "Orpheus." Such a classic concept is valid only if it

---

[1] Mme. Defarge in Dickens' *Tale of Two Cities.*

is infused with the fire of a great spirit. Claude Lorrain's landscapes are less contrived and more natural. In fact the English style of "natural" gardens came from his paintings. He used large vistas, classical architecture, and small figures. He said, "I give my figures away but I sell my landscapes." He became entranced by the diffusion of light in the atmosphere, especially at sunrise and sunset. The golden glow which he achieved was later exploited by the English artist J. M. W. Turner. "The Flight into Egypt" and the "Embarkation of the Queen of Sheba" are typical of Claude Lorrain's style.

*Perrault.* Just as Poussin and Lorrain translated into painting the old Greek precept of perfection by proportion, Claude Perrault (1613–1688) translated this principle into architectural terms in his East Front Colonnade of the Louvre (see below). Begun in 1665 and completed in 1674, it remains today the masterpiece of French Classicism, the Parthenon of French architecture. The façade is divided into five parts, with slightly projecting end and center pavilions, the latter with a decorated pediment. The architect used coupled, free-standing Corinthian pillars across the central three sections in a well-proportioned and unified design. The columns and projecting pavilions lend variety and a stabilizing balance of solids and voids, light and shadow, when the sun hits the building. The majestic dignity expresses not only the absolute power of the monarch, but also the old Greek precepts: know thyself, nothing in excess, balance by proportion, not action but contemplation. These abiding principles of good architectural design remained a standard for public buildings in Europe, England, and the United States until the era of structural steel.

*Versailles.* Louis XIV left a far greater legacy in the Louvre

CLAUDE PERRAULT: *East Colonnade of the Louvre,* Paris. (Marburg—Art Reference Bureau)

than in Versailles, where his personal taste for luxury dictated every detail. The same classic principles operate here also, but they are overlaid with Baroque ornament. Almost the full length of the central block on the garden side is taken up by the Hall of Mirrors, designed by Charles Le Brun. The vaulted and painted ceiling rests on the broken entablatures of the Corinthian pilasters of the walls. Between these pilasters are the huge mirrors of which the King was so proud.

Many sculptors designed the figures which decorate the gardens of Versailles. Of these sculptors the best is probably François Girardon (1628–1715). In his "Bathing Nymphs" around the Fountain of Diana, we see the full-blown Baroque style in the fleshy nude figures reminiscent of those of Rubens, but in "Apollo Attended by the Nymphs" classic ideals are perfectly exemplified. In fact the figure of Apollo is a reproduction of Phidias' figure of the god on the pediment of the Temple of Zeus in Olympia. Girardon represents the nearest approach made by any artist in the West to the ancient Greek plastic outlook. It is also a good illustration of the meeting of two stylistic periods in the same artist.

**Literature.** We have already discussed in the previous chapter Louis' dynamic Superintendent of Music, Jean Baptiste Lully, and told of his collaboration with Molière to produce the seventeenth-century version of "musical comedies." The literary *salons*, attended by ladies and gentlemen of the court, became increasingly fashionable. Courtiers assumed classical names, chattered in elegant language, and wrote polished sonnets to their lovers.

*Molière.* This "preciousness" in courtly life was ridiculed with gentle wit and irony by Molière (see p. 183). There were, no doubt, many courtiers surrounding Louis XIV who were just as unscrupulous in love affairs as Don Juan although perhaps not so openly defiant. Nor did Molière's comedies spare the uncultured life of the rising bourgeois class that aped the standards of the court. The most delightful comedy of this type is *Le Bourgeois Gentilhomme* (*The Bourgeois Gentleman*) (1670) for which Lully (see p. 171) wrote the incidental music. In this play the hero, Monsieur Jourdain, son of a wealthy cloth merchant, is anxious to become a courtier and hires a music teacher, a fencing master, a dancing master, and a philosopher to teach him court etiquette. He is also determined that his daughter Lucille shall marry a nobleman. Lucille's lover Cleante invents a prank to deceive the father. Cleante's valet introduces his master to Monsieur Jourdain as the Grand Turk who has come expressly to marry Lucille. To legalize the match, they elevate Jourdain to the rank of "mamamouchi," after which, highly flattered, he gives his daughter to the disguised Cleante. The piece ends with a Turkish ballet, which was much in vogue because the Turks had recently been driven out of Europe.

*Corneille.* With his play, *Le Cid* (*The Cid*) Pierre Corneille (1606–1684) ushered in the Classic period of French drama, comparable in importance to the Elizabethan period in England. The play was produced in 1636, seven years before Louis XIV came to the throne. Corneille was a transitional writer who accepted the Greek precept "Nothing in excess" and the three unities *in principle,* but his independent spirit led him to strain these concepts almost to the breaking point. He borrowed from the Spanish not only plot and characters but also their well-known theme of conflict between love and honor.

The action of *The Cid* covers twenty-four hours. In that span of time Rodrigo declares his love for Chimena, fights his first duel to avenge his father's honor, kills Chimena's father, repels a national invasion by the Moors, wins a trial by combat, and loses and regains the favor of his king and his lady. The characters are larger than life size, their language is exalted, their struggle enormous. The audience loved it, but the French Academy did not. When Corneille first went to Paris he worked in Cardinal Richelieu's "play factory," but he couldn't stand domination and left in a huff. Corneille's enemies accused him of plagiarizing the story and violating the unities. The case was submitted to the Academy, which decided against the playwright. Corneille wrote three excellent psychological dramas: *Horace* on the problem of divided loyalties in time of war, *Cinna* on the theme of self-mastery, and *Polyeucte* on Christian martyrdom. After these plays Corneille turned to religious poetry, and when he returned to drama he could not compete with Racine. He died impoverished and embittered.

*Racine.* At the same time that Molière was making an intellectual type of comedy out of the popular farce, Jean Racine (1639–1699) began to refine tragic drama. The plays of Corneille did not suit the taste of Louis XIV's more cultivated audience who wanted polished and elegant poetry concerned with love and passion. Racine chose the Alexandrine (iambic hexameter) for his meter. This form, dating from twelfth-century poems about Alexander the Great, was revived by Ronsard and the *Pléiades* group of poets because of its stately dignity. With Racine it reflected the formalism of Louis XIV's court, but Racine also showed how emotional tensions and violent passions can disrupt the precarious order of this society.

Racine had been educated by Jansenists, a strict religious sect (somewhat similar to the Jesuits) whose aim was to strengthen the Catholic faith and to combat free thinking. The Jansenists held that man was naturally weak and could be saved only by Divine Grace, a free gift of God. In their school he had obtained excellent training in the Greek language and literature. For the story of his greatest play, *Phèdre* ("Phaedra") Racine went back to Euripides' *Hippolytus*. A comparison of these two plays should show to what extent the French Classicists could recapture the classic ideals, and to what extent they were bound by their own ethnic outlook on life.

First, note the titles of the two plays. The Greeks were primarily concerned with the hero, Hippolytus; Racine shifted the emphasis to the woman, Phèdre, because he believed that women best demonstrate human weakness when they are aroused by powerful emotions.

In Euripides' play, Aphrodite, goddess of love, is angry because Hippolytus will have nothing to do with women, but prefers to worship Artemis, chaste goddess of the hunt. Aphrodite, goddess of love, decides to retaliate by having Phaedra, young second wife of Hippolytus' father, Theseus, fall madly in love with Hippolytus. In her malady, Phaedra preserves the majesty of grief and tries to remain faithful to her husband. But her nurse worms the truth out of her and advises her to tell Hippolytus in order to save her life. When the nurse herself tells him he curses all women. Theseus rushes in because an oracle has warned him that his house is burning. Phaedra, consumed by hatred and shame, hangs herself, leaving a letter accusing Hippolytus of seducing her. Theseus, in fury and injured pride, asks the god Poseidon to kill his son, and Hippolytus is killed since Artemis arrives too late to defend his innocence. Thus Euripides stresses the eternal, terrifying struggle between the opposing forces in men and divinities alike, which determine man's destiny.

In Racine's play Phèdre is not an unsympathetic figure. She has heard the rumor that Theseus may have left her for another woman (an idea quite understandable to a French audience), and she reveals her love to Hippolytus only when her husband is reported dead. But there are flaws in her character which are intensified by passion. She is too easily swayed by the nurse to act against her reason, and when Theseus returns and is made suspicious of his son, she fails to save him because she has learned of his love for Aricie. In Phèdre's great confrontation scene with Hippolytus, her jealousy causes her to lose classic poise and restraint completely. She blames herself to arouse his pity, tries to make him kill her, even tries to bribe him with an offer of her crown. Believing that Hippolytus will tell his father of her love, she accuses Hippolytus of the crime. Theseus, blinded by fury and injured pride, calls on Poseidon to kill his son. After taking poison, Phèdre confesses to Theseus that Hippolytus is innocent. The nurse gives the Jansenist doctrine of original sin when she says: "If you love, you cannot escape your destiny. You were ensnared by charms that were predestined."

How is Racine a Classicist? He holds to the Greek unities; except for one scene he preserves the noble dignity of the ancients; deaths are kept out of sight; flaws in human character bring destruction; evil is punished and virtue exalted; passions are exhibited only to show the disorder into which they lead us. The new character, Aricie, is introduced to accent Phèdre's jealousy and also Theseus' goodness (he takes the young girl under his wing at the end of the play). It is understandable that serious French actresses aspire to play Phèdre as English-speaking actresses aspire to play Lady Macbeth.

## The Rococo

The Rococo style, emanating from the pleasure-loving court of Louis XV, expressed itself in a type of decorative interior ornamentation that required meticulous workmanship. The word Rococo stems from the French *rocaille,* meaning artificial rock-work and pierced shellwork. The walls of symmetrically square or rectangular rooms were divided into panels by thin pilaster strips; then upon these flat, empty panels the decorator embroidered stucco arabesques of interlaces, leaves, acanthus scrolls, flowers, sprays, and tendrils. These delicate and fragile passages were either painted or, more often, gilded. There is occult balance rather than mathematical symmetry because one side of a panel never exactly repeats the design of the opposite side. Mirrors between some of the panels tend to wipe away the volume of the room and make the visitor feel that he is moving through constantly changing infinity. Even the juncture between walls and ceilings is disguised by curved and ornamented covings. This is an art of exquisite refinement, politeness, and taste, designed for jaded courtiers who lived only to be amused. Rococo decoration can be seen at its best in the Parisian *hôtels,* which were not hotels in our sense of the term but luxurious town houses for noblemen and wealthy merchants. It takes no great imagination to picture courtiers dressed in satin and brocade as they engage in amorous dalliance in such rooms or wander about formal gardens decorated with marble statues, little pavilions, and sentimental, artificial ruins. If one lacks such imagination he has only to examine the paintings of Watteau.

**Fine Arts.** What do Rococo painters do to give the sense of freedom and spontaneity to their paintings? They break up the masses, allowing empty space to enter the foreground, and open infinite distances behind their little garden parties. The figures are grouped casually with plenty of freedom to move at will to another group or location without constraint or effort, "as those move easiest who have learned to dance," said Pope, the perfect Rococo poet.

*Watteau.* By far the most outstanding painter of the Rococo period was Jean Antoine Watteau (1684–1721), who was born of Flemish parentage. Watteau had powerful friends among the wealthy courtiers, who took him into their homes, where he had opportunity to paint their garden parties and musical functions. He needed to be cared for because he was frail, poetic, and aloof. He died of tuberculosis at the age of thirty-six.

Watteau certainly knew the amorous intrigues and sensual pastimes that went on in the great houses, but he took no part in them and never painted them. He pictures instead a life of pleasant idleness—gay, tender, unstudied, chaste. "The Embarkation for Cythera" (see p. 197), the painting which gained Watteau entrance to the Academy, pictures discreet lovers ambling slowly toward a gilded boat which will take them to the realm of love. Watteau was constantly studying and sketching people and their casual gestures—the lift of an arm, the tilt of a head, as these revealed mood and character. In this quality he anticipated the later Impressionists. Watteau has left us a picture of eighteenth-century French high society which is poetic and refined although not quite accurate.

*Boucher.* The graceful play-acting pictured by Watteau goes hand in hand with a highly artistic portrait art of great naturalism, as you can see if you examine the portrait of Madame de Pompadour, mistress of Louis XV, painted by François Boucher (1703–1770). She was the model of all the court ladies and virtual ruler of France until her death in 1764. She is portrayed here impeccably gowned, with a book symbolic of her role as patroness of learning. The opened letter and quill pen on her bed table bespeak the interest of the period in intelligent and spicy correspondence. Behind her is a clock supported by a fat cherub.

ANTOINE WATTEAU: *Embarkation for Cythera.* Louvre, Paris. (Alinari —Art Reference Bureau)

Boucher also painted "Sprawling O'Murphy," another mistress of Louis. In Boucher's painting she looks scarcely more than a child perhaps twelve or thirteen years old. She has flung herself down nude, on a *chaise longue,* legs distended, in a pose which would be seductive in a grown woman, but in a child is unstudied and natural. On her face there is a look of both innocence and wonder.

*Sculptors.* Sculptors were kept busy making charming little statuettes to stand on tables, mantels, or pedestals in the boudoirs. The two best were Étienne Falconet (1716–1791), who did "Punishment of Cupid," and Claude Michel (1738–1814), called Clodion, who did "Nymph and Satyr" and "Bacchante and a Faun."

*Chardin.* At the same time in an obscure corner of Paris, an unpretentious painter by the name of Jean Baptiste Chardin (1699–1779) was busily creating simple genre and still-life scenes in his own home and selling them in open-air stalls on the street. Chardin captured the reality of ordinary objects and people. "The Market Girl" represents his wife coming home from market with a loaf of freshly baked bread and a chicken for Sunday dinner; "The Blessing" pictures his younger daughter saying grace while her mother puts the food on the table. Every composition shows painstaking attention to details of organization, texture, and light, and also reveals the artist's love for his simple home. Chardin's paintings are in a certain sense prophetic because they reveal the spiritual force of the submerged bourgeoisie which was soon going to overturn the whole graceful and courtly establishment.

**Music.** Music, too, was touched by the Rococo spirit of play. The sturdy pomp and majesty of Lully's operas no longer appealed. *Sensibilité*, artificial and stylized, is called in music the *style galant*, best represented by the tinkling little clavecin. This music is simple in melody and harmonic structure, but so loaded with grace notes and embellishments that the original melody is all but lost. Everything depends on suggestive titles like "The Hen," "The Cuckoo," and "The Clock." Louis Daquin (1694–1772) composed witty and elegant little pieces, drenched with a shower of ornaments which, Dr. Lang says, "linger in the air like confetti."[1] François Couperin the Great (1668–1733) was the musical counterpart of Watteau, and a real poet at the keyboard. (We call him "the Great" to distinguish him from an earlier François Couperin, a Louis and a Charles, all brothers; Couperin the Great was the son of Charles. All were masters of the organ and clavecin.) In the nineteenth century the Impressionist Claude Debussy was influenced by Couperin. Many of the little ornaments of the *style galant* found their way into the music of Haydn and Mozart.

We have already noted the French penchant for fighting about artistic matters. Here is an instance. In 1733 an Italian opera troupe brought to Paris an amusing little trifle called *La Serva Padrona* ("The Maid as Mistress") by a young Neapolitan named Giovanni Pergolesi (1710–1736), who, despite his short life, left the world some very fine music and was one of the contributors to the symphonic style. The opera calls for two singing characters and one speaking character. A serving maid convinces her master that he should marry her by disguising his valet as a handsome captain who pretends to be in love with her. It just suited the frivolous taste of the French court, and was a resounding success. But it started a war: the "war of the buf-

---

[1] Paul Henry Lang, *op. cit.,* 541.

foons." Buffoons were singers in Italian comic opera (*opera buffa*).

Everybody jumped into the fray. The King declared himself for Lully and French opera; the Queen favored the Italian buffoons and Italian opera. Jean Jacques Rousseau became a champion of the "Queen's corner." Rousseau was a self-taught musician without much technical knowledge, but he could write scathingly. He brought out a manifesto about the future of French music, in which he claimed to have annihilated the "King's corner." "Music," he wrote, "should be allied with nature." To demonstrate this thesis he composed a little opera called *Le Devin du Village* ("The Village Soothsayer"). It also was successful, and was imitated by Mozart in his *Bastien and Bastienne*. As a matter of fact, the only thing new about it was its rural setting. As in Poussin's paintings, nature was idealized rather than natural, but it did set the stage for modern French comic opera.

**Poetry.** It is easy to deprecate the "vain frippery" of the Rococo, and this was the fate of Alexander Pope (1688–1744) at the hands of the nineteenth-century Victorian critics. He has only recently begun to return to his rightful place in the hierarchy of English poets. It is true that Pope was a malicious satirist whose wit was devastating when directed against his enemies, but in his lighter moments his work bears a curious analogy to French Rococo decoration and painting.[1] He probably never visited the French court, although he was entertained in the homes of English courtiers, where life must have been quite similar. This passage from "Windsor Forest" might describe almost any one of Watteau's pastoral scenes:

> *Here waving groves a chequer'd scene display,*
> *And part admit and part exclude the day;*
> *As some coy nymph her lover's warm address*
> *Nor quite indulges, nor can quite repress.*
> *There, interspers'd in lawns and op'ning glades,*
> *Thin trees arise that shun each other's shades.*

It is in the "Rape of the Lock" that Pope shows himself most Rococo, and the greatest master of the heroic couplet in English.

---

[1] The author is indebted to Mr. Wylie Sypher for calling attention to the parallelism between the French Rococo and Pope's poetry. Wylie Sypher, *Rococo to Cubism in Art and Literature* (New York: Random House, Vintage Books, 1963).

This is not a matter of poetic diction, for there is nothing pedantic or pretentious or learned in the poem. The sensitive details are as apparent as the total unity, as simple and minutely precise as the Rococo arabesque:

> *Teach Infant cheeks a bidden blush to know,*
> *And little hearts to flutter at a Beau.*

The poem started out to be only a clever trifle, but Pope broadened it into a charming mock-heroic persiflage on the foibles of fashionable society:

> *With varying vanities, from ev'ry part,*
> *They shift the moving Toyshop of their heart.*

And again:

> *Hither the heroes and the nymphs resort,*
> *To taste awhile the pleasures of a Court;*
> *In various talk th'instructive hours they past,*
> *Who gave the ball, or paid the visit last. . . .*

Pope never plunges to the depths of human emotion or agony of soul. The loss of a husband is no more serious than the loss of a lap-dog:

> *Not louder shrieks to pitying heav'n are cast,*
> *When husbands, or when lap-dogs breathe their last . . .*

Even in the more serious "Eloisa to Abelard," Eloisa stands apart and surveys her own feelings, a practice, as any psychologist will tell you, that dissipates the emotion:

> *Tears that delight, and sighs that waft to heav'n.*

If the poet points a moral, it is more like an observation than a sermon:

> *How vain are all these glories, all our pains,*
> *Unless good sense preserve what beauty gains.*

Compare these lines with Boucher's "Toilet of Venus":

> *The busy Sylphs surround their darling care,*
> *These set the head, and those divide the hair,*
> *Some fold the sleeve, whilst others plait the gown;*
> *And Betty's prais'd for labours not her own.*[1]

---

[1] All lines quoted are from Alexander Pope, *Selected Works,* ed. Louis Kronenberger (New York: Random House, Modern Library, 1951).

## Neoclassicism

In 1764 some volumes were published which enormously stimulated the Neoclassic revival throughout Europe, England, and America. The author was Johann Joachim Winckelmann (1717–1768), a Prussian archaeologist, who had traveled in Italy and explored in Pompeii and Herculaneum. He intended to go to Greece but apparently did not get that far. It was through Winckelmann that the Greek ideals of Apollonic poise and noble restraint came to be generally accepted. Even Goethe was partly influenced by him to return to classicism. Winckelmann has been called the "Father of Archaeology," but "Father of Tourism" might be a better title. His writings were so enthusiastic that he started a perfect mania to "see Europe." Every affluent young Englishman and German had to take the "Grand Tour" as a part of his education. They all came home with souvenir works of art. Presto! Women's clothes resembled the robes of Roman matrons, and Josiah Wedgwood of England began making pottery decorated by John Flaxman with Greek figures. The Neoclassic revival was particularly strong in England as we shall see later in this chapter.

**French Fine Arts.**  Despite the Rococo interlude in France, the Classic style in architecture had not died out. It continued throughout the eighteenth century for the finest public and some private buildings. Jules Hardouin-Mansart (1646–1708) used Classic style in the church of *St. Louis des Invalides* ("St. Louis of the Sick"), although there are Baroque spatial effects in the cupola. The same is true of his *Chapelle du Palais* (Chapel of the Palace) at Versailles. In 1762 Ange-Jacques Gabriel (1698–1782) began the Petit Trianon with its stately portico upheld by Corinthian columns. This was the "little chateau" given by Louis XV to his mistress Madame du Barry as a *maison de plaisance* (pleasure house).

It is significant that Marie Antoinette, queen of Louis XVI, had her salon decorated in the Classic taste: this meant that for the court the Rococo was finished. It was, however, not a servile imitation of Classicism, for the proportions are noble, the manner refined and dignified. Classicism continued in vogue through the Revolution and the Napoleonic era.

*David.*  Jacques Louis David (1748–1825) was the greatest Neoclassic painter. These were troubled times and he cannot be blamed for being something of a political opportunist. Although at first loyal to the King, as a member of the 1792 Convention, he was one of those who voted death for his former patron. When his friend Robespierre fell, he was threatened with trial and imprisonment in the Luxembourg palace. After being out of favor for several years, he was released to become Napoleon's official painter. When Napoleon fell, David fled to Brussels and died there.

David was a product of the classical training of the Academy both in Paris and Rome. The times created a demand for heroic subjects, especially those devoted to sacrifice for a noble cause. The "Oath of the Horatii" and "Death of Socrates" (see below) were both hailed as Revolutionary paintings. In "Paris and Helen," the two figures look like sculpture. David painted Madame Récamier, leader of French society, as a Roman matron in classic gown and coiffure, but she was a capricious lady who did not like the painting. However, when the Louvre purchased it in 1826, it was regarded as one of David's finest paintings. Such works were just what the bourgeois revolutionists wanted: everything clean and clear, with nothing left to the imagination. But from an artistic standpoint they are cold, the color schemes mechanical, the figures sculpturesque, the backgrounds like a stage set.

David was such an artistic dictator that revolt against him was inevitable. All his pupils espoused the rising Romanticism except one, Jean Auguste Dominique Ingres, but even Ingres'

JACQUES LOUIS DAVID: *Death of Socrates.* Metropolitan Museum of Art, New York. (The Metropolitan Museum of Art, Wolfe Fund, 1931)

Classic forms are more flexible. His individual portraits like "Artist Granet" and "Madame Leblanc" are excellent. The sculpturesque nudes "Oedipus and the Sphinx" and "Odalisque" show his master's draftsmanship, but the lines are softer. He did not paint directly from a model, but he studied the model, dismissed her, and painted from memory. You can see that the Greek ideals behind eighteenth-century Neoclassicism led to great plastic clarity, but the artists could not recapture the spirit of the ancients, either because they were too far removed or because they were too self-conscious or because they tried too hard.

*Sculpture.* An interesting example of a sculptor who followed Winckelmann's theories of "pure beauty" of form regardless of "content" is the Italian Antonio Canova (1757–1822). You remember that Napoleon, after a successful campaign, was in the habit of leaving some member of his family in the conquered territory with the idea of consolidating his holdings. His sister Pauline "consolidated" in Italy by marrying Prince Camillo Filippo Ludovico Borghese, inheritor of the vast fortunes of the ancient Borghese family. He had joined the French army and was rewarded by being made Governor General of Piedmont. He sold the Borghese collection of art treasures to Napoleon for thirteen million francs and received the Piedmont domains as part payment. In 1815, when these lands were reclaimed by the King of Sardinia, the Prince took back part of the collection. The Borghese Palace in Rome still contains one of the finest art collections in Italy. This is an instance of how art gets mixed up with politics; it has a parallel with some of Hitler's moves in World War II.

Canova sculpted Pauline in classic hairdress, stretched out on a Roman chaise longue in a position similar to that of Madame Récamier, which was painted about the same time. Pauline's head is attached to the half-draped body of Venus, whose flesh ripples in Rococo fashion. The affectation makes it unsatisfactory as a work of art by any standard. Canova's other well-known piece of sculpture is "Cupid and Psyche," which is in the Louvre. The line pattern is pleasing, and the flesh is firm, but it is sentimental enough to make young ladies swoon.

In the Louis XVI period, the return to Neoclassicism led to an elegant formalism with a touch of sentimentality heightened by the discoveries in Pompeii. Étienne Maurice Falconet (1716–1791) did his "Punishment of Cupid" (now in the National Gallery, Washington) and Claude Michel Clodion (1738–1814) his "Nymph and Satyr" (now in the Metropolitan Museum, New York) in this style. But the best sculptor of the whole century was Jean Antoine Houdon (1741–1828), who sculpted three statues of Voltaire. He has caught the wicked glint in the eyes, the sparkle of half-cynical, half-benevolent amusement, the same spirit which we sense in *Candide*. Houdon was a great portraitist in sculpture. He portrays not just how people looked 'but also how their personalities affected those who came into contact with them. After the American Revolution, he came to the United States and executed the statue of Washington now in the Capitol in Richmond, Virginia, and also busts of Franklin, Jefferson, John Paul Jones, and Robert Fulton. His busts of children are very lifelike.

**Les Philosophes and the Enlightenment.** Throughout the eighteenth century in France there were writers who saw that the rising bourgeois class was demanding a place in the sun and that France was heading for insolvency unless something drastic were done. These men, questioners of authority, are sometimes referred to as *Les Philosophes* ("The Philosophers") and sometimes as the *Encyclopédistes* because most of them wrote articles for Diderot's *Encyclopedia*.

In 1721 Montesquieu published his *Lettres Persanes* ("Persian Letters"), a biting diatribe against European society in matters of religion, politics, finance, commerce, even marriage. Upon his return from London, he wrote in praise of the English constitution. His last work, *L'Esprit des Lois* ("Spirit of the Laws"), argued that laws should conform to the temperament and history of a people. Most modern constitutional governments are indebted to this book.

In 1735 René Lesage completed his picaresque novel *Gil Blas* (see p. 180), which was modeled on Spanish picaresque tales but satirized French social conditions. Between 1751 and 1776 Denis Diderot brought out his twenty-eight volume *Encyclopédie*, which contained the radical doctrine that the common people should be the main concern of the governing classes.

*Voltaire.* The most dangerous of these political writers was François Marie Arouet, called Voltaire (1694–1778). Voltaire was keen, inquisitive, skeptical, and ambitious. He tried every form of literature, seventy volumes of it, but is best known for his satire *Candide* (1759). This clever blend of novel and essay permitted the author to camouflage dangerous ideas by an atmosphere of nonsense. Jonathan Swift had used the same trick thirty years earlier in *Gulliver's Travels* to point out defects in English society and character.

Voltaire wrote *Candide* when he was sixty-five years old, after life had given him some hard knocks. He had been badly treated by the King, dismissed from Frederick the Great's court, imprisoned in the Bastille three times for insults to courtiers. His mistress Madame du Châtelet had deceived him with his best friend and had died in childbirth. He had been exiled to London, a fate shared by most liberal French writers. Then came 1755, the year of the Lisbon earthquake, when most of the city's population had been killed while attending church on Sunday morning. Every sect tried to explain the earthquake in terms of its own prejudices. The Jesuits said it was a demonstration of the wrath of God against heretics; the Jansenists believed it was due to the evils of the Inquisition; the Methodists averred that it was a warning against papal practices.

*Candide* is a rollicking parody on the romance of adventure, with a series of preposterous episodes that give the author an opportunity to satirize intolerance, oppression, tyranny, fanaticism, and superstition. But the most important butt of his satire is the German philosopher Leibnitz, who believed that "all is for the best in the best of all possible worlds." This philosophy is put into the mouth of Pangloss, Candide's tutor.

Candide is a well-brought-up young man, but naïve and unsophisticated. An indiscretion with Cunégonde, the daughter of the Baron in whose castle he has been reared, causes him to be kicked out to experience at first hand "the best of all possible worlds." He enlists in the Bulgarian army, but because of the tyranny of army life he deserts and flees to Holland, where he finds Pangloss in wretched condition but still optimistic. A Dutch Anabaptist takes them to Lisbon just in time to witness the devastating earthquake. They are brought before the tribunal of the Inquisition and condemned. Pangloss is sentenced to be hanged but Candide is rescued by Cunégonde who arrives opportunely. After killing the Grand Inquisitor, who has designs on Cunégonde, Candide and the girl escape by ship to Buenos Aires. Still pursued, he leaves Cunégonde there and takes refuge among the Jesuits of Paraguay who are fighting Spain and Portugal. He spends some time with cannibals, then finds the happy land of Eldorado, where there is no church, no prison, no court of justice. He regretfully leaves, laden down with gold, but the treasure is soon dissipated—lost, stolen, or given away.

Candide turns up next in France, where he is threatened with imprisonment at the hands of an unscrupulous priest. He goes to London, where he gets mixed up with politics, then to Venice, where he talks with several former kings who have lost their jobs and a wealthy nobleman who has everything but is bored with life. He finally gets to Constantinople, where he discovers Cunégonde, now old and repulsive; Pangloss, who had escaped the noose; and Martin, his other tutor, who is a pessimist and an agnostic. They buy a little farm and settle down to till the soil. Pangloss still clings to his optimistic philosophy, but Candide merely says, "mais il faut cultiver notre jardin" (we must cultivate our garden).

Voltaire's conclusions are inevitable: man is a vicious animal, absurd, unintelligent, and infamous, but even so the tale ends on a note of optimism. Human stupidity can be alleviated by resolute action and hard work. Although some of his ideas changed the thinking habits of the civilized world and destroyed the complacency of the ruling class, Voltaire was not a great philosopher, nor a revolutionary, nor a democrat. He believed in the monarchy and probably would have been amused to know that the revolutionists took him for their hero. His motto "Écrasez l'infâme" ("crush the infamous thing") did not refer to religion or the Church, but rather to injustice, superstition, and bigotry. His *Dictionnaire Philosophique* (*Philosophical Dictionary*) contains short essays on such subjects as the Soul, Beauty, and Glory, and also his views on the clergy and Catholic dogma. In the essay on intolerance he says in effect: "We are all subject to error, so let us pardon each other's follies and respect each other's opinions."

On July 10, 1791, when the revolutionists transferred his body to the Pantheon with great pomp, Jacques Louis David inscribed these words on the hearse: "He taught us to be free." Twenty-three years later, when the Bourbons came back to power during the "Hundred Days," according to one scholar,[1] his body and that of Rousseau were disinterred and burned with quicklime. Whether the story is true or not, it shows how much the Bourbons hated these men. When the sarcophagus was opened in 1864, it was empty.

*Beaumarchais.* Beaumarchais, the pen name of Pierre Augustin Caron (1732–1799), was the most important French dramatist of the late eighteenth century. He knew court life because he taught music to the court ladies. Later he entered the diplomatic service, was ennobled, and amassed a fortune which he spent aiding the American Revolution. He returned to France and died in poverty.

Beaumarchais wrote two excellent plays which are important in their own right and are still played in France, but they are

---

[1] Harold Nicolson, *The Age of Reason* (Garden City, N.Y.: Doubleday & Company, 1961), p. 90.

best-known and loved all over the world in their operatic form. *Le Mariage de Figaro* (*The Marriage of Figaro*), which Mozart made into his most amusing opera, "sounded the tocsin of Revolution," as one critic observed. The author had to wait three years before he could produce the opera. In it Figaro bids open defiance to the arbitrary power of authority, and a minor character, Bridoison, is satirized as a worshiper of rules. The other play, made into a favorite comic opera by Rossini and called *Le Barbier de Séville* (*The Barber of Seville*), has for protagonist a spirited plebeian who gets the best of a dull-witted nobleman, a jealous guardian, and a stupid priest. When the hero pokes fun at rules he is really satirizing Neoclassicism itself, and when a style begins to satirize itself it is finished.

*Rousseau.* Jean Jacques Rousseau (1712–1778), like the composer Beethoven and the poet Goethe, stands at the crossroads of two styles and, like the god Janus, looks in two directions at once: back to the Classic and forward to the Romantic. Rousseau's influence was more profound and more enduring than that of Voltaire. He spoke as his inmost spirit prompted him, and his impassioned emotions are turned against the conventions of "civilized" life. The full flood of romantic passion is loosened in his long novel *Julie ou la Nouvelle Héloïse* (*Julie or the New Heloise*), which, like Richardson's *Clarissa Harlowe,* is told in letter form. The heroine Julie sacrifices her right to happiness because of an austere notion of duty. But nature as a universal principle becomes the source of all good and the guide of all healthy motives. In *Le Contrat Social* (*Social Contract*) Rousseau argues that all social injustices can be corrected by an awakened reason. *Émile* gives his ideas on the education of children, ideas upon which most of our modern educational psychology and pedagogy rest. The force of Rousseau's prose and the balance of his style are still Classic, but his impassioned language is Romantic.

**English Fine Arts.** The position of English artists in the eighteenth century was not enviable. English people are by nature conservative and reserved. They had accepted the foreigners Holbein and Van Dyck after they had established their reputations abroad.

*Hogarth.* Ironically, probably the best artist England ever produced earned his living as an engraver of books because he was unable to get commissions for paintings from the people who were able to pay for them. This artist was William Hogarth (1697–1764). The English middle class felt that a picture should have some use; that is, it should tell a story or preach a sermon.

Hogarth's series of dramatic "moralities," *Rake's Progress* and *Marriage à la Mode,* make him one of the greatest social satirists in all art and give us as adequate an idea of the seamy side of eighteenth-century London as do Dickens' novels in the next century.

Hogarth knew his London and it was certainly picturesque. Ladies of fashion were carried about in sedan chairs to do their shopping while those less fortunate dumped their slops from upstairs windows into the street. Gentlemen wore their swords at all times and settled their grievances in the dueling field behind the British Museum. Rakes boasted of being "six-bottle" men and gambled away their ancestral estates. In spite of John Wesley's preaching, unwanted babies were flung on dunghills.

This was the London Hogarth painted in his series of picture sermons, in "Gin Lane" and "Night in Charing Cross." The public thought the pictures amusing, as they thought *Gulliver's Travels* entertaining, but they never considered it was their responsibility to correct any of these wrongs. You should know Hogarth's painting of the actor David Garrick and his pretty German wife and "The Shrimp Girl," a vendor he saw one day on the street.

*Portrait Painters.* Other portraitists of the eighteenth century catered to the aristocratic demand for beautiful pictures of their subjects decked out in sumptuous silks and satins. Sir Joshua Reynolds (1723–1792), first president of the Royal Academy (founded in 1768), studied in Italy and was classically correct in his compositions. But his pictures of children like "Miss Bowles with Her Dog" look insipid and sentimental today. Sir Thomas Gainsborough (1727–1788) was largely self-taught. His sense of naturalness came from his early life in the country. Examine "The Honorable Frances Duncombe" for texture of skin and gleaming fabrics. George Romney (1734–1802) spent two years in Italy, where he became a Neoclassicist. Although his portraits are sometimes cold, "Miss Constable" is quite pleasing. Sir Henry Raeburn (1756–1823) remained in Edinburgh, where he painted Scottish men in their formal kilts and the pink-cheeked women in less formal attire. Everybody knows his ingratiating "Boy with the Rabbit." An interesting expatriate from America was Benjamin West (1738–1830), who did historical paintings like "Death of General Wolfe" and "Penn's Treaty with the Indians" before those of the Frenchman David.

*Wren.* Neoclassic architecture in England is best represented by Sir Christopher Wren (1632–1723). Note that his dates lie well within the Baroque period on the Continent. The English were too conventional to be intrigued by the exuberance of the

Baroque, but the formality of the Classic style suited them perfectly. And having found a style they liked, they stayed with it through the life span of three good architects: Inigo Jones (1573–1652), the Palladian classic; Sir Christopher Wren, the Georgian classic; and Robert Adam (1728–1792), the Neo-Hellenic. In the first period the Banqueting Hall in Whitehall seemed almost like the Rucellai Palace transplanted to London. Wren was not trained as an architect but as a mathematician. However, he had been to Italy, and had also studied Bernini's plans for the east front of the Louvre. After the devastating London fire of 1666, Wren was appointed to plan the reconstruction of the city. His plans were not followed, but he did design St. Paul's Cathedral and many other churches.[1] The main features of St. Paul's are the huge dome over the crossing and a pedimented façade with two symmetrical towers at either end. The dome, in fact, was the one which Bramante had designed for St. Peter's. The smaller churches with their porches supported by classic columns and a tower over the main entrance are in the "colonial" style seen in so many New England churches. There is a well-proportioned one in Kennebunkport, Maine, for which Wren himself designed the tower. Robert Adam was influenced by Winckelmann's formulas; hence his classical buildings are more elegant. A good example is the portico at Osterley Park, London.

**English Literature.** Neoclassicism arrived in England in 1660 with the restoration of Charles II and the return of the courtiers who had been sojourning in France. The change was immediately evident in the theaters which had been closed for eighteen years. The lid was off; the usual English decorum was tossed to the winds; and the people were entertained with comedies far more licentious than Molière's. The trend toward satire, together with the increasing tendency to write for a middle-class rather than a courtly audience, were the most distinctive features of the period.

*Dryden.* The pivotal figure for the future was John Dryden (1631–1700). His best comedy is probably *Marriage à la Mode* (1672); and his best tragedy is *All for Love*, based on the story of Antony and Cleopatra, which is written in blank verse and preserves the unities. Dryden's essays and literary criticism, which show consummate craftsmanship, vigor, and sensible thinking, won him the title of "Father of English Prose." His poetry formed Pope; his prose formed Addison.

---

[1] Seventeen churches designed by Wren were destroyed in the World War II bombings of London.

*Swift.* Jonathan Swift (1658–1745) has been called the English Voltaire, because he too was intolerant of the stupidities and vices of man and directed his malicious and witty satire against politics and morals. He would be amused and perhaps chagrined to know that his satirical masterpiece *Gulliver's Travels* has become children's fiction. *Battle of the Books* depicts a literary controversy between the ancients and the moderns. Swift's satire is less abrasive than Voltaire's.

*Addison and Steele.* The names of Joseph Addison (1672–1719) and Richard Steele (1672–1729) are usually linked because together they published two famous periodicals, the *Tatler* and the *Spectator,* which contained mildly critical essays. The *Spectator* popularized Sir Roger de Coverley, the portrait of a perfect country squire of the period. Addison's essays have the elegant and graceful style of the polished courtier (see p. 172).

*Defoe.* Daniel Defoe (1661–1731) wrote tracts on religious questions, and as a journalist brought out *The Review* every day for nine years. *Robinson Crusoe* (1719) is the prototype of the British empire-builders, who maintained British standards even on a desert isle. *Moll Flanders* is a picaresque tale with a toothsome female as protagonist. Her moral standards are different from but no whit superior to those of Lazarillo de Tormes.

*Dr. Johnson.* Given a choice most people today would rather meet Dr. Samuel Johnson (1709–1784) than any other literary figure of this period. Johnson fought poverty most of his life. Quite alone, he compiled his immense English dictionary, the great work which made him famous but did not drive the wolf from the door. In an age which sought rules and models his dictionary standardized speech and writing throughout the country and made him the dictator of literary London. His definitions are crisp, the thought content precise, and the pertinent quotations readable. He sometimes introduced his own prejudices, such as this definition of "pension"—"The pay given to a state hireling for treason to his country." When his mother died he wrote a romance, *Rasselas, Prince of Abyssinia,* in order to get money to pay her funeral expenses. It is a tale of a Happy Valley, unspoiled by contact with the outer world. It makes one think of Rousseau, and oddly enough Johnson wrote it at the same time that Rousseau was writing *Émile.* (It was the inspiration for the modern English novel *Lost Horizon.*)

At last a government pension brought Dr. Johnson ease and independence. He formed the Literary Club, a circle of friends, one of the most brilliant groups in all history, dedicated to the study of mankind. This fusion of intellectual and social life had the effect of turning the whole English society toward literature. Johnson's devoted biographer James Boswell (1740–1795) was present at the meetings at the Turk's Head Tavern, and recorded the discussions. It was Boswell who invented the art of intimate biography.

*Gay.* John Gay (1688–1732) wrote sprightly poetic satires, especially on the artificial literary pastorals. His *Beggar's Opera* (see p. 172) satirizes the prime minister, Sir Robert Walpole, and the court of George II. Gay himself wrote the epitaph carved on his tomb in Westminster Abbey:

> *Life is a jest and all things show it,*
> *I thought so once and now I know it.*

Gay's friend Alexander Pope (1688–1744) was the most quoted poet of the century. While his light verse is Rococo (see p. 199), his more serious poems, especially his translations of the *Iliad* and the *Odyssey* and his *Essay on Criticism,* have been called the English epitome of Neoclassicism because of their technical perfection.

*Gray.* The poet Thomas Gray (1716–1771) was transitional. He is thought to have worked ten years polishing "Elegy Written in a Country Churchyard," his masterpiece. Stylistically it is the essence of Neoclassicism, but the love of nature, the brooding melancholy, and the preoccupation with death found in it mark it as Romantic.

*Drama.* Even in the mid-eighteenth century, manners in the theaters were as bad as they had been in Shakespeare's day until the famous impresario David Garrick with the influence of Mrs. Siddons, the supreme tragic actress of the century, ended these theatrical abuses. Then the audience calmed down and actually listened to the comedies of manners by Oliver Goldsmith (1728–1774) and Richard Brinsley Sheridan (1751–1816). The best of Goldsmith's comedies is *She Stoops to Conquer,* and the best of Sheridan's is *The School for Scandal.*

**Music.** The triumph of Neoclassic music is the symphony, a perfect fusion of form and content. For one hundred and fifty years artists had struggled to rejuvenate the spirit of the classics in art and literature, but they never succeeded. It was the Germans who found it in music, unconsciously and without ever realizing that they had found it. But great art forms do not arise quickly, nor are they the achievement of one genius. The form and language of the symphonic style were germinating throughout the eighteenth century in the minds and work of many worthy composers before a culminating synthesis was reached in the symphonies of Haydn, Mozart, and Beethoven. It is beyond our time and not necessary to our purpose to trace all of these developments, but it is safe to say that most of the stylistic elements of the symphony can be traced to Italian opera.

The essence of drama is conflict: the tension produced by the struggle between two forces. This struggle takes place in the development section of a symphony, which therefore requires two themes or motifs. When you listen to a Mozart opera and follow the libretto, you will note that every time there is opposition between two characters, or two forces in the same character, the music tends to sound symphonic. The Italians also contributed to the symphony the ingratiating lyrical elements, while the French threw in some of the ornamental stylisms of the *style galant* from their clavecin pieces.

All this sounds very deliberate, as though a German might say: "Come, let us make a stew. Will you contribute the potatoes, and will you contribute the onions, and I'll contribute the meat and put it all together." Great art is never that simple, and its creators did not know exactly what they wanted to make. These symphonic composers were just good, practical musicians, who had been hired by a wealthy prince to furnish music at mealtimes or for evening entertainment. They had the status of servants, and all too often were treated with condescension. Karl Philipp Emanuel Bach (son of Johann Sebastian) was chief clavier master for Frederick the Great. His brother Johann Christian had a job in London as music master to Queen Charlotte Sophia. The so-called Mannheim School was centered at the court of the Elector Palatine Duke Carl Theodor, whose musicians included Italians, Austrians, and Bohemians as well as Germans. The largest group surrounded the Emperor's court in Vienna. We still have the names of forty-four of these men, and there were undoubtedly others, all working together in a sort of *Gemütlichkeit* ("good fellowship"). If you look at the map, you will see that Vienna is the logical place for the symphony to reach maturity, because it is midway between Italy and Germany. Haydn was not the "Father of the Symphony," although he had much to do with the organization of the orchestra. Haydn, Mozart, and Beethoven came at the end of a long period of development. This does not imply that there were no symphonies composed after Beethoven. We are here dealing with the *Classic* symphony, and in the next chapter we shall see how the symphony changed under the impact of Romanticism and Romantic Realism.

It is important to understand the difference between the chief

Baroque form, the fugue, and the chief Classic form, the symphony. Any well-organized piece of music might be said to consist of tension and relaxation, or action and rest. Our physical nature demands a certain balance of these two elements, but the Baroque and the Classic had very different ways of achieving it. In the chapter on the Baroque it was pointed out that Baroque architects did everything possible to break the horizontal rest lines so that tension would not be resolved until the senses had achieved unity in eternity. In a fugue the tension created by the collision or crossing of the melodic lines is never resolved until the very end. This is a completely psychological organization. In Classic architecture like St. Paul's in London or the *Hôtel des Invalides* in Paris, there are alternating periods of vertical columns which are active and horizontal separations which are restful. This gives the building a logical or mathematical organization. In a symphony tension is achieved by altering or developing the thematic material as well as by using dissonances in the harmony which drive the action forward to a rest point or cadence, or to a repetition of the theme as we have originally heard it. Hence we can enjoy a symphony which lasts for an hour, but a fugue no longer than fifteen or twenty minutes.

For easy reference while listening, we give in outline the form of a Classic symphony, although many symphonies do not follow this pattern precisely. The same form also applies to the Classic sonata for piano or solo instrument with piano accompaniment; the Classic string quartet: two violins, viola, and cello; the Classic trio: two violins and cello, or other combinations; the Classic concerto: solo instrument accompanied by orchestra; and the clarinet quintet: string quartet with clarinet.

First movement: Allegro sonata form in fast tempo:
    Slow introduction, cadence.
    Exposition: presentation of thematic material.
        First theme virile in tonic key. Bridge passage.
        Second theme lyrical in dominant key. Complete cadence.
        Repetition of entire exposition.[1]
    Development: thematic material undergoing various changes and explorations, and ending in such manner that the listener demands a return to the original statement.
    Recapitulation: both themes restated in tonic key.
    Coda or ending to underline the tonic key.

---

[1] In some recordings the exposition is not repeated in order to save space on the record. When in doubt it is best to consult a miniature score.

Second movement: slow and lyrical, like an operatic aria.
Usually A B A song form: da capo aria.
Sometimes theme and variations.

Third movement: light and dance-like, usually a minuet in a
related key. Three part song form with trio:
A A B A B A.
Trio: C C D C D C. Originally for three instruments.
A B A.

Fourth movement: very rapid.
May be another allegro sonata form.
May be a rondo form: A B A C A D A, etc.
Usually a long coda to give finality and key feeling.

Characteristics of the Classic idiom or style:
1. Thematic material: not a tune but a motif: a few notes
   capable of many changes and transformations.
2. Sense of driving force, hurry, propulsion, chiefly in allegro-
   sonata movements.
3. Tension built up to a point where the hearer feels that a
   return to the original statement is inevitable.
4. Very little extraneous material (unity of action).
5. Strong sense of tonic-dominant relationship (unity of place).
6. Parts and sections organized in closed form.
7. Small, balanced orchestra.

Characteristic differences in the style of Haydn, Mozart, Beethoven:

*Haydn:*
Exuberance: rollicking atmosphere of the peasant and the
folk.
Slow introduction like a personal soliloquy.
Short statement of themes, long development section.
Themes whittled down to elemental simplicity.
Second theme sometimes omitted entirely.
Thin texture so that light and air circulate freely.
Reinstatement of polyphony in musical construction.

*Mozart:*
Apollonian: freshness, flexibility, charm, grace, poetry.
Often omits the slow introduction.
Some thematic development in the exposition; hence this
section is long, development section short.
Singing melodies and accompanied recitative taken over from
Italian opera.

*Beethoven:*

Dionysian: demonic power and urgency, but always controlled.

Obsession with freedom and liberty.

Themes more tense, compressed, concentrated, subjective.

Uses suspense to create tension and expectancy.

New themes often presented in development section.

Larger orchestra, thicker texture.

Transition from movement to movement sometimes without a cadence.

The courtly minuet changed to the driving scherzo.

Extremes in dynamics.

These styles may be summed up in the following generalizations. Haydn—galloping fun and sparkling vivacity; Mozart—lyrical charm and youthful buoyancy; Beethoven—Utopian grandeur and demonic fury. Although the symphony is the greatest achievement of the Classic era, Hadyn's *Creation,* Mozart's *Marriage of Figaro,* and Beethoven's only opera *Fidelio* are classic in their charm and poise.

It would be well worth while to read the biographies of these three composers. Accounts of their lives and personalities will do much to help you differentiate and understand their music.

*Haydn.* Franz Joseph Haydn (1732–1809) genial, fun-loving peasant, spent most of his life at the court of two Prince Esterhazys in Hungary. Pensioned at sixty, he took his first real vacation in London, where he composed two magnificent oratorios: the *Creation* and the *Seasons,* then settled in his beloved Vienna for the rest of his life.

*Mozart.* Wolfgang Amadeus Mozart (1756–1791), the most precocious musical prodigy in history, played the violin and harpsichord at four, composed music before he could write, and went off on an international exhibition tour before he was six. He came in contact with all styles of music, but it was Italian opera that won his heart. For a time he worked for the Archbishop of Salzburg, whose grim, forbidding castle looks down on Mozart's birthplace. The Archbishop was as grim and forbidding as his castle, and so Mozart resigned and took to the road again. Never able to find a patron who would give him financial security and temperamentally unable to manage finances, he lived in poverty, barely able to feed his family. He died at thirty-five and was buried in a pauper's grave.

Mozart's musical creed certainly does not reveal his private hardships. He said: "As passions, whether violent or not, must never be expressed in such a way as to incite disgust, so music even in the most terrible situations, must never offend the ear, but must please the hearer, or in other words, must never cease to be music.[1]

Mozart thought primarily in terms of opera, and he composed all kinds: serious and comic Italian operas, and the German *Singspiel*, comic with some spoken lines. *Le Nozze di Figaro* (*The Marriage of Figaro*) is an Italian *opera buffa*, an absurd entanglement of nobility and servants, all pursuing love and life. It involves mistaken identities, servants disguised as nobles, and nobles taking the part of servants. The librettist, Lorenzo da Ponte, was imperial court poet in Vienna. He was shrewd enough to realize that the social satire implicit in Beaumarchais' comedy was not adapted to operatic treatment or to Mozart's lyrical temperament. So he took it all out and left nothing but rollicking fun and poignant melancholy. The orchestra aids the voices, but never predominates over them.

*Beethoven.* Ludwig van Beethoven (1770–1827) was born just after the *Storm and Stress* period in Germany. This was a brief period of violent subjectivism which foreshadowed the later Romantic movement. Its greatest poet was Goethe, but even he could not comprehend Beethoven's "untamed personality" and his "grandiose and mad music." The son of a humble musician, Beethoven refused to wear a wig or to be subject to the whims of any prince. As the last and greatest son of the "Enlightenment," his highest purpose in life was to express in music his faith in the freedom and dignity of man. His personality was never gentle, and as complete deafness overtook him, he was often like a caged animal, but, by the force of his will power his music is always under control. You can see that Beethoven was not by nature a Classicist but he achieved Classicism by self-discipline.

---

[1] Mozart, letter to his father, September 26, 1781; quoted by Paul Henry Lang, *op. cit.*, p. 674.

# Chapter 10 / The Romantic Era

Pure Classicism, the pursuit of perfection by means of rules and order, appealed primarily to a sophisticated, courtly taste. In 1781, on the first page of Rousseau's *Confessions*, he wrote: "I am not made like anyone I have seen; I dare believe I am not made like anyone in existence. If I am not better, at least I am different." This statement might well be taken as the slogan of the Romantic Movement. It is the creed of subjective individualism.

After the revolutions in America and France, and the later uprisings in 1830 and 1848 in a number of other European countries, the ordinary man found, probably for the first time in history, that he had a right to express his own opinions, to reveal his own emotions, and especially to exercise his own imagination. The repercussions of this realization caused a wave of individualistic expression to spread over the civilized world and to be mirrored in all the arts. The revolutions were not the cause of Romanticism, but they gave the movement a powerful impetus. Once started, it was like a virus which was caught by one country after another. With the new nationalism came patriotic fervor and the desire to glorify ancient national heroes. Some artists indulged in weird and morbid fantasies, the result of dreams or visionary experiences.

Another Romantic tenet was belief in the restorative power of nature. Rousseau had both preached and practiced this doctrine, saying that unspoiled nature is good and that what passes for progress is actually corruption, but Rousseau had exerted little influence on his contemporaries. The Classicists wanted their nature laid out in regular patterns; in fact one of them thought that the Creator might have made the Alps more "regular," and another described Niagara Falls as "horribly wild." In contrast, the Romantic lyric poets clasped nature to their hearts and poured out their love in lines of matchless beauty.

Most Romanticists lived constantly at a high emotional pitch, a prey to violent love affairs or to violent involvement in social wrongs. When their dreams failed to materialize, they fell victims of melancholia, drink, drugs, or physical illness. One could almost count on the fingers of one hand those who lived to a ripe old age. Most of them died young: Byron fighting for Greek independence, Shelley by drowning, Keats of tuberculosis, Bizet partly over the cool reception of *Carmen,* Schumann in a mental institution, Mendelssohn of grief for his sister, Musset of debauchery. They paid with their lives that we might enjoy their legacy of beauty.

### England

The Romantic movement seems to have started in England with advance intimations of its approach even before mid-eighteenth century. By this time the new mercantile middle class was sufficiently educated to enjoy reading and sufficiently affluent to have leisure time to devote to reading.

**Literature.** In literature the period was marked by the development of the novel and an emphasis on lyrical poetry.

*Richardson.* In 1740 Samuel Richardson (1689–1761) published his novel *Pamela, or Virtue Rewarded.* In this book Pamela is the fifteen-year-old daughter of poor and humble parents who has become lady's maid to the rich widow of a country gentleman. Pursued with unwelcome attentions by the son and heir, Pamela maintains her personal integrity until her master learns to admire her character as well as her beauty and asks her to marry him. Thus a daughter of the middle class triumphs over the loose-lived aristocracy and wins wealth and position by her own sober standards of decency.

*Fielding.* Nine years later *Pamela* was followed by *Tom Jones,* a novel by Henry Fielding (1707–1754). In this novel Tom is a foundling with the manners and morals of his age, but with admiration for virtue when he sees it. The tale follows his many escapades and moral lapses until he is united to the beautiful Sophia Western, daughter of a country squire who might be descended from Chaucer's jolly Franklin.

*Gray and Goldsmith.* "Elegy Written in a Country Churchyard" by Thomas Gray (see p. 211) was published in 1751. So great is its fame that many tourists would not think of leaving England without a visit to the little church at Stoke Poges and the grave of the poet who touched the heart of England with his "short and simple annals of the poor." A companion poem to Gray's "Elegy" and almost as famous is "The Deserted Village" by Oliver Goldsmith (1728–1774), published in 1770. This is an idealized picture of the little Irish hamlet of Lissoy where Goldsmith grew up, which was drained of its inhabitants by emigration to the colonies and the factory towns. The whole picture is tinged with sentiment and melancholy.

*Macpherson.* Paradoxical as it may seem, it was not these two literary gems but the work of an obscure Scotch poet and his literary hoax which touched off the Romantic conflagration. In 1760 James Macpherson published a volume of poems which purported to be translations of a third-century Celtic bard, Ossian. Written in short sentences of poetic prose, they recount tales of fighting between the Celtic tribes of western Scotland and Ireland against Scandinavian invaders. Fingal, the brave Celtic warrior, is often assisted by the shades of heroes and maidens who have been killed. This brief excerpt will give an idea of both the style and content of the poems:

> *The third day, with all its beams, shone bright on the wood of boars. Forth moved the dark-browed Starns; and Fingal, king of shields. Half the day they spent in the chase; the spear of Selma was red in blood. It was then the daughter of Starno with blue eyes rolling in tears; it was then she came with her voice of love, and spoke to the king of Morven. "Fingal, high descended chief, trust not Starno's heart of pride. Within that wood he has placed his chiefs. Beware of the wood of death."* [1]

As you can see, there is much wild beauty in the poems. They caused such excitement that Macpherson was given money to further his "research." Subsequently, two more volumes and a collected edition appeared. Later critics, after Macpherson's death, called them an unmitigated hoax, perpetrated by Macpherson himself. The truth probably lies somewhere between the two extremes. The stories have been traced to oral traditions, passed down in the western highlands of Scotland, and even the name of a third-century bard called Ossian or Ossim, but the form and language are no doubt Macpherson's.

At any rate, the poems, which just suited the Romantic taste, were translated into German and French and influenced later Romanticists, especially Byron, Goethe, and George Sand. Even Napoleon admired them.

*Burns.* At about the same time as the Ossianic excitement, Robert Burns (1759–1796), a *real* Scottish bard, was collecting and rewriting hundreds of traditional ballads and songs. When

---

[1] *The Poems of Ossian,* translated by James Macpherson. (Edinburgh: Patrick Geddes and Colleagues, 1896).

his first edition of poems appeared in 1786, Burns became a literary sensation, and his days of dire poverty were over. He wrote with great ease and metrical grace in his own Lowland dialect. He is beloved because of his passion for freedom and his emphasis on the dignity of the humble working man. Emotion rather than reason is guide. Read "The Cotter's Saturday Night" and "A Man's a Man for a' That."

*Blake.* William Blake (1757–1827), mystic, visionary, poet, engraver, water colorist, was considered "mad" by some of his contemporaries. He was certainly not "mad"; he supported his family as an engraver of books, but he felt very strongly about religion, morals, and republicanism, and he was a nonconformist in art and poetry.

He thought of himself as an intrepid seer whose pronouncements, inspired by spiritual and intuitional vision, were not subject to argument. Small wonder that he was not acceptable in social circles.

Blake's poetry, although sometimes obscure, as in the so-called *Prophetic Books,* has freshness and charm. His water colors and engravings, although sometimes faulty in drawing, express energy, aspiration, ardor, and a curious blend of simplicity and intensity. His engravings for the Book of Job and *The Divine Comedy* are sublime. Read the *Songs of Innocence* and *Songs of Experience,* and study as many of the engravings and water colors as you can find. Blake had great artistic talent, but probably because of his temperament, his overweening belief in himself and his "visions," he exerted no influence; during his lifetime he had no followers.

*Scott.* Another Scotsman, Sir Walter Scott (1771–1832), contributed to the vogue of the historical novel. He re-created the past in adventure stories marked by vividness of detail and sometimes poignant melancholy. If you know only *Ivanhoe,* read *The Heart of Midlothian,* which is the one best loved by the Scottish people. Scott's *Bride of Lammermoor* was made into an opera by the Italian Donizetti, while the greatest French Romantic painter, Delacroix, depicted the "Abduction of Rebecca" from *Ivanhoe.* This collaboration of writers, painters, and musicians is a very important aspect of Romanticism.

*Wordsworth.* William Wordsworth (1770–1850) was the leader of the early Romantic movement in England and wrote some of the finest nature poetry in any language. His meeting with Coleridge in 1795 had a profound effect on both poets. Together they published the *Lyrical Ballads* of 1798. In the preface to the second edition of this volume (1800) Wordsworth wrote the manifesto on Romanticism which we have already quoted (see p. 15). The manifesto repudiated Neoclassic rules and defined poetry as the "spontaneous overflow of powerful feelings" arising from "emotion recollected in tranquility." The language of poetry was not to be artificial poetic diction but ordinary language in "a state of vivid sensation." Wordsworth himself was not always meticulous in following these rules. We can trace his development by following his conception of nature. As a young man his love of nature was a sensuous animal passion; later, nature was for the poet a moral influence; and still later it was a sort of mystical communion. Three of his ideas have inspired many later poets: the natural goodness of childhood, the moral value of the simple life, and the healing power of nature. Read Wordsworth's "Daffodils," "The Solitary Reaper," and "Tintern Abbey." Read also his beautiful tribute to his wife Mary in "She was a Phantom of Delight."

*Coleridge.* The life of Samuel Taylor Coleridge (1772–1834) was tragic. He was the victim of chronic neuralgia and of the opium prescribed to relieve the pain; victim also of an unhappy marriage with a sister-in-law of the poet Robert Southey. The two years of close association with Wordsworth and Wordsworth's sister Dorothy were the happiest years of his life and during this time he wrote his finest poetry: "Kubla Khan," "Rime of the Ancient Mariner," and "Christabel." In such poetry he said that he sought to express "a semblance of truth sufficient to procure for these shadows of imagination that willing suspension of disbelief which constitutes poetic faith." His best poetry proves his ability to carry out his thesis. Coleridge loved nature, but it was nature in its weird, supernatural aspects. In fact, if he were living today he would probably be found among the Surrealists.

*Byron, Shelley, and Keats.* In the next generation after Wordsworth and Coleridge came the three lyricists: George Gordon (Lord) Byron, Percy Bysshe Shelley, and John Keats.

Byron (1788–1824) probably exerted more influence outside England than any English poet except Shakespeare. He was considered everything a poet ought to be—handsome, aristocratic, talented. He was an artistic rebel, everywhere pursued by beautiful, aristocratic women. Proud, arrogant, moody, he loved mankind and hated injustice. He is the real hero of all his poems. Read *Childe Harold's Pilgrimage,* which was written during a trip to Greece, and his masterpiece, *Don Juan,* in which the Don is the victim of social corruption. Goethe believed this poem "a work of boundless genius."

Shelley (1792–1822) was a visionary idealist who believed in the perfectibility of man, once tyranny and cruelty had been removed. He excelled in form, intensity, and imagery. Read again his "Ode to the West Wind," "To a Skylark," and "Adonais," an elegy on the death of Keats, which begins:

> *I weep for Adonais—he is dead!*
> *Oh, weep for Adonais! though our tears*
> *Thaw not the frost which binds so dear a head!*
> *And thou, sad Hour, selected from all years*
> *To mourn our loss, rouse thy obscure compeers,*
> *And teach them thine own sorrow! Say: "With me*
> *Died Adonais; till the Future dares*
> *Forget the Past, his fate and fame shall be*
> *An echo and a light unto eternity."*

Keats (1795–1821) is the most sensuous of the group. It is revealing to make a list of his allusions to sounds, colors, perfumes, and even appeals to the sense of touch. His entire creed was the worship of beauty. His two most celebrated lines are: "A thing of beauty is a joy forever," and "Beauty is truth, truth beauty." He sometimes gives way to melancholy and nostalgia. Read his "Ode to a Nightingale," "Ode to a Grecian Urn," and "Eve of St. Agnes."

**Painting: Constable and Turner.** While poets were immersing themselves in the natural beauty of the English countryside and making it come alive in their verses, a poor artist had been painting this same countryside for fourteen years without selling one picture. This painter was John Constable (1776–1837), who at the age of forty-eight was struggling to care for a sick wife and son. He had been living on the five hundred pounds a year given him by his father, steadily refusing to paint the elegant portraits then so popular because he loved to paint nature. In order to meet expenses he sold his largest (six-foot) canvas "The Hay Wain" (see p. 223) and two small ones to a French dealer for three hundred and fifty dollars. They were exhibited in the Paris Salon of 1824 and Constable became the rage of Paris. The French king, Charles X, gave the artist a gold medal.

Think back for a moment. The Venetian Giorgione had painted an idyllic landscape as a background for his figures; Poussin had arranged his Italian stylized designs; the Dutch Ruisdael had dared to paint the flat landscape of Holland with its windmills and sand dunes. But there had never been anything like Constable's landscapes before. The fluid sky with its fleecy clouds sets the key; the sunlight filters down through the individual

JOHN CONSTABLE: *The Hay Wain*. National Gallery, London. (Photograph reproduced by permission)

leaves of the trees; the dew sparkles on the grass. All this may be too literal for twentieth-century taste, but it set the stage for Corot and the Barbizon School and through them for the later Impressionists. The modern critic Sir Kenneth Clark believes that Constable achieved the greatest pictures ever painted in England.

Another English landscapist leads directly to the technique of the Impressionists. J. M. W. Turner (1775–1851) was interested in Claude Lorrain's mythological scenes, so many of which were suffused with the golden glow of the setting sun. Turner reduced his subjects to barely recognizable shapes swallowed up in a fantastic whirl of mist, fog, or snowstorm. This atmosphere is fluid, swirling, and moving, with the result that Turner's paintings are very dramatic. Study especially his "Steamer in a Snowstorm," "Burning Houses of Parliament," and "Rain, Steam and Speed" (see p. 224), which portrays a railroad train coming across a bridge in a real London fog. Turner made a painting of *Childe Harold's Pilgrimage,* inspired by Byron's poem. Turner's nature reflects man's emotions when confronted by cosmic forces which man cannot control; this idea also is Romantic.

**Architecture.** The nineteenth century was the only historical

J. M. W. TURNER: *Rain, Steam and Speed*. National Gallery, London. (Anderson—Art Reference Bureau)

period which developed no architectural style of its own. The Industrial Revolution practically wiped out hand craftsmanship. The people who now paid for the arts were not kings and courtiers but the rising mercantile middle class, in France called the bourgeoisie. These people had no artistic tradition whatsoever in their background; hence their tastes were eclectic, and they were willing to accept cheap, shoddy workmanship if it fulfilled their idea of "Art." This is the situation admirably portrayed in John Galsworthy's short story "Quality."

With the rapid expansion of cities, there was a vast amount of new building going on, but it might take on almost any style, or mixture of styles, depending on who paid the bill. Some good architects found a way of satisfying the customer without sham antiques or freak inventions. The new Houses of Parliament in London, built after the fire of 1834, are in the Gothic style, but they are dignified and imposing, especially when half-shrouded in London fog. Many churches were also constructed in Gothic style, because it represented the age of mystic faith. Similarly, opera houses and moving-picture "palaces" were likely to be built in the Baroque style and city halls, post offices, and school buildings in the Classic style of the Renaissance or the eighteenth century.

## Germany

The translation of the Ossianic poems into German as well as a new translation of Shakespeare by August Wilhelm Schlegel coincided with an early, violently subjective movement in Germany called *Sturm und Drang* ("Storm and Stress"). The movement took its name from a play by Friedrich Klinger called *Wirrwarr, oder Sturm und Drang* (*Confusion, or Storm and Stress*), which was a literary declaration of independence from French Neoclassic rules. The movement lasted only about ten years, from 1770 to 1780, but it was the climate in which the young Beethoven, Goethe, Schiller, and Weber lived.

**Literature.** The guiding genius of the *Sturm und Drang* movement, Johann Gottfried Herder (1774–1803), believed that literature should be the natural, free expression of the people. Stimulated by "Ossian," he made a collection of German folk poetry which provided the Romantic composers Franz Schubert and Robert Schumann with lyrics for their songs. Herder also gathered about him a brilliant circle of writers—Johann Wolfgang von Goethe, Friedrich Schiller, Christoph Martin Wieland, Jean Paul Richter, and others, who made Weimar the literary capital of Germany.

*Goethe.* Although there was no great political upheaval in Germany (partly because there was at the time no centralized authority), nevertheless the writings of Rousseau and the French Humanists were read in Germany, and gave impetus to the *Storm and Stress* movement. Suddenly Goethe's drama *Götz von Berlichingen*, burst upon the scene. Götz was a historical nobleman, a sort of German Robin Hood, who in the late Middle Ages sided with the peasants in their unsuccessful revolt against the nobility. With its unmitigated devotion to the ideal of freedom, the play had enormous popular success, which was rivaled the next year by *Die Leiden des Jungen Werther* (*The Sorrows of Young Werther*). Written in letter form, this novel describes Werther's passionate love for the beautiful Lotte, who is already pledged to Albert. Werther takes a position in another town, but he cannot forget the girl and is irresistibly drawn back to her. He finds her now happily married to Albert. Lotte, a character drawn with excellent psychological insight, acts with good sense, understanding, and sympathy, and so does her husband until almost the end. For Werther there is no way out but death and he commits suicide. The youth of Germany was dissolved in tears, the young men dressed in Werther's characteristic garb, and at least three committed suicide as a result of the book.

But when an author spends a lifetime writing and leaves behind him one hundred and twenty volumes, he should not be judged by one youthful work. Johann Wolfgang von Goethe (1749–1832) was born in Frankfurt, the son of prosperous middle-class parents with artistic and intellectual interests. When the French forces occupied the town during the Napoleonic Wars, they brought along a French theater. The boy was exposed to French Neoclassic drama, and he was soon writing plays in the French style. After obtaining a law degree he began to practice, but spent most of his time writing lyric poetry under the stimulus of love affairs.

When Goethe was twenty-six he was invited to the court of Duke Carl August of Saxe Weimar, himself only eighteen, who gave Goethe increasingly heavy duties and responsibilities. He reorganized the army, controlled the court finances, built roads and mines, and finally became prime minister. He also managed the court theater, hired singers and actors, and supervised performances. He was in the Duke's employ for fifty-five years, and could not have found a more agreeable and appreciative patron.

Goethe had what modern psychologists would call a dual personality: Apollonian and Dionysian, contemplative and active, Classic and Romantic. The combination of the two extremes forms in his writing the same synthesis we have observed in Haydn, Mozart, and Beethoven. He needed to love more than to be loved. He fell in love many times, always with a beautiful and intellectual woman, but before the affair reached fulfillment and an offer of marriage, his "demon" drove him to run away from her. Then when the woman married someone else, he was inconsolable. Under the influence of these passions he did his best work. Once he fled to Italy for two years, and came back a Classicist.

In his multiplicity of interests Goethe resembles Leonardo. His study of human and animal skulls led him to state the doctrine of evolution seventy years before Darwin. His study of plants led him to envision cross-breeding. He sketched heads from the Sistine Chapel that he might understand form. He turned to the symbol of the macrocosm, the universe, that he might feel himself to be God; then he humbly submerged himself in his own microcosm, inner self, that he might feel God in him.

Goethe began his masterpiece, *Faust*, when he was twenty years old, and finished it two months before he died at eighty-two. This great epic-poetic drama of man's struggle for redemption sums up

Goethe just as the *Divine Comedy*, the only work to which it can be compared, sums up Dante. It mirrors man's desire to transcend his physical limitations, his search for answers to the eternal questions of the meaning of life and the universe. The two main characters are Faust, universal man, and Mephistopheles, or Mephisto, the nihilistic destructive force. The drama presents man's cultural, spiritual, and intellectual development in the face of his physical limitations.

You should read the Prologue and Part I, which is the most interesting because it contains the tragic love story of Gretchen. In the Prologue notice that Mephisto is not the devil but a servant of God, an evil force created in order that man may strive against it. God simply gives Mephisto permission to tempt Faust. You will enjoy the humorous scene of the students in the wine cellar. *The Walpurgis Nacht* (Witches' Sabbath) was. a favorite device of medieval German folk tales. It also appears in Weber's opera *Der Freischütz*. It is compassion that makes Faust return to try to help Gretchen in prison, and this is something that Mephisto cannot understand. This is the only stageworthy portion of the drama, and it is the one used in Gounod's opera *Faust*.

The high point of Part II is the Helen of Troy drama. Helen is the symbol of ideal, classical beauty. Her union with Faust, representing the romantic, medieval spirit, produces Euphorian, symbol of modern poetry, the union of Classic and Romantic, epitomized by Byron. But Euphorian refuses to be earth-bound; he soars aloft like Icarus, singing:

> *Ever higher must I wing me,*
> *Ever farther must I gaze.*
> *Now I know whereon I stand,*
> *In midst of Pelops' land,*
> *In midst the isle are we,*
> *Wedded to land and sea.*
> (Part II, lines 9821–26).[1]

He mounts still higher, then falls at his parents' feet. The chorus intones:

> *All whom this land has bred,*
> *Through dread perils led.*

---

[1] The quotations from *Faust* are from the translation by J. F. L. Raschen (Ithaca, N.Y.: The Thrift Press, 1949). Reprinted by permission of the publisher.

> *To them of dauntless mood*
> *Who, reckless, shed their blood:*
> *To the unconquerable*
> *Patriot zest,*
> *Fighters indomitable*
> *Come Freedom blest.*
>                 (Part II, lines 9843–50).

This passage refers to Byron's death in the cause of Greek independence.

But Faust, having achieved the classic ideal, is still dissatisfied. Although now an old man, enfeebled by worry and care, he wants to see himself as a man of action. He forces the disgusted Mephisto to help him in a huge land-reclamation project, land on which thousands of people can live and work happily. He looks forward to the time when this task is completed, and he can say to the moment of fulfillment, "Linger awhile, thou art so fair." But he dies of natural causes before the project is quite finished. Mephisto sends for his legions of devils, but God's angels intervene and carry off Faust's soul to heaven where Gretchen awaits him. She says:

> *Mary, grant me to instruct him,*
> *Dazzled as yet by this new day.*
>                 (Part II, ending)

The theme is pronounced at the close by the angel chorus:

> *Whoso with fervent will strives on,*
> *We angels can deliver.*
>                 (Part II, lines 11936–38)

Goethe wrote lyrical poetry throughout his lifetime. The earliest poems are full of passion. Between 1775 and 1786 the poems are calmer but filled with a yearning for spiritual peace. Those composed after he returned from Italy are humanistic, with many classical allusions. The poems of his old age are pensive and philosophical. More than seventy of his poems were set to music by Schubert, best-known of which are *Der Erlkönig* ("The Elf King"), *Gretchen am Spinnrade* ("Gretchen at the Spinning Wheel"), and *Wandrers Nachtlied* ("Wanderer's Night Song").

The favorite of all Goethe's ballads is the "Elf King." It is the pathetic story of a dying lad whose father is taking him on horseback to a doctor. The child hears the voice of the Elf King (Death) calling him, tempting him with companions and toys to come to fairyland. The boy cries out in terror while the father tries to calm him, but at the end of the journey the child is dead. Schubert's setting, published in 1815, has been a favorite with dramatic contraltos ever since. The singer must change her voice with the person speaking to portray fright in the child, soothing concern in the father, enticement in the Elf King. The agitated accompaniment represents the galloping of the horse. It was a favorite concert song of Madame Ernestine Schumann-Heink.

*Heine.* Heinrich Heine (1797–1856) was another fine lyrical poet. *Die Grenadiere* ("The Two Grenadiers") and *Du bist wie eine Blume* ("Thou Art Like a Flower") were set to music by Schumann, *Auf Flügeln des Gesanges* ("On Wings of Song") by Mendelssohn, and *Die Lorelei* by Liszt.

*Schiller.* Friedrich Schiller (1759–1805), close friend of Goethe, wrote some very excellent plays, all of them having to do with the struggle for freedom. *Maria Stuart, Die Jungfrau von Orleans* (*The Maid of Orleans*), and *Wilhelm Tell*, the Swiss festival drama of liberation, still hold the stage today.

*Story Writers.* We should mention here also the universal children's fairy tales by the brothers Grimm (Jacob and Wilhelm) and the Gothic tales of fantasy and horror by E. T. A. Hoffmann.

**Fine Arts.** When Romantic painters broke with academic tradition they fell back upon nature, but not the simple, curative nature advocated by Rousseau in *Émile*. Ideal, absolute beauty was gone, and every artist followed his own intuition, each seeking his own inspiration in solitude. It is true that Constable came close to raw nature in his English landscapes, but he was the exception. Under the impetus of subjective individualism each painter strove to become a part of nature; he sought to communicate her uninhibited quality in his paintings. He found inspiration for his art in drama and the fantasies of pure instinct.

Caspar David Friedrich (1744–1840) was the best of the German Romantic painters. In his painting "Chalk Cliffs at Rügen," the sense of space assaults the mind. The painting seems to express the remoteness of the universe from man. There is no link or transition between the three human figures at the edge of the precipice and the towering white cliffs. The cliffs are thin and flat, almost transparent. Behind them, without transition, lies the sea—unlimited because there is no horizon line. Man is only an insignificant spectator on the edge of nature. The real actor in the drama is the sky, which rushes down, both molding and destroying the forms.

**Music.** In general, the real Romanticists in music expressed themselves best in the smaller forms: art songs and short musical vignettes, usually for piano, inspired by a poetic idea and portraying an emotional mood. In Germany, Schubert, Mendelssohn, and Schumann were the best representatives.

Romanticism was primarily a literary movement. Most of the great Romantic composers, including Weber, Schumann, Berlioz, Liszt, and Wagner, had extensive literary and philosophical schooling. Some were able writers, critics, poets, and playwrights as well as composers. This literary interest shows itself in the importance of lyricism in both their vocal and instrumental works. Schumann preferred song cycles based on a poetic theme; Mendelssohn's "Songs Without Words" and the suggestive titles given to piano pieces by Schumann and Chopin acknowledge the poetic character of their inspiration.

Another characteristic of the Romantic was his dual personality with two or more conflicting sides of his nature continually at war. Schumann personified this struggle in his writing as the figures of Florestan and Eusebius, the two sides of his nature that caused the dissension in the artist's soul. When we think back to the Classic personality, so finely integrated, so calm and poised, we see at once why the Classic sonata-symphony was inimical to the Romantic artist.

*Schubert.* Franz Schubert (1797–1828) was close enough to the Classic period to be able to write symphonies. His C Major Symphony is the last symphony of Classic poise and breadth. But Schubert was a real Romanticist and one of the greatest spontaneous melodists the world has ever produced. If someone brought him a small book of poems which he liked, he set every one of them to music before retiring that same night; then he forgot about them. When a friend took Beethoven a sheaf of Schubert's songs, the older master said, "Truly he has the divine spark." Had he accepted the Romantic notion of the supremacy of the text over the music he would not have created the modern song; but in his works harmony, instrumental accompaniment, melody, and poem are fused in an organic whole which seems to have been created spontaneously. The poem is only the incentive to this creative activity. Schubert's melodies are so nearly perfect that they give aesthetic satisfaction without any accompaniment. On the other hand, Liszt transcribed some of the songs for piano alone, making of them small symphonic poems although they have no text.

This does not imply that Schubert composed his symphonies without effort. Let us take the first movement of the B Minor Symphony, for example. Parenthetically, this symphony is not "unfinished." When he had said what he had to say he stopped—a pretty good rule for most of us to apply. You remember that the Classic symphonists built their allegro-sonata movements not out of melodies but out of a short terse motif. But Schubert the song writer thought in melodies. In this first movement then he has three full-fledged tunes: an introductory tune, a first theme in B Minor, and a second theme in G Major. What will he do in the development section? We can easily follow his thinking: "I can't use the first theme because it is chromatic. The second theme is major, which is out of the question. It will have to be the introduction. Yes, I'll use two four-note motifs from the introduction." And so he did, as you will see if you can identify them. Schubert was so naturally unassuming and seemed to compose so effortlessly that his contemporaries, even his loyal friends, did not realize his true stature. He lived and died in poverty.

*Mendelssohn.* Felix Mendelssohn (1809–1847) was born into a cultured and refined home environment. His family was well-off, devoted to each other, and dedicated to all that was noble and artistic. As a youth he was equally proficient in music, languages, and painting, but music was his first choice. The family put on plays and gave concerts in the home; hence the boy could try out his youthful works there. For one such occasion he composed the Overture to Shakespeare's *Midsummer Night's Dream.* He lacked the glowing passion and profound emotions which hardship and struggle might have given him, and he turned to Classic music for his inspiration. He planned to imbue Classic form with Romantic content, but although his symphonies are polished and fluent, they have refined taste without real depth. On his travels about Europe and England as a conductor he discovered the score of Bach's *St. Matthew Passion* and had it performed. If he had done nothing else, we would be everlastingly in his debt.

*Schumann.* Robert Schumann (1810–1856) was the prototype of the romantic youth—talented in both poetry and music, sentimental in love, by turns fervid and dreamy, sometimes vehement and strong, sometimes gentle and poetic. After hearing Paganini play the violin, he decided to become a virtuoso on the piano; then he ruined his right hand by too violent exercises. He married Clara Wieck, the daughter of his piano teacher, herself a virtuoso pianist. With concertizing out of the question, Schumann turned to composition while his wife popularized his music by playing it all over Europe.

Schumann was master of the song form and kindred piano vignettes, especially when these gave him opportunity for rhythmic subtleties. He composed symphonies and concerti, which are far removed from Classic economy of material, formal logic, and thin texture. Schumann's works are more like fantasies, sometimes violent, sometimes dreamy, but always beautiful of melody and warm with emotion. He published his own musical newspaper and wrote excellent criticisms of new works. From 1851 on his mental capacities declined rapidly, and he ended his life in an institution.

*Brahms.* Johannes Brahms (1833–1897) saw clearly that under the influence of Romanticism, German music would drift down the path of weakness and sentimentality or would become only an accompaniment for poetic and philosophic ideas. Despite his own Romantic strain, he felt it his task to apply the brakes and to return to the vigor and virility of Beethoven. Even in his first compositions for piano, he spurned the wonderfully developed Romantic style and endeavored to follow in the path of Beethoven. Some of these "Sonatas" are more symphonic than pianistic. He fought to discipline his romantic dreaming and yearning by strict symphonic logic. He took the *idée fixe* principle and used it to build the unity of all the movements of his symphonies. He knew that he could not recapture the past completely, and this is why he waited until he was over forty before attempting his first symphony, then carried it around in his pocket for some time before he diffidently brought it out. He kept setting himself greater obstacles to overcome. In the last movement of his fourth and greatest symphony he went back to the Baroque period, and built the whole movement on a repeated bass motif (*basso ostinato*).

Did Brahms succeed or fail? He probably felt that he had failed, which accounts for the dark, melancholy atmosphere so prevalent in his music. In the last analysis, the question is for you to decide when you listen to this music. The symphonic logic is there, and often the driving force although it is not sustained. The orchestra is large, the texture thick, the rhythms complicated. The fact remains that the symphonic repertoire today could no more get along without the four symphonies of Brahms than without any four by Beethoven. If they required discipline from the composer, they also require discipline of the listener.

## France

France was late in casting off Neoclassicism. The turbulent political climate was unfavorable to art of any kind, and the influence of Racine and the Academy was very strong. The Enlightenment ended its process of emancipation with a storm of liberation; yet the new century opened under the aegis of a new Caesar, Napoleon. Thus the liberty of the individual ended in the reign of the boldest of tyrants, and the political movement ended with the establishment of national monarchies not only in France but in every awakened country of Europe, which became saturated with the spirit of nationalism. The aristocratic atmosphere of court and salon was forgotten in favor of parliaments, alliances, confederations, and trade unions. With capitalism's coming of age, money and goods, industry, and communications became collectivized and the new mercantile middle class held the reins. We usually think of Romanticism as the cult of the individual, but the Romantics reveled in love and friendship, widening it to universalism and the longing for the infinite. Even religion was for them but a segment of the cult of the infinite.

**Literature.** What did the new bourgeoisie want in the shape of literature? Certainly nothing deep or esoteric. They wanted poetry tinged with melancholy to make them weep, stories which were fantastic and set in faraway lands which would stimulate their imaginations, and above all drama dealing with bygone times, exotic and tragic. The theater was their most congenial atmosphere because the theater unifies and addresses itself to the multitude.

*Chateaubriand.* François-Auguste, Viscount de Chateaubriand (1768–1848), dominated French literature for nearly four decades. His love of nature especially in its wilder aspects, his love of the medieval, and his preoccupation with his own melancholy temperament mark him as the first typical French Romanticist. He enjoyed travel and in 1791 set out to "discover America." Actually he was in America only six months and saw little beyond the environs of the Great Lakes, but he found inspiration for two Indian tales which give a rather warped impression of Indian life, but which proved to be best sellers. *Atala* takes place in the wilderness of America on the banks of the Mississippi. A young Indian warrior, Chactas, has been captured by a hostile tribe. He is saved from death by Atala, a beautiful maiden of that tribe, with whom he falls in love. But Atala is a Christian convert who has promised her dying mother that she will remain a virgin. In a violent thunderstorm Atala and Chactas take refuge in the hut of a hermit, whom Chactas asks to marry them. But Atala takes poison and dies rather than break her vow. Chactas weeps over her dead body.

An early French Romantic painter, Anne-Louis Girodet-Troison (1767–1824), painted *L'Enterrement d'Atala* ("The Entombment of Atala"). He depicted the eerie darkness of the hermit's cave, the weeping Chactas clasping the dead girl, the comfort of religion, and Atala looking more like Elaine the lily maid of Astolat than an Indian. Here we have all the elements of Romanticism: exotic setting, the wildness of nature, frustrated love, and religion. We introduce Chateaubriand and Girodet not because they were great artists but because they bespeak the type of audience, different from any audience in the past, toward which the Romanticists directed their art. If they wanted to be accepted they had to gratify this audience.

*Madame de Staël.* In 1810 came a book by Madame de Staël (1766–1817), an aristocratic Frenchwoman of rather unconventional habits, who liked to travel and to associate with great literary figures. After an extensive sojourn in Germany, she wrote *De L' Allemagne* ("Of Germany") which popularized German Romanticism. In it she called Weimar the "Athens of Germany," extolled freedom of the press and scholarship in German universities, and lamented the fact that English literature, especially Shakespeare, was better known in Germany than in France. She praised the German writers Klopstock, Winkelmann, Lessing, and especially Goethe and Schiller. She commended German comedy, tragedy, philosophy, and criticism and quoted long passages from Goethe's and Schiller's plays.

In Chapter XI she for the first time contrasted the terms *Classic* and *Romantic,* saying that Classic poetry comes only from imitation, not inspiration, whereas Romantic poetry is indigenous to France. "French poetry, the most classic of all is the only poetry which has not spread among the common people. The stanzas of Tasso are sung by the gondoliers of Venice, the Spanish and Portugese know by heart the verses of Calderón and Camoëns. Shakespeare is as much admired in England by commoners as aristocrats, the poems of Goethe are sung from the Rhine to the Baltic. Our French poetry is admired by cultivated people everywhere, but remains unknown to the masses. . . . Some French critics have pretended that German literature is still barbarous; this opinion is completely false." [1] As you might expect, Napoleon decided Madame de Staël was inimical to his interests and banished her from France. Of course she exaggerated, but there was much truth in what she wrote.

*Hugo.* It was not until 1830 that the Romanticists scored their first success on the French stage. The theater was sacrosanct, guarded by the ghost of Racine. It meant much to produce a successful play: a seat in the Academy, a professor's chair in

---

[1] Mme. de Staël, *De L'Allemagne* (Paris: Librairie Marcel Didier, 1956); translation by the author of this volume.

the College of France, an office of dignity and pecuniary value under government, a knowledge that the work would be read all over the world because of the universality of the French language. In 1830, before this august tribunal, Victor Hugo placed his *Hernani,* produced in spite of Academy opposition.

Such a furor! A large and hostile audience gathered: fashion, aristocracy, and journalists combined to kill the play. They hissed and were howled at by the left-bank students, brought in to support the play. The hissing and hooting continued throughout so that nobody could hear what the actors were saying.

*Hernani* is a historical tragedy whose theme is the conflict between love and honor. The action takes place in sixteenth-century Spain in the reign of Don Carlos I, who during the play is elected Holy Roman Emperor, Charles V. The story was later used by Verdi in his opera *Ernani,* and you can look it up in a book of opera stories. To us it sounds harmless enough, but almost as ridiculous and melodramatic as a "soap opera."

Hugo used plenty of action—bloody action—on stage. There is color in the swift changes of scene from palatial hall to the gloomy caverns surrounding the tomb of Charlemagne and in the conflict of violent passions. The play flouts the unities; uses taboo expressions; and mingles comic and tragic as Shakespeare had done, but never Racine. (Incidentally, when Alfred de Vigny's translation of *Othello* was produced in 1829, the play was wrecked when an actor uttered the taboo word *mouchoir* for handkerchief, instead of "a quadrangular tissue of snowiest cambric.")

Eventually the Romanticists won out, and in 1841 Hugo was elected a member of the Academy. When he died in 1885 his funeral was a demonstration seldom equaled in solemn pomp and the proud grief of a nation.

We know Hugo chiefly through his novels, but his lyric poetry is considered his greatest legacy. Lyric poetry is seldom adequate in translations, but this poem from *Contemplations,* written just after the death of a beloved daughter, may provide an idea of the thought, if not the beauty of language. In it the poet says that he would gladly renounce inspiration and fame if he could have his daughter again.

> *O God, truly could'st thou have believed*
> *That I preferred, under the heavens,*
> *The dreadful ray of thy glory*
> *To the sweet light of her eyes?*
> *If I had known thy somber laws,*
> *That to the same enchanted spirit*

*Thou didst never give these two things:*
*Happiness and truth,*[1]
*Rather than to lift the veil,*
*And to seek, with sad, pure heart,*
*Thee in the farthest star,*
*O somber God of the world obscure,*
*I would have preferred, far from thy face*
*To follow, happy, a narrow path,*
*And to be just a man who passes*
*Holding his infant by the hand.*[2]

*Vigny.* Alfred de Vigny (1797–1863), another lyricist, was a deep and original thinker. He was a pessimist, a disillusioned idealist, who believed that everything was for the worst in the worst of all possible worlds: nobody was benevolent or trustworthy, the masses were stupid and dishonest, woman was fickle, nature was a tomb, and God was either malevolent or blind. Resignation was the only attitude for man. Here is a stanza from *La Maison du Merger* ("Shepherd's Hut"):

*Eve, who art thou? Dost understand thy nature?*
*Did'st understand thy aim, thy task?*
*Did'st know how thou hast punished man, God's creature,*
*When thou placed his hand upon the tree of knowledge?*
*God permits him for love of Himself,*
*To fulfill his supreme task in every time and age,*
*Tortured for love of Him, tormented to see Him.*[3]

*Musset.* Alfred de Musset (1810–1857) was the most tormented of all French poets. In 1833 he fell violently in love with the novelist George Sand and accompanied her to Italy. The affair ended two years later when she transferred her affections to a Venetian doctor. Musset sank into despair and debauchery, and died at forty-seven. Here is his lyric called *Tristesse* ("Sadness"):

*I have lost my spirit and my life,*
*My friends and my gaiety,*

---

[1] When Romanticists use the word "truth," they usually mean artistic inspiration.

[2] L. Cazamian, *A History of French Literature* (London: Oxford University Press, 1960); translation by the author of this volume.

[3] The quotations are from *Nineteenth Century French Verse*, eds. Joseph Galland and Roger Cros (New York: Appleton-Century-Crofts, 1959); translations by the author of this volume.

*I have lost the fire*
*That made me confident of my genius.*
*When I knew truth*
*I thought it was a friend.*
*When I had understood it and felt it,*
*Then I was weary of it.*
*Nonetheless, truth is eternal,*
*And those who are satisfied without it*
*Have ignored all else here below.*
*When God speaks, we must reply.*
*The only good left to me in the world*
*Is to have sometimes wept.*[1]

Now do you understand what is meant by the *mal de siècle?* The "disease of the century" was melancholia.

**Fine Arts.** The plight of the painter, the composer, and the writer was not enviable. They either had to make concessions to popular taste at the expense of their own artistic integrity or glory in their isolation and starve unless they had a private income. The French Academy was as usual on the side of conservatism. If a nude was exhibited, unless it was called "Diana" or "Venus," there was a great hue and cry about "public morals." Once Napoleon III slashed at one of Courbet's paintings with his whip, and his wife Eugénie inquired whether the buxom nudes were "Percheron mares." Paris was the battleground on which all divergent views were fought out. The French always get excited about artistic matters, and there were fireworks throughout the whole century. Fortunately there were many sincere artists who chose to defy convention not for the sake of notoriety, but to explore new paths in their chosen medium. These are the people who blazed new trails.

*The Barbizon School.* Around 1830 artists began to gather in the small village of Barbizon on the edge of the Fontainebleau forest on the outskirts of Paris. They included Jean-Baptiste-Camille Corot (1796–1874), Charles François Daubigny (1817–1878), Theodore Rousseau (1812–1867), and Jean François Millet (1814–1875). The first landscapes which they exhibited in the Salon of 1831 were not vehemently realistic, because they were in the tradition of the English Constable and the Dutch Ruisdael, based on a classical substructure derived from Claude Lorrain and Poussin. After the Revolution of 1848 their paintings became more frankly realistic and not so noble.

---

[1] *Ibid.*

With the dying gasps of the aristocracy came a new social consciousness as the middle class came into power, and this called for an art of actuality as a means of communicating with the masses. Moral and social truth gradually became synonymous with contemporary life. However, the Barbizon artists turned their backs on the real contemporary phenomenon, the urban worker, and concentrated on the peasant. In fact their whole output was an impassioned outcry against the onrushing urban-industrial revolution.

Corot was the most classical of the Barbizon group. He usually included small figures of nymphs among his trees. Daubigny was more romantic, full of poignant melancholy. Rousseau was more realistic, painting oaks which look permanently fixed to the earth. Millet's figures are often tragically enslaved by toil, as in *Le Faucheur* ("Man with the Hoe"), the inspiration for Edwin Markham's poem. His open form suggests infinity.

These landscapes are not simply a sentimental return to nature, nor are they merely the cradle of Impressionism. If we study them with at least a portion of the love with which they were created, we will find a reality higher than the small events of daily life. The artist finds poetry in his soul, and if we let him, he can transport us to the privacy of intense artistic experience.

*Géricault.* Théodore Géricault (1791–1824), a painter of independent means, cared not a whit about the Academy. His *L'Officier de Chasseurs à Cheval* ("Officer of the Imperial Guard") depicts an actual horse and rider in battle. Notice the terrific rhythmic sweep and speed that it portrays. (Géricault loved horses; he was accidentally killed in a horse race when he was only thirty-three.) The Academy did not approve his *Le Radeau de la Méduse* ("Raft of the Medusa"), which was inspired by a shipwreck off the coast of Africa. Fifteen people managed to survive for three weeks on a raft before they were rescued. Géricault depicted the moment when the rescue ship was first sighted. This is an excellent painting to analyze for form and movement.

*Delacroix.* The greatest of all the Romantic painters was Eugène Delacroix (1799–1863). The poet Baudelaire described him as "passionately in love with passion in the most visible manner." [1] Delacroix hated academic recipes, and in the course of his experiments, especially with color, discovered so many new

---

[1] Quoted by Harold Nicholson, "The Romantic Revolt," in *Horizon Magazine of the Arts*, Vol. III, No. 5.

techniques that all modern painters invariably go back to his findings. He practically eliminated black and earth colors from his palette, because he found that shadows take on the complementary color of the objects nearest them and that the local color is reflected from one object to another nearby. Splotches of complementary colors next to each other heighten the color of both. Flesh, Delacroix discovered, reveals its true color only in open air and sunlight; hence he would not paint in a studio. These are just a few of Delacroix' revolutionary findings.

Delacroix took his subjects from history or from writers, including Shakespeare, Scott, Dante, Burns, and Goethe. All his work bristles with speed, air, light, and emotion. *Le Massacre de Scio* ("Massacre at Scio") depicts an incident in the Greek war in which Byron lost his life. Critics called it "Massacre of Painting." Three years later he finished *La Mort de Sardanapale* ("Death of Sardanapalus"), portraying an Assyrian king, threatened with death at the hands of his generals, who had his wives, servants, and animals slaughtered on his own funeral pyre. Sardanapalus was a legendary figure previously treated by Byron in a poetic drama. Even the painter's artist friends called the paint-

EUGÈNE DELACROIX: *Bark of Dante*. Louvre, Paris. (Alinari—Art Reference Bureau)

ing confused and unrestrained. It is. Another famous Delacroix painting, "Taking of Constantinople by the Crusaders," depicts an incident of the Fourth Crusade. In Delacroix' unfinished portrait of George Sand, enamorata of Alfred de Musset and later of Chopin, the artist pictures her with face averted from the sundial to suggest that her novels would be timeless. It is a delicate compliment, but, withal, wishful thinking.

In 1832 Delacroix made a memorable trip to Morocco and came back with sketches for future paintings. His paintings of lions and tigers are so real that they make one shiver. See, for example "The Lion Hunt," painted two years before he died.

**Music: Chopin.** The truest instrumental lyricist of Romanticism was Frédéric Chopin (1810–1849). In Chopin's music a songlike theme expresses a state of mind or mood, and this theme may be expanded within the narrow framework like a lyrical confession. The modern piano became for Chopin the only means of self-expression, and so fresh and improvisatory are these little pieces that one would never know they had been subjected to rigorous filing and polishing. Chopin lived his whole life in the turmoil of society, but his music speaks to us out of the solitude and loneliness of his soul. He is often referred to as the "Poet of the Piano."

## Spain

Throughout the French Revolutionary and Napoleonic eras, Spain figured very little in international affairs. When Napoleon decided not to invade England but to cut off her lifeline to India, he invaded Spain and his troops conquered most of Spain and Portugal. The Spaniards could do little more than use guerilla tactics, supported by the English. Many young Spaniards in exile from the oppressions of King Ferdinand VII, traveled or lived abroad, especially in England and France. When Ferdinand died they returned to Spain, bringing Romantic ideas as well as translations of foreign Romantic literature with them.

**Literature.** The result of these circumstances was that Spanish Romantic literature was largely an imitation of foreign commodities. In fact there was no native Spaniard who could touch the genius of Calderón and Lope de Vega in the Spanish Golden Age. Most of the lyric poets imitated Byron, Hugo, or Ossian; the novelists patterned their works after Sir Walter Scott or Alexander Dumas, Père; the dramatists followed Hugo and Dumas. Goethe's *Werther,* translated in 1803, brought forth a wave of melancholia and suicide.

A lyrical poet, José de Espronceda (1808–1842), lived a short and violent life on the model of Byron and Alfred de Musset. He was a skillful versifier on themes of death, disillusionment, and cynicism. His *Himno al sol* ("Hymn to the Sun") is Ossianic in inspiration. According to his critics, "when the romantic chaff is swept away, there still remains a true essence of lyric feeling and expression." [1] A longer poem called *El estudiante de Salamanca* ("The Student of Salamanca") portrays a young libertine who, after his own funeral, dances off with his skeleton bride with the same romantic swagger he had displayed in life.

José Zorilla (1817–1893) wrote a popular play on the Don Juan theme, called *Don Juan Tenorio* (1844), which is performed regularly on All Souls' Day throughout Spain. In it Don Juan is saved after death through the intercession of Dona Ines. Their souls issue from their mouths and fly up to heaven. The play has sparkle, zest, and ringing verse. The Duke of Rivas produced in 1835 *Don Alvaro, o la Fuerza del Sino* ("Force of Fate"), which is the basis of Verdi's opera *La Forza del Destino* (*Force of Destiny*), a mixture of prose and verse, comedy and tragedy. The innocent heroine is stabbed to death by her brother, who is stabbed by Don Alvaro, who in turn plunges over a cliff screaming, "Curses! Extermination! Punish the human race!" while chapel bells toll, lightning flashes, and thunder roars.

**Fine Arts: Goya.** Spain's most original painter was Francisco de Goya (1746–1828). Goya was a real individualist, belonging to no school. He started out by painting tapestry cartoons in which the figures look unstable, as if they would topple over. Then he became court painter to three kings: Charles III, Charles IV, and Ferdinand VII. He did not aim to caricature his victims, but he could not hide his feelings, and painted the grandees as vain, ugly, greedy, empty, in spite of their fine clothes. Unaccountably, his patrons accepted these highly critical portraits, and he continued in favor until the political crisis of 1808 when Napoleon's troops entered Spain and forced Charles IV to abdicate.

The people rose in revolt, and on the third of May the French troops retaliated with terrible atrocities. Goya was an eyewitness, and he recorded the scene in a painting called "The Third of May" (see p. 242), the most scathing denunciation of man's inhumanity to man ever painted. It was the point of departure for Delacroix' "Massacre at Scio" and later for Picasso's "Guernica." The executioners suggest automatons, impersonal figures of blind

---

[1] N. B. Adams and John E. Keller, *Spanish Literature* (Totowa, N.J.: Littlefield, Adams & Company, 1960).

FRANCISCO GOYA: *The Third of May.* Prado, Madrid. (Mas—Art Reference Bureau)

force. The young man facing them seems to suggest that although he dies, the cause for which he dies will triumph. He might be the spirit of all revolt against oppression.

Another powerful painting by Goya is called "The Lunatic Asylum." In it there is no spatial continuity or perspective, no line where floor meets wall. The background seems limitless. The figures are crowded on a narrow foreground with no organic connection with each other or with the room; they are trapped in isolation.

In middle age, at the height of success, Goya was struck by an illness which left him blind, deaf, and paralyzed. He recovered except for his hearing and went on painting, but always with an urgency and fear of death. In 1819, after the deaths of his wife and four of his five children, he retired to a house outside Madrid, the so-called House of the Deaf. On the walls of this house he painted his inner world of demons, phantoms, memories of cruelty, horrors, and vanities. These "Black Paintings" were removed to a museum after his death. One portrays Saturn devouring his sons, another two wasted old people eating supper, another a Witches' Sabbath. They show Goya's late technique of slashing and jabbing the surface, and dragging a heavily loaded brush across the wall. In the late nineteenth century the Expressionists copied these techniques.

## America

There was no Romantic Era, as such, in America. After the Revolution the problems of organizing the new national state required realistic thinking rather than fantasy. The earliest national idea of the United States was that of an Atlantic community, and it was thought that the culture of the Atlantic seaboard was or ought to be the culture of the nation. It was not until after the Civil War that this idea of American nationalism broadened to include the whole country. The literary men and the painters presented the American as an individual, alone, pitted against the elemental realities of existence. Nevertheless, at least some of the earmarks of Romanticism crept into literature, later into painting, and still later into music.

**Literature.** Coinciding with the Romantic movement abroad, the United States for the first time began to produce literature with enough power and originality to command respect outside the country. Cooper, Irving, Hawthorne, and Poe were the most important representatives, and they continued in vogue at least until the Civil War. Even after the war, Bret Harte, by making tenderness a foil for the hardness of the Western frontiersman, became as complete a Romantic as can be found. (Read his short story "Luck of Roaring Camp.")

*The Lyricists.* The major poets of this era were Bryant, Whittier, Longfellow, Holmes, and Poe. Since they should be well-known to you from your school experience, we shall suggest one or two poems by each poet to read as a refresher.

BRYANT. William Cullen Bryant (1794–1878) was chiefly the author of nature poetry in which he was influenced by Wordsworth. His best-known poem is "Thanatopsis" (a musing on death), considered by some critics to be the first great poem written by an American. It says that since nature claims all living creatures in death, one should so live that death is as gentle as falling asleep.

WHITTIER. John Greenleaf Whittier (1807–1892) wrote poems of nature and the intimate life of New Englanders, under the influence of Robert Burns and Oliver Goldsmith. Some of his poems sound banal today, but the best describe the natural scenes which he knew and voice his respect for common humanity. Perhaps his greatest poem is "Snowbound," in which each member of the family is characterized with warm sympathy but not sentimentalized.

LONGFELLOW. Henry Wadsworth Longfellow (1807–1882) poet and professor of languages at Harvard, studied in France, Spain, Germany, and Italy. Influenced by the German Romantic poets, he glorified nature and the simple joys and sorrows of ordinary upright folk such as "The Village Blacksmith." Longer poems like "Courtship of Miles Standish" and "Evangeline" are perhaps too sentimental for modern taste, but they instruct youth about American pioneer life. The regularity of Longfellow's meters makes the poems easy reading and also monotonous.

HOLMES. Oliver Wendell Holmes (1809–1894) was a professor of anatomy and physiology at Harvard. In his essays and some verses, he was a humorist and satirist. His best-known poems are "Old Ironsides," "The Chamber'd Nautilus," and the "One Hoss Shay," whose actual title was "The Deacon's Masterpiece" (the wagon was so well constructed that it lasted a hundred years and then disintegrated completely into a heap of dust). "The Chamber'd Nautilus" has a beautiful thought: that just as this crustacean, as he matures, walls up his old shell and builds a larger one, so man's mind as it matures should discard outworn ideas and build larger,

> *Till thou at length art free,*
> *Leaving thine outgrown shell by life's unresting sea.*

POE. By far the best of the nineteenth-century poets was Edgar Allan Poe (1809–1849), who, contrary to popular opinion, was not a depraved genius but a hardworking journalist, storyteller, and poet whose worth was not adequately assessed. Like some French Romantic poets, he succumbed to alcohol and drugs. He always considered himself a poet, but he was also an excellent literary critic. He perfected his weird and gruesome tales because his magazine audience liked them. Tales like "The Gold Bug" might be called the progenitors of the modern detective story. Poe was one of the first to preach that the low state of culture in America was due to a preoccupation with money-grubbing.

Poe's first genuine taste of success followed the publication of "The Raven" in the *New York Evening Mirror*. The weird, melancholy atmosphere and no doubt the pervasive alliteration struck the public fancy. "Ulalume" tells of the death of a beautiful woman and the attempt by her bereaved lover to establish communication with her spirit. "Annabel Lee" also mourns the death of a beautiful woman in lucid and musical language.

The best of Poe's so-called "synthetic" tales attempt, as Coleridge did, "to give the semblance of reality to shadows of the imagination." This technique presupposes realities deeper than superficial appearance, which are only fleetingly glimpsed by ordinary men, and discovered by the feelings rather than the senses. Such a tale is "The Fall of the House of Usher," in which the last of the family dies at the moment when their decrepit mansion is demolished by a whirlwind and collapses into the sinister stream. The story intimates that there is some preternatural power which triumphs over the family. Poe never locates the precise time and place of his stories, a fact which makes them more readable today.

*The Novelists.* There are three writers of "romances" which are a part of America's cultural heritage: Cooper, Irving and Hawthorne.

COOPER. James Fenimore Cooper (1789–1851) was the first to achieve fame abroad with his historical novels of romance and adventure, especially *The Last of the Mohicans* (1826), *The Pathfinder* (1840), and *The Deerslayer* (1841). Cooper created the character of the Indian Natty Bumpo, the noble savage with his delicacy of sentiment and fancy, fierce pride, and shame at loss of face. In his unequal struggle with the encroaching white man he is pushed ever farther west until we see him last at the age of ninety on the western prairies.

IRVING. Washington Irving (1783–1859) was born in New York City, and although he spent much of his life in Europe, he was loyal to the Hudson River Valley, built himself a fine manor at Tarrytown, and collected the legends of the early Dutch settlers which were published in the *Sketch Book of Geoffrey Crayon, Gent.* (1820). Many of the sketches are real short stories. Among them are "Legend of Sleepy Hollow" about Rip Van Winkle's magic sleep in the mountains, and what happened when he wakened fifty years later, and the "Spectre Bridegroom," which tells how the villagers got the better of a bumptious schoolmaster. Even before Irving became Ambassador to Spain, he collected Moorish tales about Grenada and the Alhambra. They are full of magic, fantasy, and humor. Read the "Legend of the Enchanted Soldier." Irving's style is urbane, easy to read, and his tone is lighthearted.

HAWTHORNE. Nathaniel Hawthorne (1804–1864) is the best of these early novelists. He was influenced by Gothic tales and by Walter Scott's novels. His family loved him but did not understand his literary endeavors. He withdrew in spirit and lived in isolation. Hawthorne is difficult to classify: Is he Puritan or rebel,

Romantic, or anti-Romantic, humanitarian or individualist, realist or idealist? It is best to read his greatest novel *The Scarlet Letter* with some one so that you may discuss its meaning.

In the opening scene of *The Scarlet Letter* the young and beautiful Hester Prynne stands on the scaffold of the pillory in seventeenth-century Boston, with her three-months-old baby Pearl in her arms. Her husband, an elderly medical man, crooked in mind as well as body, had sent her to Boston two years previously, intending to follow her, but she had received no news from him. When the baby was born Hester had been convicted of adultery and imprisoned but had refused to declare her lover. She was sentenced to stand for three hours in the pillory and ever thereafter to wear on the front of her dress a scarlet letter *A* (signifying adulteress). Afterwards her husband comes, guesses that her seducer is the young minister, and moves in with him to corrupt his moral energies so that he cannot repent and find forgiveness. Seven years pass. Pearl has grown into a charming but rebellious child with a strange attachment for the letter on her mother's breast and an intuitive distrust of her unacknowledged father. Meanwhile Hester has devoted herself to her child and to the good works in the community. She has never repented of her adultery because she loves the minister, who has become renowned for his talents and piety. Finally Hester and the minister decide to run away with Pearl to Europe. But at the last minute the minister takes Pearl and Hester by the hand, mounts the scaffold, and after confessing his sin and asking the forgiveness of God, he dies. The doctor, balked of vengeance, withers away and also dies within a year. Pearl is no longer an outcast, but when Hester dies, a scarlet *A* is inscribed on her tombstone. What is the central theme: the Puritan doctrine of Original Sin; Romantic naturalism and the "right to happiness"; the animal nature of man; the right to vengeance when honor is violated; salvation through suffering and confession? Or are all of these points of view part of the American conscience?

**Fine Arts.** It seems incredible that European stylistic impulses should have crossed the Atlantic in spite of the meager communication between the two continents. Our pioneer forefathers were too busy subduing a big, rawboned continent to indulge in art. Nevertheless, the aesthetic sense was there and the urge to perpetuate themselves in portraits to hang on the parlor walls. Itinerant painters, without benefit of academic training, earned a livelihood by wandering from one pioneer settlement to another. Their pictures are often laughable, but always genuine and sincere.

*Copley.* John Singleton Copley (1738–1815) in his youth sold tobacco to sailors on the Boston waterfront. He was left to support his mother at fourteen, and turned "professional" painter. His portrait of Mrs. Seymour Fort might at first glance be taken for a portrait by Reynolds or Gainsborough, but there is something American about it, a forthright honesty and solidity. English aristocrats believed that to do manual labor was a disgrace; yet Copley painted Paul Revere in his work clothes, his tools beside him, admiring a teapot he had just made (see p. 248). The painting is a perfect example of Classic style.

*Stuart.* Gilbert Stuart (1755–1828) went to London, where he learned how to paint gleaming silks, satin, and lace, but he also painted faces with great psychological penetration and character analysis as in the portrait of Mrs. Richard Yates. His portrait of Washington is the best one we have, although it was never finished.

*Sully.* The portrait of the beautiful Rebecca Gratz, friend of Washington Irving, was painted by Thomas Sully (1783–1872), who was not above flattering his subjects. Irving is said to have described her to Walter Scott, who made her the prototype for Rebecca in *Ivanhoe.* The way the figure is modeled and the way it melts into the background mark the painting as the beginning of Romanticism.

*The Hudson River School.* With Thomas Cole (1801–1848) we come to the first real American Romanticist. The poet William Cullen Bryant, who was his friend, warned him to keep his eyes in America. His painting "In the Catskills" looks like Corot transplanted to New York state. Cole started the whole Hudson River School of painters. One of them, Asher B. Durand (1796–1886), did a painting called "Kindred Spirits" showing Cole and Bryant standing on a rocky ledge overlooking a waterfall in the Catskills. It is a well-organized landscape, calling attention to the puniness of man against the grandeur of nature.

*Innes.* More significant than the Hudson River School is the Pennsylvanian George Innes (1825–1894). Innes was self-taught at home, but on his frequent trips to Europe he learned from the paintings of Constable and Corot, taking from them what he wanted but remaining true to his American vision. He contracted with the Delaware Lackawanna Railroad to do a painting of the Lackawanna Valley and the roundhouse near Scranton. The railroad sent it back because it showed only one track instead of three. Innes needed the promised seventy-five dollars and put in the extra tracks. Late in life he discovered the painting in a junk shop in Mexico and bought it.

JOHN SINGLETON COPLEY: *Paul Revere*. Courtesy, Museum of Fine Arts, Boston.

*Architecture.* Our observations on English nineteenth-century architecture apply equally to America. In nearly every city of the United States you can see Gothic churches, Baroque theaters, Renaissance or Classic post offices and schools. There are even "wedding-cake" houses in the most exuberant Rococo style. But when the architect had to design a dwelling for the little (but successful) merchant on Main Street, he really had to produce "Art" for his money. You have only to examine the nineteenth-century dwellings in your home town to see the results. Fortunately, many of these buildings are now coming down in urban renewal projects. The machine-made "decorations" plastered on the outside of buildings without rhyme or reason were called brackets. They supply the title for Edith Wharton's novel *Hudson River Bracketed,* and you can see them in Grant Wood's painting "American Gothic." Then there are the mansions of the wealthier clientele which may resemble a Norman castle, a Renaissance palace, or even the Taj Mahal. It is fortunate that the era of glass and structural steel came to put an end to such monstrosities.

**Music: MacDowell.** Why did America produce literature and painting in the nineteenth century which stand up well in comparison with European products, but no music? The only possible exception is Edward MacDowell, and even he is seldom performed today. We can only attempt an answer to this riddle.

While all the arts reflect the same traits of the cultural complex in their own stylistic period, a musical style usually takes longer than the other arts to attain complete maturity. For instance, it took six hundred years for the polyphonic style to reach maturity in the High Renaissance. In that length of time Byzantine, Romanesque, and Gothic art had flowered and passed; Renaissance painting was over. In literature the heroic epics, chivalric romances, Dante, and Shakespeare were already ancient history. Similarly, it took some three hundred years for all the stylistic elements of the symphony to reach complete maturity in Haydn, Mozart, and Beethoven. Our nation is not yet two hundred years old. How much can we expect?

Edward MacDowell (1861–1908) was a true Romanticist who can best be compared with the Norwegian Edvard Grieg. Both had a feeling for individual melodic and harmonic combinations; both were best in the smaller forms. MacDowell's "Woodland Sketches," "Sea Pieces," and "Piano Sonatas" are more creative than his symphonic poems based on Shakespeare, or Tennyson, or Keats. When MacDowell was studying in Germany, Liszt gave him a great deal of encouragement. Even though much of this music sounds dated, if not definitely derivative, today, it contributed to America's musical awareness, and we can afford to be as generous toward it as was Liszt.

## Italy

Romanticism in Italy is closely bound up with the struggle for national unification. The Austrian domination of north Italy following the Napoleonic wars created a political reaction in a country already stirred with patriotic fervor by the French

Revolution. In 1848 Charles Albert, King of Savoy, drove the Austrians from Milan, united Piedmont and Sardinia (see p. 203), and then abdicated in favor of his son Victor Emmanuel. Lombardy was wrested from Austria with the help of Napoleon III; then it was a matter of taking south Italy away from the Bourbons and driving Napoleon out of the Papal States. Count Camillo di Cavour, prime minister of Piedmont, was the determining factor in the north, and Garibaldi, a free-lance soldier, in the south. Not until 1870 was the entire country united.

The cult of the past and the exotic sifted in from France and was applied to Italian patriotism. The Italian classics were revived, especially Tasso's *Jerusalem Delivered*, while translations of Ossian, Shakespeare, Goethe, and Walter Scott were eagerly read by the people.

**Literature: Manzoni and Leopardi.** *I Promessi Sposi (The Betrothed)*, an immensely popular romantic novel by Alessandro Manzoni (1785–1873), played no small part in Italian unification. Originally written in the author's own Milanese dialect, it was translated into Tuscan for the definitive edition of 1840. Hence Tuscan became the standard literary language of Italy and assisted in standardizing the literary qualifications for voting. Children in the Italian public schools begin to study this book at the age of nine; it has gone into more than five hundred editions, and has been translated into every other important modern language.

*The Betrothed* is a historical novel of the second quarter of the seventeenth century when northern Italy, the district around Milan, was under the harsh domination of the Hapsburgs. Essentially it is the love story of two peasants, Lucia and Lorenzo, who must surmount the incredible obstacles of war, plague, bread riots, and especially the designs of a Spanish nobleman on Lucia. After some six hundred pages the two lovers at last are free to marry. The book is far more than just an entertaining adventure story in the style of Walter Scott. It might be interpreted as the story of a search for justice, or a commentary on the inhumanity of the governing classes, or a celebration of the poor and humble people, who are the innocent victims of historical events. Manzoni's indictment of evil is devastating, but at the same time the story sparkles with humor.

Giacomo Leopardi (1798–1837) is considered Italy's greatest lyrical poet since Tasso, but his poems are usually pessimistic. His love of liberty and his pessimism recall Byron; his love of beauty and yearning for human love remind us of Keats.

**Music: Rossini.** The great traditions of Classic opera had declined in the nineteenth century. The bourgeois audiences could not appreciate its subtleties, and they wanted pure entertainment and glitter. Germans, French, and Italians were struggling for the leadership. French libretti were becoming more popular and Paris had become the musical capital of the world. English Romanticism, already lapped up by Germany and France, now reached Italy. The Italian is not an imitator; when he finds something useful he will match it with something Italian. The Italians took the romantic characters of Shakespeare, Byron, and Scott and surrounded them with completely Italian music. Donizetti and Bellini had already composed Italian Romantic operas of this nature, but they were not sufficiently strong composers to halt the decadence of opera. This role was played by the much misunderstood Rossini.

Gioachino Rossini (1792–1868) had a clear knowledge of the problems of romantic opera. In 1816 he produced *Il Barbiere de Siviglia* (*The Barber of Seville*), a work worthy of Beaumarchais' comedy and a worthy companion to Mozart's *Figaro*. The music, sparkling with merriment, beautiful melodies, and irresistible rhythms, captured the entire musical world. When Rossini visited Vienna in 1822, Beethoven, Mozart, and Schubert were forgotten as the people went wild over the new operatic hero. Other operas followed in rapid succession. In 1829 he produced *William Tell* based on Schiller's drama, which had the pathos of serious opera and the bombast of French grand opera. Then something curious happened: at the age of thirty-seven and at the height of his powers, Rossini stopped composing altogether. One historian accused him of "inveterate laziness," and that verdict has been copied by many subsequent writers. Rossini was not lazy. He had been in Paris for the first performance of *The Huguenots* by Giacomo Meyerbeer and decided that if the audience wanted thrillers then his operas were no longer needed. Although Meyerbeer was a gifted musician as far as orchestration and dramatic accompaniment are concerned, he used his superb craftsmanship to conceal the emptiness of an art lacking integrity and entirely based on effect. His operas were a pompous spectacle of dancers, staging, and lush scenery calculated to overwhelm the bourgeois audience. Mendelssohn, Schumann, Wagner, and even Alfred de Vigny judged this "grand spectacle" correctly; but most of the French, including Balzac and George Sand, declared it to be consummately beautiful. Opera, which had caused the decline of classical tragedy, now practically destroyed French drama.

## Russia

Russian literature and music became known to the West only in the second quarter of the nineteenth century; hence we are likely to imagine that these arts arrived at maturity almost overnight. Such was not the case. The arts in Russia went through a long and slow development which has an amazingly similar parallel to their western counterparts.

The Christianization of Russia began with the baptism of Prince Vladimar in A.D. 988. After he married the sister of the Byzantine Emperor, Basil II, he took back to Kiev, besides his bride, a Bulgarian bishop and many priests, monks, and singers of Byzantine chants. Churches were built; choirs were instructed in the Byzantine liturgy; and clerics laid the foundations of the written language which became known as Church Slavonic. Thus Russia became the heir of the Hellenic civilization.

The literature written in Church Slavonic was religious, didactic, and practical, with emphasis on moral and social problems. It existed alongside but apart from the many folk dialects of the people. The chants of the Russian Church, however, still called today the *znamenny* chants, soon became infused with folk elements.

The pagan traditions of the people were preserved in folklore: fairy tales, love songs, and proverbs which expressed their fantasy and emotions. These have survived in oral tradition into the twentieth century. The songs of the "Men of Might" are not unlike the King Arthur stories; the struggle against the Asian Tartars is similar to Roland's battles with the Saracens. From 1240 to 1480 Russia was dominated by the Mongols, who isolated the country from Western civilization, at the same time tending to unify it. Moscow became the chief center, and when Constantinople fell in 1453, the Moscow rulers called themselves czars (Caesars). The Mongols were driven out, and Italian builders were called in to design the Kremlin.

In the seventeenth century occurred the Russian equivalent of the Reformation. The supporters of Church reform, backed by the Czar, became the Greek Orthodox denomination, while the "Old Believers" clung to the ancient books and ritual. Rather than make a pact with Western ideas of harmony and polyphony, the znamenny chant buried itself in the haunts of the Old Believers, and in doing so escaped the fate of Gregorian chant, which was mutilated beyond recognition in the course of the centuries.

The Westernization of Russia began under Peter the Great (1672–1725). Peter wanted to break the rigidity and isolation of the Byzantine tradition and to promote secular progress, but he was a tyrant who would brook no opposition. Schools, science, and the arts were freed from Church domination, while translations of Western philosophers, scientists, and statesmen were read by the educated class, who were also compelled to practice French manners. The result was to widen the gap between the upper class and the masses.

In the eighteenth century there developed a classic style of writing which observed the unities but was more realistic than that of the West. Under Catherine the Great the cultural advance increased rapidly. Because the Italians dominated music, unison singing was abandoned in favor of thick harmony. The French dominated literature, and even Catherine corresponded with Voltaire, Diderot, and the *Encyclopédists* until she became frightened by the French Revolution. Then the Empress and the aristocrats decided on protective measures against the pernicious ideas which seemed to threaten their position. Freedom of the press was abolished, and liberal educators were arrested. But it was too late. Very soon thereafter the rulers found themselves opposed by the very educated minority they had created.

After Napoleon's 1812 invasion was thwarted, Russia gained a position of respect in the West. National consciousness and increased wealth among the upper classes brought an increased demand for literature, music, and the arts. The young nobles who fought in Germany, Austria, and France during the 1812–1815 campaign absorbed ideas of freedom and equality, and when they returned they took a new look at the despotism, serfdom, and social injustice which they had previously taken for granted. On the very day that Nicholas I was to be enthroned, the young nobles started a military uprising. It was crushed, the leaders hanged, and several hundred "Decembrists" were sent to Siberia in exile.

**Literature: Pushkin.** In the early nineteenth century, classical odes and tragedies were replaced by melancholy tales of unrequited love, while poetry celebrated nature and idyllic love. Vassily Zhukovsky (1783–1852) translated Ossian, Scott, Byron, Goethe, and Schiller. The Romantic Age had dawned on Russia, too. The currents of Russia's past converge in Alexander Pushkin (1799–1837); he was the inspiration of all the following writers who have made the nineteenth century Russia's Golden Age of literature. All of the cultural and political changes, as well as Russia's spiritual and artistic growth, are mirrored in his writing. Pushkin led a wild life but never let his excesses interfere with his devotion to literature. He suffered exile for attacking serfdom and ridiculing the ruling regime. His first long poem, *Russlan and Ludmilla*, is a mock-heroic epic, a blend of folklore and classical forms. *Eugene Onegin* was written under the inspiration of Byron, and *Boris Godunov* under that of Shakespeare. *Boris* is a historical tragedy in blank verse, based on the life of a sixteenth-century czar.

It is the musical quality of Pushkin's verse that attracted composers to him. It might almost be said that he directly inspired Russian Romantic composers. Glinka based an opera on *Russlan and Ludmilla*. Tschaikowsky used *Eugene Onegin* and the *Queen of Spades*. Rimsky-Korsakov made an opera out of *The Golden Cockerel*, and Moussorgsky from *Boris Godunov* (see p. 268). Read some of Pushkin's lyric poems, his short story "The Queen of Spades," and the plot of *Boris* in a book of opera stories.

**Music: Glinka.** The first significant Russian composer was Mikhail Glinka (1804–1857). After some musical training in Italy and Germany, Glinka went back to Russia, where his literary friends selected him to compose the national opera. The result was *A Life for the Tsar*, first performed in 1836 and received with enthusiasm. Glinka proved that Russian folk music could be utilized by the serious composer and hence paved the way for Moussorgsky.

# Chapter 11 / Realism, Romantic Realism, and Naturalism

The Revolutionary year of 1848 is a convenient date to remember as marking the end of Romanticism *per se* as an art movement. But the popularity of such figures as Superman, the Lone Ranger, and Batman indicates that Romanticism is not dead even today. Perhaps these elements of the fantastic are necessary as antidotes for the harsh realities of contemporary life.

By mid-nineteenth century violent emotionalism had burned itself out and had produced the antithetical reaction in Realism in art and literature and Romantic Realism in music. While Romanticism emphasized values of the imagination, Realism portrayed life as it really is, Naturalism the seamier side of actual life. Naturalism was largely a preoccupation of the literary artists, although painters sometimes chose sordid subject matter to point up flaws in the social order. Millet had already done this in "Man with a Hoe." During the Realistic era, which lasted well into the twentieth century, the ambitions of artists became more grandiose and were expressed in long series of novels on one subject, huge canvases with esoteric meanings, and symphonic poems or series of operas weighed down with extraneous literary elements. The symphony orchestra assumed staggering proportions; musical texture became thick with chromatic harmony and dissonance. The number of significant works in all the arts is enormous, but for lack of space, we shall here limit ourselves to a few representative examples.

## Realistic and Naturalistic Painting

The rapid development of an industrial civilization in the large cities created acute political and social unrest. The pressures of modern life fell heaviest on the lowest classes, cut off from the benefits of materialistic culture. Realistic artists professed to portray only objects and situations which they had seen and experienced at first hand. With artistic sincerity they wanted their paintings to be a protest against accepted conventions and traditional clichés. Most of them scorned their real audience, the mercantile middle class, and championed the peasants.

**France.** French Realism received a powerful impetus from

the eccentric and indigent painters and writers who led Bohemian lives in the Latin Quarter of Paris, scoffing at the melancholy of the romantics and the mediocrity of the bourgeoisie. Another impetus came from the Barbizon School of painters (see p. 237), who had turned against violence and picturesqueness and gone back to landscape and peasant subjects.

*Daumier.* Honoré Daumier (1808–1879) was in close touch with the social situation, contributing satirical lithographs to leading journals. There are some four thousand of these prints, which show not only keen insight and warm sympathy for humanity but also excellent draftsmanship and mastery of line. When these radical publications were suppressed by the government, Daumier went to jail for six months, and when he came out he faced hunger, eviction from his home, and unemployment. It was then that the aged Corot came to the rescue with the gift of a simple house. Daumier lived in poverty and neglect and was buried in a pauper's grave. He never suspected that within a generation he would be hailed as the first of the modern artists, his works eagerly sought and purchased for handsome sums.

Daumier's paintings not only communicate ideas; at the same time they are masterpieces of design, form, receding and advancing planes, and underlying rhythmic patterns. Daumier laid bare the life of the poor and starving, the washerwoman, the prostitute, the corrupt judge, the venal attorney. We respect him for his utter truth, and his genuine talent. "The Laundress" depicts a mother and child climbing up the embankment. The mother carries a bundle of clothes, but her concern is whether the wobbly youngster is going to "make" the top step. No Madonna was ever painted to depict greater spiritual relationship between mother and child than is shown in this simple scene. Daumier's "Print Collector" represents everyone who enjoys pictures but is too poor to buy an original. The scene is repeated daily at the bookstalls along the Seine. If you have ever traveled third class in France or Spain, you will appreciate Daumier's "Third Class Coach" showing humble people stoically enduring boredom, discomfort, and the lurching of the train just to get where they have to go. They might be all mankind, hopelessly imprisoned, "condemned to life."

Occasionally it is worth while to discuss an artist's failure. Daumier's *Rue Transnonain* depicts an entire family dead after some sort of violent fracas in a bedroom. Unlike Goya's "Third of May," it has no impact upon the observer (except repulsion) unless we know the circumstances which prompted it. In 1834, there was a strike of laborers at Lyons. Paris workmen staged a sympathetic strike, and troops were called out to keep order. They were fired upon from the windows of number 12, Rue Transnonain. In retaliation, the troops killed every person in the building, including the family shown in the painting. When these circumstances are known the painting becomes a powerful. condemnation of brute force, but without this knowledge it is meaningless.

*Courbet.* Gustave Courbet (1819–1877) was a big, hearty man in love with life. His family supported him, reluctantly, in his artistic career. He claimed that nature was his only teacher; like Caravaggio he wanted truth. In *Bonjour Monsieur Courbet* we see him in his shirt sleeves, his back laden with canvases, tramping along, doffing his hat to his immaculate dealer. In 1848 when the power of the Academy was temporarily diminished, the Salon was open to all and Courbet won a second-class medal. The next year he exhibited a huge canvas, ten by twenty-one feet, called *Enterrement à Ornans* ("Funeral at Ornans"), which depicts a peasant funeral in a rural churchyard. Although the scene is quiet and devotional, the picture was pronounced vulgar by critics and public.

Courbet spent the rest of his life fighting academism and Romanticism. Every new canvas aroused a fresh storm, but his friends the novelist Zola and the poet Baudelaire jumped into the fray to fight for him. He traveled around proclaiming the gospel of Realism whenever he exhibited his paintings, with the result that he became the best-known living artist, and sold more than a hundred paintings in the Paris World Exhibition of 1867. When Napoleon III fell, the Republican regime made Courbet Director of Fine Arts. Soon the Germans bombarded Paris, the Republic fell, and Courbet was again on the wrong side of the political fence, because the Academy was back in power. He was accused of failing to protect French Art during the bombardment; his possessions and paintings were confiscated; and he was driven into exile. It was not until the beginning of World War II, long after his death, that he was exonerated.

Courbet's most controversial painting is called *L'Atelier* ("The Painter's Studio") and subtitled "Real Allegory" (see p. 258). This huge canvas was rejected by the Salon jury of 1855, and hung in a wooden pavilion outside. Most of Courbet's friends called it "terrifying foolery," while only Delacroix admired it. Courbet has here reduced to a formula the entire artistic development of the first half of the nineteenth century and foreshadowed the second half.

"The Studio" divides into three parts like a triptych. In the

GUSTAVE COURBET: *The Painter's Studio*. Louvre, Paris. (Agraci—Art Reference Bureau)

central panel are the artist, Courbet himself, painting a realistic landscape; a little boy (the innocent eye) who stands absorbed in the painter's work, and a sympathetic nude figure representing "truth." On the right you see an affluent couple, the type of bourgeois people who frequent expositions out of curiosity; two lovers completely absorbed in each other; some of Courbet's friends who are not concerned, just there; and on the extreme right the poet Baudelaire, engrossed in a book. On the left is a collection of ordinary people: the prostitute nursing her child half behind the easel, the merchant, some old soldiers, the grave-digger with a skull, a priest, a hunter with his dog and gun. The nude figure tied to a pillar is Classicism. The fact that strikes you forcibly is that each of these figures is alone, absorbed in his own thoughts, unconcerned with those around him. There are representatives of society's upper, lower, and middle strata: poverty and wealth, exploiters and exploited, ignorant and intellectual, the elite and the outcasts, in fact all the dissonances that are hidden within the structure of society. It is a social indictment, but it is more than that. In this disparate world all stand with empty hands; that is, all except the artist. He alone has control over reality, his canvas, and he alone expresses compassionate understanding. The indefinite and unreal background seems to be a haphazard collection of abandoned pieces of stage scenery. The pictorial space is not governed by perspective, but seems to flow and float almost like infinity. However, this intangible background becomes upon the easel tangible reality. Thus it is the artist alone who is an active agent, mastering the real world and giving it form. Only the artist can co-ordinate all the elements in society, connect them, and give them spiritual meaning.

*Manet.* Following the lead of Courbet, an ever larger group of left-wing (or rather Left Bank) radicals, painters, and writers gathered by night in the Montmartre cafés to fulminate against the Academy with its sterile ideas and crushing tradition. Then came the fatal Salon of 1863 which, stricter than usual, threw out four thousand paintings by the avant-garde group. The ensuing uproar was heard by Napoleon III, who decreed a *Salon des Réfusés* in the same building for the rejected paintings. More than six hundred paintings were withdrawn by the artists themselves and the remaining paintings were hung.

This was the best kind of publicity. All Paris came to see and jeer. One painting was Whistler's "White Girl," now in the National Gallery in Washington. But the picture that created the greatest sensation was *Le Dejeuner sur l'herbe* ("Luncheon on the

ÉDOUARD MANET: *Luncheon on the Grass.* Louvre, Paris. (Agraci— Art Reference Bureau)

Grass") (see p. 259) by Édouard Manet (1832–1883). Manet was a Realist and must not be classed as an Impressionist, although he was the friend and hero of the latter group. He had studied the technique of Hals, Velásquez, and Goya, especially their method of using clear colors unseparated by artificial blends which produce muddy tones. His "Luncheon on the Grass" was an experimental exercise such as those often undertaken by Renaissance artists to demonstrate their ability to blend clothed and nude figures with landscape and still life in the same picture. (Compare it with Giorgione's "Out-of-Door Concert.") He avoided heavy modeling, painting landscape and figures with large areas of color, fresh and clean. The painting told no story; it made no comment. What was the bourgeois audience expected to think? "The painting is indecent"; and the critics agreed.

Two years later when Manet exhibited "Olympia," there was an even more violent storm. It was quite in the tradition of Titian's "Venus of Urbino," but what startled and annoyed the public was its frankness. The model, obviously a courtesan, is not embarrassed but perfectly composed, not coy or seductive but frankly naked. The light strikes the figure from the front making modeling in shadows unnecessary. The flesh tones are clear and warm against the cool linen. A painter could hardly dream up a simpler design, and yet it is perfectly integrated. The Negress who has brought in the flowers is a necessary part of the design, but is slightly set off from the reclining figure by a line which is probably the edge of the bed curtain. This vertical line is necessary as a foil for the predominantly horizontal lines of bed and girl.

Manet said that he tried to express the inward reality by the outward appearance. Contrast the depravity expressed in the face of *Le Buveur d'Absinthe* ("Absinthe Drinker") and the quiet contentment expressed in the face of the mother in *Gare St. Lazare* ("St. Lazare Station"). This is one of Manet's most ingratiating paintings. A young mother and her little girl are waiting in the station. The mother, holding a tiny puppy in her arms glances up from the book she is reading; the little girl in an immaculate white dress and blue sash peers through the grating at a train concealed in a cloud of steam. The painting gives the impression of being spontaneous and natural, and yet it is emotionally empty. There is little modeling and no depth. No wonder the contemporary audience was puzzled.

**America.** America produced many excellent Realistic painters in the nineteenth century; in fact most of them were Realistic. The hard facts of life were too ever present to allow for prettifying art.

*Homer.* Winslow Homer (1836–1910) began his career as a magazine illustrator and painter of the loneliness of the Civil War soldier's life. He delighted in the raw pastimes of rural Americans. A brilliant water-colorist, he painted powerful pictures of the sea on the Maine coast and around Bermuda. You can actually feel the wind in "Breezing Up." The expatriate novelist Henry James, on the eve of his departure from "raw" America to "refined" Europe, asked Homer, "Why do you stick around here? Do you think the Maine coast as paintable as Capri?" The answer was, "Yes."

*Eakins.* Thomas Eakins (1844–1916) was a scientific realist who believed artists should study anatomy by dissecting cadavers as Michelangelo had done. He loved to paint anything that moved: nude boys swimming, horses prancing, sailboats in a brisk wind. He was discharged in disgrace from the Philadelphia Academy of Art because he had his students paint from a nude model. Walt Whitman said that people who like Eakins best are those who have no prejudices. Eakins' portrait of "Miss Van Buren" is a superb painting not because the technique is flawless, which it is, or because it is a realistic likeness, which it probably is, but because it finds within the everyday world a poetry which does not need to be pretty or ornamental. Eakins' Americanism was genuine and spontaneous. His paintings have a soundness, a vigor, a rejection of pretense, a natural warmth, and a perception of the spiritual concealed within the ordinary. Examine for example, his painting called "The Swimming Hole."

*Naturalists.* About 1910, while Teddy Roosevelt was breaking trusts and Dreiser was writing his novels of social protest, a Naturalistic school of painters known as "The Ashcan School" came into being in New York City. John Sloan (1871–1951) painted scenes of New York saloons, like "McSorley's Bar," which were sold and hung in the same saloons. George Bellows (1882–1925) painted prize fighters in the ring, like "Stag at Sharkey's," and scenes in the slum sections of the city. His portraits are real character analyses.

*Wood.* After World War I the Atlantic seaboard ceased to be the exclusive domain of painters. Other sections of the country produced their characteristic painters with their characteristic local color. Iowa was the locale of Grant Wood (1892–1942), who might almost have been a character in Sinclair Lewis' *Main Street.* But Cedar Rapids was not like Gopher Prairie; its citizens were proud of their painter. They bestowed upon him a free studio, and they bought his paintings. Examine "American Gothic" and decide why Wood gave it that title. "Dinner for Threshers" looks like a stage set because the front wall of the house has been removed to reveal the kitchen where the women are serving the food, and beyond a partition some twenty or thirty men, all in blue overalls, seated around the table doing justice to the food. It is a homely American scene. "Daughters of Revolution," however, earned for the painter some enemies. The three women presented are austere, unyielding, and narrow. The social satire is implicit.

*Benton.* Thomas Benton (1889–    ) came from the Missouri of Mark Twain. His father was a congressman with enough money to send his son to Paris to study. He came back in clothes of a Paris artist and for ten years tried to paint like one. Then suddenly he found himself, turned about-face, and became the self-appointed spokesman for American Art. Examine his "Jealous Lover of Lone Green Valley" and "Cradling Wheat."

*Ryder.* America also produced a mystic in Albert Pinkham Ryder (1847–1917). His "Death on a Pale Horse" is probably his best-known canvas. "Temple of the Mind" was inspired by Poe's "Haunted Palace."

## Romantic Realism in Music

Just as Courbet tried to encompass all contemporary Parisian society on one enormous canvas, the three composers whose works we shall consider also tried to achieve a grandiose, universal art form. Later we shall see that the writers had equally colossal ideas. It was an impossible goal, and they all failed; but their struggle has left us works of imperishable beauty, and if Goethe was correct, they are redeemed by their struggle.

**Berlioz.** Hector Berlioz (1803–1869) was a great composer in spite of his limitations. He was not a melodist; there are only a few great melodies in his entire output. He composed what he called symphonies, but the symphonic form is only a frame for poetic ideas. He ignored Beethoven's advice on the title page of the *Pastoral Symphony: "Mehr Empfindungs-ausdruck als Tonmalerei"* ("more expression of feeling than tone painting"). There is no dramatic tension in the development, no symphonic drive because chromatics and dissonances obscure the tonal logic. Excitement is no substitute for dramatic conflict. To make up for a lack of inner unity and coherence, Berlioz' symphonies are built around a story or program.

His greatest achievement lies in exploring the sonorities of the enlarged symphony orchestra. His *Requiem Mass,* for example, calls for a chorus of several hundred voices, a minimum of one hundred strings, twenty woodwinds, and twelve French horns, reinforced at times by four choirs of brasses, and eight sets of timpani. The total effect sounds as though it might wake the dead, but hardly comfort the mourners. Berlioz wrote a textbook on instrumentation which is still standard in musical conservatories today.

While studying at the Paris Conservatory he was hit by three lightninglike strokes: Goethe's *Faust,* Shakespeare's plays, and Beethoven's symphonies. The *Symphonie Fantastique* was inspired by his love affair with an Irish singer, Harriet Smithson. He became engaged to her, then won the *Prix de Rome* and went off to Italy. When he heard she had married someone else, he bought poison and pistols and started back. But he fell in love with the Italian countryside and decided to remain. When he returned to Paris she was divorced; he married her and was miserable.

In the *Symphonie Fantastique* a rather nebulous tune representing his beloved appears in each section in a slightly changed form. This tune is not woven into the musical fabric, but appears in a solo instrument alone while the rest of the orchestra is nearly silent. The first movement is called "Reveries and Passions," the second, "Ball," the third, "Scenes in the Country," the fourth, "March to the Gallows" (he dreams he has killed her), a fifth, "Dream of a Witch's Sabbath" (shades of Faust; she is now a witch).

Berlioz contributed much to modern orchestral technique. The reason we designate such music Romantic-Realist is that while the subject matter is highly imaginative, its literal transcription into music attempts to be realistic. The tune or motive used to characterize a literary idea is called by the French the *idée fixe* (fixed idea), by the Germans the *leitmotif* (leading or guiding theme).

**Liszt.** The religious music of Franz Liszt (1811–1886) was designed to "lead man back to God." In his essay on the "Church Music of the Future," written in 1834, Liszt defined "humanistic music" as dramatic and churchly. Here again is an impossible romantic goal. Liszt was a great virtuoso at the keyboard, a prodigy at the age of nine. Born in Hungary, educated in Paris, he toured Europe as a virtuoso pianist and settled in Weimar as Court Conductor. His daughter Cosima married Richard Wagner. Liszt was kind and unselfish, and always ready to help struggling composers.

Liszt was a more original innovator than Berlioz. His achievement proved that it was possible to create a logically organized piece of music without forcing poetic ideas into the traditional symphonic form. The symphonic poem which Liszt created made use of the *idée fixe* principle, but instead of being a separate adjunct to the musical syntax, as Berlioz used it, it became with Liszt the germ out of which grew the entire work: the harmonic and rhythmic development as well as the form. Put succinctly, Berlioz used the *idée fixe* like mayonnaise in potato salad, to make a mechanical mixture; Liszt used it like baking powder in a cake, to form a chemical fusion.

To demonstrate Liszt's achievements examine his symphonic poem, *Les Préludes*, based on one of Lamartine's *Poetic Meditations*. The poem likens life to a series of preludes to death. The enchanted dawn of life is love, but love is soon shattered by a storm which disperses its illusions. After the storm the bruised soul seeks respite in rural calm. But when the trumpet signals, the soul is recalled to the battle of life in whose struggle he finally achieves self-mastery. Almost any active man's life could be poured into this mold.

The music is continuous, but you can readily discern the four sections:

1. Introduction with statement of theme. The love experience.
2. The storm which destroys love's illusions.
3. The retreat to the bosom of nature.
4. The call to action in which man finds self-fulfillment.

If you get acquainted with the three-note motif, you will have no difficulty in following its metamorphoses.

**Bizet.** The death of Georges Bizet (1838–1875) at the age of thirty-seven deprived the world of a very great composer. He is known and admired today largely for just two scores: the incidental music which he composed for Daudet's play, *L'Arlesienne* ("Woman of Arles"), and the opera *Carmen*, which critics believe to be the finest French opera ever written.

When *Carmen* was first produced in 1875, it was not a failure, but for several reasons it did not receive the acclaim it deserved. Since it had some spoken dialogue it could not "defile" the Paris Grand Opera House, and had to be given at the *Opéra Comique*, which "important people" did not attend. It also had a Spanish locale, and made use of the Wagnerian leitmotif principle. But these were all excuses. The real reason was that it offended "nice" bourgeois sensibility just as Manet's paintings had done. The protagonist of the opera is a gypsy who works in a cigarette factory, smokes cigarettes, and dances on the table.

The story, based on a tale by Prosper Mérimée, is a simple love and jealousy triangle involving two men (a soldier and a toreador) and a flirtatious gypsy. There is no sentimentality; love is a primitive force like fate in classic drama. The picturesque choruses, dances, and soldier and smuggler scenes drive the action forward to the point where the fatal stabbing of Carmen in the last act is inevitable. Carmen has the voluptuous quality of the French female voice. Bizet has contrived to change her melody, mood, tempo, and spirit according to the man she is addressing. José, the light, soft French tenor, is whipped into passionate action by the girl. His vocal line ends in the cry of the animal as he sings, "Yes, it is I who have killed her, my beloved Carmen." The choruses set the atmosphere of foreboding which foreshadows the ultimate tragedy. The orchestra provides the light and air in which the characters live and breathe. One might say that the entire opera is built around Carmen's voice, the typical French mezzo-soprano, as it expresses melancholy and frivolity, sensuality and contempt for death. The philosopher Friedrich Nietzsche said of *Carmen:*

> *Yesterday—would you believe it?—I heard Bizet's masterpiece for the twentieth time. Have more painful, more tragic accents ever been heard on the stage before? I know no case in which the tragic irony which constitutes the kernel of love is expressed with such severity, or in so terrible a formula, as in the last cry of Don José.*[1]

**Wagner.**   The one asset which Richard Wagner (1813–1883) did not possess was modesty. He believed himself to be the greatest composer, poet, and philosopher who had ever lived. The fact that his contemporaries did not at first share this conviction caused him much suffering until Liszt performed his *Lohengrin* and mad King Ludwig of Bavaria pulled him out of the financial doldrums by giving him money for his own theater in Bayreuth.

Wagner was influenced by Nietzsche's philosophy of the Superman, the self-disciplined perfectionist. And Nietzsche saw in Wagner the incarnation of his Superman, destined to re-create the ancient Dionysiac tragedy from the spirit of music, the creator of a *Gesamtkunstwerk* (universal art form) which would draw to itself all the arts of poetry, drama, painting, and philosophy, and

---

[1] Quoted by Paul Henry Lang, *op. cit.,* p. 908.

make their separate existences redundant. It took just three years for Nietzsche to become disillusioned because he detected insincerity and theatricality in Wagner's life and work. Nietzsche's disappointment was so keen that it probably contributed to his ultimate insanity.

It is not fair to blame Nazism and its subsequent evils on Richard Wagner and Friedrich Nietzsche. But the fact remains that the German people and Hitler were quite willing to claim Nietzsche as their prophet and Wagner as the re-creator of the ancient drama of their race. There is a photograph of the Emperor William II standing with his Lohengrin helmet before a swan, the "Knight of the Grail of German imperialism." And in 1933, if you will forgive a personal allusion, the author was present for the opening of the Bayreuth Festival, and saw Madame Siegfried Wagner, the High Priestess at the shrine of her father-in-law, welcoming Hitler, Goering, Goebbels, and the rest of the Nazi hierarchy to worship at Wagner's altar. And with that international throng, I too was moved to ecstatic tears when the hidden orchestra came crashing down on the Prelude to *Meistersinger*. This is not a digression, but an object lesson in the influence of an artistic idea on the destiny of mankind, a potential force far greater than that of the atomic bomb because it can destroy not the body but the soul.

The musico-dramatic unity in Wagner's music dramas was accomplished by the *leitmotif* principle already worked out by Berlioz and Liszt. But Wagner extended its use to include objects, people, and ideas (such as renunciation and retribution), and even to express the thinking of his characters. He used all these intertwined motives to build up the musical structure of the work. Most of this complex musical material must be manipulated by the orchestra while the voices declaim the text in a sort of speech-song above it. The orchestra, overburdened with the thick texture resulting from the interweaving of the motifs, completely dominates the singers. In fact, in the most climactic scenes the voices are eliminated altogether.

Perhaps the *Liebestod* (Love-Death) scene at the end of *Tristan and Isolde* is as good a sample of Wagner's style as any that might be chosen. It is not morbid, but a joyous consummation of ecstatic rapture. Dr. Lang has described it as the *Missa Solemnis* of love. "In it Romanticism culminates and falls, for in it the longing of a century reaches its fulfillment and then perishes in the embrace." [1] Musically, it is chromatic harmony built

---

[1] *Ibid.,* p. 878.

up to a climax by prolonged suspensions which do not resolve into consonance until the very end.

Whether we approve of Wagner or not, we must admire him as an artist. To quote Dr. Lang again: "To go ahead composing, with the mighty but unperformed scores of *Rhinegold, Valkyrie, Tristan,* and *Meistersinger* buried in the drawers of his desk, required a Herculean artistic integrity against which all of Wagner's insincere acts pale to insignificance." [1] The world could ill afford to lose the music of Richard Wagner.

**Verdi.** In the operas of Giuseppe Verdi (1813–1901) we find the highest expression of Italian arts and letters contemporary with the German Wagnerian era. Verdi's music is human, dramatic, and intrinsically Italian. His operas were born out of nationalistic fervor and supreme musical genius. In the face of strictly enforced censorship, Verdi found libretti which embodied the idea of liberty and which would have allegorical significance for his countrymen. *Rigoletto* (1851), *Il Trovatore* (*The Troubadour*) (1853), and *La Traviata* (*The Lost One*) (1853) were all based on celebrated French plays, but they are poles apart from the conventional Romantic grand opera with its insistence on spectacular display. Nor is there the formidable amalgamation of leitmotifs with which Wagner built up his musical texture. Verdi rather developed the motives and actions of his characters through the harmonic and tonal relationships of the music. *Aïda* (1871) is more lavish in pomp and display than the most spectacular grand opera, but these features are not responsible for this opera's enduring esteem. It is rather the development in the characters of passion *as mirrored in the music* which gives it its universal appeal. In 1874 came Verdi's tribute to his friend Carlo Manzoni in the *Requiem Mass,* which is as dramatic as any opera. At the age of seventy-three Verdi composed his *Otello* (1887), which is "one throbbing story of the catastrophe of a great love." [2] He finished his life work with *Falstaff* (1893), a comic opera. It is not mere entertainment music, however, because this dreamer of beauty and greatness hides under a cloak of merriment. Thus Verdi translated human emotion into music.

**Russian Composers.** We have already seen the beginning of a Russian national art music in Glinka's *Life for the Tsar* (see p. 254). Following Glinka, Russian composers divided into two groups: those who consciously followed Western musical tradi-

---

[1] *Ibid.,* p. 888.
[2] *Ibid.,* p. 911.

tions and those who believed in building on their own Pan-Slavic heritage.

*Tchaikovsky.* In the first group Peter Ilich Tchaikovsky (1840–1894) is the most eminent. Tchaikovsky had an unhappy life and a morbid, introspective personality, but he was a thorough musician who left a few works which rival even Beethoven's symphonies in popular appeal. He worked very hard at composition and handled the symphony orchestra with marvelous technique. He wrote some beautiful melodies, showed great rhythmic freedom, and avoided exaggerated nationalism.

It was the *Sixth Symphony,* the *Pathétique,* which sold Tchaikovsky to the general public. Why is this? Because in our age it is popular to be pessimistic and gloomy. When this attitude ceases to be general, his music will cease to be so popular. Like Byron, Tchaikovsky wore his heart on his sleeve, and *he* is the hero of every program overture, whether it be *Hamlet* or *Manfred,* or *Paolo and Francesca* or *Romeo.* Gaiety and charm are to be found in the *Italian Caprice* and the *Nutcracker Ballet,* but these are the exceptions that prove the rule. *Marche Slave* and *1812 Overture* are blatantly bombastic. His chamber music is intimately personal, and always morbid.

*Moussorgsky.* None of the five composers who formed the Pan-Slavic group (Balakirev, Borodin, Cui, Rimsky-Korsakov, and Moussorgsky) was a professional musician. All had other professional jobs and composed music as a hobby. We shall consider only Moussorgsky, who was the most talented and came closest to achieving the aspiration of the entire group by deriving inspiration and subject matter from Russian history and culture. Moussorgsky composed in *Boris Godunov* the finest opera to come out of eastern Europe. Since he believed that song should arise out of the natural singable quality of the Russian language, he took the style of Russian folk songs for his arias, and the speech-melody and harmony from Russian church chants for the recitatives.

The singing by men's voices always predominates in Russia. Hence the center of *Boris Godunov* is the baritone who is opposed by the counter force in the chorus. The love episode and even the tenor voice of the false Dimitri remain secondary to the stark conflict between Boris and chorus. The bass monk-evangelist provides the frame for the action in the introduction and conclusion.

The story, based on Russian history and first told in Pushkin's play of the same name, is concerned with the inner torment of a czar who has killed the real heir to the throne. The shifting Russian people (the chorus) alternately support and repudiate him. Boris dies a prey to fear and remorse. When first presented in 1874 the opera was too rough even for Russian taste. When it was revised in 1904 Rimsky-Korsakov refined away much of Moussorgsky's characteristic harmonic and orchestral language. Today audiences are used to dissonance, and Moussorgsky's original edition is the one usually presented. The coronation scene is the most colorful one in the opera. The music contains discords, primitive rhythms, and abrupt transitions, but musicians realize now that these were due not to Moussorgsky's ignorance, but to his deliberate attempt to make the music more expressive.

## Nineteenth-Century Literature

The nineteenth century is the great period of the novel; hence one can best trace the development from Romanticism to Realism to Naturalism through the novels of the period. The second half of the century also marks the beginning of the short story as a literary form. We are therefore suggesting short stories by the same authors which can provide a quicker comparison of points of view and style.

The word *Realism* comes from the Latin word *res* ("thing"), the same derivation as *real estate*. The movement arose out of the French Revolution when the rising capitalist society was intent on becoming socially important, a status which it equated with the accumulation of *things*. (The Victorian poet and critic Matthew Arnold used the term "Philistines" for people of low culture who aspired to greatness and power through wealth.) Thus "property" came to have an absolute value, and competition became the way to accumulate it. This concept is basic to an understanding of the nineteenth and twentieth centuries, especially as they are mirrored in the novel.

Following the Realists came the Naturalists, who professed to subject the life of men and women to a medico-literary clinic. They denied romantic love and emphasized the brutal and often revolting aspects of existence. They even denied the artistry of writing, but we must respect them for their honesty and intellectual integrity.

**France.** Because the French are by nature individualistic, we must first trace the development of Realism in the French novel.

*Hugo and Stendhal.* As a sort of bridge between Romanticism and Realism it is interesting to compare the description of the

Battle of Waterloo found in Stendhal's *Charterhouse of Parma* (1839) and that in Victor Hugo's *Les Misérables* (1862).[1] Stendhal (Henri Beyle, 1783–1842) was not entirely a Romanticist; indeed in many ways he anticipated the modern psychological novel. The long life of Victor Hugo (1802–1885), like that of Michelangelo, spanned more than one stylistic period. When Hugo wrote most of his lyric poems and his play *Hernani* (see p. 235), he was living in the full tide of Romanticism. When he wrote *Les Misérables* he was living in the full tide of Realism. Stendhal gives us a few fragmentary episodes of the battle, which are completely confusing and baffling to his main character, who had anticipated being in the thick of the "glorious fray." Hugo gives us a minute play-by-play account of the actual battle, which is as precise as the description of a football game. Hence the first account is subjective and Romantic, the second objective and Realistic.

*Balzac.* Honoré de Balzac (1799–1850) was the first and perhaps the greatest of the Realistic novelists. He was himself a curious blend of idealist and materialist. He wanted fame and fortune and would have achieved both of them sooner but for his concern with get-rich-quick schemes which invariably led to disaster. He formulated a grandiose scheme of novels which was to depict every facet of French society and was to be called *The Human Comedy* as opposed to Dante's *Divine Comedy*. When he died he had completed ninety-five novels and had planned forty more.

Balzac is at his best in character analysis, but his characters are types rather than individuals. The same character appears in a number of novels, enabling the author to show how a person changes under changing circumstances, especially those of accumulated money and pleasure. Balzac liked to dwell on an individual dominated by a passion which causes his destruction. He was content to observe his characters and not to judge them; he did not reward virtue and punish vice as Dickens did, but his characters are never false to their own nature. Balzac's style is often coarse, clumsy, and pedantic, but the content of his novels is both powerful and vital. He depicted one side of life as it is, although he disregarded other elements.

Balzac believed that greed was the worst and commonest vice of French character. In *Eugénie Grandet* the wealthy old father is a psychopathic miser who imposes such frugality on his wife

---

[1] *Charterhouse of Parma,* Chapters 3–4; *Les Misérables,* Part II, Book 1, Chapters 4–14.

and daughter that after both father and mother are dead, Eugénie, having paid the debts of her cousin and lover so that he can marry a titled lady, goes on living the same kind of frugal life her father had taught her. Thrift is here pushed to the loathsome excess of inhuman avarice. Eugénie is not a tragic but a pathetic figure.

*Père Goriot* ("Old Goriot") is a French King Lear, a father who loves his daughters so much that he lets them gradually filch from him every cent he has. When he dies, the girls, now married to titles and very wealthy, do not come to the funeral. He is attended only by two poor students from his rooming house who feel sorry for him.

*Flaubert.* Gustave Flaubert (1821–1880) wrote the most famous realistic novel of the period, *Madame Bovary*. By temperament Flaubert was a romantic and a perfectionist. He hated cities and bourgeois life, loved the country and the exotic Orient. He coined the phrase *le mot juste*, the one right word, and he spent days refining and polishing a single page of writing.

If Emma Bovary's character is not typical of all women, she exemplifies traits which are true not only of women of nineteenth-century France but of our own period as well. She has been made a sentimentalist by her education and by her taste for romantic fiction; she wants ecstasy and thrills. Her husband is a mediocre doctor, prosaic and boring, but a man who loves his wife dearly and who gives her what money he can afford to satisfy her taste for fine clothes. She deceives her husband with several unworthy men, neglects her child, and enters into questionable business transactions to get more money. Caught up at last by the moneylenders, she commits suicide; her husband dies of grief; and her daughter goes to work in a cotton factory.

Madame Bovary has been called the female Don Quixote, but there are many differences between the two characters. To Cervantes' hero romance means knightly adventure; to Emma it means passionate love. The Don's motives are intellectual; Emma's are emotional. (Is it not true that many shallow-minded girls today are deluded by the glamorized movie stars, the empty faces and figures that parade through magazine advertisements into thinking that life owes every girl beauty and happiness?) Certainly it is natural to dream and to wish. But where Don Quixote's dreams were altruistic because he wanted to right wrong, Emma's are sheerly egoistic. Flaubert also condemns Emma's husband because he is a poor creature who requires not much of his wife besides comfort and security. How would you express the theme and the moral of the novel?

*Zola.* Zola was not completely objective because he started with a thesis: the theory of heredity, which was in vogue among intellectuals since in 1859 Darwin had published his *Origin of Species.* The twenty volumes which Zola wrote form a study of the effects of a marriage between an alcoholic and a subnormal, degenerate woman on the later members of the family unto the third and fourth generations.

Zola made the novel *Thérèse Raquin* into a play partly on a dare by his critics who said that it would dissolve under the merciless glare of the footlights. On the contrary, the play was more successful than the novel, and it is moving to read and to see on the stage.

The entire action takes place in the tawdry sitting-room of a "flat" above a haberdashery shop. The orphaned Thérèse has been brought up by her aunt, who is such a possessive woman that she has made her only son, Camille, into a sickly, spoiled, and obstinate creature, afraid of his own shadow. Thérèse has been induced by her aunt to marry this cousin.

When a young artist comes to the flat, Thérèse pretends to despise him although in reality the two are soon passionately in love. They take Camille on an outing and tip over the canoe so that Camille is drowned. They still pretend to despise each other. After a year has elapsed, the aunt suggests that they marry. They do, but gradually come to hate each other because remorse for the murder hangs over their heads. The aunt finds out the truth, but refuses to "turn them in," because she wants to watch them suffer. Both Thérèse and her husband commit suicide.

The action lies not in the story, but in the inner conflicts of the characters. Thérèse is a passionate woman who goes from frantic love to fierce hatred, passing through moods of hypocrisy, disgust, and terror. Laurent is an idle, cautious fellow who loves Thérèse at first because she costs him nothing, then becomes a lover so passionate that he is made into a murderer, then deteriorates into a poor creature grown cowardly by suffering, his mind deranged to the point where he would commit a second crime to wipe out the first. There are three subsidiary characters, innocuous and colorless, who come to the flat once a week to play dominoes with Camille. With their bourgeois chatter they are completely oblivious to, and a foil for, the tragic drama going on around them.

For Zola, the novel involved watching people behave under pressure, and he was both the witness of the behavior and the gauge of the pressure. Although the Naturalists refused to accept ideals as a part of human character, Zola seems to be saying that people who are essentially upright cannot enjoy ill-gotten gains. *Maupassant.* A follower and admirer of both Flaubert and Zola was Guy de Maupassant (1850–1893). As a youth he was very athletic and loved the out-of-doors, but he had inherited a tendency toward a mental disease. His works, mostly in the field of the short story, were all written within a period of ten years; then he went insane and died at forty-three.

Maupassant accepted Flaubert's doctrine of *le mot juste* and wrote his gruesome stories with great care and objectivity. Some of his works which are concerned with the brutal aspects of sex were suppressed by the public censors. Maupassant never judged or censured his characters. He gave the essentials of character and situation with economy and sharp detail; not a word is wasted. A favorite among his short stories is *La Parure* ("The Necklace"). In this story the young wife of a Cabinet clerk is unhappy because she craves fine clothes and social position. Her husband procures for her an invitation to a splendid social function and buys her a new dress. She borrows a diamond necklace from a friend and is a big success at the party, but she loses the necklace. She buys another to replace it and scrubs floors for ten years to pay for it. Having become a haggard old woman, she meets the friend and learns that the borrowed necklace had been only an imitation.

**Norway: Ibsen.** A dramatist who exerted a telling influence on the French Naturalists of the 1880's, and later on English and American Naturalists, was the Norwegian Henrik Ibsen (1828–1906). Ibsen's early poetic drama *Peer Gynt,* for which Edvard Grieg later wrote the incidental music, is romantic and allegorical rather than realistic. Peer is a worthless rascal who spends his life running away from reality and chasing ephemeral goals. At last, old and weary of wandering, he returns to Norway where he meets the Button Molder (Death), who informs him that he is about to be melted down like an ill-cast button and made over into someone else. Peer is temporarily saved from this ignominious fate by the redeeming love of a peasant girl, Solveig. This play seems to point to the author's hope for a regenerated Norway.

Ibsen's prose dramas concern defects in middle-class life and morality. These "pillars of society" are interested only in feathering their own nests at the expense of the public good. Dr. Stockmann, the main character in *An Enemy of the People,* is somewhat like the author, a man who steadfastly refuses to compromise with the truth as he sees it. The town has become famous and wealthy as a health resort when Dr. Stockmann discovers that the water supply is contaminated. He stands alone against the entire town ("the confounded, compact, liberal majority"); hence he is dubbed an "enemy of the people." Although ostracized, he decides not to run away but to stay and become the teacher of the poor. The essential problem is the conflict between material and spiritual values, a problem pertinent to every age. The play also points up the acquisitive standards of the mercantile middle class.

*Pillars of Society* reveals the rottenness and hypocrisy of community leaders and establishes the thesis that the real pillars of society are freedom and truth. In *A Doll's House* a woman leaves her husband when it might be argued that she should not have done so, and in *Ghosts* the wife remains with her husband when she has just cause to leave him. Ibsen was severely criticized for bringing the subject of venereal disease into the open in this play.

The themes of all Ibsen's plays are universal: the individual versus society, the true versus the false, reality versus make-believe. Although he was a moralizer, most of his plays are stage-worthy today.

**Russia.** The great period of Russian literature began during the reign of Czar Nicholas I (1825–1855). Frightened by the Decembrist revolt (1826), the Czar determined to crush all liberalism. His autocratic and corrupt bureaucracy exacted mute obedience from peasants and minority groups. Literature and even opera scores were strictly censored. The reaction of writers to all this was exactly opposite to the Czar's intention. They became strongly realistic in their representation of life and zealous in exposing social and political wrongs. Their moral anxiety sometimes shows itself in despondency and sometimes in idealistic aspirations for Russia's future.

Writers divided into the same two groups we have already noted among the musicians. The "Westernizers" hoped that Russia would lead the world in a social revolution without the bourgeois regimes and parliamentarianism which were plaguing the West. The Slavophiles believed that traditional ways of life and customs should be preserved. Both groups criticized serfdom and autocratic abuses. During this whole period Russia produced some greatly talented writers. These men loved their country, and although most of them came from the ranks of the aristocrats, they championed the cause of the oppressed peasants. With their artistic sensitivity they were keenly aware of social injustice, and their frustration often led them to a morbid fatalism. At the same time they were more concerned with moral and

ethical problems than were the French writers of this same period.
*Gogol.* First of the great novelists was Nicolai Gogol (1809–1852), who came from an aristocratic Ukrainian family. His prose is usually a mixture of fantasy and reality. His first works were fantastic tales filled with folklore, devils, and ghosts, depicted with lighthearted humor. In *The Overcoat* he turned to the use of humor as a satiric weapon against universal injustice. It is a semifantastic tale of an insignificant little man whose ghost comes back to exact justice from the "Very Important Person" who had wronged him. Dostoevsky maintained that the whole tradition of Russian prose stemmed from *The Overcoat.*

The *Inspector General* is a riotous comedy based on mistaken identity. The corrupt mayor and officials of a small provincial town are anxiously awaiting the arrival of an inspector from St. Petersburg, who they know is coming incognito. They all mistake a young scoundrel for the inspector. The scoundrel exploits their confusion, takes bribes to cover up their dishonesty, becomes engaged to the mayor's daughter, and goes off with his ill-gotten gains. Then the real inspector arrives. The play is a *tour de force* on the subject of bribery. Indeed from the lowest citizen to the highest official, everybody seems to be swindling everybody else. The play was received with such enthusiasm as a social satire that Gogol found it expedient to leave Russia.

Gogol's masterwork is *Dead Souls,* a novel about a swindler who buys up dead serfs in order to gain social standing. In late life Gogol turned to religious meditation and was induced to burn his manuscripts. He was not a revolutionist, although later he was hailed as one; he rather sought reformation of each corrupt individual.

*Turgenev.* Ivan Turgenev (1818–1883) is the writer most revered by the West because he approached closest to Western European style. Turgenev consciously promoted Russian culture abroad, and was a friend of Flaubert, Zola, and Henry James. Like Chekhov, he was a refined craftsman, opposed to the naturalness of popular speech, and better at character analysis than at plot. Turgenev believed in the emancipation of women, and in general his women characters are the strongest.

Turgenev's novel *Fathers and Sons* is concerned with the universal conflict between the older and the younger generation. So great was the impact of the novel that all Russia was divided between those who favored the old autocratic regime and those who favored the new social order. Turgenev is thought to have coined the word *nihilist* to describe the young nonconformists. Read his weird fantasy called *Phantoms* and you will see his morbid preoccupation with doom and futility. He seems to be saying that life is always vanquished by annihilation; that youth and love, no matter how beautiful, are only vain phantoms.

*Dostoevsky.* Feodor Dostoevsky (1822–1881) has been called by some critics the world's greatest novelist, and yet he was unknown to English-speaking readers until *Crime and Punishment* was translated in 1885. He pleaded for the little man in conflict with ruthless masters, but his larger problem was man's whole condition on earth; man eternally searching for God, harmony, and truth; man who can find salvation and purification only through suffering. This is the theme of the powerful but depressing novel, *Crime and Punishment.*

Most critics would say that *The Brothers Karamazov* is Dostoevsky's most ambitious achievement, for psychological penetration, variety of characters, and intellectual subtlety. This novel is a morbid tale of suffering, crime, insanity, and cruelty. In the course of the story, the main character, Ivan, tells a fantastic tale of how Jesus came back to earth at the time of the Spanish Inquisition and was condemned by the Grand Inquisitor for offering man freedom of choice in knowledge of good and evil, because the ordinary man wants only bread and an authority to direct his actions. The Inquisitor would correct Christ's mistakes and lead man into a comfortable existence where he would even be allowed to sin so long as he obeyed his leaders.

Here we see the blueprint of the coming Communist and Fascist states. In fact, Dostoevsky in his late life went through a complete reversal of his early concepts and became a defender of autocracy and the old Orthodox Church. It is no wonder that the civil and religious leaders did not know what to make of him; and modern critics don't seem to know what to make of him, either. Read "The Christmas Tree and the Wedding," and you will see what Dostoevsky thinks about the ethics of the ordinary man.

*Tolstoi.* Leo Tolstoi (1828–1910) was a more optimistic writer than Dostoevsky. He was an aristocrat, but, orphaned at an early age, he floundered about trying to find some meaning in life. After the Crimean War he found a goal—the education of the peasants. As a disciple of Rousseau, he believed in the goodness of the common man and decried the materialism of Western civilization. These ideas led him to a concept of religion in which "there is no God other than the moral law inside man [conscience]" and a concept of history in which elemental forces and Divine Providence rather than the efforts of great leaders are shaping factors. These ideas were not fully worked out until late in Tolstoi's life, but we can see them taking shape in his two greatest novels, *War and Peace* and *Anna Karenina.*

*War and Peace* is a four-volume story woven around the lives of four families against a background of Russian history in the early nineteenth century. Individually the characters are convincing. One feels that, given similar vicissitudes, they would react in the same way in any other country at any other time. In the "war" passages, Tolstoi gives detailed accounts of several battles, the occupation of Moscow by Napoleon's forces, and the disastrous French retreat from Russia. He satirizes Napoleon and the officers and treats the common soldiers sympathetically.

*Anna Karenina,* with its definite plot, is more dramatic and more tragic than *War and Peace.* It recounts the destruction a woman brings upon herself and others because she is dominated by her emotions rather than moral principles. Anna leaves her husband and runs away with a dashing officer. She is deserted by her friends, and when the officer loses interest in her she commits suicide. The book has been called the most powerful novel of its period. In Tolstoi's short story "God Sees the Truth, but Waits," an innocent traveler is arrested for a crime, convicted, and sent to Siberia. After many years in a labor camp, where he shows kindness to fellow prisoners, the real criminal confronts him and confesses. The theme is in the title.

*Chekhov.* Anton Chekhov (1860–1904) was primarily a writer of short stories and plays. The grandson of a serf, he was interested in the commonplace man or woman who leads a dull, meaningless existence. But as with Gogol, his delicate sense of humor tended to alleviate the tragedy of the life situations that he portrayed. His drama *The Cherry Orchard* is about the decayed aristocracy who realize that their day of glory is over, but are powerless to do anything about it. Their decadence contrasts with the crude but businesslike ex-serf representing the new social order, who ruthlessly buys up the land and cuts down the cherry trees which were the status symbol of the aristocratic owner and represented what she and her family held dear.

Many of Chekhov's stories, for example "The Darling," are more in the nature of character sketches than real short stories. Chekhov made a kind of impressionistic use of understatement which requires us to search for his meaning after we have finished a story. He was an excellent interpreter of his people and time.

**England.** When the young Queen Victoria came to the throne of England in 1837, the Industrial Revolution had already started. The upper middle class profited most from the rapid expansion of industry and commerce. They built drab houses filled with horsehair furniture, decorated with what-nots and useless bric-a-brac. The industrial barons found their way into politics, and soon industry was setting the styles, guiding the policies, and furnishing the philosophy of the era. Progress meant business progress, and its evidence was the accumulation of material possessions. The result was a materialistic, utilitarian philosophy which measured everything by its practical use. Some writers defended this philosophy and some were outspoken against it.

*Thackeray.* William Makepeace Thackeray (1811–1863) was neither an apologist for nor a critic of industrial civilization. He was content simply to picture its effects on his characters. In all his novels he waged an unremitting war on hypocrisy and sham. His uncompromising realism serves to reveal Victorian smugness and satisfaction with material progress. When his first novel, *Vanity Fair*, came out in 1847, he was feted by the same fashionable society which he satirized in the novel. Becky Sharp, the heroine, is the original "gold digger" in literature, a girl who continually tries to wrest from the social world the position and wealth she craves. She fails because in Thackeray's view life does not reward selfishness and deceit.

Thackeray's masterpiece is usually considered to be *The History of Henry Esmond*, an historical novel of the eighteenth century involving one of the Stuart plots to regain the English throne. In Beatrix, Thackeray created a character as real and as unpredictable as life itself. When she spurns Henry's love and runs off with the Pretender, thereby ruining his chances to the English throne, Henry repudiates him, marries Beatrix' mother, and brings her to America. The sequel novel, *The Virginians*, continues the story of the family in Revolutionary America. Thackeray's other well-known novel, *The History of Pendennis*, is largely autobiographical.

*Dickens.* The most successful assault upon the complacency of the Victorian era was made, in the name of simple human decency and fairness, by Charles Dickens (1812–1870). The hundreds of characters in Dickens' novels are more alive and vivid than the real people were who walked the streets of London. With the exception of Shakespeare there is probably no greater example of creative force in English literature. Dickens has left a legacy of human comedy (and tragedy) more vast and irreplaceable than Balzac's.

Dickens wrote about the life he knew. He had suffered the privations and humiliations of dire poverty; his father, the model for Mr. Micawber, had been sent to a debtor's prison; he himself had worked in a factory potting and labeling shoe blacking.

Many of the incidents in the early life of David Copperfield are autobiographical. And yet Dickens never indulged in resentment or self-pity. Today he is criticized for being sentimental. However, the Victorians liked sentimentality. His characters are termed caricatures, but in order to caricature it is first necessary to create character. Dickens was always interested in exposing oppression and injustice, and if this crusading spirit sometimes got the upper hand over the artist, we must forgive him. In spite of all his faults, his stories will live because of their vitality, their humor, and their variety. Regardless of how evil a character is painted, Dickens finds some vestige of good in him. Nevertheless, the author's hatred of cruelty and meanness and his pity for the downtrodden produced some of the bitterest satire in English.

In the twenty or more novels and stories which Dickens wrote there is something for every taste. In *Oliver Twist* he shows the life of the poorhouse and the criminals; in *Bleak House* the agonizing delays of the law; in *Little Dorrit* the suffering of those consigned to debtor's prison; in *Nicholas Nickleby* the brutality and ignorance of schoolmasters; in *David Copperfield* the struggles of the self-supporting child. Many of these abuses have been rectified today, but we still read the novels for their inimitable characterizations. If you do not care to read about suffering, *A Tale of Two Cities* has an excellent plot centered on the physical resemblance of Charles Darnay to Sidney Carton, both of whom are in love with the same girl. To many people this story gives the essence of the French Revolution. Another novel with a suspenseful plot is *Great Expectations*. The hero Pip goes through the fire of many illusions to emerge a mature individual. All this simply proves that a great work of art is not great because of its subject matter, but it is great because of what a great artist does with it.

*The Brownings.* The beautiful and true love story of Elizabeth Barrett (1806–1861) and Robert Browning (1812–1899) has been told so often in the movies and on the stage that we tend to forget that they were real people and great poets. Elizabeth Barrett was a famous poet before they met and before Robert had published anything. In fact, it was a volume of her poetry which brought them together. Her "Cry of the Children," a passionate appeal on behalf of child laborers in mines and factories, was influential in securing laws for their protection. But she is remembered today for her series of sonnets written during Robert's courtship. Read the sonnet beginning, "How do I love thee?"

No other poet ever attained such a vogue during his lifetime as did Robert Browning. His great interest in personality encouraged him to attempt drama, but his ability at character analysis led to the creation of a new form of poetry, the dramatic monologue, in which the speaker addresses a listener whose responses must be imagined. Now that you know some of the paintings of Fra Filippo Lippi and Andrea del Sarto, read these two companion monologues and see how Browning has interpreted the character of each.

*Tennyson.* The writer who perhaps best synthesizes the entire Victorian era is Alfred, Lord Tennyson (1809–1892). Tennyson realized the importance of industry, but he deplored its vulgarity. Like Dickens, he hated cruelty, and like Thackeray and Browning, he was revolted by materialism. He felt, too, that science had called into question old religious dogmas. He protested against the artist who kept himself apart from life. Tennyson was not a seer and we do not turn to him for prophetic utterance; his was a troubled, sensitive soul, whose lyrical gift never deserted him. Read his poem "Ulysses," in which the ancient Trojan hero represents the spirit of progress.

You no doubt had the *Idylls of the King* thrust at you in high school. Probably you thought the King Arthur stories "old hat" in the modern period. Are you sure? King Arthur was defeated by flaws of character, greed, and selfishness, which are as prevalent today as they ever were. In Arthur's kingdom Tennyson depicted an ideal government designed for the people's good. And into the mouth of the dying Arthur he put a challenge to build a new and better world.

**America.** In the mid-nineteenth century, American literature was largely New England literature. Its major writers espoused not a philosophy but a doctrine, or point of view, which they called Transcendentalism. The period during and after the Civil War was one of Romântic Realism in fiction and poetry.

*Emerson and Thoreau.* The best-known exponents of Transcendentalism were Ralph Waldo Emerson (1803–1882) and Henry David Thoreau (1817–1862). Emerson's small book *Nature* (1836) became the Bible of the movement, whose main theses were the following: God reveals Himself everywhere at all times here and now. Historical Christianity shuts out God now. Nature is the revelation of God, matter a manifestation of spirit. Man beholds spirit in nature through intuition, which is higher than understanding. Communion with nature as spirit can redeem man through his spiritual affinities, which are more direct and effective than the ritual of priests and churches.

This eclectic doctrine seems to have taken elements from the

German Idealistic philosophers, especially Kant, as interpreted by Coleridge and Carlyle; from Neoplatonism; and from Oriental mysticism. At first sight, Transcendentalism seems utterly remote from Realism, but actually it is not, because it represents the New Englander's final break with the stranglehold of Puritanism's narrow and exclusive dogma, and also with Calvinism and Unitarianism. Emerson himself was a Unitarian minister, but he left the Church because he could not conscientiously administer the sacraments. Thereafter he supported himself by writing and lecturing. Probably his most famous essay is the one on "Self-Reliance": "To believe your own thought, to believe that what is true for you in your private heart, is true for all men—that is genius." Emerson wrote some good, if not great, poetry. "The Rhodora" (a plant of the azalea family) contains the lines:

> *If eyes were made for seeing*
> *Then beauty is its own excuse for being.*

"Threnody" is a gentle elegy to his son Waldo. The "Concord Hymn" memorializes the battle of Concord and contains the lines:

> *Here once the embattled farmers stood,*
> *And fired the shot heard round the world.*

In later life, Emerson became more liberal and tolerant, and was generally accepted as a "Great American." He was not eminent in talent or originality, but he was great in sympathy and sincerity.

Thoreau, early friend and disciple of Emerson, was also a Transcendentalist, and he was a greater writer than Emerson. When he died, he left thirty-nine volumes of manuscript journals from which he had refined his literary works. Thoreau was a more rugged individualist than Emerson. He tried schoolteaching but resigned because he was expected to flog the students; he spent a night in jail rather than pay a poll tax. Eventually he became a surveyor because he could be alone and close to nature. Once he built a fire to cook some fish he had caught. The fire spread and consumed a hundred acres. The townspeople were furious because of the destruction of property; Thoreau was unhappy because he had destroyed the trees. Every American should read *Walden*, which describes the two years he spent in the cabin he built on Walden Pond in Emerson's woods in order to find out basically how best to spend his life. He wanted to escape not the company of men but the oppression of institutions which he believed were beneath the absolute morality of the individual.

His basic conclusion in *Walden* is that the man who simplifies his life will find that the "higher laws" begin to operate when convention and superficiality cease. His essay on "Civil Disobedience" is one of the world's classic treatises on political justice.

*Stowe.* Suddenly, in 1852, the slavery question that had been hovering on the threshold of American consciousness burst into the open with the publication of Harriet Beecher Stowe's *Uncle Tom's Cabin,* which became an immediate best seller. Within a year hundreds of thousands of copies had been sold, and it had been translated into twenty languages. The work had tremendous sentimental appeal for not very critical readers. The characters are exaggerated types; the plot is a succession of improbable coincidences; most of the scenes are melodramatic. Nonetheless, it aroused the moral indignation of the North; stiffened the defense of slavery in the South; and contributed the characters of Uncle Tom, Little Eva, Topsy, and Simon Legree to American folklore. The work takes on added significance in the light of the modern racial crisis.

*Melville and Whitman.* In the crucial decade before the Civil War when the intellectual hegemony of the Atlantic seaboard was breaking down, appeared two literary geniuses, perhaps greater than any others this nation has produced: Herman Melville (1819–1891) and Walt Whitman (1819–1892). Both were born in the same year in New York; both came of New England ancestry on the father's side and Dutch ancestry on the mother's side; and they died within six months of each other. Both men dreamed of an ideal American who would be "natural," that is, free from puritanical restraints and free from the materialism that made the acquisition of property and wealth the sole aim in life. Both men believed in brotherhood not only among men but among all the creations of God.

MELVILLE. Some of Melville's ancestors had been seafaring men, and so when financial reverses overtook his family he went to sea. For about five years he wandered over the seven seas as a whaler, mutineer, prisoner, inhabitant of cannibal islands, sailor in the United States Navy. He returned with material enough to inspire some fifteen volumes, but of them all *Moby Dick* is his masterpiece. You can read *Moby Dick* for the thrilling adventure story that it is, and also for its symbolic meaning. Possibly you will want to skip certain chapters about the techniques of the whaling industry, which keep the action from proceeding too rapidly. John Huston made an excellent movie version of the story.

Briefly, *Moby Dick* is the epic struggle of man against the brute strength of the whale. Ahab, the protagonist, is like the Biblical Ahab who, because he worshiped false gods and stole Naboth's vineyard, was slain in battle and his blood was licked by dogs. This Ahab too worships a false god, the god of revenge, because the whale Moby Dick had, on a previous voyage, sheared off his leg. From the point when Ahab swears on the quarter deck to hunt the whale to the death, we are assured of the final catastrophe. He throws away his pipe (comfort), and his quadrant (science); defies the lightning; and forges his harpoon in blood, baptizing it in the name of the devil.

Ishmael in the Bible was an outcast and a wanderer. In the story Ishmael is the narrator, Melville himself. Only he has the intelligence to oppose the search. He grows in respect for humanity, human dignity, and tolerance. He is the only one on the *Pequod* who is saved. The whale is the personification of evil. Early in the book, in Father Mapple's sermon, the author says: "If we obey God, we must disobey ourselves; and it is in this disobeying ourselves wherein the hardness of obeying God consists." The events of the book bear out the truth of the statement. Melville himself wrote to Hawthorne: "I have written a wicked book." Do you think that it is?

WHITMAN. Whitman had about five years of formal schooling and spent a great deal of time rambling, loafing, and reading. He worked for a time as a journalist; then when he was twenty-nine he took a trip down the Ohio and Mississippi to New Orleans and returned by way of the Great Lakes and the Hudson. He came back full of the greatness of America and her people.

You have no doubt read in school Whitman's poem, "O Captain, My Captain," written on the death of Lincoln, and perhaps you have sung the beautiful arrangement of "I Hear America Singing," but these are simple poems written for popular taste. Now it is time to penetrate the more deeply philosophical *Leaves of Grass*.

The first edition of *Leaves of Grass*, which came out in 1855, contained twelve poems, and from that time on the book grew with the poet, each edition showing the added maturity of his personality and the influence of changing conditions. For instance, the fifth edition (1872) contains the poems on the Civil War. The seventh edition of 1881 is the definitive one.

*Leaves of Grass* is not easy reading (great poetry seldom is). Here are just a few keys to Whitman's symbolism. His "I" in the poems means body and soul fused into an *identity*, a *Shape*. As the poet is the *Shape* of the American, America is the *Shape* of democracy, and democracy is the *Shape* of all humanity. *Grass* is a symbol of life and also a symbol of democracy. *Lilacs* are a symbol of *love*, and *stars* stand for individual existences. The *Shape* of the poet is also fused with all nature. *Nature* in America is so large that without a corresponding largeness and generosity in man, the country would be monstrous. Just as past, present, and future are fused into an identity or *Shape*, so birth, love, and death are fused. Hence death is a purifier and renewer of life. The human form is so great that it must never be made ridiculous. All that a person does or thinks is of consequence and never dies. Hence an individual is as superb as a nation when he has the qualities which make the nation superb.

With these helps, read "Out of the Cradle Endlessly Rocking," "There Was a Child Went Forth," and "Grass." If you cannot grasp his meaning, just enjoy the beauty of the lines. Whitman's best work has become the common property of Western civilization, and there is hardly a modern poet—American or European —who is not in his debt.

*James.* Henry James (1843–1916) repudiated his Puritan heritage and the growing Philistinism of New York and went to London, eventually becoming an English citizen. He was well-equipped to be the first cosmopolitan novelist, but he could not escape Philistinism because it was pervasive in both London and Paris. In Paris Turgenev introduced him to Flaubert, Zola, and Maupassant. Turgenev also taught him that character was more important than plot.

James found the English novel only a tale. He changed it to a subtle and profound analysis of developing character. It is almost amusing that James, who went abroad to escape Puritanism, should have taken it right along with him. In his two best novels, *The Portrait of a Lady* (1881) and *The Ambassadors* (1903), the main characters reject personal happiness to return to their self-chosen "duty." So the true American doctrines of individual freedom, moral purpose, and the capacity for human betterment prevail.

# Chapter 12 / The Modern Period

*New occasions teach new duties,*
*Time makes ancient good uncouth;*
*They must upward still and onward*
*Who would keep abreast of truth.*
James Russell Lowell, 1845

As we have seen, the arts arise out of the life and thoughts of man and they depend on man for acceptance or rejection. Only the best which earlier eras produced has survived, while a far larger share has been measured by time, found wanting, and consigned to the rubbish. That elimination process is going on all the time, and it will take care of much that has been produced in the twentieth century. In the meantime it is unfair to make a sweeping condemnation of all modern art, music, and literature.

A sensitive critic is just as capable of discerning a fine work of art today as he would be if he were living fifty years hence, but as to whether the work of art is *valid* fifty years hence will depend in no small measure on the trend of our whole civilization. The world moves ever more rapidly. Styles emerge, mature, disintegrate, and merge into something else before we have had time to assimilate them. This makes for confusion and frustration. We should not be misled by charlatanism such as "Auto-Beatnik" poetry written by an electronic computer, a collage made out of a kitchen sink, or a musical composition determined by throws of dice. These are only efforts to avoid making decisions. We are living in a very creative period, and right here and now somebody is painting the pictures, composing the music, writing the poetry, dramas, and novels which will point the direction which the arts will take in the twenty-first century. Romanticism and Realism were very strong movements, and just as always happened before, modern art forms have arisen as a protest. A clean break with the past was necessary, and a fresh start along new lines.

Edward T. Cone, a progressive but sound musician, has this to say: "When chance is invoked as an element of construction, logic is largely inoperative. A work of art ought to imply the standards by which it demands to be judged."[1] Just so. Fundamental artistic principles such as unity, order, balance, coherence, harmony between matter and means of expression, personal and articulate meaning—these principles have been embedded in man's physical and psychological make-up for hundreds, perhaps thousands, of years, and no art work which ignores them can hope to endure. We must believe that serious artists will eventually find their way to new and vital art forms.

## Impressionism and Symbolism

A movement which arose around 1863 in France developed into Impressionism when applied to painting and music, and as Symbolism when applied to literature. The movement arose as a reaction to the specific character of realistic art and aimed to portray the effects of experience upon the consciousness of the artist and audience rather than the objective characteristics of things or events. Painters were more concerned with the technique of suggesting light and color than with subject matter. Composers were more interested in the shifting atmosphere of the sea or clouds than in an integrated musical structure, and poets spoke in clustered images and metaphors suggesting vague or obscure meanings. Such poetry exerted some effect on the stream-of-consciousness technique in the twentieth century.

Impressionism is thoroughly French; no other temperament could have created it. It is Romanticism carried to the final degree, but it led down a blind alley and ended, because it could not evolve.

**Painting.** In 1863 when Manet was being castigated for his "Luncheon on the Grass," displayed in the *Salon des Refusés* (see p. 259), his artist friends gathered about him for moral support. These men found they had much in common. They were verifying and extending the effects of brilliant sunlight in breaking up color, which Delacroix had already discovered. They also went back to painters like Frans Hals and Velásquez and found that their details of such things as lace and embroidery were not actually depicted but only suggested, thereby forcing the observer to re-create the experience of the artist and to supply in imagination the missing details. Perhaps the gravest fault with their technique is that painting only what the eye records in a casual glance seldom reveals character, but their use of glowing color was handed down to the moderns as an accomplished fact.

---

[1] In *Problems of Modern Music,* ed. Paul Henry Lang (New York: W. W. Norton & Company, 1962).

CLAUDE MONET: *Japanese Footbridge and Water Lily Pool.* Collection of Mrs. Albert D. Lasker, New York. (Courtesy French Reproduction Rights, 1966)

By 1874 these artists were calling themselves "Impressionists," a term taken from a composition by Monet called "Impression: Rising Sun." Leaders of the movement were Claude Monet (1840–1926), who concentrated on landscapes depicting sunlight playing on water (see above) or on the carved façade of a cathedral; Auguste Renoir (1841–1919), who liked to paint human figures, especially women, glowing with vitality and health; and Camille Pissarro (1830–1903), who was called the "Village Impressionist" because he painted peasant scenes.

Monet's canvases express the poetry of nature with amazing life and brilliance. Renoir applied his color in little hooked daubs which set the forms vibrating. By applying the paint directly to the canvas without underpainting or glazing, he gave his paintings spontaneity and unstudied naturalness. Georges Seurat

(1859–1891) carried the technique a step further by painting an entire composition out of tiny dots of pure color, suggesting mass and receding space by varying the intensity of the color. Critics called his technique *pointilism*. Seurat did not want to show movement but rather suspended animation as if all the figures had suddenly been stopped in their tracks. His most famous painting is "Sunday Afternoon at the Grande Jatte."

**Poetry.** While the painters were experimenting with the sensuous effects of pure color, Symbolist poets were concerning themselves with the suggestive quality of words. They tried to divorce themselves from rhyme, verse, strophe, strict rhythm, and even meaning so far as that was possible. The meaning is to be found *between* rather than *in* the lines. As you can see, all they have left is ephemeral and attenuated sound, which is the sphere of music. Hence the Symbolist poets go hand in hand with the Impressionistic composers. Read some poems of Paul Verlaine (1844–1896) and Stéphane Mallarmé (1842–1898).

**Music: Debussy.** Impressionistic music can be summed up in one composer: Claude Debussy (1862–1918). He invented it, perfected it, and finished it. Others tried, but could not capture the technique or atmosphere. The best imitations are probably "Nights in the Gardens of Spain" by Manuel De Falla and "Daphnis and Chloë" by Maurice Ravel.

How did Debussy get his effects? His programmatic titles do not suggest literal descriptions, but rather subjective moods awakened by these concepts. Elements that we have come to expect in music (melody, rhythm, and articulated formal structure) are discarded or made inapparent in favor of shifting harmony made up of chromatic and altered chords which merge but seldom resolve. This vibrating sound complex changes with the color of the instrumentation. Debussy used the whole tone scale or one of the medieval modal scales which sound to us unfamiliar and slightly exotic. The orchestra is large but muted; the strings are divided into many parts; woodwinds play outside their normal register; brasses are muted. If there are any straight edges or clear outlines left, they are blurred by harp glissandos. Debussy's most familiar compositions are *Clair de Lune* ("Moonlight"), based on a poem of Verlaine, and *L' Après-midi d'un Faun* ("Afternoon of a Faun") based on Mallarmé's poem of the same title.

### Paul Cézanne, the Lone Artist

Paul Cézanne (1839–1906) had for a time belonged to the Impressionist camp, but he was dissatisfied. He admired the way

VINCENT VAN GOGH: *The Starry Night*. Museum of Modern Art, New York. (Collection, The Museum of Modern Art, New York, acquired through the Lillie P. Bliss Bequest)

they painted "nature," but he felt that this was not enough. Where was the sense of order, harmonious design, perfect balance which old masters like Poussin had achieved? Cézanne wanted to realize the rich, unbroken tones that belong to nature without destroying the impression of depth. He went off by himself to southern France to wrestle with his problems of how to get intensity and architectonic form and still retain the vivid colors of nature. Study his Mont Sainte-Victoire landscapes and you will see that they are bathed in light and color, and yet they are firm and solid. Cézanne worked out many problems in his still lifes. He found that he could often get solidity and depth by ignoring conventional draftsmanship. He certainly did not realize that this indifference to "correct drawing" would start a landslide in modern art and earn for him the title of "Father of Modern Painting." Study "The Card Players" and "Boy in the Red Vest" and you will see that he has achieved solidity, color, and balanced design. But Cézanne was never satisfied; he kept struggling until the very day he died.

## Expressionism

The Expressionistic movement arose in Germany shortly before the turn of the twentieth century and invaded all fields of art. The Expressionists replaced a rational conception of nature or life with one based on nonrational and emotional concepts. The movement came about partly as a result of the Machine Age, which seemed to demand an entirely new artistic orientation. As opposed to terms like "vague," "fleeting," and "transitory," which we applied to French Impressionism, terms like "harsh," "brutal," "introspective," and "morbid" characterize the German Expressionistic style.

**Painting.** In painting Expressionism is characterized by the free distortion of form and color through which the painter gives visual form to inner sensations or emotions. These emotions often involve pathos, morbidity, violence, and tragedy. Since the movement lasted through the two world wars, it reflected the neurosis of defeat. Hitler condemned it as degenerate and had the works of many painters confiscated.

*Van Gogh.* Like Cézanne, Vincent Van Gogh (1853–1890), another strange, tormented genius, criticized the Impressionists for their shallowness and lack of emotional commitment. Although Van Gogh's best paintings were done in the south of France, we must remember that he was not a Frenchman but a Hollander, an artist with northern blood in his veins. In the strong sunlight of Provence, Van Gogh poured out his turbulent spirit in strong color and writhing forms. But even as he approached insanity the artist in him was always in control. We know from sketches and letters to his brother that he spent months organizing his painting "The Starry Night" (see p. 289). He probably never heard of Expressionism, but his violence and subjective attitude are expressionistic.

*German Expressionists.* About 1905, there were two organized German groups of painters: one in Dresden called *Die Brücke* (The Bridge), and the other in Munich called *Der Blaue Reiter* (The Blue Rider). All these men were rebels against the dullness and sentimentality of German academic painting. Their interest in bold woodcuts came from their own medieval Gothic inheritance, Grünewald, and Dürer. Other influences were primitive South Seas art and African tribal masks.

Ernst Ludwig Kirchner (1880–1938) wanted to express emotion and experience with large, simple forms and clear colors. His canvas "The Street" (see p. 291) represents the emotional state of a German city following World War I. The "soul-sickness of

ERNST KIRCHNER: *The Street*. Museum of Modern Art, New York.
(Collection, The Museum of Modern Art, New York)

defeat" is everywhere apparent. The witchlike figures wearing
clothes that were once fashionable, the unearthly flesh tones, the
toy taxi—all contribute to an effect of ominous foreboding. The
black lines give the painting the effect of a woodcut.

Emil Nolde (1867–1956) built up his designs with blotches of strong color: yellow-orange, blue-green, and red-violet, the ugliest colors a painter can use. He said that he portrayed depravity "in order to show that God's unfathomable wisdom is present even in dereliction." See "Christ and the Children" and "St. Simeon and the Women." Notice how much the faces look like masks.

*Kokoschka.* Oskar Kokoschka (1886–    ), a teacher in the Vienna School of Arts and Crafts, in 1908 began to produce paintings so radical that he lost his job. He almost starved and later was wounded in World War I but kept on painting. Recognition came to him in 1924, but in 1938 Hitler declared his painting degenerate and had more than four hundred of his canvases burned. He fled to England. "The Tempest" represents two people, protective male and trusting female, being whirled about in a stormy sky. The figures are twisted and deformed, but the love and goodness they show on their faces are a refuge from evil.

*American Expressionists.* George Grosz came to the United States from Germany in 1932. His "I Was Always Present" shows hatred and greed as a ravenous skeleton riding a mad horse through the flames of war. Other American Expressionists are Max Weber (1881–1961) and Ivan Albright (1897–    ). Weber's colors are usually dark and rich, his forms distorted as in "Tranquility." Albright's pictures, for example "Into the World There Came a Soul Named Ida," usually imply social indictment and often seem brutal and vulgar. Albright made surgical drawings in World War I, and he paints with the same exactitude.

**Music.** Expressionistic music goes hand in hand with painting in that both tend to ignore or cover up rational structural relationships. You will recall the battle over equal temperament which took place in the late Renaissance (see p. 145). Once this was settled, until the twentieth century all serious composers wrote within the tonal framework. But the tonic-dominant relationship, upon which all tonal music is based, brought with it chromaticism, which was increasingly exploited by post-Romantic composers and Impressionists. Debussy did not hesitate to introduce chords which were unrelated to the old harmonic system and foreign to the key. In fact, this is what makes his music seem to wander around without a sense of key, which, of course, was exactly his intention.

*Stravinsky.* At the turn of the century, we find composers complaining of the "slavery" of the tonic-dominant relationship and experimenting with bitonality and polytonality. Then in 1913 came the explosion which rocked musical Paris: the first performance of Igor Stravinsky's (1882–1971) *Le Sacre du Printemps* ("Rite of Spring"), which had for its subject the ancient fertility rites of Russia. It was not the superb choreography by Diaghilev nor Nijinsky's dancing, but Stravinsky's musical score (filled with strange colors, distorted lines of sound, superimposed rhythms, and bursts of cacophony) which excited and enraged the audience. Both critics and audience called it a blasphemous attempt to destroy music as an art. Pandemonium reigned in the theater, and at least one duel was fought as a result.

Although *Le Sacre* seemed defiantly indifferent to tradition and heritage, using polyrhythms, polytonal harmony, and unhackneyed instrumental combinations, its purpose was not to shock. Its setting in pagan Russia called for an atmosphere by turns coldly mystic and calculatingly savage. The score does have logic and coherence, and even scraps of repeated melody. It does not completely abandon tonality, but it paves the way for Schönberg to do so later. After fifty years it no longer shocks; indeed it will probably remain as one of the masterpieces of this century.

*Schönberg and the Twelve-Tone Row.* In the period following World War I, music seemed to have lost faith in its tonal roots and to demand some other method of securing coherence. A piece of music must be unified in some way if it is to have validity, and if key feeling is thrown out, what then? The Viennese composer Arnold Schönberg (1874–1951) meditated long on this problem, and finally came up with a solution: the *twelve-tone row,* or so-called "serial" technique. We shall give here a brief explanation of this system.

First, in the old tonal system, certain tones in the diatonic scale had preferential treatment: that is, the first (tonic), the fifth (dominant), the fourth (subdominant), and the third (mediant) were the stable tones of the scale. The other tones of the scale, together with the chromatic tones between them, create tension because they want to move toward 1, 5, 4, or 3. In the twelve-tone row, all of the twelve half-tones of the scale are equal in importance, and no note has the power to attract any other note. Before he begins, the composer sets up an arbitrary sequence of these twelve tones. He can use this sequence horizontally (melodically), vertically (harmonically); he can invert it; he can use it backwards; or he can invert it backwards. He can begin on any tone of the row, but he cannot change the sequence once set up. None of the twelve tones which make up the row may be repeated until all the eleven others have been heard. The function of the row is to establish order or unity in the composition, because the listener (hopefully) perceives the sequence and follows it. Mathematically, this system gives the composer forty-eight different ways of using the row without affecting the fundamental unity of the musical discourse. Schönberg also rejected the huge orchestral apparatus of the Romantic period in favor of a small, so-called chamber orchestra, and he favored a return to a texture based on counterpoint rather than on vertical chords.

Neither Schönberg nor either of his pupils, Alban Berg (1885–1935) and Anton Webern (1883–1945), seems to have been resourceful enough really to make music out of serialism. Their music is a dialectic rather than an art. Later, however, the Frenchman Pierre Boulez (1925–    ) and the Italian Luigi Dallapiccola (1904–    ) were able to create music out of the twelve-tone row. It is worth while for the student to hear either the *Marteau sans Maitre* ("Hammer without a Master") by Boulez or Dallapiccola's *Variations for Orchestra,* first performed in 1954. Stravinsky and Aaron Copland have also composed successfully in serial technique.

If some student is searching for an esoteric topic for a term paper, here it is: "What is the connection, if any, between the stream-of-consciousness novel and the twelve-tone row in music?" In 1951, Dallapiccola wrote: "My progress along the route of the twelve-tone system is a rather strange and a very long progress. Outside the works of Schönberg, Berg, and Webern, I have received very extraordinary explanations, exactly in the twelve-tone domain, through the literature of Proust and James Joyce. Such a declaration, strange as it may seem, should lead us to the conclusion that the arts, in a specific moment of history, have a common problem. If I were competent in painting, I am sure that even in this art I could find very striking analogies with twelve-tone music." [1]

Dallapiccola avoids the angular leaps which create painful tensions and somber colors typical of the Viennese Expressionists. True to his Italian heritage, he prefers a luminous aura with a climate of fervor, faith, and enthusiasm.

Boulez in his "Hammer without a Master" uses the twelve-tone row both horizontally and vertically. In addition, he uses rhythmic series, dynamic series, and a serial distribution of timbres or densities. The work is scored for flute, viola, vibraphone, xylorimba, guitar, and percussion. A contralto singer connects the sections, each of which is scored for a different combination. Rarely does he use all the instruments at the same time.

**Literature.** Expressionistic literature was influenced by the

---

[1] In London *Music Survey,* October, 1951.

plays of August Strindberg (1849–1912), a brilliant but erotic Swedish dramatist, whose fantastic and perverted "dream plays" were popular in Germany. The German movement was at its height after World War I. It attempted to express the sordid reality of society rather than its superficially attractive exterior. Under the influence of Dostoevsky, Freud, and to a certain extent Marxian socialism, it relied on distortion, dynamism, and the cryptically baffling to make its powerful appeal. The German Expressionists tend to de-emphasize the individual and to obliterate individual character. The protagonist is often an amorphous mass of humanity submerged in brooding pessimism, or in sinister forces in nature, or crushed by machines. In Gerhart Hauptmann's play *The Weavers* (1892), the people destroy the machines, but their plight is thereby worsened rather than improved. The author, however, seems to approve the action of the workers. In Ernst Toller's play *The Machine Wreckers* (1922), the author blames the corrupt and callous bosses rather than the machines themselves. Many of the best Expressionistic writers forsook the movement for a less iconoclastic attitude toward life. While predominantly north European, the movement found disciples elsewhere such as the Irish novelist James Joyce, the English poet T. S. Eliot, and the American dramatist Eugene O'Neill, whose *Hairy Ape* (1922) and *Great God Brown* (1925) are expressionistic.

*Capek.* The only play on the theme of the crushing of individuals by machines still enjoyed by English-speaking audiences is *R.U.R.* by Karel Capek (1890–1938), a Czech who was zealous in trying to win freedom for his country. The initials stand for "Rossum's Universal Robots," a firm that manufactures mechanical automatons to replace human laborers. The play, a fantasy with a happy ending, gave the word *robot* to our language. The author believed that machines must be controlled or they will master mankind. The play was probably the inspiration for Huxley's *Brave New World* and Orwell's *Nineteen Eighty-Four*.

*Wedekind.* Frank Wedekind (1864–1918) was obsessed with sex, which he personified as a primitive life force (*Erdgeist*), always waiting to destroy men through wiles. His play *Pandora's Box* is clearly based on Turgenev's *Phantoms*, but where the Russian touched his subject lightly, even ethereally, the German play is brutal and sordid. *Frühlings Erwacken* ("Awakening of Spring"), which is considered Wedekind's masterpiece, deals with the harm of keeping sexual information from adolescents.

*Werfel.* Franz Werfel (1890–1954), an Austrian-Czech whose tender novel *Song of Bernadette* you have perhaps read, wrote

Expressionistic dramas in the 1920's. One of them called *Bock-gesang* ("Goat Song") has the consequences of Dionysiac passion for its theme. The play is gruesome in the extreme. Werfel ardently believed in human brotherhood, a theme charmingly portrayed in his farcical comedy *Jacobowsky and the Colonel* (1944), which you should read for pure enjoyment (see p. 346).

## Modern Painting

In the art epochs of the past we have always found a certain homogeneity of style among artists of a certain period and a certain "school" which has enabled us to "relate" an unknown work to similar known works of a given time and place, and to interpret or judge a work of art against its stylistic background. Today there are so many different techniques and styles that the viewer is sometimes left confused and baffled.

However, no matter what may be your attitude toward modern art, you must admit that it is exciting. It may excite you to violent antipathy or to extravagant praise, but if you are at all perceptive, it never leaves you cold. It is tremendously alive, dynamic, forceful.

**Abstract Art.** The techniques of representation, canonized by the Renaissance masters, were accepted by artists until the late nineteenth century just as the musicians had accepted the rules of tonality. However, constant repetition had weakened their effectiveness, and change seemed to be demanded. The beginnings of change we have already noted in Impressionistic painting, which put the emphasis less on the subject represented and more on the attitude of the artist toward his subject. This changed emphasis led artists to *Abstraction*, which must be thoroughly understood because it is the basis of much of modern art.

The verb "abstract" has two meanings: "to take away" and "to summarize." Both meanings were known and employed by the old masters. In Raphael's "Sistine Madonna," for instance, the sky seems to be filled with heads of little angels. Although we see only the heads, we assume that the bodies which have been abstracted are really there. This is the first meaning of the term. In Botticelli's "Birth of Venus" the artist painted some little ripples near the shore and we assume that a gentle breeze is rippling the entire surface of the sea, although we do not see the ripples farther away. He has summarized the effect of the breeze. Similarly, no painter has found it necessary to paint every branch, twig, and leaf on a tree.

*Mondrian.* There is a series of paintings by the Dutch Abstractionist Piet Mondrian (1872–1944) which shows a horizontal tree in successive stages of abstraction until all similarity to tree is gone, and we have nothing but a pleasing assemblage of lines and planes without any reference to anything in the visible world. They represent only the sense of order, harmony, and balance in nature. The artist thus expresses the feeling that in our age man is becoming increasingly depersonalized, subject to the power of the science which he has discovered.

*Kandinsky.* Wassily Kandinsky (1866–1944) was a Russian who at first worked with the Expressionist *Blaue Reiter* group. Their free distortion of shapes and arbitrary use of color led him to the idea that shape and color, not subject, are the expressive elements in painting. He therefore eliminated subject and became an Abstractionist. He called his paintings either "Composition" or "Improvisation."

*Cubism.* Cubism is a form of abstraction in which objects are first reduced to cubes and then flattened into two-dimensional shapes arranged in overlapping planes. The movement started in 1906 with conversations among Pablo Picasso (1881–1973), Georges Braque (1882–1963), and, later, Juan Gris (1887–1927) in a Montmartre café. These men were interested in breaking down classical form and proportion, and in so doing were influenced by Cézanne's precepts and African Negro sculpture. In the first, or *analytical,* style their interest in form led them to abandon color for an almost monochromatic palette. By presenting an object as if viewed from different angles, as in Picasso's "Girl Before a Mirror," the artist is inviting the observer to step into the painting and walk around. They called this effect simultaneity of vision. *Synthetic Cubists* reversed the process, taking an abstracted form and building a two-dimensional composition around it. A good illustration is Braque's "Musical Forms."

Picasso's *Demoiselles d'Avignon* ("Ladies of Avignon") is an important Cubistic document although it was never completed, and the vertical forms are not completely co-ordinated. By the time that Picasso had gone back to Cubism in 1921, the year of the "Three Musicians," color had returned and it is the strong colors that make the whole picture sing. In "Nude Descending a Staircase" by Marcel Duchamp (1887–1968) we find another preoccupation of analytical Cubism: that of expressing sequential movement in time. The Cubists thus opened up many new possibilities in visual experience.

**Surrealism.** The Surrealist movement is the most original school to have emerged since World War I. It began as *Dadaism,* a movement of protest against reason itself, springing from the anguish of war. It appeared almost simultaneously in Zurich, New York, Cologne, and Madrid. The adherents came together in Paris in 1919, and under the aegis of the French poet André Breton the nihilism of Dada was abrogated, and *Surrealism* was born. The name derived from an early play by the French poet Apollinaire. Drawing on the Freudian theory of psychoanalysis, the Surrealists try to bring elements of the subconscious to the surface, expressing them in symbolic forms. Surrealism is almost the antithesis of abstraction because it tends to sacrifice plastic values to the symbolic power of the image. The deliberate intention to shock the consciousness seemed to elicit such a response from a war-weary world that the movement attracted artists from many countries. Among the most important are: Swiss, Paul Klee (1879–1940); German, Max Ernst (1891–1976); French, Yves Tanguy (1900–1955); Spanish, Joan Miró (1893– ) and Salvador Dali (1904–    ); Italian, Giorgio de Chirico (1888–    ); Russian, Marc Chagall (1887–    ); American, Man Ray (1890–1976). By way of illustration we will consider a few Surrealist paintings.

*Dali.* In Salvador Dali's "Persistence of Memory" a number of limp watches hang over a dead tree growing out of a table on a beach. Insects attack one of the watches without success. The watches, symbolizing time and eternity, are bent to the will of the artist. Hence the painting suggests that by the artist's created works he defeats time and achieves immortality.

*Chagall.* Marc Chagall is a merry little Russian with a zest for life and a very deep love for his wife Bella. Never has love been more joyously celebrated than in "The Bride and Groom of the Eiffel Tower" and "Birthday." In the former painting, the two float together above the Eiffel Tower; in the latter, Chagall's dream image of himself, upside down with delight, bends over to kiss his Bella from the heights of ecstasy.

*Klee.* Paul Klee, who was also a poet and sculptor, represents in "The Twittering Machine" his fear that machines might reduce men to the role of twittering birds. The collage developed out of his paintings.

*Miró.* Joan Miró has a genius for delicate absurdity. Both "Person Throwing a Stone at a Bird" and "Dog Barking at the Moon" represent various forms of human frustration.

*Ernst.* Max Ernst painted the most gruesome of Surrealist documents in a series of paintings called "Europe after the Rain." Done at the close of World War II, they portray his idea of what the world would look like after total atomic destruction. It is a nightmare world of complete upheaval.

**Picasso.** Pablo Picasso (1881–1973) was probably the most important twentieth-century painter. An artist who keeps on turning out paintings, ceramic figurines, and sculpture when he is more than eighty years old deserves some kind of medal for heroism. But anyone who turned out work as rapidly and as prolifically as Picasso cannot expect to hit the bull's eye every time. His work is uneven, and it is unfortunate to hear people rave as soon as they discover Picasso's signature on a canvas. It is necessary to analyze each painting carefully before we judge it a great work of art.

We could study all of the modern styles so far discussed by examples from Picasso's work because he tried them all exhaustively. It is significant, however, that after a period spent on one of the modern "ism's" he felt the need to go back to the classic style of representational painting with its order, restraint, and poise.

Picasso was born in Málaga on the southern Mediterranean coast of Spain. Because his father was an art teacher, he started painting in early childhood. He shuttled back and forth between Barcelona, Paris, and Madrid for many years and finally settled in Paris, where he spent much of his life. He spent his last years in a chateau on the French Riviera with his young wife, Jacqueline Roque. Probably due to her influence, his last works are vigorous and gay. In considering Picasso, it is convenient to divide his work into time periods.

In the "Blue Period" (1901–1904) Picasso painted poor people, dejected and forlorn: underfed children, work-weary women, blind beggars. He used little background detail, and his color is a grayish-blue monochrome shading from light to dark. See "The Old Guitarist" (1903).

In the "Harlequin or Rose Period" (1905–1906) Picasso's fortunes had improved and his palette took on brighter colors. He was interested in circus people, or *Saltimbanques,* families of acrobats who wandered from town to town putting on shows for a pittance. These figures begin to have more classic roundness and solidity than do the emaciated figures of the first period.

The period of 1907–1908 is known as Picasso's "Iberian-African Negro Period." Picasso studied this archaic sculpture in the Louvre, and one can see in *Les Demoiselles d'Avignon* the distortions, the barbaric interplay of angles, and the hatched shadings of the masklike faces which resulted from his study.

From 1909 to 1914 Picasso and Georges Braque worked out the formal language of Cubism. "Girl with Mandolin" is a good example. What a meeting of great minds took place in Rome in 1917! Picasso went there with Jean Cocteau (1889–1963), French poet and dramatist, to design the curtain and sets for Cocteau's ballet *Parade*. Music for the ballet was by the modern. French composer Eric Satie. Picasso also met the Russian composer Igor Stravinsky, who was working on the *Firebird* score, as well as Diaghilev and the members of his Ballet Russe and the dancer Massine, who became his special friend. More important he married one of the ballerinas, Olga Koklova. None of these men was as yet at the height of his career, but all would become famous later in the century. *Parade* was joyously avant-garde and highly successful, and the whole experience gave Picasso international standing.

While in Rome Picasso studied the old masters with the result that his next period (1918–1924) is his "Classic Period." The "Lovers" and "Woman in White" are good examples. In the middle of this period he produced his Abstraction "The Three Musicians" about which we have already spoken. Around 1928 he produced some grotesque distortions of bathers on a beach which look like a heap of bones, then after reverting to the classic again he went into his "Double-Image Period" (1932), of which "The Girl Before a Mirror" is one example. The artist claimed that the girl is shown "simultaneously clothed, nude, and x-rayed."

Then in 1937 in the white heat of anger and revulsion at Hitler's senseless bombing of a Spanish town, Picasso produced his greatest masterpiece, "Guernica" (see p. 301). It is composed in the form of a triptych; every line, every mass, is almost mathematically balanced, and the colors are confined to black, white, and gray. The distortions of natural forms reflect the dislocation of Fascism with its accompanying brutality and terrorism.

After "Guernica" Picasso did many humorous sculptures of animals and birds. Again and again he took his inspiration from the old masters. You might say he adapts or paraphrases or distorts them with almost diabolical skill. In 1954 he did fifteen paintings based on the "Women of Algiers" by Delacroix. They are Cubistic with large geometric planes, colorful and exciting. That same year he married Jacqueline Roque and did many abstract and realistic portraits of her. In 1956 Matisse was "treated"; in 1957 he painted twenty pictures derived from Velásquez's "Maids of Honor"; in 1962 came a series based on Manet's "Luncheon on the Grass." He toyed with David's "Rape of the

PABLO PICASSO: *Guernica.* Museum of Modern Art, New York (on extended loan to the Museum of Modern Art, New York, from the artist). (Courtesy French Reproduction Rights, 1966)

Sabine Women" as well as lithographs and drawings after Cranach and Altdorfer. Interspersed between the old masters are lithographs, lineoleum blocks, and paintings of bull fights.

How shall we evaluate Picasso as an artist? Anyone can see that he was powerful, skillful, and audacious. Hordes of painters followed him in taking nature apart and putting it back together again in unorthodox arrangements. Picasso was commercially successful, sometimes realizing $200,000 for a single painting. His good draftsmanship and bold patterns show up well in reproductions, where his less outstanding technique of applying paint is hidden. His technique covered up the fact that he had no profound spiritual insight. There is no indication that he felt deeply about any work except "Guernica." In the perspective of history he may rank as one of the most important figures of this period, but how this period will measure alongside the Italy of Michelangelo is another matter.

**Modern Art in America.** Just as in Europe, avant-garde art in America developed as a protest against industrial society and the *nouveaux riches* who lived in wedding-cake houses and wanted, in the words of Flaubert, "little statuettes, little music, and little literature." Mass democracy led to popularization, and popularization was the enemy of the independent artist. So-called critics praised the pretty salon paintings and sentimental novels geared to bourgeois taste. Novelty and bad taste were the essence of American society.

The need to find a more congenial climate sent American writers and painters fleeing to Europe, where at least some artistic institutions were preserved. When they returned home they were even less sympathetic with the American moral climate and adopted more belligerent attitudes toward it than did their European confreres. Their only sense of solidarity came from the photographer and art dealer Alfred Stieglitz, who exhibited their works and published a little art journal called *Camera Work*. Max Weber, an early twentieth-century commentator, expressed standards common to the group: art freed from classical ideas, derived from the infinite world of experience, without concrete limitations, and with a strong respect for the element of chance in creation.

Many of these artists had been in Paris, and were familiar with early Cubism, the "Wild Beasts," and the "Blue Rider" groups (see p. 290). Some had studied in the studio of Matisse. But the rank and file of Americans never came to the Stieglitz exhibitions and knew nothing about what was going on in Europe.

*The Armory Show and Its Aftermath.* In 1913 came the big explosion: the Armory Show, sponsored by the Association of American Painters and Sculptors and held in the Sixty-ninth Regiment Armory in New York City. Its official title was "International Exposition of Modern Art"; but after the opening day it became "Armory Show" and has been so called ever since. On display were some sixteen hundred representative foreign works by the French Impressionists, Picasso, Matisse, Cézanne, Duchamp, Kandinsky, Van Gogh, Gauguin, and many others. In addition some four hundred American works were displayed, many by Americans who had studied abroad. Childe Hassam and Maurice Prendergast had been strongly influenced by Impressionism; there were the Realists of the Ashcan School, John Sloan, George Luks, and William Glackens; George Bellows was a younger and very vigorous Realist; then there were the exponents of the School of Paris: James McNeill Whistler, Albert Pinkham Ryder, and Max Weber. Walt Kuhn had fathered the idea of the show and Arthur B. Davies had organized it. Overnight the Armory Show became front-page news and the center of heated controversy.

The *New York Times* called the show "pathological," the *Herald* "unadulterated cheek"; the official magazine of the American Federation of Arts compared the artists to "anarchists, bombthrowers, lunatics, depravers"; even Theodore Roosevelt felt called upon to denounce the "lunatic fringe." Art students were advised to stay away from the Armory. The Cubists came in for the most scathing denunciation. The most shocking exhibit was Marcel Duchamp's "Nude Descending a Staircase," which was derisively called "Explosion in a Shingle Factory" and "Rush Hour in the Subway." This painting sold for $324.00.

It is doubtful whether the American public has yet really accepted modern art, but never again after the Armory Show could the public claim ignorance. This exhibition also served to put the traditionalists on the defensive. Moreover, many of the canvases were purchased by courageous souls, and these paintings form the nucleus of modern collections such as those of the Whitney Museum and the Museum of Modern Art, both in New York City.

There are American painters who derived from each of the stylistic groups we have mentioned, but none of them slavishly followed their European progenitors. They took what they wanted and adapted it to their own individual outlook.

*Cubist Influence.* One can see the influence of Cubism in the diaphanous shafts of light that play over "Grain Elevators" by Charles Demuth (1883–1935) and over "Mouth of the River Riga" and "Steamer Odin II" by Lionel Feininger (1871–1956). Whereas Demuth's paintings are solid, Feininger's seascapes are mystical and contemplative.

*Surrealist Influence.* Morris Graves (1910–     ) is a recluse and mystic who lives near Seattle. His subjects are usually bird and plant forms derived partly from Surrealism and partly from Zen Buddhism. See his "Little Known Bird of the Inner Eye" and "Preening Sparrow." Peter Blume (1906–     ) painted a canvas called "The Eternal City," a Surrealist Rome with Mussolini's violent green head jumping out of a jack-in-the-box.

*Abstract Expressionism.* But most of the Americans derive from the "Blue Rider" group (see p. 297), especially Kandinsky. These artists call themselves *Abstract Expressionists*. Since the most vigorous creative artists today belong to this group, we had better understand the term. These people believe that color and form can be expressive without imitating visual reality. They may tell you that they start painting without any preconceived idea, that the painting evolves by chance. However, most of them have had formal academic training and have been subconsciously guided by ideas of color harmony, coherence, and formal organization. Of course, there is an element of chance in any painting. An artist may make a blunder and find later that his "mistake" is the most expressive element in the painting. (For example, one water-colorist was so frustrated with a painting that he put the painting in the bathtub and turned on the water; he took it out and found he had something finer than what he had been struggling to achieve.)

The Abstract Expressionist feels that he can better express his own individuality, experience, or emotion when he is completely unconfined by subject matter. By the same token, the observer may enter into the painting more freely when he need not search for the artist's meaning. The meaning of the painting for you will be commensurate with the amount of time, thought, and feeling that you are willing to put into it. But don't try to put the meaning into words any more than you would put the intrinsic meaning of a piece of music into words. Approach it on its own terms as a visual experience.

Willem de Kooning, who is talented, trained, and experienced, attacks his canvas vigorously. Philip Guston paints in a more concentrated fashion. Jackson Pollock put his canvas on the floor and dribbled the paint on it. Each achieved a characteristic style. Why does this form of modernism appeal to American artists? Because it is the most personal, hence the most romantic form of utterance. And in spite of efforts to be "hard-boiled," Americans are the most romantic people on earth.

Here are a few American Abstract Expressionists and an outstanding painting of each:

John Marin (1870–1953): "The Singer Building"
Mark Tobey (1890–    ): "Tundra"
Mark Rothko (1903–1970): "Earth and Green"
Willem de Kooning (1904–    ): "Composition"
Franz Kline (1910–1962): "Chief"
Jackson Pollock (1912–1956): "Number 12"
Philip Guston (1913–    ): "The Return"
Robert Motherwell (1915–    ): "The Voyage"

*Representational Painting: Wyeth.* Although they are less sensational, the *Representational* artists should not be overlooked because they express America, too. Representational painting seems to be staging a comeback, especially among a group of painters on the West Coast.

Many people would argue that Andrew Wyeth (1917–    ) is the finest painter in America today. He was born in Chadds Ford, Pennsylvania, the son of N. C. Wyeth, a famous illustrator of children's books. Illnesses in childhood kept him from the usual occupations of American boys, and so, tutored by his father, he spent his time drawing, painting, and rambling through the countryside. He still lives in Chadds Ford, spends his summers in Cushing, Maine, and paints the homely, familiar scenes around him. In his first show, in 1937, people quickly bought every picture, some selling for $17.00. Recently a Wyeth painting sold for $65,000, and they have gone all over the world.

Wyeth's subjects are people—not the affluent, "successful" people, but the ordinary folk who form the backbone of America. He likes to paint in winter and late fall, "when the bloom is off." His art is not photographic, for there is always a psychological penetration which is personal and never obvious, which must be caught and interpreted from the observer's own experience. One critic calls this quality "remembered emotion."

Perhaps Subjective Realist is as accurate a label as any for Andrew Wyeth. He says that he tries to express the quality of the country he lives in, a sort of organic representation, symbolic of the way he feels about a person or scene. The first thing that strikes the observer is his consummate and meticulous draftsmanship in details—a rotten log, a milk pail, a cracked plaster ceiling, wind from the sea blowing the window curtains, bird tracks in the sand. But when one has ceased to wonder at the obvious skill of the painter, then the deeper truth begins to reveal itself.

Study his painting of his son "Nicky"—a tall, gangling, eighteen-year-old youth, standing barefoot in the sand, wind blowing open his shirt, lost in contemplation as he gazes far out to sea. All the aspiration of young America is expressed in the painting. Or study the strong but gentle face of "Albert's Son," perhaps fourteen years old, peering out of the barn door. This young lad runs the household for his alcoholic father. Or study "Christina's World." Christina, a victim of infantile paralysis, lies in the grass and looks up proudly at her home, her castle, her "world." Then there is "Citizen Clark," an elderly Negro who expresses frankness and honesty on his weather-beaten face. These are some of the people whom Wyeth knows and loves.

Here are some other Representational artists with examples of their work:

Edward Hopper (1882–1967) : "Early Sunday Morning"
Ben Shahn (1898–1969): "Handball"
Reginald Marsh (1898–1954) : "They Pay to be Seen"
Charles Burchfield (1893–1967) : "Backyards in Spring"

## Modern Sculpture

In the nineteenth century sculpture was commissioned by the state to adorn public buildings and parks, and the results were usually academic and rhetorical. A few years ago critics were prophesying the demise of sculpture, but today there seems to be a great resurgence of interest in this ancient form of art.

It is difficult to know what to do with a piece of sculpture. The interest in it today has come largely from industrial concerns and institutions which want to use sculpture as part of the landscaping. The best solution is to find a sculptor in whom one has implicit faith and commission him to design the figures to conform to the interior or exterior spaces to be decorated. Alec Miller, English sculptor and critic, says: "Today artists turn too readily to the expression of personal idiosyncracy. The artist must return to the idea of service, and instead of making his art a sterile and esoteric expression of himself, make it a revelation of his love of earth and man." [1]

**Rodin.** The enormous productivity and popularity of August Rodin (1840–1917) exerted a nefarious influence on modern sculptors. Rodin deliberately left parts of his statues rough-hewn for effect, when there was no technical justification for the practice. He willfully ignored the character of his material because he did not do the actual sculpturing himself. He made the clay figure and his assistants transferred it to stone or bronze, sometimes both. Rodin's "Thinker" is the embodiment of male brute strength. His "Hand of God" and "The Kiss" are so exaggerated that they incline to sentimentality. Hence modern sculptors in repudiating him have tried to reveal the "stoneness of stone."

**Post-Impressionists.** Many of the Post-Impressionist painters, especially Matisse and Picasso, also worked in sculpture. Matisse's reclining nudes are deliberately crude, but have great power. Picasso's sculptured birds have captured the essential character of the model (the cockiness of the cock, the gravity of the owl) which makes them humorous. Kirchner's "Recumbent Cat" is satiric.

**Lehmbruck.** Wilhelm Lehmbruck (1881–1919), a German sculptor, respected the traditions of realistic classical form, and achieved its idealism with a certain amount of stylistic elongations, but he always utilized correct anatomical structure. See his "Standing Woman" (1910) and "Kneeling Woman" (1911).

**Maillol.** Aristide Maillol (1861–1944) was perhaps the most important sculptor after Rodin. He brought back the pure classic ideals of repose, serenity, balance, and stability that had been forgotten by the Realists. His female nudes are monumentally simple in contour, dignified and unsensual. See his "Leda" (1902) and his standing nude done in lead which is in the Tate Gallery, London.

**Brancusi.** It was inevitable that the sculptors should follow the painters in their desire to experiment. Constantin Brancusi

---

[1] Alec Miller, *Tradition in Sculpture* (London: Studio Publications, 1949), pp. 165–166.

(1876–1957), a Rumanian, is usually considered the father of modern abstract sculpture. Brancusi said that when he had reached a point of virtuosity and could surpass his rivals in translating reality into forms, he felt that his previously explored paths could yield no further spiritual experience. This is a sincere statement of the reason why serious, accomplished artists go on to experiment. Their motive is self-realization rather than a desire to startle or shock. Brancusi's well known "Bird in Space" (1925), done in polished bronze, was the subject of the owner's contest with the United States Customs, who wanted to tax it as bric-a-brac instead of allowing it to enter the country duty-free as a work of art. The dispute was settled in favor of the sculptor. "The Kiss" (1908) shows the influence of primitive forms. The egg-shaped "Sculpture for the Blind" is meant to convey its beauty of form and texture by being handled.

**Zorach.** William Zorach (1887–1966) was born in Russia but came to the United States when he was four years old. Zorach was a successful painter before he turned to sculpture in 1916. He never turned his back on Representation, although his simplified mass and emphatic planes show the influence of Cubism, especially in "Child with Cat" (1926). The spiritualized "Mother and Child," "Head of Christ," and "Prophet" are in the Metropolitan Museum, and you may have seen "Spirit of the Dance" in Radio City Music Hall.

**Archipenko.** The Ukranian sculptor Alexander Archipenko (1887–1964) was a pioneer in adapting Cubist methods to sculpture. In "Woman Combing Her Hair" (1915) (see p. 308), he opposes rounded planes to sharply concave ones, which are rendered convincing by the play of light on the edges. He makes a vacuum, an actual hole, substitute for a human head. Observing that "empty space should never be of less importance than solid mass" he was one of the first exponents of "open sculpture." His terra-cotta figure "The Bride" is more abstract and stylized, but still graceful.

**Moore.** The idea of treating space as volume instead of as emptiness brings us to the English sculptor Henry Moore (1898– ), who many critics believe is today's outstanding sculptor. Moore began by saying that his medium (block of wood or piece of stone) determined his subject, but he later discarded this idea. His hollowed-out forms require us to appreciate shaped voids as well as masses. In other words, holes are negative volumes. When he works in wood, these voids strongly suggest the action of wind and weather. For this reason a purely abstract figure like "Internal and External Forms" (1954) is more convincing than his

ALEXANDER ARCHIPENKO: *Woman Combing Her Hair*. Museum of Modern Art, New York. (Collection, The Museum of Modern Art, New York. Acquired through the Lillie P. Bliss Bequest)

reclining or seated human figures with their ponderous, elephantine limbs and small heads. To see three of these figures—father, mother, and child—sitting on a stone bench in the middle of an open field in England's usually inclement weather approaches the ridiculous. Moore prefers to work out of doors and likes his sculpture, which is usually more than life-size, displayed out of doors. Of the many Moore sculptures in the United States, four are in the Albright Knox Art Gallery in Buffalo. Moore did all the sculptures for the UNESCO Headquarters in Paris.

**Welding Sculptors.** Today welding is as frequently used as casting in metal sculpture. The inventor of this trick was Julio Gonzales (1876–1942), compatriot and friend of Picasso. See his abstraction called "Seated Woman I" (1935). Another abstraction called "The Horse" (1914) combines the anatomy of a real horse with the anatomy of a locomotive, an iron horse. It is by Raymond Duchamp-Villon (1876–1918), the brother of Marcel Duchamp, who painted "Nude Descending a Staircase." With these two Abstractions as a background, study Seymour Lipton's (1903–    ) "Archangel," which was commissioned for Philharmonic Hall in Lincoln Center, New York City, and unveiled in 1964. See also his Abstraction "Thunderbird." Arch-angel" is nine feet high, a size related to the architectural dimensions of the hall. Its gold-bronze finish, tempered surface, and recessed hollows give it great beauty whether or not one has imagination enough to see its connection with an archangel. Lipton has been concerned with "hero images" since 1948. "The hero is the potential force in Everyman, the continued renewal of life. 'Archangel' is the winged messenger from on high surmounting dark forces of evil in a clash of cymbals." [1]

**Calder.** The American Alexander Calder (1898–1976) invented the *mobile,* a form of sculpture made out of wire, string, and small, light objects such as plastic balls. These are either suspended or mounted so that they will move in air currents or by a motor. Typically American, they are buoyant, humorous, and exuberant, based on the vernacular of science, engineering, and mechanics. It was Duchamp who gave Calder's 1932 suspended figures the name of "mobiles." Some are related to the free curves and bright colors of Miró. Calder's 1937 "Whale" is a curvilinear abstract with a dynamic concept of space. The rhythmically moving parts describe arcs which constantly shift but make us aware of the areas both within and without their orbits.

## Modern Architecture

While modern painters and sculptors have gone off on unpredictable flights of fancy, the architects have kept their feet firmly planted on the ground of functionalism. In building, sound construction must take precedence over the aesthetic. (You remember how the Gothic architects weakened their walls with windows to such an extent that the walls sometimes collapsed). To understand modern architecture and what is meant by functionalism, we must go back to London in 1851.

By the mid-nineteenth century the Industrial Revolution had produced an array of preposterous machine-made furniture and household gadgets which were the wonder of the world. England decided to hold a "Great Exhibition of the Works of Industry of All Nations" in London's Hyde Park. An enormous pavilion which could be built quickly and cheaply was needed to house the exhibit, and Joseph Paxton, a designer of greenhouses, was given the job. Out of iron rods, sheathed by panes of glass, Paxton built the sensational Crystal Palace, which was not only the

---

[1] Quoted by Katherine Kuh in *Saturday Review,* February 20, 1964.

world's first prefabricated building but also the prototype of steel skeleton and glass skyscrapers of today. However, no one then guessed its architectural possibilities.

**Frank Lloyd Wright.** America's greatest architect, Frank Lloyd Wright (1869–1959), was the first one to understand the implications of the domestic revolution. It was an earlier architect, Louis Sullivan, who coined the slogan, "Form must be based on function." But Sullivan could not rid himself of the excessive ornamentation so dear to the nineteenth century. Wright was a romantic who believed that a man's home should express his personality and that it should be adapted to the natural surroundings of its location. As Wright developed and matured, he came to regard all ornamentation, even his beloved Japanese prints, as superfluous and insisted that the natural textures of wood and stone must not be violated by paintings or sculpture. One of his best-known homes is the Kaufmann House at Bear Run, Pennsylvania, which is built over the bed of a stream and clings to the gorge on each side of it. The owner must surely feel the security and privacy and also the unity with nature which the architect intended. Another beautiful example of a private home is the Taliesin House in Green Spring, Wisconsin.

Wright's Johnson Wax Company buildings in Racine, Wisconsin, form perhaps the most beautiful industrial plant in existence, but he was not always so successful. The Guggenheim Museum of modern art in New York reveals the visitors better than the paintings, but Wright was the wrong architect to design such a building, because he didn't like paintings. As you travel about the country, ask to see the Frank Lloyd Wright buildings. You will have to ask because there are no two alike.

**The Bauhaus.** In 1919 a young German architect, Walter Gropius, established at Weimar a school called the *Bauhaus* to teach the visual arts for the purpose of serving the needs of mass production. Klee, Kandinsky, and Feininger all served on the faculty. The school was so successful that it was moved to Dessau, where Gropius designed a magnificently modern building that became a sort of manifesto of functionalism. The workshop wing of the building was a steel and glass cage, which became the prototype of the modern style of skyscraper construction. When Hitler came to power the school was disbanded, and teachers and students fled into other lands to spread the gospel of the new functional architecture.

**The Skyscraper and Its Influence.** The skyscraper was demanded by the necessity of city space utilization. Architects were unprepared for its construction because old devices like the buttress, the column, and the arch could not solve the problems. It was like trying to hold back Niagara Falls with a row of peanuts. Most of the structural problems were solved in Chicago; then it was only a matter of duplicating that success in every city in the country. In the 1920's the skyscraper became *the* American symbol, and even small towns which had plenty of room to expand had to build at least one skyscraper just to be "in the swim." In New York there was a humorous contest between the Empire State Building and the Chrysler Building in which each added lightning rods, flag poles, and mooring masts to try to outdo the other in height. The latest innovation is the development of the cantilever construction, which allows architects to indulge in flights of fantasy in projections and roofs.

So many architects and engineers from foreign countries (Austria, Russia, Holland, France, and Scandinavia) have contributed to skyscraper construction that the style has been called the International Style. Whether the building is used for offices, department stores, private apartments, or schools, the same assets and liabilities are apparent once the building is put to use. Frank Lloyd Wright, having contributed to the style, fought it to the day he died. Why? First, monotony: every building looks like every other building, and all look like an exercise in geometry. Second, the glass-walled rooms cost a small fortune to be kept warm in winter and cool in summer. Third, if your apartment has glass walls it has no privacy; if you have to close draperies to get privacy you may just as well have an opaque wall. And most important of all, the International Style, no matter how efficient it may be, is cold, inhuman, and forbidding. It may have the clarity, purity, and unity of a Greek temple, but it lacks warmth and humanity.

All over the length and breadth of America we are watching urban renewal projects pull down the jerry-built, gingerbread-decorated homes and stores which were erected in the nineteenth century. This is good, but the question that concerns every one of us is: what kind of building will replace them? Will they be steel, glass, and concrete cubes as sterile, cold, and dehumanized as a surgical dressing, or will we encourage our architects to use a little imagination so that our houses are not just like every other house but express something of our personality and blend with the natural setting? Do we want our business establishments, our office buildings, our schools to be functional, but at the same time livable? These are questions for us the public to decide, because in the long run the public will get what it wants.

**Church Architecture.** There is another problem which may

be controversial but which seems to demand attention: the problem of church architecture in the twentieth century. Certainly no style of church building is more beautiful or more spiritual than the Gothic. The National Cathedral in Washington, D.C., although far from being finished, is in the pure Gothic style. But the era of the twelfth and thirteenth centuries which conceived the Gothic was an era of mystic faith, and the church was meant as a palace for the Queen of Heaven, where she could be approached by her suppliants. Today for many people the purpose of the church is functional: how to bring the knowledge of the love of God to bear upon the complex moral, ethical, and social problems of our society. If the modern church is functional, then it would seem to demand a functional architecture, and many such churches are being built in the modern idiom. Coventry Cathedral near London was partially destroyed in World War II. It has been rebuilt in the modern style, but the Gothic portion which escaped the bombs has been incorporated in the modern church. It is a happy marriage of the two styles.

**Modern Architects.**   Following is a list of the most important of the modern architects, the country of their birth, and some of their outstanding contributions. References are to books, magazines, or University Prints where these buildings are pictured.

Frank Lloyd Wright (1869–1959), U.S.A.
> Unity Church, Oak Park, Illinois. Un. Print GM 80
> Kaufmann House, Bear Run, Pennsylvania. Un. Print GM 366
> Johnson Wax Building, Racine, Wisconsin. Un. Print GM 367
> Guggenheim Museum, New York, N.Y. Un. Print GM 392

Walter Gropius (1883–1969), Germany
> Bauhaus, Dessau, Germany[1]
> Harvard Graduate Center, Cambridge, Mass.[2]

Eero Saarinen (1912–1960), Finland
> TWA Terminal, Idlewild, N.Y.[3]
> University of Chicago Law School, Chicago, Ill.
> Ingall's Rink, Yale University, New Haven, Conn.[3]
> Gateway Arch, St. Louis, Mo. (not completed) [4]
> M.I.T. Chapel and Auditorium, Cambridge, Mass. Un. Print GM 387

---

[1] John Canaday, *Mainstreams of Modern Art* (New York: Simon and Schuster, 1959).

[2] *Encyclopedia of Modern Architecture,* ed. Wolfgang Pehnt (New York: Harry N. Abrams, 1964).

[3] *Saturday Review,* January 23, 1965.

[4] *Reader's Digest,* March, 1964.

Christ Lutheran Church, Minneapolis, Minn. Un. Print GM
**376**
Dulles International Airport, Washington, D.C.[5]
Mies Van der Rohe (1886–1969), Germany, of Dutch parents
Sometimes called a modern classicist. Fine teacher, directed
the Bauhaus at Dessau, 1930–1933.
Tugendhat House, Brno, Czechoslovakia. Un. Print GM **121**
Seagram Building, New York, N.Y.[1 and 3]
Crown Hall, Illinois Institute of Technology, Chicago [3]
Charles Édouard Le Corbusier (1887–1965), France
Also painter and sculptor. Liked buildings on piles, open to
air and sunlight.
Walls appear to be thin screens.
U.N. Secretariat, New York, N.Y.[6]
Monastery at La Tourette, France [7]
Notre Dame du Haut, Ronchamp, France [6]
Block of Houses in Marseilles, France [8]
Pier Luigi Nervi (1891–      ), Italy
Called "Poet in Concrete." Has three sons who are architects
and another who is an engineer.
Exhibition Hall, Turin, Italy[2]
Stadium, Florence, Italy[2]
UNESCO Headquarters, Paris [10]
Olympic Sports Palace, Rome, Italy[9]
George Washington Bridge Bus Station, New York, N.Y.[3]
Port of New York Authority Bus Terminal [9]
Edward Stone (1902–      ), U.S.A.
U.S. Embassy, New Delhi, India [11]
U.S. Pavilion, Brussels World Fair, Belgium [11]
National Geographic Society Building, Washington, D.C.[11]

## Modern Music

The problem of sterilized, dehumanized musical performance is
what is involved every time we listen to a concert on radio, television, or records today. We are not hearing the sounds produced
by the performer, but rather what the production engineer, the

---

[5] *Time Magazine,* November 30, 1962.
[6] Nickolaus Pevsner, *Outline of European Architecture* (Baltimore, Md.:
Penguin Books, 1961).
[7] *Horizon Magazine of the Arts,* March, 1961.
[8] Seton Lloyd, *World Architecture* (New York: McGraw-Hill, 1963).
[9] *Reader's Digest,* February, 1964.
[10] Bodo Cichy, *Great Ages of Architecture* (New York: G. P. Putnam's
Sons, 1964).
[11] *Reader's Digest,* February, 1965.

314 / The Modern Period

A and R (Artist and Repertory), thinks we ought to hear. He has recorded the performer or performers on tape, and then with his vast array of technological equipment he has performed plastic surgery on that tape. He has splintered, spliced, multiplied, filtered, equalized, taken out the "clams" (wrong notes), and made a master tape which goes out on the air waves or is recorded on vinyl. This engineer, not the performer, is the real artist. What do we want, a mechanically perfect sound, or a live performer?

Haydn encouraged his men to play and have a wonderful time doing it. Presumably they sometimes played wrong notes. So what? The spontaneity, the joy of performing music, is expressed in everything that Haydn composed. In a recent New York Philharmonic Youth Concert, the French horns flubbed a passage. That was good; it proclaimed that even those consummate artists were human, and that the "A and R" had not doctored the tape. Some performing artists believe that there will be no "live" concerts by the end of this century. On the other hand, a great violinist says, "Name me the recording that can provide the electricity, the magnetic quality that you get from a great live performance."

The plight of the modern composer is not enviable either, because for the first time in history he has a commodity which the rank and file of consumers don't like and don't want. It is true that the real stature of certain great composers (Bach, Schubert, and Brahms, for instance), was not recognized during their lifetimes, but their music was undervalued rather than repudiated. In order to understand the contemporary situation, let us review some of the characteristics of "modern" music.

When composers felt that the language of Romanticism was worn out, they began to experiment. They threw out lush melody (and most people remember a piece of music by its tune) in favor of loosely connected color patches involved in incessant chromatics. Or else the melodies were angular, involving wild leaps which could neither be sung nor remembered. Then they threw out tonality, which had governed the harmonic structure which in turn governed the formal logic. As a substitute they returned to a contrapuntal style of writing in which the conflicting voices produced acid dissonances which, unlike Baroque counterpoint, were never adequately anticipated or resolved.

When tonal order and logic had been eliminated (see p. 293), it was necessary to get rid of the sensuous singing voice in favor of speech-song. With gargantuan harmonic chords gone, the big orchestral apparatus was unnecessary, and so the nineteenth-century symphony orchestra was discarded in favor of a small chamber orchestra, or unlikely combinations such as flute, viola, vibraphone, xylorimba, guitar, and percussion called for by the composer of a specific composition. Even Stravinsky discarded his magnificent pagan colors and his superimposed rhythms (which we admired in *Le Sacre*) in favor of serial music, cold, inhuman, and objective. When serial organization is extended to rhythmic and dynamic values, we might as well leave everything to machines and send the composers on a vacation.

One more outcome of all these tendencies must be mentioned. There are no longer any nationalistic schools to provide variety, but only two or three main trends, which may be adopted by the composer from Paris, Milan, New York, or Timbuctoo. This is like the skyscraper to be found in New York, Barcelona, and Tokyo, or the Hilton hotels which look alike everywhere except for a few decorative elements to tell you whether you are in Cairo or Istanbul.

The human ear is a very strange organ. The first time you hear "Hammer without a Master" by Pierre Boulez, you will be shocked, but you can't be shocked again, because you will know what to expect. This makes it necessary constantly to invent new shocks. In 1913 the dissonances in "Le Sacre" created an uproar; now we like them. This means that the more we hear dissonance the less dissonant it becomes. We remember the practical joker who when Brahms's music was first performed in Boston, put signs on the exits saying, "This way out in case of Brahms." Could it be that some day we will *like* "The Hammer without a Master" or some electronic composition by Karlheintz Stockhausen? One thing is clear: most people don't like them now.

This situation puts the conductor in a dilemma. The avant-garde painter can put his picture in an exhibition room where people will see it. The avant-garde writer can usually manage to get his work published. But the avant-garde composer must have his work performed. Conductors are reading new works all the time, and choosing very few for performance. The conductor must keep his eye on the box office. He wants to encourage the budding composer, but if he programs too many new works he will lose some subscriptions next year. One hearing is not enough anyway. Some years ago the conductor of the Philadelphia orchestra used to repeat a new work at the end of a concert. What happened? People refused to stay to hear it again and went home. There are a great many composers in America today, but they can't earn a living composing. Most of the good ones have left New York and are teaching composition and theory in colleges. With this general discussion as a background, we submit the names of a few twentieth-century composers whose works you are likely to hear on concert and radio programs. These compositions are not ultra-modern, but are pieces which we believe you will enjoy.

**Bartók.** Early in life Bela Bartók (1881–1945) discovered the indigenous folk tunes of his native Hungary. These were not the gypsy tunes which Liszt and Brahms had used, but were a much truer expression of the Hungarian people. Bartók traveled from village to village, living and working with the people until he had collected more than five thousand of these tunes, which he published. He did not use them in his own compositions, but many of their characteristics are discernible: melodies based on modal scales, parlando-rubato rhythms which came from the extemporization of the performer, a polyphonic texture in which the voices are completely free and produce striking dissonances when they cross.

Bartók's *Music for String Instruments, Percussion and Celesta* (1936) is in four movements. The first movement is in the form of a fugue with a very chromatic subject. After moving to a climax on E flat, the subject is inverted and the ground retraced back to the beginning. The other three movements (impetuous, somber, gay) are all derived from the fugal subject. Bartók was a superb craftsman, but his music was too modern to have wide appeal during his lifetime.

**Bloch.** Ernest Bloch (1880–1959), born in Geneva, the son of a Swiss clock merchant, consecrated himself to music in the same spirit of service as had prompted the old Hebrew prophets. To uplift man, to reveal new conceptions of beauty and truth through his innate Jewish ideals, became his lifelong goal. With savage sincerity and idealism, he was sometimes brutally critical of shams and postures in music, and he denounced those who broke musical laws for effect. Romain Rolland, the French author of *Jean Christophe*, after hearing his first symphony became convinced of his genius and encouraged him in his creative work.

After 1916 Bloch spent most of his life in America, where his music was performed and appreciated. His "Quintet for Piano and Strings" is probably his masterpiece, his most successful attempt to express his race. In this composition sometimes provocative harmonies are balanced by passages of meditative counterpoint. The work both purifies and exalts.

**Vaughan Williams.** After the death of Sir Edward Elgar, Ralph Vaughan Williams (1872–1958) became the dean of English composers. Like many English composers, Vaughan Williams was most at home in the choral idiom. He collected and arranged a number of beautiful English folk songs and incorporated them in his original works until he realized that they were stifling his creativity. You will enjoy his "Fantasia on a Theme of Tallis" (1910) because of its rich sonority, which sounds very conservative today. Thomas Tallis was court organist to Henry VIII and on into the reign of Elizabeth I. His beautiful old hymn tune "Lent" is the basis of Vaughan Williams' "Fantasia," which is handled much like Gabrieli's multiple-choir works. It is scored for three string choirs, which sometimes echo each other antiphonally, and sometimes combine in broad, massive chords.

**Britten.** Benjamin Britten (1913–1976) is perhaps the most original of the modern English composers, although not in any sense avant-garde. His opera *Peter Grimes,* produced in 1945, is a successful experiment in re-creating the atmosphere of a small English coastal fishing village. Listen to his popular "Variations and Fugue on a Theme of Purcell," which offers an opportunity to pick out the instruments of the symphony orchestra, because in it each one has a turn at the Purcell tune. (Lest you have forgotten, Purcell was the seventeenth-century composer of the opera *Dido and Aeneas.*)

**Hindemith.** Paul Hindemith (1895–1963) was undoubtedly the greatest of the modern German composers. Hindemith's parents were so opposed to a musical career for him that he ran away from home when he was only eleven and while studying music supported himself by playing in dance bands and movie houses. For his orchestral suite based on his opera *Mathis der Maler,* Hindemith was found "objectionable to Nazi philosophy," and his works were banned. He went to Paris, London, and finally to America.

It is the *Mathis der Maler* score that we recommend for your listening. It is not long, but is more complicated musically and more modern. The three sections of the suite are based on three panels of the Isenheim altarpiece, painted in the sixteenth century by the so-called Mathias Grünewald (see p. 130). The three panels are called "The Angel Concert," "The Entombment," and the "Temptation of St. Anthony." Find pictures of the altarpiece before you hear the music. Hindemith's music is a fusion of the polyphonic principles of Bach with the rhythmic and melodic innovations of the twentieth century. The style is crisp and clear; the dissonances are sometimes acid; but the structure is sound and coherent.

**Milhaud.** Darius Milhaud (1892–    ), the most important of the new generation of composers in France, is essentially a lyricist in his love of simple, folklike tunes and clear-cut rhythms. He can, however, be quite perverse when using polytonality and polyrhythms which have strong overtones of the jazz idiom. He is very prolific and has tried his hand at all musical forms including opera, oratorio, and ballet, as well as instrumental numbers. Without any comment whatsoever we suggest you listen to "Frenchman in New York "(1963).

**Prokofiev and Shostakovich.** Soviet composers have had the difficult task of maintaining their artistic integrity in the face of many changes in requirements imposed by official circles. The most successful have been Serge Prokofiev (1891–1953) and Dmitri Shostakovich (1906–1975). Shostakovich is probably the greater artist. His symphonies (twelve to date), sound in workmanship and monumental in proportion, express the highest ideals of his country. Nevertheless, he has been in and out of government favor because he likes to be daring and experimental. His opera *Lady Macbeth of Mzensk* is a remarkable work, but it was condemned because it conflicted with "socialistic realism," whatever that means. Thereafter for a time he composed conservatively. Then in 1945 his *Ninth Symphony* produced another storm; it was too "light and humorous." It is this choice "spoof" which we suggest for your listening. It is a take-off on the conventional form and language of an eighteenth-century classic symphony.[1] Both Beethoven and Schubert had completed their life achievement of nine symphonies with a monumental work; Shostakovich makes his ninth—a joke. It starts off conventionally with a slow, calm introduction. All goes well until one instrument stumbles on a "wrong note"; then the music starts adding a beat or skipping a beat while the harmony jerks you from key to key without preparation. The second theme, instead of being sweet and lyrical, is a silly little piccolo tune which the solo violin repeats in the recapitulation accompanied by a whole brass band. The trombone keeps insisting on two wrong notes until the rest of the orchestra finally catches up with it. The second movement is a melancholy waltz which has no place in a conventional symphony. The last three movements are short and connected. The third movement (scherzo) sounds like a Spanish bull-fight tune, but it peters out and runs into a pompous and tragic largo. A passage by cellos and basses sounds like the introduction to Beethoven's "Ode to Joy," but it doesn't introduce anything. It

---

[1] For these details we are indebted to the comments by Leonard Bernstein on his Youth Concert of January 5, 1966, given in Philharmonic Hall, Lincoln Center, and televised.

runs into the closing allegretto, which is a joy ride, closing with a bassoon parody on a traditional coda. The more familiar you are with the classic symphony, the funnier this one is.

**Harris and Copland.** For two interesting twentieth-century American works we suggest that you listen to Roy Harris' (1898– ) *Symphony 1933*, and Aaron Copland's (1900– ) *El Salon Mexico* (1936). Both are popular concert numbers. Harris is the product of a Western pioneer farm and Copland of an Eastern city (Brooklyn). Both studied with the famous French teacher Nadia Boulanger. In the 1930's there was more active interest in the young American composer than there seems to be today. The International Composers' Guild, the American League of Composers, the Guggenheim Memorial Foundation, the Victor and the Columbia Phonograph companies, and especially the Boston conductor, Serge Koussevitzky, all assisted with grants, commissions, and sponsorship of new scores. Both Harris and Copland blossomed under this encouragement.

Harris' music is the more intellectual, but it expresses healthy American vitality. His melodies are likely to be long and angular, his rhythms irregular, but he knows how to expand and develop them. There is none of the nervousness and restlessness of ultramodern music. Copland, on the other hand, is closer to the people, with references to folk and jazz idioms. *El Salon Mexico* is based on Mexican tunes and calls for Mexican percussion instruments. Copland never stands still. He has tried opera, ballet, and music for movies as well as instrumental forms; he has even used the twelve-tone row, but not too successfully.

**Musical Comedy.** The musical comedy, while not American in origin, has received its widest development in the United States. This musical genus probably began with the *Beggar's Opera* of 1728 (see p. 172). But the American species came from such Austrian operettas as Franz Lehar's *Merry Widow*, the younger Johann Strauss's *Gypsy Baron*, and Oscar Straus's *Chocolate Soldier* in the late nineteenth and early twentieth centuries. The stories are romantic and improbable; the music sometimes operatic, sometimes folkish.

We think of Victor Herbert (1859–1924), Rudolph Friml (1881–1972), and Sigmund Romberg (1887–1951) as American composers of light opera, although all were born abroad (Herbert in Dublin, Friml in Prague, and Romberg in Hungary). But they came to America early in their careers, and won their laurels here. In an age of sentimentality their operettas were vastly popular and contained songs which still appear on radio and television today. From Victor Herbert's *Babes in Toyland* (1903) come "March of the Toys" and "Toyland"; from *Mlle. Modiste* (1905), "Kiss Me Again"; from *Naughty Marietta* (1910), "I'm Falling in Love with Someone" and "Ah, Sweet Mystery of Life"; from *Eileen* (1917), "Thine Alone." In 1912 Friml brought out *The Firefly*, which contained the songs "When a Maid Comes Knocking at Your Heart" and "Sympathy." In 1924 the smash hit *Rose Marie* included "Indian Love Call." In 1925 came *Vagabond King*, based on the life of the fifteenth-century French poet François Villon (see p. 124). This operetta popularized "Song of the Vagabonds" and "Only a Rose." The last successful operetta by Friml, *The Three Musketeers*, based on the novel by Dumas, contained the song "March of the Musketeers." In 1917 Sigmund Romberg produced *Maytime*, which popularized the song "Will You Remember?" In 1921 came *Blossom Time*, based on the life of Franz Schubert, with the beautiful "Song of Love" made out of the second theme of the first movement of Schubert's *Symphony in B Minor. The Student Prince* was produced in 1924, with its popular "Deep in My Heart"; *The Desert Song* in 1926 started everyone singing "Blue Heaven" and "One Alone." Romberg's last great success was *New Moon* (1927) with "Lover Come Back to Me" and "Stout-Hearted Men." Also in the 1920's came Vincent Youmans' *No, No, Nanette* (its "Tea for Two" is still popular), Jerome Kern's *Show Boat*, and George Gershwin's *Of Thee I Sing*.

The era of collaboration began in the 1930's and then musical comedies became more musically solid and more original. The team of Richard Rodgers and Oscar Hammerstein produced in the '40's *Oklahoma, Carousel*, and *South Pacific* and in 1959 *Sound of Music*. In these comedies the music is generally better than the dialogue. The other team, Frederick Loewe and Alan Lerner, produced *Brigadoon, Camelot*, and *My Fair Lady*. In these the dialogue is usually better than the music. But the best of all American musical comedies is probably Leonard Bernstein's *West Side Story* (1957). The music, dancing, dialogue, and story are all excellent. Musical comedy is more popular than drama today on Broadway. There is too much of the sordid in real life for people to want to go to the theater to see more of it, and musical comedy is good, popular entertainment.

**Jazz.** It is unfortunate that we must perpetuate a misnomer by referring either to "popular music" or "jazz." Someone really should invent a generic term that would cover all of the various forms of the species. Since no one has, we make this apology and refer to all the varieties of "popular music" as "jazz." That jazz is a distinctly American development no one would deny.

The music sprang from the black people: their songs, dances, religious shouts, laments, and work songs. It was born in New Orleans in the closing years of the nineteenth century. Since New Orleans was an "open" town, tolerant of blacks, and a center of the manufacture of wind instruments, blacks flocked there, bought cheap instruments, organized bands, and earned a livelihood playing for carnivals, prize fights, and funerals. Early in its career jazz became improvisational. Jazz bands were soon found in Chicago, and from there jazz spread over the country.

While there are almost no jazz tunes good enough, musically, to survive the ravages of time, the movement as a whole has had a very salutary effect on "classical" music. Every time in history that music has become overcultivated, lush, and precious, it has been revitalized by an injection from folk sources. Such overcultivation characterized the end of the nineteenth and the beginning of the twentieth centuries. This may well be the reason that jazz developed so rapidly and became so all-pervasive in American life.

Rhythmical subtlety and complexity are the most striking features of jazz. The tunes are banal and lifeless, often poorly constructed. This is why popular songs are laid away on the shelf for a few months while the public has a chance to forget them before they are put back into the repertoire. Up until rather recently the harmony also has been stereotyped. One always knew what chord was coming next. In the last few decades jazz has borrowed dissonance, diminished and augmented chords, and chromatics from classical music. There has been a fair exchange since at the same time classical music has been enriched by the rhythmic complexities of jazz.

The best jazz bands have also adapted counterpoint to their own needs. The instruments are divided into two categories: rhythm instruments (piano, guitar, bass, and drums) and melody instruments (clarinets, saxophones, trumpets, and trombones). Over the firm, basic pulse of the rhythm section, the melody instruments impose independent melodic and rhythmic counterpoint. This makes for great rhythmic and color subtlety.

Popular and classical music have contributed much to each other. It is probably safe to say that no contemporary composer has been immune to jazz influence. George Gershwin (1898–1937) was the first to take jazz into the concert hall. In 1924 in New York the first symphonic jazz concert took place, directed by Paul Whiteman and featuring Gershwin's "Rhapsody in Blue." Gershwin's untimely death robbed America of a fine composer. His *Porgy and Bess* is probably the best opera built on an American theme. If you have listened to Milhaud's "Frenchman in New York," you really should also hear Gershwin's "American in Paris" (1928).

## Modern Literature

The sheer quantity of literature published since 1900 far exceeds that of any comparable period in history. There is little logical relationship which ties together these fragments into a consistent stylistic pattern. Nevertheless, this century has produced some very fine, if not great, literature. If the prevailing tone of some of this literature is amoral, frustrated, and hopeless, we can perhaps lay the blame on "the bomb," two devastating world wars, loss of faith in conventional religious concepts, and even in reason. But we see also in the distintegration mirrored in some literature a poverty of values and not a serious but vain search for meaning in life. The literary critic Edmund Fuller says: "You can't have a vital literature if you ignore or shun evil. . . . The individual, not society the abstraction, did the act and has responsibility. . . . Mercy follows a judgment; it does not precede it." [1] The conflict between good and evil has been the basis of great literature from the Greeks on down to our own day. If writers say of murder, rape, and perversion, "What's wrong with it?" they are not being compassionate, but arrogant, because they are tending to undermine the social and moral order.

As a matter of fact, never before in history has so much been done to assist the unfortunate to change his condition, and this effort is world-wide, from the government, the Peace Corps, and private industry on down to the humble Oregon farmer who has taken a dozen derelict children into his own home. Some modern writers are again finding the literary value of the courageous and the unselfish.

It is at once apparent that American literature predominates. The enormous rise in the number of secondary and college graduates has produced an audience of more discerning readers than that of any country in the world. If this is the "Age of Anxiety," as W. H. Auden suggests, then these literate young people are looking to literature for guidance.

An increased audience has also produced a better social and economic status for the author. Many have found on college campuses economic stability and opportunities to get their works

---

[1] Edmund Fuller, "The New Compassion in the American Novel," in *Five Approaches of Literary Criticism,* ed. Wilbur Scott (New York: The Macmillan Company, 1963), p. 63.

published in paperback editions and magazines. This situation has created in some a more optimistic attitude toward their society, a realization that the institutions of democracy are still valid and that inhuman conditions are worth changing. You remember what was said about the medieval period, that an age is not dark unless the urge to create and the will to change one's environment cease.

If modern literature is geared to a more intellectual audience, by the same token it is more difficult to grasp, and requires more effort on the part of the reader. Never admit that an author's meaning eludes you; dig until you find it. Today reading is not a pastime to fill otherwise empty hours. The kind of story in which the conventional villain reaped his just deserts while the good hero got his girl and lived happily ever after has gone along with the Victorian what-not, and we are not advocating its return.

**The Stream-of-Consciousness Novel.** The modern novel is concerned with two issues: technique or method and the social relevance of its material. We expect an author to be master of his craft, but craftsmanship alone does not produce fine literature. Before we consider the Americans, let us examine some important Europeans and a new technique called *stream of consciousness,* which stems from modern psychology, particularly Freud and Jung. According to the theory of the fluidity of time, the human mind in confronting any situation is constantly influenced by what has happened in the past and what it hopes for the future. The action and plot of such a novel develop in the mind of a character as he is aware of these associations and recollections.

*Proust.* The first great novelist to use this technique was the French author Marcel Proust (1871–1922) in his seven-volume work, *À la Recherche du Temps perdu,* usually translated *Remembrance of Things Past.* The first novel, *Du Côté de chez Swann,* translated as *Swann's Way* (1913) is considered best. In it Marcel, the hero, as a child stays awake long hours until his mother, entertaining a guest, can come upstairs to bid him goodnight. The theme of tormented love, especially the person who loves more than he is loved in return, is established. Each of Marcel's later experiences of love follows this same pattern. To re-create the free play of mind, Proust uses metaphors and symbols; hence the work is Symbolic as well as Naturalistic.

*Joyce.* A more exact term for the stream-of-consciousness technique as used by the Irish novelist James Joyce (1882–1941) is the *interior monologue.* The author's interest was in recording the impact which events in the exterior world have on the psychological and mental processes of his hero. This is an Impressionistic approach. In his *Portrait of the Artist as a Young Man,* which is more or less autobiographical, we have to wait until page one hundred and sixty-six before we learn that Stephen Dedalus is sixteen years old. But if we are sensitive to Stephen's thoughts as they develop we will see that through his confused images of love and rejection he is slowly developing into a sensitive artist. The narrative follows strict chronological order: Stephen's school days in which he gets into trouble because of his independent thinking and religious doubt; his first experience with sex in a brothel with the resultant disappointment and conviction of "sin"; the sermon he hears and his confession to a strange priest; his estrangement from his classmates because he cannot share their Irish patriotism and piety; his resolve to leave Ireland for some foreign land where he can develop a literary career. The many mythical allusions make the work more difficult and at the same time more interesting. For instance, the hero's name is identified with that of St. Stephen, the first Christian martyr, who was stoned to death, although guilty of no crime. Dedalus is associated with the Greek Daedalus, the artist maker of wings whose son plunged to earth through disobedience. Stephen is far from perfect; he has many bad qualities: priggishness, arrogance, conceit, and disobedience to God, country, and mother.

*Woolf.* Virginia Woolf (1882–1941) was another leading exponent of the stream-of-consciousness technique. She believed that the modern generation of writers should get out of the stuffy atmosphere of Edwardian fiction. She represented the mind as a disorganized mass of impressions received from environment and mixed with chance notions from memory and recollection.

In *To the Lighthouse* (1927) Mrs. Woolf was concerned with the meaning of life. The novel involves the Ramsay family: Professor Ramsay, Mrs. Ramsay (an intuitive and understanding woman), their six-year-old son James, daughter Camilla, and other children, who have a summer cottage on one of the Hebrides Islands off the coast of Scotland. A guest of the family is Lily Briscoe, an amateur painter. In the first section of the story the children want to make an expedition to the lighthouse, but Mr. Ramsay answers James rather flippantly that the weather will not permit it. The boy holds this resentment against his father for ten years. The pattern (of family life) is spoiled, and Lily's pattern will not come clear upon her canvas. In a short interlude called "Time Passes" Mrs. Ramsay and two of her children have died and the cottage has aged. The lighthouse, however, which is the central symbol of the book, still punctures the darkness, guides the seafarer, gives dreams of mystery to children, and provides stability in its recurrent rhythm. In the final section the expedition to the lighthouse is consummated, and when Mr. Ramsay compliments his sixteen-year-old son on his seamanship, James's old resentment against his father is dissipated. At the same time the pattern of life is completed on Lily's canvas, and Lily as artist and creator becomes the rightful heir to Mrs. Ramsay. She says at the end: "I have had my vision."

*Lawrence.* The novels of D. H. Lawrence (1885–1930) created a violent controversy in England in the 1920's because they were the first novels to bring the subject of sexual relationships into the open. They do not sound very shocking today, and most people would probably agree with Lawrence that a really satisfactory love relationship consists of a balance between the physical and the spiritual which Lawrence calls "polarity." In *Lady Chatterley's Lover* (1929) there are three types of male: Clifford Chatterley, the successful businessman who is paralyzed physically from a war injury and symbolically because his love is an intellectual convenience; Michaelis, who is capable only of a thin, artificial sensuality; and the game-keeper Mellors, who is well-balanced sexually and capable of real tenderness. Connie Chatterley becomes pregnant by Mellors, whose wife returns, finds out about his "transgression," and causes him to be dismissed from his job. Clifford Chatterley is not concerned with his wife's "transgression" but with the lower social status of Mellors. At the end of the book Connie and Mellors look forward to their eventual reunion.

*Conrad.* Probably the finest English novelist of the twentieth century is Joseph Conrad (1857–1924), who was born in Poland and became a seaman in the British merchant marine. Although his stories are placed in exotic lands, Conrad was not a Romanticist. He did not use stream-of-consciousness technique, but his oblique point of view, showing incidents through the minds of several different characters, creates much the same effect. He was most interested in revealing character, but his dramatic situations are simple. Because the plot is given bit by bit, often in inverted time order, his novels must be read carefully. He was adept at creating mood, especially of the sea; hence his settings become actors in the drama. His characters are psychologically convincing.

*Lord Jim* (1900) is usually considered the best of Conrad's novels. One of the finer qualities of British character is a rigid sense of personal honor and integrity. In *Lord Jim* the hero devotes his life to an attempt to expiate a youthful breach of honor. The key incident occurs in the Red Sea on a ship called the *Patna,* which is loaded with Moslem pilgrims. The ship hits a derelict, and in the moment of panic Jim and the rest of the English officers jump into a lifeboat. But the *Patna* does not sink, and the officers find themselves in the humiliating position of having abandoned ship, leaving the passengers to their fate. This "sin" torments Jim ever afterward; his notoriety always seems to catch up with him. He finally settles on a remote Maylayan island and, as adviser to the chief, he becomes virtual ruler of the island. He takes a wife and begins a new life in the jungle. Then Brown, a ne'er-do-well pirate, comes to loot the town. Jim tries to get Brown to depart peaceably, but when he leaves one of his men kills the chief's son. Jim takes the blame and is killed by the boy's father. In dying to preserve his honor, Jim at last expiates his early mistake.

**The American Novel in the Early Twentieth Century.** American novelists who began writing before World War I were still concerned with the Western expansion of the country and the fortitude it entailed and also with the impact of industrialization on the Eastern seaboard. Novelists of this period tried to explain the motivation of their characters from within a character's mind rather than from the point of view of an observer.

*Wharton.* Edith Wharton (1862–1937) knew the society life in New York and Boston intimately, but her chief interest was the impact of this life on the inner struggles of the characters. For instance, certain conventions must be observed: it was all right to have a secret affair, but to marry out of one's class was inexcusable. Sensitive people rebelled against this duplicity. In *The Age of Innocence* (1920), Ellen Olenska, a fashionable New York debutante, marries a Polish nobleman and goes to Europe with him. She finds his character is ignoble and comes home. She falls in love with Newland Archer, who is engaged to her cousin May. Ellen's parents are opposed to the scandal of a divorce, and Archer is bound by his promise to May. They abide by the conventions of society, but Archer is disgusted with its hypocrisy.

*Cather.* Willa Cather (1875–1947) was a Romanticist and a reactionary, although her point of view was psychological. Herself a product of the southwestern prairies, she admired pioneer life because it was stimulating and revealed noble traits of character. In *My Ántonia* (1918), Ántonia Shimerda and her father come to Nebraska from Bohemia and buy bad farming land. The father, an impractical musician, can't stand the rigorous life and commits suicide. Ántonia, optimistic and energetic, assumes the entire burden of the farm. She marries and becomes a tower of strength to her large family.

*Roberts.* A similar tale of dauntless pioneer womanhood in the eighteenth century is told by Elizabeth Madox Roberts (1886–1941) in *The Great Meadow* (1930). The husband is more interested in avenging the killing of his mother by an Indian than in providing for and protecting his wife. While he goes off looking for the Indian she wards off an Indian attack.

**The American Novel between the Wars.** The great period of disillusionment began after World War I. In the view of many writers the war had bred more troubles than it solved. Fighting was not "heroic"; goodness and respectability were shams; the "average American" was mean and petty; success often eroded character. Some writers depicted people on the fringe of respectability: victims of alcohol, narcotics, or sexual perversion. Some authors pictured the effects of the Great Depression: laborers brutalized and stupefied by machines, the disintegration of the South due to the effects of machine labor. The preoccupation of novelists with these themes has given the epithet "the Lost Generation" to this whole period. Such topics surely do not make for "pleasant" reading, but nevertheless the period produced some very fine writers, and it is important to understand why they wrote as they did.

*Anderson.* Sherwood Anderson (1876–1941) was torn between affection and bitterness toward America. He was scornful of respectability and hypocrisy, especially among religious persons. His style attempts to capture the colloquial atmosphere of folklore. *Winesburg, Ohio* (1919) is a group of sketches of neurotic misfits in a small town. In every case Anderson shows that it is the intolerance and uncharitableness of the respectable people that have made wrecks out of individuals who might have been happy and successful.

*Lewis.* Sinclair Lewis (1885–1951) was a satirist after the manner of Balzac. Indeed his novels taken together might be called "The American Human Comedy," because each one satirizes some phase of contemporary American life. But Lewis was not destructive in his criticism; he had a warm feeling of affection, even of kinship, toward his characters. Every Lewis novel that came out aroused angry protests from the type of people he satirized, but the books were widely read and through one of them the words *Babbitt* and *Babbittry* found their way into the dictionary. *Babbitt* is a penetrating study of the suburban middle class in Zenith, a small midwestern city. The description of the Zenith Athletic Club recalls what we said in the section on architecture (see p. 248). "The entrance lobby of the Athletic Club was Gothic, the washroom Roman Imperial, the lounge Spanish Mission, and the reading-room in Chinese Chippendale." George F. Babbitt is a real-estate salesman, a go-getter and a booster for the town, but devoid of culture. He is rigidly moral in his family life, but doesn't mind having a bit of a fling when he goes away to conventions. At middle age he becomes aware of the superficiality of his life and tries to lift himself by an interest in culture, politics, and illicit love. He can't escape his limitations and drifts back into his former complacency.

*Fitzgerald.* F. Scott Fitzgerald (1896–1940) was the spokesman of the Jazz Age. He was not a shocking Naturalist, nor was his work very deep. He wrote about what he knew: the activities of the leisure class, especially of the flappers of the age of Prohibition. His wife Zelda became the model for a whole series of his heroines. In *The Great Gatsby* the hero has become wealthy as a Long Island racketeer and bootlegger. He throws expensive parties and tries brutally to rearrange his friends' lives to suit his schemes. When Daisy Buchanan, a youthful flame, re-enters his life, he tries to take up the affair where he left off, but Daisy is now married and lacks his aggressiveness. Gatsby is shot trying to protect Daisy from the consequences of an automobile accident. The book is a powerful study of the debilitating effect of success on character. Fitzgerald is best in dialogue.

*Dos Passos.* John Dos Passos (1896–1970) was more of a sociologist than a novelist. He does not attempt to interest us in individual characters but rather in conflicting social masses. The effect of *Manhattan Transfer* (1925) is a pessimistic sense of futility because the characters are bitter and disillusioned, without the ability to find any meaning in life. Ellen Thatcher, an unhappy actress, who weds two other main characters and whose life touches many more, provides what little continuity there is. After this early work Dos Passos went on to a Marxist denunciation of the entire capitalistic system.

*Faulkner.* According to many critics William Faulkner (1897–1962) is the most important American writer of this century. The great subject which he knew from his own family background and which concerned him in all of his novels is the moral and economic disintegration of the old Southern aristocrats at the hands of the progressive and materialistic Philistines. The Sartoris family is typical of the aristocratic Southern type and the Snopeses of the parvenu encroachers. In each of the novels the Sartoris type struggles valiantly but vainly against the Snopes type. Faulkner did not idealize either type but analyzed them psychologically and convincingly. Stylistically Faulkner novels are difficult because he uses stream-of-consciousness technique, the interior monologue, and often an oblique point of view through confused chronology, recollections, and flashbacks. His novels are, however, worth the effort it takes to read them.

We suggest beginning with *The Unvanquished* (1938) because it is easy reading, romantic, and important to the subsequent novels since it pictures the maturing of young Bayard Sartoris to the point where he can make independent moral judgments. *Intruder in the Dust* (1948) is suggested because it gives Faulkner's attitude on the racial question. It might be considered an adventure story with a long sermon or editorial tacked on the end. It contains a murder, a threatened lynching, a risky trip by night to dig up a corpse, a nip-and-tuck race with death, and an exciting trial. Lucas Beauchamp, the old Negro, is a very real person. Faulkner was no pessimist; he believed in the resurrection of the South, and he also had faith in the eternal verities. In his speech accepting the Nobel Prize in 1950, he said: "I believe that man will not merely endure: he will prevail. He is immortal, not because he alone among creatures has an inexhaustible voice but because he has a soul, a spirit capable of compassion and sacrifice and endurance."

*Hemingway.* The life and death of Ernest Hemingway (1898–1961) were so spectacular, well-nigh theatrical, that it is easy to become more interested in the man than in his work. He was, however, a careful and conscientious writer, with a terse economy of language and brilliance of imagery which mark his individual style and which other writers have tried to duplicate without success. Hemingway was a subjective novelist who wrote about experiences which he had personally encountered. These he transformed into artistically heightened episodes in his novels and stories. He was an intensely active person, traveling widely and passionately fond of dangerous sports: sport-fishing, big-game hunting, bull-fighting, skiing, even warfare. He was so intensely masculine that his female characters suffer by comparison with the men. In his novels Hemingway never comments or philosophizes, nor does he resort to pathos or sentimentality. He did believe, however, that each activity, such as fishing, hunting, fighting, and loving, has a certain ritual associated with it and that these rituals must be followed or the contest is monstrous.

In 1917–1918 Hemingway went to Italy to serve as an ambulance driver on the Austrian front and was severely wounded. Out of these experiences came one of his best novels, *A Farewell to Arms*. The theme of the story is the problem of identity. Fred-

erick Henry, the protagonist, is at the beginning of the story
rootless. He has had many experiences: drinking, sex, and fighting, but none of these have left any impression on his real self.
The symbol extensively used at the beginning of the story is that
of the masquerade. Even the idea of an American wearing an
Italian uniform is part of the masquerade. When he meets
Catherine Barkley, he has no intention of caring for her; she too
is a part of the masquerade. He is severely wounded and Catherine nurses him back to health. They are ideally happy during
his convalescence. He goes back to his ambulance outfit, but at
last deserts. Frederick and Catherine escape to Switzerland,
where Catherine dies in childbirth. But on his way to his meeting
with her in Stresa he realizes for the first time that he cares.
Hence there are two opposite movements in the novel: the inexorable movement toward doom and death, and for Frederick the
movement toward self-realization through real love.

*Steinbeck.* John Steinbeck (1902–1968) was similar in interests
to Willa Cather. He admired the foreign elements in the American population, especially the mixture of Mexicans and Orientals
found in central California. He believed that country life is more
stimulating than that of the city. He sometimes presents scenes
of cruelty and passion, but these acts are committed inadvertently
or ignorantly. *Grapes of Wrath,* although not written as propaganda, directed public attention to the problem of the migrant
worker and excited a torrent of indignation. The story tells of
the hardships of the Joad family, who leave the Oklahoma Dust
Bowl to drive to California in search of work. They are beset by
police, hunger, strikes, and death, but at the end are undefeated.
This is a survival of the old pioneer spirit in modern times.

**The American Novel since World War II.** Another period
of ideological battle fatigue followed World War II, but now we
are beginning to notice changes. Some authors are becoming
concerned about the people of foreign lands; others are again
treating the age-old concerns of every individual: identity, responsibility, suffering, compassion. At least some are returning to
the saving graces of enlightenment, beauty, and goodness.

*Mailer.* One of the most ambitious novels to come out of
World War II is *The Naked and the Dead* (1948) by Norman
Mailer (1923–    ). Set on a small South Pacific island, this
novel explores the personalities and backgrounds of the men of
an infantry platoon and shows how these factors impinge on the
major action. The main conflict is between Lieutenant Hearn, a
skeptic and a liberal, and General Cummings, representing the
conventional military mind.

*Hersey.* John Hersey (1914–    ) presents the humanitarian

side of war in his *A Bell for Adano* (1944). The novel tells how the Americans win the confidence of an Italian village by procuring a bell for its church.

*Richter.* Conrad Richter (1890–1968) wrote *The Lady* (1957), a tale of the old Southwest. According to the Southern code of aristocratic honor, a lady must always be defended, regardless of her actions. This lady is a moral coward and by refusing to admit murder, she is responsible for the deaths of her family and friends.

*Salinger.* Whatever may be the ultimate place of J. D. Salinger (1915–    ) in American fiction, he has certainly caught some of the outstanding traits of the contemporary adolescent. Holden Caulfield, hero of *Catcher in the Rye* (1951), hates pretense—in his school chums, in religion, in the movies, in most of the people he meets. But he is not a snob, for he is capable of great compassion. His conflict is between compassion and the high standards he sets for himself and others.

*Malamud.* The central theme of Bernard Malamud (1914–    ) is suffering, and his dominant attitude is compassion. In *The Assistant* (1957), the protagonist Frank Alpine attacks and robs a poor Jewish storekeeper and later tries to make amends secretly. He comes to identify himself with Morris Buber, the man he has injured, and from him he learns that a man can live a good life in spite of inevitable suffering.

*Bellow.* Many critics believe that Saul Bellow (1915–    ) is the outstanding novelist in America today. Bellow is more concerned with man as an individual than with his relation to society. Important to an understanding and appreciation of Bellow's longer works is the novelette *Seize the Day* (1956). Wilhelm, the protagonist, has led a false and irresponsible life, and now has his back to the wall. He realizes his defects and wants to change but cannot. He meets a Dr. Tamkin, a rather nebulous figure who plays a role similar to that of Sir Edward in T. S. Eliot's *The Cocktail Party* (see p. 341). The doctor's philosophy is better than his knowledge of the stock market, and although he gives Wilhelm no tangible aid, he at least holds out the possibility of redemption through suffering. In the final scene Wilhelm accidentally enters a funeral parlor and pours out his grief for someone he had never known. This experience is symbolic of the fact that he is beginning to break out of the prison of "self."

**Recent British Novelists.** British novelists representative of recent trends include Somerset Maugham, Aldous Huxley, Alan Paton, Brian Moore, and Evelyn Waugh.

*Maugham.* When Somerset Maugham (1874–1965) died, he

had completed fifty years of writing—novels, plays, short stories, essays, dealing mostly with middle- and upper-class English society. He was a master craftsman in all his writing, but three works stand out for their penetrating psychological insight. First is *The Moon and Sixpence* (1919), a novel based on the French painter Paul Gauguin, which was made into a successful play; next is the intense short story "Miss Thompson" (dramatized as *Rain*), which tells of the encounter of Sadie Thompson, a prostitute, with Alfred Davidson, a Puritanical missionary on a South Sea island, who is destroyed because he cannot resist her attractions. Maugham's masterpiece is *Of Human Bondage* (1915), which the author wrote from personal experience. The dominant theme is the effort of Philip Carey to find his own nature and his place in life. Orphaned at nine, Philip is brought up by an austere vicar and his childless, possessive wife. He grows up sensitive and repressed, hating school because the students ridicule his club foot. He studies first to become an artist but on being told by his instructors that he has no talent, decides to become a physician. Naturally compassionate, he takes up with inferior women because he feels sorry for them. His involvement with a crude waitress, Mildred, causes him to fail his examinations. His money gone, he is befriended by Thorpe Athelny, who gets him a job and invites him to dinners with his large family. When Philip's uncle dies, he uses his inheritance to get his medical degree, marries Sally Athelny, and settles down to practice in a small fishing village. He is thus freed from the "human bondage" into which every person is in some way born, as well as from his own insatiable struggle for fame.

*Huxley.* Aldous Huxley (1894–1963) wrote *Brave New World* (1932) and *Brave New World Revisited* (1958). These are not typical novels, but horrendous pictures of the debilitating effects of machines.

*Paton.* Alan Paton (1903–    ) set his novel *Cry, The Beloved Country* (1948) in his native South Africa. It is a beautiful and tragic story of racial unrest. The protagonist is a Zulu clergyman who goes to Johannesburg to try to rescue his son from prison. But the boy had killed a white man, son of a man who was trying to help the Negroes. The two fathers find release from their sorrow in mutual understanding and love.

*Renault.* Mary Renault (1905–    ) spent many years in Greece and wrote three exciting tales about the ancient Greek hero, Theseus, telling of his struggle to find out who his parents were, his love affairs, and his battle with the Minotaur. These novels are called *The Last of the Wine* (1956), *The King Must*

*Die* (1958), and *The Bull from the Sea* (1961). Her latest novel, *The Mask of Apollo* (1966) deals with historical Athens during the period between the death of Socrates and the rise of the Macedonian Empire. The protagonist is Niko, an actor in Greek tragedy who feels a strong sense of relevance between the great tragedies and his own life. He carries on imaginary conversations with a mask of Apollo, which symbolizes his profession and his devotion to the good, the true, and the beautiful. The struggle for the control of Syracuse convinces Niko that in spite of Plato's teaching, no man can be both a philosopher and a king. Many of the philosophical and political problems which Niko had to face are still unsolved today.

*Moore.* Brian Moore (1921–   ), born in Ireland, is now living in the United States. The hero of his *Emperor of Ice Cream* (1965) is a seventeen-year-old Belfast boy who stands on the edge of life, a failure. On the outs with his family because he has lost faith in the Catholic Church and has failed his examinations for college, and because his father prefers Hitler to the hated English, he joins the Air Raid Precautions, a rag-tag collection of drunks, loafers, and prostitutes. The entire book is a crescendo, building up to the air raid in the last chapter.

*Waugh.* Evelyn Waugh (1903–1966), like many another contemporary English novelist, was a great debunker. Nothing was too sacred to escape the irony of his pen. Waugh was mainly concerned with the leisure classes, because he felt that only these people are sufficiently cultured to have ideas. The middle-class people in his novels are either money-grubbers or self-made men; the plebeians are for the most part either deferential servants or ruffians. His novels are read because he is a skillful and witty technician. *Brideshead Revisited* (1945), considered by many critics his best novel, treats of the decline of a proud but degenerate family of British aristocrats. The Marquis goes off to Italy with his mistress. The eldest Brideshead son thinks of becoming a monk, but instead marries an elderly widow, who can provide him no children. His brother Sebastian becomes a hopeless alcoholic. The younger sister, Cordelia, once witty and enthusiastic, becomes a plain and consecrated social worker. The older sister, Julia, the most intelligent of the family, marries a vulgar parvenu simply out of boredom, later realizing her love for the narrator, Charles Ryder. Despite their failures, the family is sustained by the Roman Catholic faith, to which Waugh had converted in 1930. The characters are well drawn and there are some expert pictures of dissipation among British aristocrats.

**Recent European Novelists.** Outstanding recent European

novelists include the Frenchmen André Gide, André Mauriac and Albert Camus; the German Thomas Mann; the Russian Boris Pasternak; and the Italians Ignazio Silone and Lorenzo Mazzetti.

*André Gide.* (1869–1951). Like the typical French artist that he was, André Gide tried many of the modern 'ism's, and at different times was labeled a Symbolist, a Puritan, a hedonist, a Neoclassicist, a Communist, an iconoclast, and an aesthete. He was associated with a magazine *La Nouvelle Revue Française*, in which many of his works were published. For pure entertainment *Les Caves du Vatican* translated as "The Vatican Swindle" or as "Lafcadio's Adventures" (1914) is without parallel in modern fiction. The protagonist, Lafcadio Wluiki, is an iconoclastic and amoral individual who reminds us of the hero of Stendhal's *Characterhouse of Parma*. He is comic to the point of being farcical. There is quite a complicated plot involving swindlers who have bilked religious Frenchmen of money with a preposterous tale that the Free Masons have kidnapped the Pope and are holding him in the Castel St. Angelo. One naïve devoté, Amédee Fleurissoire, who has never been outside his native town, sets out for Rome to right matters. He is bitten by bedbugs, fleas, and mosquitoes, caught by the criminals he has come to catch, and seduced by a wily prostitute. He begins to wonder who the real Pope is, and whether when he gets to Heaven he will be able to tell the difference between God and Satan. On the way home Lafcadio throws him out of the train window as a demonstration of the unmotivated act.

*Mauriac.* François Mauriac (1885–1970) is considered among the greatest contemporary Catholic novelists. He was a poet, with the poet's urge toward sensual enjoyment, but he repudiated physical love and the world itself. He said in his *Journal II:* I am a metaphysician working on the concrete. . . . I try to make the Catholic universe of evil perceptible, tangible, odorous. The theologians give us an abstract idea of the sinner; I give him flesh and blood." This he did in *Thérèse Desqueroux.* The heroine, who attempts to murder her husband, is probably the most tragic, most sinful, most passionate woman in modern literature. The author sees her as the epitome of the common guilt of mankind, a woman whose mysterious currents carry her violently toward death. Without God's grace, says Mauriac, all of us are as Thérèse.

*Camus and Existentialism.* We have already seen how prone are the French to analyze, theorize, and rationalize about their arts. The theory of the Danish philosopher Søren Kierkegaard (1813–1855) that each man is isolated, existing independent of his fellows, provided a point of view which expanded into a literary cult. Artists everywhere rebelled against increasing industrialization with the shabbiness and "hollowness" it precipitated. Put these two ideas together and you get the basis of the literary existentialists. Man exists alone in the midst of a chaotic world and must work out his own catharsis by direct acts of will. There is nothing new here. We can trace it back to Goethe's redemption through struggle, to Aristotle's character determined by choices, and even to the Hebrew prophet Jeremiah, when he said, "The whole land shall be a desolation." Jean Paul Sartre was the first French writer to exploit the doctrine, but Albert Camus (1913–1960) was its best literary artist.

Camus was born in French-controlled Algeria of poor, unlettered parents. His sensitivity was awakened by the beauty of the sea, the color and strong light of the desert, and the uncomplaining love of his widowed mother. His teachers in high school and college encouraged his passion for literature. He launched an amateur theater group and, around 1932, began to write plays. He had a deep concern for social justice and took an active part in the French underground during the German occupation. After the liberation, the savage Algerian conflict tore at his heart. He died in an automobile accident before this conflict was resolved. All of the intense emotional, political, and intellectual ferments of his life are mirrored in his novels and plays, but we also find his buoyant love of life, for he is essentially an optimist and an idealist.

*The Plague,* considered his best novel, is about a pestilence which completely isolates the city of Oran, and about a small group of men who forge a solidarity to defeat the physical and psychological evil. It bespeaks faith in man's capacity to endure and triumph.

*Mann.* Thomas Mann (1875–1955) was the last of the German "intellectual" novelists. Before embarking on the rough seas of *Der Zauberberg* (*The Magic Mountain*) (1924), it would be well to read an analysis of Mann's psychological and ethnic theories. Although he was not a great philosopher, one can see in his works the influences of Freud, Goethe, and the Russian novelists.

*The Magic Mountain* has very little plot. The protagonist, Hans Castorp, goes to a tuberculosis sanitarium in the Swiss Alps to see his cousin and finds that he too has the disease. He remains seven years, not only seeking a cure but trying to reach an awareness of his true personality embedded in his subconscious. While Mann believed in Freudian psychoanalysis, he made the psychoanalyst Krokowsky a charlatan. At the end of his stay Castorp has come into contact with every phase of European culture and has reached a kind of synthesis of the opposing forces.

*Pasternak and Communism.* The theme of the novel *Doctor Zhivago* (1957) by the Russian Boris Pasternak (1890–1960) is man's inhumanity to man. Suppressed in Russia, the book was first published in Italy. Similar in pattern to Tolstoy's *War and Peace,* it follows the life story of a doctor who is also a poet through the outbreak and aftermath of the Revolution, and shows how difficult it is for him to keep his religious faith amid this deliberately created chaos. The scenes of Siberian deportation camps, of cities starving and freezing, and of villages burned and depopulated are graphically portrayed. Against this background is woven the doctor's own love story. Pasternak was awarded the Nobel Prize for literature in 1958 but was forced to decline it for political reasons.

*Silone.* The Italian novelist Ignazio Silone (1900–    ) was an effective anti-Fascist propagandist during the thirties and forties and wrote for several leftist publications, but he abandoned the Italian Communist party in 1930 and became as vigorously anti-Communist as anti-Fascist. He went into exile in Switzerland, where he wrote many of his novels. His detailed and sympathetic pictures of Italian peasant life and character mark him as a socialist and humanitarian. Since 1950 he has not been associated with any political group. *La Volpe e le Camelie (The Fox and the Camellias),* translated into English in 1961, is a slight but effective story which takes place in the Ticino, that beautiful district of Italian Switzerland bordering on Lake Locarno. The father Daniele cherishes his family and adores his elder daughter. He has returned to his father's Swiss farm in order to preserve his children's patrimony, but he is engaged in some sort of political activity against the dictator across the border. His position becomes hazardous when his beloved daughter Silvia falls in love with a spy symbolized by the fox that has been maurauding the chicken coops and spoiling the idyllic life (the camellias). The "fox," somewhat ambiguously (conflict between love and duty?) drowns himself in the lake.

*Mazzetti.* Lorenza Mazzetti (1933–    ), a young Italian novelist, has written in her second novel *Furore (Rage)* (1965) as penetrating a revelation of the adolescent girl as Salinger's of the adolescent boy. The heroine Penny is angry, bewildered, death-haunted because she has seen her Jewish foster family machine-gunned. By the method of the continuous interior monologue, Penny tells her own story, by turns pathetic, by turns hilariously funny. She is a bundle of contradictions: she wants to be adored and to do away with everyone; she is curious about sex and contemptuous of boys; she questions the conventions of polite society—about sin, death, love, God. She is certain of one thing: that her younger sister Baby will not desert her. Then Baby falls in love, and Penny, in despair, pursues a young American who proves a traitor too. At the end she says: "I hadn't yet fallen into the great lethargy right-thinking people call sensible."

**The Short Story.** Today short stories usually appear first in magazines and afterward in collections or anthologies. Many novelists have also written fine short stories; other writers specialize in this medium. One such is Frank O'Connor, who has written an excellent study of the form called *The Lonely Voice* (1963). He says that the short story is a distinct art form because the author "has a greater effect to achieve in a smaller compass"; hence he must seize upon "a basic situation that has within it a maximum of significance." At the heart of the story is a revealed truth which may be stated as its theme or felt by the reader. Thus it becomes the revelation of a unique personal vision. Here is a reperesentative collection taken for the most part from three readily available paperback anthologies.[1]

1. Stephen Vincent Benét—"The Devil and Daniel Webster"
2. John Collier—"Witch's Money"
3. A. E. Coppard—"The Third Prize"
4. John Galsworthy—"Quality"
5. Ernest Hemingway—"The Killers"
6. Ernest Hemingway—"The Old Man and The Sea" (long short story)
7. W. W. Jacobs—"The Monkey's Paw"
8. Katherine Mansfield—"The Garden Party"
9. W. Somerset Maugham—"Rain"
10. Flannery O'Connor—"Everything that Rises Must Converge"
11. Frank O'Connor—"My Oedipus Complex"
12. O. Henry—"A Municipal Report"
13. Katherine Anne Porter—"Theft"

---

[1] *Fifty Great Short Stories,* ed. Milton Crane (New York: Bantam Books, 1959).

Pocket Book of Short Stories, ed. Edmund Speare (New York: Washington Square Press, 1966).

*Short Story Masterpieces,* eds. Robert Penn Warren and Albert Erskine (New York: Dell Publishing Company, 1963).

**Drama.** During the past seventy-five or eighty years there have probably been more experimentation and change going on in the field of drama than in that of any of the other arts. Victor Hugo's Preface to *Cromwell* (1827) threw over the last remaining principles of Neoclassic drama as laid down by Aristotle (see p. 38). This document not only set the program for the Romantic theater but also gave dramatists their charter of freedom for subsequent playwriting. In the battle over *Hernani* three years later the Classicists were successfully routed (see p. 234). By 1850 Realism had replaced Romanticism, and a play was supposed to be a "slice of life" in which reality sprang from the roots of character. The audience was well isolated from the action by the "frame" of the stage, but the action itself, including the costuming and scenery, was as realistic as the inevitable stage conventions would allow.

Émile Zola's Preface to *Thérèse Raquin* (see p. 272), the first important manifesto of Naturalism for the theater, predicted that the scientific spirit of the century would enter the domain of the drama and called for an inquiry into the twofold life of the character and his environment. It set the stage for Ibsen's dramas of social protest such as *Pillars of Society* and *Enemy of the People* (see p. 273). In the dramas of the Expressionists the social idea (for instance, the enslavement of workers by machines, as in Hauptmann's *The Weavers* [1893]) rather than the conflict of a single character with his environment became the concern of the dramatist. In the meantime the lyric or poetic element had been ignored; hence the Impressionists and Symbolists had a virgin soil for their labors. Maurice Maeterlinck's *Pélleas and Mélisande* is an example of poetic Symbolism in drama. Even Ibsen entered a more or less Symbolist phase in *The Wild Duck* and *The Master Builder*.

By the turn of the century the Norwegian Ibsen was no longer writing, and the Irishman George Bernard Shaw had replaced him as the leading realistic and satiric dramatist. After a brief return to Romanticism with Edmond Rostand and Sir James Barrie (see p. 341), the theater's Age of Innocence closed; there followed what critic Robert Brustein calls the "Theater of Revolt." Some new scientific techniques had enhanced the effectiveness of staging; the use of electricity, beginning about 1885, increased the possibilities of lighting for both naturalistic and atmospheric purposes; and the invention of the revolving stage in 1896 made it possible to produce multiscened plays with ease. These innovations led to more stylized and "theatrical" (less realistic) staging, especially in a number of *Intimate Theaters* established for modernistic experimentation.

By the second decade of the twentieth century conventional staging was being discarded in some plays in favor of a three-level platform with connecting steps, and the distinction of lighting between stage and auditorium was sometimes eliminated, thus making the audience a part of the drama. The pictorial possibilities of the cinema soon made stage naturalism seem inadequate and superfluous. In 1917 the first Surrealist play, Guillaume Apollinaire's *Les Mamelles de Tiresias* (*The Breasts of Tiresias*) was produced in Paris. In the same year came *Parade*, Jean Cocteau's Surrealist ballet with music by Eric Satie and designs by Picasso. In 1921 Pirandello produced his theatricalist masterpiece *Sei Personaggi in cerca d'autore* (*Six Characters in Search of an Author*). Three years later André Breton published his first Manifesto of Surrealism with emphasis on "pure automatism," requiring the elimination of intellectual, moral, and aesthetic factors from the creative process. Gertrude Stein's *Four Saints in Three Acts* (1927) is a good example of Surrealist drama and a forerunner of the Absurd play. In the New York production of Eugene O'Neill's *The Great God Brown* (1926), masks were first used to symbolize modern man's dual personality. At the same time central Europe, especially Germany, began to experiment with *Epic Theater* style, notably under Erwin Piscator. In Epic Theater the play depicts a long series of events without regard for the unities of place and time. Piscator used this style to dramatize savage social conflicts and Brecht's *Mother Courage* used it to depict an awareness of the power of the irrational moral choice in a given character. Around 1940 Thornton Wilder's theatricalist plays *Our Town* and *Skin of Our Teeth* were produced in New York. In the late 1940's the arena theater or *Theater in the Round* began to appear. In this type of theater scenery is entirely eliminated and there is almost total involvement of audience with actors.

The avant-garde *Living Theater* made its appearance in New York between 1954 and 1964 with such plays as Pirandello's *Tonight We Improvise* and Brecht's *A Man Is a Man*. This type is usually referred to as *Theater of the Absurd*. "Absurd" in this sense does not mean ridiculous but rather "out of harmony" with reason or propriety: incongruous, unreasonable, illogical. Absurdist theater was influenced by the preceding Dadaist and Surrealist movements, which were all products of postwar disenchantment and reaction against "middle-class realism." Plays in this style are unconcerned with social or psychological problems except in parody and mockery. They use bohemian shock tactics with coarse speech, freakish simplifications and exaggerations, clowning, naïveté, and calculated incredibility.

Albert Camus used the word "absurd" when trying to diagnose the human situation in a world of shattered beliefs. The Rumanian-born French playwright Eugène Ionesco used it to mean man lost: that is, "cut off from his religious, metaphysical, and transcendental roots." Such "anti-theater" dramatists do not believe that logic can be superimposed on an illogical world; hence they try to express nonlogically modern man's efforts to come to terms with the world in which he lives. Recurrent themes have been the impossibility of communication between people, the falsity of human values, man's isolation, the living who are really dead. For example, Ionesco's *Rhinoceros* is a fantasy about people whose desire to conform turns them into a herd of rhinoceroses.

Such drama can be effective; on the other hand it can easily degenerate into the condition described by John Mason Brown, drama critic emeritus for *Saturday Review:* "I for one am sick of the theater of the living dead, of derelicts, spongers, drug addicts, illusion-seekers in brothels, and conversationalists trapped in sand or emerging from ashcans. I resent having the theater offer me a fraction of truth, pretending that it is the whole truth." [1] Real decadence, in our century is marked by the dissolution of character. It is not the emphasis on obscenity, morbidity, or decay and death, but the disappearance of *man* that undermines the drama today. When *man* returns to the drama then we will once again have great plays.

*British and American Drama.* Drama in England and America has been for the most part realistic, but it has picked up ideas from all of the styles and techniques that we have been discussing.

SHAW. The Irishman, George Bernard Shaw (1856–1950), was primarily a satirist; but he was also a rebel against muddy think-

---

[1] *Saturday Review,* August 29, 1964.

ing and smug prudishness. He stripped bare cherished notions about conventional religion, sex, military heroism, high society, and professional charity; he offered in their place an intellectual confrontation of life itself. But he was never malicious; his witty satire makes good theater even today. While making fun of Romanticism, he is himself an archromanticist. This is Shaw's paradox. For an understanding of this duality, read the early *Candida* (1895) and the late *Saint Joan* (1923).

BARRIE. Sir James M. Barrie (1860–1937), a Scot, wrote whimsical and sentimental comedies which although dated are still popular. *What Every Woman Knows* (1908) says that woman is the real power behind her husband's throne. *The Admirable Crichton* (1902) concerns the sharp cleavage between aristocrats and servants. At home Crichton is the perfect butler, but when the family is shipwrecked on a desert island, where the primitive situation ordains that only those who work will eat, the resourceful Crichton becomes the master and the aristocrats become servants. Before Crichton's love affair with Lady Mary can be consummated, the family is rescued, and he becomes once more the "perfect butler."

SYNGE. John Millington Synge (1871–1909) was probably the greatest of the Irish nationalists. He was urged by his compatriot William Butler Yeats to learn the language and lore of the far western Irish peasants and to use them in his plays. He followed this advice, turned sharply away from the bourgeois realism of Shaw, and found the basis of his material and the key to his style in the character of the peasants. In his greatest play, *The Playboy of the Western World* (1907), he spoofed man's susceptibility to hero worship. Christy, the protagonist, has run away to a strange village because he thinks he has killed his father. To the villagers he is a glamorous hero, and to Pegeen and the Widow Quinn he is a desirable suitor. But the father had not been killed, only stunned, and when he comes looking for his son, Christy finds it necessary to do the deed all over again. This repetition at close range is another story and the villagers run him out. The father is not killed this time either, and he goes off chastising his son.

ELIOT. The American-born British poet T. S. Eliot (1888–1964) demonstrated a strange ambivalence in *The Cocktail Party* (1949). The play mingles sacred and profane, realism with the supernatural, poetry and prose, the dullness of cocktail parties with the modern fetish of psychiatry. At the first cocktail party, the marriage of Edward and Lavinia is nearing divorce; Lavinia has left Edward because of his affair with Celia Coplestone. Ed-

ward wants his wife back since she has dominated him so long
that he can't get along without her. Sir Henry Harcourt-Reilly, a
psychiatrist and kind of mystic priest, helps these characters
to understand each other and their possible choices. Julia and
Alex are a couple of busybodies who are very annoying until we
discover at the end that they are assistants of Sir Henry's, whose
work is incomplete without them. At the second cocktail party,
Edward and Lavinia are smugly happy because they have learned
to find and accept their destiny. Celia has accepted a life of self-
sacrifice and has been martyred in a jungle. Sir Henry is the
best-drawn character. He has a fine sense of humor and mixes
Christian and Eastern mysticism.

BOLT. Robert Bolt (1924–     ), whose chief influence was
Bertolt Brecht (see p. 346) wrote an outstanding epic drama in
*A Man for All Seasons* (1962). Although somewhat discursive,
the play was enormously popular for its excellent delineation of
Sir Thomas More as played by Paul Scofield. More, a man of
angel's wit, great learning, of mirth and pastimes, sometimes
sad, sometimes grave, was truly a "man of all seasons." Chan-
cellor of England under Henry VIII, he was a great lawyer and
Humanist, but like his contemporary Erasmus, he was opposed
to withdrawal from the Catholic Church. Henry wanted More to
give public approval of his sovereignty over the Church of England, but More felt that this act would betray himself and God.
He suffered death rather than violate his principles. As we see
him in the play, More is wise, witty, gentle, affectionate, often
perplexed, pathetic but never ignoble. Bolt used a character
called "The Common Man," who plays the part of narrator,
commentator, executioner, and a host of minor roles. Some of
the sets and costumes are conjured up before our eyes. The
author seems to be saying that we must resist the compromise
that corrupts, the conformity with society that becomes defor-
mity of the soul. The play has serious intent, pertinent theme, and
sound theatrical construction.

O'NEILL. One of the first major American dramatists was Eugene O'Neill (1888–1953), whom we have already mentioned
under "Expressionism." O'Neill went through a long career of
changing styles (Romanticism, Expressionism, Social Realism)
and perhaps attained true greatness only at the end of his life.
*The Emperor Jones* (1920) concerns a former Negro Pullman
porter who sets himself up as a god over an island in the West
Indies and dies a prey to his fears. *A Long Day's Journey into
Night* (1940) is considered by many critics a great tragedy. The
Tyrone family which it portrays is a single organism with four

branches. No character trait is revealed that does not have a bearing on the lives of the entire family, and nothing happens that does not have its roots in the past. The father is parsimonious and concerned with his career as an actor. He has sent his wife to a quack doctor, who has introduced her to drugs. Son Edmund is to be sent to a state farm for tuberculosis treatment. Son Jamie, an alcoholic, is envious of his brother's literary gifts and has lost faith in his own capacities because of his mother's inability to give up drugs. Although no one can move without hurting the others, the family is also bound by the chains of love. Compassion and understanding alternate with anger and recrimination. All four seek solace for the shocks of life in nostalgic memories. As the mother says, "Only the past when you were happy is real." At the end of the play she comes in carrying her wedding dress. The entire play takes place in one day, in mist and fog.

ANDERSON. Maxwell Anderson (1888–1959) wrote two good historical tragedies, *Elizabeth the Queen* (1930) and *Mary of Scotland* (1933). Historical drama is often valuable because it brings us close to the people and events that it portrays, but there are usually so many attendant circumstances to explain that it tends to be discursive. It takes a very good writer to make great theater out of history; even Shakespeare did not always succeed. The success of such works depends on the skill of the actor or actress who plays the title role.

MACLEISH. Archibald MacLeish (1892–    ) wrote one of the most controversial plays of this century in *J.B.* (1958), a modern adaptation of the Biblical book of Job. J.B. is a prosperous American business man whose faith in God is sorely tried by the loss of his family and possessions. The theme is the old problem of human suffering. At the end J.B. recognizes that God does not operate by the laws of human justice.

JEFFERS. Robinson Jeffers (1887–1962), although primarily a poet, wrote a fine poetic drama on the Hippolytus-Phaedra story which he called *The Cretan Woman*. We include it here so that the reader may compare it with the versions by Euripides and Racine (see pp. 194–195). While the rhythms and cadences of poetry are lacking, the language is poetic in a way that we have come to expect in English tragedy. The part of the chorus is taken convincingly by three old beggar women who, like their Greek prototypes, sense the supernatural presence emanating from the altar before the main characters do. Their earthy talk about food is a good foil for the supernatural.

In this version of the tragedy, classic pride and restraint are completely gone. Phaedra has little pride or reserve and even says that her love is ridiculous. Hippolytus jokes about love, saying, "The world is full of breeders: a couple in every bush: disgusting." When he tells Phaedra that we control our own wills and acts for good or evil, she replies that philosophy bores her. These are modern attitudes: the feeling that life is a game of chance and an unwillingness to come to grips with basic moral and ethical problems. Hippolytus judges Phaedra correctly when he says: "There is not one hair of difference between the extremes of love and hate." Our pity goes out to Theseus in the final scene when he says: "She was in trouble and I did not help her." The chorus supplies the theme: "The worst wounds that we suffer we inflict on ourselves." The old Greek story is still a powerful theme.

WILDER. Thornton Wilder (1897–1975), both playwright and novelist, experimented with the idea of the fluidity of time. *Our Town* (1938) celebrates in unconventional staging the heroism of ordinary small-town folk as they face the normal events of birth, life, and death. *The Skin of our Teeth* (1942) is a sort of allegory of mankind represented by the Antrobus family as they jump from the Stone Age, when Mr. Antrobus has just invented the wheel, to modern times when he is judging a beauty contest at Atlantic City. The mood becomes more serious when Mr. Antrobus tries to teach his children the accumulated wisdom of the ages, and when he fights the Fascist spirit in his son. This play, rich in amusing and serious comments on modern life, abounds in deliberate anachronisms, theatricalism, and rapid changes in mood.

SHERWOOD. Robert Sherwood (1896–1955) wrote a very popular play in *Abe Lincoln in Illinois*. It is one of the discursive historical plays mentioned above, but unforgettable as Raymond Massey played the role of Lincoln. Sherwood was concerned with the passing of systems and the death of societies. In *Idiot's Delight* (1936) an odd assortment of international characters are detained in a Swiss resort just before World War II, which Sherwood foresaw. Upon the outbreak of war, the Europeans succumb to extreme nationalism and reveal their smallness and banality in their effort to escape the impending disaster. The play is a satiric and mournful evocation of the madness of war and the chauvinism which it produces even in the most intelligent people.

STEINBECK. John Steinbeck (1902–1968), best-known as a novelist (see p. 330), wrote an experimental play in *Of Mice and Men* (1937). It is a sympathetic story about two migratory farm laborers in California who are struggling to acquire a bit of land of their own. The feebleminded Lennie is such a giant that he breaks everything he touches, even a girl. The good-natured George is powerless to save Lennie and kills him to keep him from being lynched. These two characters have an inarticulate nobility.

WILLIAMS. Few American dramatists have been as daring in experimentation as contemporary Europeans. Tennessee Williams (1914–     ) might be considered one of the exceptions. In *The Glass Menagerie* (1945) Williams explores time and memory. Tom Wingfield, who is both narrator and participant, evokes his early home in St. Louis, his domineering Southern-belle mother, and his crippled sister, who finds refuge in the imaginary world of her glass animal collection. The play combines realism with the subtle moods of reminiscence. This is the stream-of-consciousness technique pictorialized. Tom addresses the audience in plain violation of the realistic "fourth-wall" convention. He says in the first lines of the play: "I am the opposite of a stage magician. He gives you illusion that has the appearance of truth. I give you truth in the pleasant disguise of illusion."

MILLER. In *Death of a Salesman* (1948) Arthur Miller (1915–     ) wrote one of the finest dramas in American theater. The salesman, Willy Loman, has been all his life the victim of self-delusion. He believes that back-slapping and perseverance are the keys to success in business and life. At the age of sixty-three when he loses his job, he realizes that all his life he has pursued wrong goals. Although his wife loves him for what he is, she is powerless to prevent his suicide.

*European Drama.* European drama in the twentieth century has explored a wide variety of styles and methods. A number of playwrights were deeply affected by the wars and political upheavals of the period.

ROSTAND. Edmond Rostand (1868–1918), a French dramatist who repudiated the Naturalism of his generation created a great romantic play in *Cyrano de Bergerac* (1897). The play is virile, fanciful, exuberant, delightfully humorous, and perfectly constructed. It makes one feel that there is still room in the world for romance. It reminds one of Alexander Dumas, but Dumas was not subtle and never could have conceived the delicately tinted death scene.

PIRANDELLO. In *Sei Personaggi in cerca d'autore* (*Six Characters in Search of an Author*) (1921), the Italian Luigi Pirandello (1867–1936) wrote a satire on realism. To his fellow dramatists the author is saying in effect: "You think you are being realistic, do you? I'll show you what life is really like." In the play six characters invade a theater during a rehearsal of another play. Each character strives for a kind of part necessary to him and impossible for him to achieve. The manager is forced to listen to their story, a gruesome family imbroglio. As soon as they begin to act it out, the truth is distorted, theatrical conventions intrude, and the story ends by being more artificial than the actual play. To Pirandello, no virtue, truth, or convention is reliable, and he leads the audience also to question its own deep-seated convictions.

WERFEL. Franz Werfel (1890–1945), an Austro-Czech Jew, escaped from Germany during Hitler's purge, was in France until the Nazis took over, then went to Spain, and in 1940 to America. His only political credo was the search for humanity everywhere, and the avoidance of barbarism. Although primarily a novelist, he wrote the most successful European antiwar play. *Jacobowsky und der Oberst* (*Jacobowsky and the Colonel*) (1944) is a witty tragicomedy describing the reactions of German, French, Polish, and British minds to the war. The two main characters are Jacobowsky, a shrewd and witty Polish Jew who has fled Hitler all over Europe and is finally caught in the fall of Paris, and the flashy but incompetent Polish Colonel. They flee toward the Allied lines, first picking up the Colonel's French mistress Marianne, symbol of *La Belle France*. The two men become Don Quixote and Sancho Panza to each other, always conscious of being actors in a grotesque farce. The play is saved from sentimentality by the farcical and candid scenes.

BRECHT. Bertolt Brecht (1898–1956) was a satiric dramatist of fierce intensity. Driven out of his native Germany by Hitler, he went to Denmark, where he wrote *Mother Courage*. He came to the United States and wrote *The Caucasian Chalk Circle* here. Subpoenaed by the House Un-American Activities Committee because of his alleged Communist sympathies, he returned by invitation to East Germany, where he was given excellent facilities for staging his plays.

*Mutter Courage und ihre Kinder* (*Mother Courage and Her Children*) (1939) reveals the ironies and contradictions that attend man's acceptance of war. It is a quasi-historical kind of Epic Theater dealing with the Thirty Years' War, but its emphasis is on an individual human being who both lives by war and is destroyed by it. The scenes in which greed and cowardice are exposed alternate with scenes depicting perseverance and sympathy. Mother Courage is an itinerant peddler who lives off both sides in the struggle. Her wagon is her status symbol and her only possession. She loses her entire family, each a victim of his own heroic actions. She alone survives, still pulling her wagon, not realizing that because she lives off war she is partly responsible for the deaths of her children. Songs and war pictures cast upon a screen intensify the atmosphere.

*Der Kaukasische Kreidekreis (The Caucasian Chalk Circle)* (1945) is another epic play. It is an amalgam of many elements: comrades of collective farms contending for the valley and trying to work out the terms of ideal community; an ancient Chinese play about a child who is stolen by a maid, who loves him, from his own mother, who cares more to save her clothes than her child. It is a modern version of the Biblical story of the Judgment of Solomon. At the end of the play the circles close; the serving maid Grusha is awarded the child even though she refuses to pull him violently out of the circle that the judge has drawn to test the strength of the two claimants. She has become the mother in an organic way: by serving as mother. Similarly, the peasants who have watered the land get it.

LORCA. Federico García Lorca (1899–1936) was a Spanish poet who turned to the stage to gain a wider audience. His two principal themes were the Spanish peasant temperament as seen in folk literature, and the artificial preciosity of the Spanish Golden Age. His works are in the style of Lope da Vega (see p. 180): blood and pain, passionate and sensual love, fertility and barrenness, sin and cruelty. His characters are unnamed; they are types rather than individuals. More than half of *Blood Wedding* (1933) is poetry—folk songs which establish the mood of a scene or foreshadow one to come. Lorca also used the symbolism of color: rose for a wedding, blue-black for murders. As in Synge's *Riders to the Sea*, the young people all get killed and the old people are left to suffer. The play is gruesome but strangely beautiful.

GIRAUDOUX. Jean Giraudoux (1882–1944) was a life-long pacifist and foe of nationalism, and also a patriotic Frenchman with a very original mind. His characters are simple souls who enjoy food, wine, and love. They are pitted against the fanatics who resort to cruelty to defend their "ideals." *La Folle de Chaillot (The Madwoman of Chaillot)* (1943) is in essence a farce exemplifying reason-charged fantasy and fantastic reason. A group of speculators believes that there is oil under Paris and plots to destroy the city to get the oil. The "mad" woman sends the greedy men down a secret stairway through her cellar and they never come back. Then beauty and love return to earth. The colorful Parisian street characters are superbly delineated. The author says that the only truly sane people are the "mad" ones.

ANOUILH. Perhaps the most prolific European dramatist is the Frenchman Jean Anouilh (1910–    ). Anouilh is a psychological playwright who revived the classic idea that the downfall of a character is due to a tragic flaw (*hubris*) in his modern settings of *Antigone, Euridice,* and *Medea.* In his excellent play *Becket* (1959) he avoided the discursive pitfall of epic drama by concentrating only on Becket and King Henry. Even the vivid Queen Eleanor is given only a minor part. His version of the story of Joan of Arc called *L'Alouette* (*The Lark*) (1955) begins with her trial and dramatizes various events in her life through flashbacks. The play was intended to demonstrate Joan's triumph over the petty demands of worldly institutions.

BECKETT. Samuel Beckett, a Parisian Irishman (1906–    ), is the most avant-garde of this group of European dramatists. His *En Attendant Godot* (*Waiting for Godot*) (1952) has provoked endless discussions and critical analyses. Nothing happens in the play, and yet audiences find it vastly appealing. Beckett extracts from the idea of boredom the most genuine pathos and enchanting comedy. His message is not that of bleak despair, surely; on the contrary, it may be a message of religious consolation. Two tramps, Didi and Gogo, who have come from nowhere in particular and have nowhere in particular to go, are waiting for Godot (God?) to come but, although he sends messages, he never comes. Their attitude toward Godot is partly hope and partly fear. The ambiguity of their position may represent the state of tension and uncertainty in which modern man lives. The other two characters, Pozzo and Lucky, are "practical," but they become blind and dumb and must be helped by the contemplative "waiters." Pozzo and Lucky are drawn together by hate and fear, but Didi and Gogo are held together by something like charity. If they are not any better off at the end of the play, neither are they any worse off. The Christian element in the structure of the play is constantly underlined in symbolism and dialogue. The play is worth thoughtful reading.

**Poetry.** For poets the modern era has been a time of experimentation. They have abandoned familiar techniques and aimed at new effects made imperative by states of mind unknown to the Romantics and Symbolists, whose noble and sweet harmony couched in regular verse and sonorous music was not adapted to the dissonances of modern life. Hence, the new poets were dubbed eccentrics and their poetry was held suspect.

To express the complexity of his thought and feeling, the modern poet needs a new vocabulary, imagery which can express unusual states of mind, and forms which are not the result of an orderly mental exercise but which fit the emotional experience, no matter how contradictory or ambiguous it may be. All this imposes well-nigh insurmountable difficulties for many readers. In addition, by its very nature poetry is so personal a form that what appeals to one person may not appeal to another. The poet may not be particularly concerned as to whether or not he communicates his meaning to you, but there is meaning there or else the words are just so much gibberish and hence not a poem. The best approach is to read a difficult poem several times, decide what the poem means to you, and then express that meaning in a lucid prose sentence. Then go back and isolate the *images* (pictures) and *symbols* (words which stand for ideas) to discover how these contribute to or illustrate the meaning. To do this conscientiously will soon reveal the beauty of the language and the significance of the poem.

*European Poets.* Europe has produced some fine modern poets whom, because of the inadequacy of translation, we shall list but not discuss. They are: Guillaume Apollinaire (French, 1880–1918); Rainer Maria Rilke (German, 1875–1926); Constantine Cavafy (Greek, 1868–1933); Vladimir Mayakovsky (Russian, 1894–1930); Boris Pasternak (Russian, 1890–1960) (see p. 336); Federico García Lorca (Spanish, 1899–1936) (see p. 347); and Raphael Alberti (Italian, 1902–    ).

*Housman.* Alfred Edward (A. E.) Housman (1859–1936) was an eminent Latin scholar as well as a poet. After the publication of *A Shropshire Lad* in 1896, Housman's influence on the young poets was far-reaching. He abandoned conventional poetic imagery, used symbols sparingly, and concentrated on verbs and nouns instead of adjectives and adverbs. This style gives his work a starkness and directness of expression. Having lost his beloved mother when he was only twelve, he was always conscious of the imminence of death. This feeling is apparent in "Loveliest of Trees" and "To an Athlete Dying Young." "When I was One-and-Twenty" says that youth cannot learn from age but only from experience. Housman's later poems are more melancholy and sardonic: "Let us endure an hour and see injustice done." He calls upon man to assert even the values that appear to be doomed.

*Yeats.* William Butler Yeats (1865–1939) was one of the founders of the Irish Renaissance movement (see p. 341). He was influenced by the French Symbolists and by the folklore of his country. Throughout his life he was conscious of ambivalences in his nature: a recluse and a man of action, a symbolist and a realist, looking backward to youth and forward to age. In "Leda and the Swan" the swan is the symbol of poetic inspiration or spirit; Leda stands for the flesh. Their union produces Helen of Troy, who precipitates the Trojan War but also provides the inspiration for Homer's poem.

In "Sailing to Byzantium" Yeats sees himself as an old man leaving his homeland, which is the land of the young and the sensual, a land concerned only with procreation, birth, and death. He is going to Byzantium, the ancient repository of Greek and Oriental art, and the symbol of the mind and the spirit: all that is left after the sensual has been surmounted. These "monuments" alone are permanent and transcend the limitations of the flesh. He invokes the artists of the golden mosaics to pierce the whirlwind of the flesh and to make of him a golden bird: that is, to give him fresh poetic inspiration so that he can be a monument to an aging intellect.

*Eliot.* Probably the most significant twentieth-century poet was Thomas Stearns Eliot (1888–1965), an expatriate from America to England, who described his creed as "classicist in literature, royalist in politics, and Anglo-Catholic in religion." No modern artist has been more extravagantly praised and more extravagantly maligned than Eliot. He found a vocabulary which is sharp and unequivocal, couched in a form of stark, rocky directness, which he himself called "poetry standing naked in its bare bones." This was the tonic that modern poetry needed, the only style that could express the dissonances of the modern world.

Eliot's best poetry, exemplified by "The Hollow Men," "Gerontion," and "Waste Land," pictures the emotional starvation, purposelessness, and shallowness of our time, a kind of life divested of meaning and imagination. These poems are so full of symbolism, obscure allusions to the classics, and quotations from other languages as to be largely incomprehensible except to a small group of intellectuals. In them the poet is condemning the common, unlettered, "hollow" man. He seems to say that democracy is vulgar, ugly, and barbarous, without feeling compassion or desire to change the situation. Another of Eliot's concerns is with the general perversion of love. Prufrock, a tea-party-frequenting aristocrat, is unable to love or to act because of shyness, self-consciousness, and fear of rejection. Among the humbler people in Eliot's poems, either the men are unable to satisfy the women or the women are deserted by their lovers. Their experiences show the gulf between one human being and another.

Eliot's late poetry, written after his conversion to Anglo-Catholicism, has fewer classical allusions and is more concerned with morality and religion. These poems contain lines of great beauty, but they are less astringent than those of the early period. In "East Coker," Eliot celebrates a happy marriage among the lowly, and in "The Dry Salvages" there is a strong note of compassion. Read "The Love Song of J. Alfred Prufrock," "The Hollow Men," "Marina," and "East Coker." Eliot's poetry is pessimistic; even his religious experience did not bring him joy, but nonetheless it is great poetry.

*Graves.* Robert Graves (1895–     ) first became known for his poetry protesting the horrors of World War I. His poems are rough, direct, and powerful. He professed admiration for punctilious and intuitive realism, but his poetry is more likely to be eerie and fantastic. Read "The Legs," which seems to say that man is on a treadmill, everlastingly moving but without purpose or direction.

*Auden.* Wystan Hugh (W. H.) Auden (1907–1973) was an English poet who emigrated to the United States in 1939 and later became an American citizen. Before Auden left England his poetry made a cult of obscurity and was directed toward a small group of intellectuals. After coming to America, he deliberately tried to write for the general public. Auden was very intellectual and apparently had a profound knowledge and love of music and the fine arts. His range is great, from relatively simple ballads to elaborate symphonies and fugues. His "Song for St. Cecilia's Day," with its intricate rhythm and rhyme patterns, celebrates the legendary Christian martyr who was supposed to have invented the organ. The saint here represents life itself evolving in humankind the capacity for music, the art which seems to intimate superhuman excellence and to make prayer acceptable. Auden's "Musée des Beaux Arts" ("Museum of Fine Arts") is a poetic analysis of tragedy based on Brueghel's painting representing the fall of Icarus (see p. 143). It suggests that tragedy does not affect the whole world but is a personal affair of little concern to eyewitnesses who are busy with their own interests. Poetry, Auden says, makes nothing happen but makes suffering endurable by regarding it aesthetically.

"September 1, 1939" was written in a New York restaurant on the eve of World War II. It is a personal soliloquy on war and human degradation, ending with the admonition that "we must love one another or die." In this poem Auden affirmed the Christian beliefs that all created existence is good, that evil is the perversion of created good, and that all men are sinners when the will is perverted.

*Thomas.* The poetry of the Welsh Dylan Thomas (1914–

1953) is full of exuberant vitality and energy. Thomas was the inheritor of long centuries of Welsh bards, and his poems are meant to be read aloud or perhaps sung. He heaped metaphor upon metaphor and rhyme upon rhyme so that the thread of his discourse is sometimes lost. His early poems are obscure because they are based on a sort of private mythology which he never bothered to explain. In later poems the images become simpler, as when he describes the October wind that "With fists of turnips punishes the land." Thomas sang of life and death, love and nature. Read his "Fern Hill," which tells about the farm replete with growing things, where Thomas dreams of having spent his childhood. He suggests that when the child grows to manhood, he loses the sensuous delight in the world around him unless that world is restored and vivified by the poet. In "Refusal to Mourn the Death, by Fire, of a Child in London" (during an air raid), the poet says that life is passion and passion is suffering; had the child lived, she would have had to endure evil that her childish innocence did not know. For sheer pleasure we suggest that you read *Under Milk Wood,* a long dramatic poem which describes a day in the life of a little Welsh fishing village. It introduces us to its people, some good, some bad, all human. The poem expresses with humor and sympathy the poet's sense of the flavor and variety of life.

*Robinson.* Edwin Arlington Robinson (1869–1935) was a down-East Yankee with the New Englander's restraint, cynicism, and dry humor. He viewed life as a drama in which each person assumes a certain role before his fellows. Sometimes the mask is torn away as in the case of Richard Cory, who was gentleman to the manner born, but who ended a suicide. Sometimes the deception fails as for "Miniver Cheevy," who is such a romantic misfit that he never makes anything of himself. But Robinson's happiest characters are those who continue to maintain their illusions even when they realize them to be false. With true New England idealism, he believed that worldly failure may result in spiritual triumph.

*Frost.* Perhaps no poet has so endeared himself to a nation as did Robert Frost (1874–1963) to this generation of Americans, probably because of his unshakable independence and his large sympathy for all humanity. He lived in close touch with everything that was going on in the lives of his countrymen. Although he represented the old rural New England, his poetry is tougher than Robinson's. It is based on the facts of experience and is couched in a language which is plain and simple, not literary. His characters maintain their stubborn courage until they break in drudgery or isolation. His dramatic monologues might be about his own neighbors: the farmer who sees no reason to mend a wall, the woman whose mad uncle was housed in a cage in the attic until his fate crawls toward her. But there are also happy scenes that have a salty quality not found in Robinson. Frost writes of nature as one who loves it deeply (read "Stopping by Woods on a Snowy Evening") and who believes there is reason even in its apparent waste, as in the woodpile left in the swamp "to warm the swamp with its smokeless burning of decay." He wrote tenderly of young life: the runaway colt, the nest of young birds exposed by the cultivator.

But Robert Frost was not blind to evil and pain. In some of his late poems he confronted the anguish of existence and the presence of the malign. "Provide, Provide" treats the malice of fate with wry humor. In "The Constant Symbol," he sees his own poetic life as "straight crookedness," and says that every experience may begin in either delight or anguish, but it is bound to end in wisdom.

*Masters.* Edgar Lee Masters (1869–1950) was the mid-Western Frost. He was a realist who combined provincialism and universality. His *Spoon River Anthology,* a collection of epitaphs, is a microcosm of industrial America with its good, bad, and mediocre people, who are the victims of an economic system based on exploitation and stupidity; Masters did not conceal the sewage, the empty barrels, and the garbage cans. One of the characters who speak from the graveyard is "Lucinda Matlock," who worked hard beside her husband for seventy years, and who says to her children: "Life is too strong for you;/It takes life to love life." Read, too, the beautiful poem "Ann Rutledge."

*Sandburg.* Carl Sandburg (1878–1967) is sometimes called "The Poet of the Commonplace." He had vast sympathy for "The People," and did not hesitate to denounce their betrayers. He knew the Swedes, the "Dagos," the "Hunkies" who work in the stockyards and on the railroad, and these he celebrated in his poetry. His work has brought about a renewed awareness of ordinary life and language, including slang. His *American Songbag* is a comprehensive collection of American folk songs, over a hundred of which Sandburg copied down from hoboes, farmhands, and hill people. One of Sandburg's best poems is "Four Preludes on Playthings of the Wind," in which he sees civilization itself as ephemeral. The poem says that the past is a "bucket of ashes." In addition to poetry, Sandburg wrote a monumental biography of Lincoln.

*Lindsay.* Vachel Lindsay (1879–1931) is generally remembered as the poet of jazz rhythms. He had a zeal to reform the world and also a delight in his chosen art. He traveled about the country reciting his poetry and accompanying himself on a guitar. Young people especially enjoy the strong rhythms and savage simplicity of his "Congo" and "General William Booth Enters Heaven." However, his work is marred by the facile phrase, the shopworn metaphor, and the exuberance that mark the sentimentalist. He had a visionary feeling for his birthplace, Springfield, Illinois, and wrote a poem about Lincoln's ghost walking there in wartime.

*Millay, Benét, and Cummings.*   Here are three poets especially chosen for young people. Edna St. Vincent Millay (1892–1950) was one of the best-known and most financially successful poets of her day. Read her poem "Recuerdo," which celebrates two young lovers who ride back and forth on the ferryboat all night long just to be together. Stephen Vincent Benét (1898–1943) was interested in fantasy and in American themes. One of his finest poems is *John Brown's Body*, a long narrative poem on the Civil War. One section of it called "Lee" is a beautiful tribute to the Confederate General, who was heroic in defeat. Edward Estlin Cummings (or e.e.cummings) (1894–1962), known for the eccentricity of his typography and punctuation, wrote love poems, humorous character sketches, and satires on the foibles of his time. Boys especially like "I Sing of Olaf" in which an unsoldierly soldier is punished by his commanding officer, but he has the courage of his convictions and is braver than the officer. Now go back and read "The Balloon Man" (p. 16).

*Stevens.*   Wallace Stevens (1879–1955) has been called a sensualist and a "voluptuary of the mind." He had the painter's delight in colors and the musician's delight in sounds. In the first stanza of "Sunday Morning" notice how the poet has juxtaposed colors: coffee, oranges, "the green freedom of a cockatoo," "waterlights," "Dominion of the blood." He praises sunlight because it makes the sea sparkle and the river flash. The sounds of an autumn evening, the colors of a summer morning, the cry of a bird or the undulation of the sea increase the sensuous pleasure of the reader through the poet's experience of them.

But "Sunday Morning" is not just a nature poem. The lady, apparently seated on porch or patio enjoying a leisurely breakfast along with the beauty of the summer morning, keeps returning to thoughts of Sunday: the sepulchre of Jesus in "silent Palestine," of death not clothed in horror but as the mother of beauty. This leads to the thought of Paradise as the kingdom of enduring beauty and love, the "fulfilment of our dreams and desires." On earth the rock (truth) is covered; hence she feels the "need of some imperishable bliss."

To Stevens, poetry was the closest approach to religion. Even an Irish wake that is gawdy and rakish can still show love and devotion to the dead, as in "The Emperor of Ice Cream." This is the poem which Brian Moore used for the title of his novel (see p. 333).

*Williams.* William Carlos Williams (1883–1963) was a medical doctor who wrote poetry in his spare time. His poems are set in the life of the provincial town which he knew, Passaic, New Jersey. In poems which are much easier to read than those of Stevens, he speaks of suburban homes with their neat grass plots, the roads, the ferry, the glittering city across the river, all the sights and sounds of suburbia. He is just as objective when he talks of housewives, servant girls, children. He takes something as commonplace as a suburban street and gives it the quality of Botticelli's "Spring." This is sheer wizardry, but it is a wizardry that we can all understand, because the scenes are familiar. Williams has a deeper purpose in "The Yachts." The poem is an exciting account of a yacht race, but it ends in the disaster of torn and mangled bodies. The poem leaves one with a sense of both pleasure and grief, attitudes which are so often mingled in life itself.

As you read poetry, especially poetry as difficult as that of Eliot and Wallace Stevens, don't forget what Archibald MacLeish said: "A poem should not mean/But be."

## Conclusion

In concluding our survey of the arts, the author can see no reason for frustration or despair, or for the easy attitudes of cynicism or boredom. This is a glorious age in which to live; every field of endeavor is wide open and waiting for the courageous, vibrant soul to extend our far horizons. We say glibly: "the sky's the limit," but the sky has now become limitless. Remember, however, that Dante attained his vision of Paradise only *after* he had gone through Hell and Purgatory. Goethe's Faust was redeemed not because of his accomplishments, but because of his struggle. Hemingway's Old Man was not defeated by the sea but was planning to go back the next day for another try, and the young lad promised to go with him on his future expeditions. The boy is the symbol of renewal. When we have reached the end of our resources, then it is up to the next generation to carry on. This is the secret of all human progress.

August Heckscher, New York City Recreation and Parks Commissioner, has this to say: "As I move about the country I notice a dim, inarticulate but growing feeling that in the arts is to be found a kind of happiness which nothing else in our national life has been able to fulfill." [1] It is my earnest hope that you may find this happiness.

---

[1] *Life Magazine*, July 20, 1962.

# Bibliography

This Bibliography comprises first, a chapter-by-chapter listing of books related to the topics discussed in each chapter and, second, a Reference Bibliography in which are included the more difficult and more expensive volumes, as well as general histories. Books such as *Art in the Western World, The Story of Art, Music in Western Civilization,* and *Outline of European Architecture* are excellent references for every stylistic period. Paperback editions are designated by an asterisk.

## Chapter 1: The Meaning and Importance of the Humanities

Clark, Kenneth. *Civilisation.*\* New York: Harper & Row, 1970.

Hagen, Oscar. *Art Epochs and Their Leaders.* New York: Charles Scribner's Sons, 1927.

Lang, Paul Henry. *Music in Western Civilization.* New York: W. W. Norton & Co., 1941.

Miller, Alec. *Tradition in Sculpture.* New York: Studio Publications, 1949.

Moore, Douglas. *A Guide to Musical Styles.*\* New York: W. W. Norton & Co., 1962.

Pevsner, Nikolaus. *Outline of European Architecture.*\* Baltimore, Md.: Penguin Books, 1958.

Zucker, Paul. *Styles in Painting.*\* New York: Dover Publications, 1963.

## Chapter 2: Elements of the Arts

Apel, Willi, and Daniel, R. T. *Harvard Brief Dictionary of Music.*\* New York: Washington Square Press, 1961.

Drew, Elizabeth. *Discovering Poetry.*\* New York: W. W. Norton & Co., 1962.

Gardner, Helen. *Art through the Ages.* 6th ed. by H. De La Croix and R. O. Tansey. New York: Harcourt Brace Jovanovich, 1975.

Rosenheim, Edward. *What Happens in Literature.*\* Chicago: University of Chicago Press (Phoenix), 1960.

## Chapter 3: The Greeks

Gombrich, E. H. *The Story of Art.*\* 12th ed. New York: Oxford University Press, 1974.

Grant, Michael. *The Birth of Western Civilization*. New York: McGraw-Hill Book Co., 1964. Pp. 52–166.

Hamilton, Edith. *The Greek Way to Western Civilization.*\* New York: New American Library (Mentor), 1961.

Kaplan, Justin D. (ed.). *The Pocket Aristotle.*\* New York: Washington Square Press, 1961.

Kitto, H. D. *The Greeks.*\* Baltimore, Md.: Penguin Books, 1951.

Renault, Mary. *The Bull from the Sea.*\* New York: Pocket Books, 1963.

———. *The King Must Die.*\* New York: Pocket Books, 1958.

———. *The Last of the Wine.*\* New York: Pocket Books, 1964.

———. *The Mask of Apollo.*\* New York: Bantam, 1974.

Robinson, C. A. (ed.). *Anthology of Greek Drama,* Series I.\* New York: Holt, Rinehart & Winston, 1962.

Rosenmeyer, Thomas G. *The Masks of Tragedy: Essays on Six Greek Dramas*. Austin, Tex.: University of Texas Press, 1963.

Rouse, W. H. D. (trans.). *Great Dialogues of Plato.*\* New York: New American Library (Mentor), 1956.

## Chapter 4: The Romans
## and the Early Medieval Period

Beckwith, John. *Early Medieval Art.*\* New York: Frederick A. Praeger, 1965.

Bloch, Raymond. "In Search of the Etruscans," *Horizon Magazine of the Arts,* May, 1960.

Busch, Harald, and Lohse, Bernd. *Pre-Romanesque Art*. New York: Macmillan Co., 1966.

Dawson, Christopher. *The Making of Europe.*\* New York: New American Library (Meridian), 1956.

Guinagh, Kevin (ed. and trans.). *The Aeneid of Virgil.*\* New York: Holt, Rinehart & Winston, 1953.

Hinks, Roger. *Carolingian Art.*\* Ann Arbor, Mich.: University of Michigan Press, 1962.

Kessel, Dmitri. *The Splendors of Christendom*. Lausanne, Switzerland: Edita Lausanne, 1964.

*Medieval Epics*. Ed. W. S. Merwin and others. New York: Random House (Modern Library), 1963.

Power, Eileen. *Medieval People.*\* 10th ed. New York: Barnes & Noble, 1963.

Runciman, Steven. *Byzantine Civilization.*\* Cleveland, Ohio: World Publishing Co. (Meridian), 1956.

Sherrard, Philip. "Byzantium: The Other Half of the World," *Horizon Magazine of the Arts,* November, 1963.

Volpe, Carlo. *Early Christian to Medieval Painting*. New York: Golden Press, 1963.

## Chapter 5: The High Middle Ages

Adams, Henry. *Mont-Saint-Michel and Chartres.** New York: New American Library (Mentor), 1961.

Auberjonois, Ferdinand. "Gislebertus Hoc Fecit," *Horizon Magazine of the Arts*, September, 1961.

Chaucer, Geoffrey. *The Canterbury Tales.** Trans. R. M. Lumiansky. New York: Holt, Rinehart & Winston, 1954.

――――. *Troilus and Cressida.** Trans. G. P. Knapp. New York: Random House (Vintage), 1959.

Closs, August. *Medusa's Mirror: Studies in German Literature.* Chester Springs, Pa.: Dufour Editions, 1957.

Coulton, G. G. *Chaucer and His England.** New York: Barnes & Noble, 1963.

Dante Alighieri. *The Divine Comedy.* Trans. J. B. Fletcher. New York: Columbia University Press, 1951.

――――. *The New Life (La Vita nuova).** Trans. Mark Musa. Bloomington, Ind.: Indiana University Press, 1962.

Gilson, Étienne. *Heloïse and Abelard.** Ann Arbor, Mich.: University of Michigan Press, 1960.

Hutter, Heribert. *Medieval Stained Glass.* New York: Crown Publishers, 1963.

Kelly, Amy. *Eleanor of Aquitaine and the Four Kings.** New York: Random House (Vintage), 1957.

Lewis, C. S. *The Allegory of Love.** New York: Oxford University Press (Galaxy), 1963.

Lorris, Guillaume de, and Meun, Jean de. *The Romance of the Rose.** Trans. Harry Robbins. New York: E. P. Dutton & Co., 1962.

*Medieval Romances.** Ed. R. S. Loomis. New York: Random House (Modern Library), 1957.

## Chapter 6: The Renaissance

Artz, Frederick B. *From the Renaissance to Romanticism.** Chicago: University of Chicago Press (Phoenix), 1962.

Baroni, Constantine (ed.). *All the Paintings of Leonardo da Vinci.* Trans. Paul Colacicchi. New York: Hawthorn Books, 1961.

Bianconi, Piero (ed.). *All the Paintings of Piero della Francesca.* Trans. Paul Colacicchi. New York: Hawthorn Books, 1962.

Bishop, Morris. *Ronsard, Prince of Poets.** Ann Arbor, Mich.: University of Michigan Press, 1959.

Boccaccio, Giovanni. *The Decameron.** Trans. Richard Aldington. New York: Dell Publishing Co., 1949.

Byrne, M. St. Clare. *Elizabethan Life in Town and Country.** New York: Barnes & Noble, 1961.

Camesasca, Ettore (ed.). *All the Paintings of Raphael.* Trans. Luigi Grosso. New York: Hawthorn Books, 1963.

Canaday, John. "The Flowering of Flemish Art," *Horizon Magazine of the Arts,* Winter, 1966.

Castiglione, Baldassare. *The Courtier.** Trans. C. S. Singleton. Garden City, N.Y.: Doubleday (Anchor), 1959.

Chastel, André. *The Genius of Leonardo da Vinci.* Trans. Ellen Callmann. Orion Press, 1961.

Coletti, Luigi (ed.). *All the Paintings of Giorgione.* Trans. Paul Colacicchi. New York: Hawthorn Books, 1961.

Denis, Valentin (ed.). *All the Paintings of Jan van Eyck.* Trans. Paul Colacicchi. New York: Hawthorn Books, 1961.

Huizinga, J. *The Waning of the Middle Ages.** Garden City, N.Y.: Doubleday (Anchor), 1954.

Leonardo da Vinci. *Notebooks.** Ed. Pamela Taylor. New York: New American Library (Mentor), 1960.

Machiavelli, Niccolò. *The Prince.** Trans. George Bull. Baltimore, Md.: Penguin Books, 1961.

Naylor, E. W. *Shakespeare and Music.* New York: E. P. Dutton & Co., 1931.

Origo, Iris. "The Education of Renaissance Man," *Horizon Magazine of the Arts,* January, 1960.

Procacci, Ugo. *All the Paintings of Masaccio.* Trans. Paul Colacicchi. New York: Hawthorn Books, 1962.

Rabelais, François. *Gargantua and Pantagruel.** Trans. S. Putnam. New York: Viking Press, 1946.

Reade, Charles. *The Cloister and the Hearth.** New York: E. P. Dutton (Everyman), 1933.

Ross, J. B., and McLaughlin, M. M. (eds.). *The Portable Renaissance Reader.** New York: Viking Press, 1953.

Salvini, Roberto. *All the Paintings of Botticelli.* Trans. J. Grillenzoni. New York: Hawthorn Books, 1965.

———. *All the Paintings of Giotto.* Trans. Paul Colacicchi. New York: Hawthorn Books, 1963.

Schmitt, Pierre. *Mathias Grünewald and Other Masters of Colmar.* New York: A. S. Barnes, 1961.

Schneider, Laurie, ed. *Giotto in Perspective.** Englewood Cliffs, N.J.: Prentice-Hall, 1974.

Sidney, Sir Philip. *Selected Prose and Poetry.**New York: Holt, Rinehart & Winston, 1969.

Stevens, John E. *Music and Poetry in the Early Tudor Court.* Lincoln, Neb.: University of Nebraska Press, 1931.

Stone, Irving. *The Agony and the Ecstasy* (fictionalized life of Michelangelo).* New York: New American Library (Signet), 1963.

Tusiani, Joseph (ed.). *The Complete Poems of Michelangelo.** New York: Ivan Obolensky, 1960.

Valcanover, Francesco (ed.). *All the Paintings of Titian.* Trans. Sylvia Tomalin. New York: Hawthorn Books, 1964.

Villon, François, *Complete Works.** Trans. A. Bonner. New York: Bantam Books, 1960.

## Chapter 7: Mannerism

Baroni, Costantino (ed.). *All the Paintings of Caravaggio*. Trans. A. F. O'Sullivan. New York: Hawthorn Books, 1962.

Campbell, Lily Bess. *Shakespeare's Tragic Heroes*.* New York: Barnes & Noble, 1960.

Cellini, Benvenuto. *Autobiography*.* Trans. John Addington Symonds. New York: Bantam Books, 1956.

Cervantes, Miguel de. *Don Quixote*.* Trans. Walter Starkie. New York: New American Library (Signet), 1957.

Denis, Valentin (ed.). *All the Paintings of Pieter Bruegel*. Trans. Paul Colacicchi. New York: Hawthorn Books, 1961.

Fletcher, J. B. *Literature of the Italian Renaissance*. New York: Macmillan Co., 1934.

Gowing, Lawrence. *Vermeer*.* New York: Harper & Row (Icon), 1975.

Grimmelshausen, H. J. C. von. *Simplicius Simplicissimus*.* Trans. G. Schultz-Behrend. Indianapolis, Ind.: Bobbs-Merrill (Liberal Arts), 1965.

Montaigne, Michel de. *Complete Essays of Montaigne*.* Trans. Donald M. Frame. Stanford, Calif: University of California Press, 1958.

Shakespeare, William. *King Lear*.* Random House (Arden Shakespeare), 1964.

Stubbe, A. *Rubens*.* Trans. Albert J. Fransella. New York: Barnes & Noble, 1966.

Tasso, Torquato. *Jerusalem Delivered*.* Trans. Edward Fairfax. New York: G. P. Putnam's Sons, 1963.

Zesmer, David M. *Guide to Shakespeare*. New York: Barnes & Noble, 1976.

## Chapter 8: The Baroque

Addison, Joseph, and Steele, Richard. *The Spectator Papers*. New York: E. P. Dutton & Co., 1964.

Beeren, William. *Hals*.* Trans. Albert J. Fransella. New York: Barnes & Noble, 1963.

Bukofzer, Manfred. *Music in the Baroque Era, from Monteverdi to Bach*. New York: W. W. Norton & Co., 1947.

Flores, Angel (ed.). *Masterpieces of the Spanish Golden Age*.* New York: Holt, Rinehart & Winston, 1960.

Lang, Paul Henry. *George Frederic Handel*. New York: W. W. Norton & Co., 1966.

Manzoni. Alessandro. *The Betrothed*.* Trans. Archibald Colquhoun. New York: E. P. Dutton (Everyman), 1961.

Milton, John. *Paradise Lost*.* Ed. Meritt Y. Hughes. New York: Odyssey Press, 1962.

Molière (Jean Baptiste Poquelin). *Five Plays*. Trans. John Wood. Baltimore, Md.: Penguin Books, 1960.

Pirro, André. *J. S. Bach*. Trans. Mervyn Savill. New York: Crown Publishers, 1957.

Schmitt, Gladys. *Rembrandt* (fictionalized life).* New York: Dell Publishing Co., 1962.

Wölfflin, Heinrich. *Principles of Art History* (differences between Renaissance and Baroque styles).* Trans. M. D. Hottinger. New York: Dover Publications, 1932.

Zumthor, Paul. *Daily Life in Rembrandt's Holland.* New York: Macmillan Co., 1963.

## Chapter 9: The Classic Period

Barbaud, Pierre. *Haydn.** Trans. Katherine Sorley Walker. New York: Grove Press (Evergreen Profile), 1959.

Dryden, John. *Poetry, Prose, and Plays.* Ed. Donald Grant. Cambridge, Mass.: Harvard University Press, 1952.

Einstein, Alfred. *Mozart: His Character and His Work.** Trans. Arthur Mendel and Nathan Broder. New York: Oxford University Press (Galaxy), 1965.

Houghton, Norris (ed.). *Masterpieces of Continental Drama.* Vol. I, *The Golden Age* (Corneille, Racine, Molière).* New York: Dell Publishing Co., 1963.

Mitford, Nancy. *The Sun King* (Louis XIV). New York: Harper & Row, 1966.

Nicholson, Harold. *The Age of Reason.* Garden City, N.Y.: Doubleday & Co., 1961.

Pope, Alexander. *Selected Works.* Ed. Louis Kronenberger. New York: Random House (Modern Library), 1951.

Rousseau, Jean-Jacques. *Émile.** New York: Teacher's College, 1962.

Sullivan, J. W. N. *Beethoven: His Spiritual Development.** New York: Random House (Vintage), 1960.

Sypher, Wylie. *Rococo to Cubism in Art and Literature.** New York: Random House (Vintage), 1960.

Tempko, Allan. "The Louvre: 1180–1871," *Horizon Magazine of the Arts,* September, 1960.

Voltaire (François Marie Arouet). *Candide.** Trans. Lowell Bair. New York: Bantam Books, 1961.

Winwar, Frances. *Jean Jacques Rousseau.* New York: Random House, 1961.

## Chapter 10: Romanticism

Blake, William. *Selected Poems.* Ed. F. W. Bateson. New York: Barnes & Noble, 1957.

Clark, Kenneth. *The Romantic Rebellion: Romatic versus Classic Art.* New York: Harper & Row, 1974.

Dumas, Alexandre. *The Three Musketeers.** Baltimore, Md.: Penguin Classics, 1952.

Goethe, Johann Wolfgang von. *The Sorrows of Young Werther.** Trans. Catherine Hutter. New York: New American Library (Signet), 1962.

Gowing, Lawrence (ed.). *Turner: Imagination and Reality.* New York: Doubleday & Co. and Museum of Modern Art, 1966.

Hawthorne, Nathaniel. *The Scarlet Letter.** Boston: Houghton Mifflin (Riverside), 1960.

Herbert, Robert L. *Barbizon Revisited.* New York: Clarke & Way, 1963.

Houghton, Norris (ed.). *Masterpieces of Continental Drama.* Vol. II, *The Romantic Influence* (Goethe, Schiller, Hugo, Rostand).* New York: Dell Publishing Co., 1963.

Johnson, Lee. *Delacroix.* New York: W. W. Norton & Co., 1963.

Manzoni, Alessandro. *The Betrothed.** Trans. Archibald Colquhoun. New York: E. P. Dutton (Everyman), 1961.

Poe, Edgar Allan. *Selected Prose and Poetry.** Ed. W. H. Auden. New York: Holt, Rinehart & Winston, 1956.

Pushkin, Alexandre. *Poems, Prose, and Plays.* Ed. A. Yarmolinsky. New York: Random House (Modern Library), 1936.

Schiller, Friedrich. *William Tell.** Trans. Sidney Kaplan. Great Neck, N.Y.: Barron's Educational Series, 1954.

Stendhal (Marie Henri Beyle). *The Charterhouse of Parma.** New York: New American Library (Signet), 1962.

Williams, Oscar (ed.). *Immortal Poems of the English Language* (Gray, Goldsmith, Burns, Wordsworth, Coleridge, Byron, Shelley, Keats).* New York: Washington Square Press, 1962.

## Chapter 11: Realism, Romantic Realism, and Naturalism

Balzac, Honoré de. *Eugénie Grandet.* Trans. D. Walter and J. Watkins. New York: Random House (Modern Library), 1950.

————. *Old Goriot.** Trans. Henry Reed. New York: New American Library (Signet), 1962.

Browning, Elizabeth Barrett. *Sonnets from the Portuguese.** New York: Doubleday (Dolphin), 1954.

Browning, Robert. *Selected Poems.** Ed. J. Reeves. New York: Barnes & Noble, 1955.

Callow, James T., and Reilly, Robert J. *Guide to American Literature from Its Beginnings through Walt Whitman.** New York: Barnes & Noble, 1976.

Chekhov, Anton. *The Cherry Orchard.** Trans. T. Guthrie and L. Kipnis Minneapolis, Minn.: University of Minnesota Press, 1965.

Dickens, Charles. *A Tale of Two Cities.** New York: New American Library (Signet), 1960.

Dostoevsky, Fyodor. *The Brothers Karamazov* (abridged).* Ed. Edmund Fuller. New York: Dell Publishing Co., 1956.

Flaubert, Gustave. *Madame Bovary.** Trans. Francis Steegmuller. New York: Random House (Modern Library College Editions), 1957.

Glackens, Ira. *William Glackens and the Ashcan School.** New York: Grosset & Dunlap (Universal Library), 1957.

Guerney, B. G. (ed.). *The Portable Russian Reader* (Gogol, *The Overcoat;* Turgenev, *The Specters).** New York: Viking Press, 1964.

Houghton, Norris (ed.). *Masterpieces of Continental Drama.* Vol. III, *Seeds of Modern Drama* (Zola, Ibsen, Chekhov).* New York: Dell Publishing Co., 1963.

Ibsen, Henrik. *Four Great Plays (A Doll's House, Ghosts, An Enemy of the People, The Wild Duck).** Ed. John Gassner. New York: Bantam Books, 1959.

James, Henry. *Portrait of a Lady.** New York: New American Library (Signet), 1964.

Melville, Herman. *Moby Dick* (abridged).* Ed. Maxwell Geismar. New York: Washington Square Press, 1956.

Selinko, Annemarie. *Désirée.* New York: Pocket Books, 1953.

Seltzer, Thomas (ed.). *Best Russian Short Stories* (Dostoevsky, "The Christmas Tree and the Wedding"). New York: Random House (Modern Library), 1918.

Speare, M. E. (ed.). *Pocket Book of Short Stories* (Maupassant, Chekhov, Tolstoi, Poe, Twain).* New York: Washington Square Press, 1941.

Tennyson, Alfred, Lord. *Poems.** Ed. Clyde de L. Ryals. Philadelphia: University of Pennsylvania Press, 1966.

Thackeray, William Makepeace. *Henry Esmond.** New York: Washington Square Press, 1963.

Thoreau, Henry. *Walden.** Ed. Owen Thomas. New York: W. W. Norton & Co., 1966.

Tolstoi, Leo. *War and Peace* (abridged).* Ed. Edmund Fuller. New York: Dell Publishing Co., 1955.

Whitman, Walt. *Leaves of Grass and Selected Prose.** Ed. John Kouwenhoven. New York: Random House (Modern Library College Editions), 1960.

Williams, Oscar (ed.). *Immortal Poems of the English Language* (Elizabeth Barrett Browning, Robert Browning, Poe, Tennyson, Lowell, Whitman).* New York: Washington Square Press, 1961.

## Chapter 12: The Modern Period

Anderson, Sherwood. *Winesburg, Ohio.** New York: Viking Press (Compass), 1958.

Anouilh, Jean. *The Lark.* Trans. Christopher Fry. New York: Oxford University Press, 1956.

Barrie, James M. *Representative Plays.* New York: Charles Scribner's Sons, 1954.

Beckett, Samuel. *Waiting for Godot.** New York: Grove Press (Evergreen), 1956.

Brecht, Bertholt. *Mother Courage and Her Children.** Trans. Eric Bentley. New York: Grove Press (Evergreen), 1963.

Callow, James T., and Reilly, Robert J. *Guide to American Literature from Emily Dickinson to the Present.*\* New York: Barnes & Noble, 1977.

Camus, Albert. *The Plague.*\* New York: Random House (Modern Library College Editions), 1965.

Canaday, John. *Mainstreams of Modern Art.* New York: Simon & Schuster, 1959.

Conrad, Joseph. *Lord Jim.*\* New York: New American Library (Signet), 1961.

Deri, Otto. *Exploring Twentieth-Century Music.* New York: Holt, Rinehart & Winston, 1968.

Eliot, T. S. *The Cocktail Party.*\* New York: Harcourt, Brace & World (Harvest), 1964.

Faulkner, William. *Intruder in the Dust.*\* New York: Random House (Vintage), 1972.

————. *The Unvanquished.*\* New York: New American Library (Signet), 1961.

Fitzgerald, F. Scott. *The Great Gatsby.*\* New York: Charles Scribner's Sons, 1925.

Gide, André. *Lafcadio's Adventures.*\* New York: Random House (Vintage), 1925.

Hemingway, Ernest. *A Farewell to Arms.*\* New York: Charles Scribner's Sons, 1923.

————. *The Old Man and the Sea.*\* New York: Charles Scribner's Sons, 1952.

Houghton, Norris. *Masterpieces of Continental Drama.* Vol. III, *Seeds of Modern Drama* (Strindberg, Hauptmann).\* New York: Dell Publishing Co., 1963.

Hunter, Sam. *American Art of the Twentieth Century.* New York: Harry N. Abrams, 1973.

Huxley, Aldous. *Brave New World Revisited.*\* New York: Bantam Books, 1960.

Jeffares, Alexander N. *W. B. Yeats: Man and Poet.* New York: Barnes & Noble, 1949.

Jeffers, Robinson. *The Cretan Woman.* (In the Modern Repertoire, Series III). Ed. Eric Bentley. Bloomington, Ind.: Indiana University Press, 1956.

Joyce, James. *Portrait of the Artist as a Young Man.*\* New York: Viking Press (Compass), 1964.

Lawrence, D. H. *Lady Chatterley's Lover.*\* New York: New American Library (Signet), 1954.

Lewis, Sinclair. *Babbitt.*\* New York: New American Library (Signet), 1949.

MacIntyre, C. F. (trans.). *French Symbolist Poetry.*\* Berkeley, Calif.: University of California Press, 1961.

Mann, Thomas. *The Magic Mountain.* New York: Alfred A. Knopf, 1927.

Mailer, Norman. *The Naked and the Dead.** New York: New American Library (Signet), 1954.

Malamud, Bernard. *The Assistant.** New York: New American Library (Signet), 1958.

Maugham, Somerset. *Of Human Bondage.** New York: Pocket Books, 1942.

Mazzetti, Lorenza. *Rage.* New York: David McKay, 1965.

Miller, Arthur. *Death of a Salesman.** New York: Viking Press (Compass), 1949.

Moore, Brian. *The Emperor of Ice Cream.** New York: Bantam Books, 1966.

Newmeyer, Sarah. *Enjoying Modern Art.** New York: New American Library (Mentor), 1960.

O'Neill, Eugene. *A Long Day's Journey into Night.** New Haven: Yale University Press, 1956.

Pasternak, Boris. *Doctor Zhivago.** New York: New American Library (Signet), 1959.

Paton, Alan. *Cry, the Beloved Country.** New York: Charles Scribner's Sons, 1948.

Proust, Marcel. *Swann's Way.** New York: Random House (Modern Library College Editions), 1956.

Renault, Mary. *The Mask of Apollo.* New York: Pantheon, 1966.

Sherwood, Robert. *Idiot's Delight.* In *Twenty Best Plays of the Modern American Theatre.* Ed. John Gassner. New York: Crown Publishers, 1965.

Silone, Ignazio. *Bread and Wine.* New York: Atheneum, 1962.

Speare, M. E. (ed.). *Pocket Book of Short Stories* (O. Henry, Hemingway, Benét, Maugham).* New York: Washington Square Press, 1941.

Steinbeck, John. *The Grapes of Wrath.** New York: Viking Press (Compass), 1958.

———. *Of Mice and Men.** New York: Viking Press (Compass), 1963.

Synge, J. M. *The Playboy of the Western World and Riders to the Sea.** New York: Barnes & Noble, 1962.

Thomas, Dylan. *Under Milk Wood.** New York: New Directions, 1959.

Waugh, Evelyn. *Brideshead Revisited.** New York: Dell Publishing Co., 1956.

Wharton, Edith. *The Age of Innocence.** New York: New American Library (Signet), 1962.

Wilder, Thornton. *Our Town* and *The Skin of Our Teeth.* In *Three Plays.** New York: Harper & Row (Harper's Modern Classics), 1957.

Willams, Oscar (ed.). *Immortal Poems of the English Language* (Eliot, Yeats, Auden, Masters, Robinson, Frost, Lindsay, Millay, Williams, Graves, Stevens).* New York: Washington Square Press, 1961.

Williams, Tennessee. *The Glass Menagerie.** New York: New Directions, 1949.

Williams, William Carlos. *Selected Poems.** Rev. ed. New York: New Directions, 1969.

Woolf, Virginia. *To the Lighthouse.** New York: Harcourt, Brace & World (Harvest), 1949.

Wright, Frank Lloyd. *On Architecture.** Ed. Frederick Gutheim. New York: Grosset & Dunlap (Universal Library), 1960.


# REFERENCE BIBLIOGRAPHY

## Aesthetics and History

Barr, Stringfellow. *The Pilgrimage of Western Man* (history of Europe, 1500–1961).* Philadelphia: J. B. Lippincott (Keystone), 1962.

Berenson, Bernard. *Aesthetics and History.** Garden City, N.Y.: Doubleday (Anchor), 1954.

Bronowski, Jacob. *The Ascent of Man.** Boston: Little, Brown & Co., 1974.

Calmette, Joseph. *The Golden Age of Burgundy, 1364–1477.* New York: W. W. Norton & Co., 1962.

Davidson, Kerry. *Twentieth-Century Civilization.** New York: Barnes & Noble, 1975.

Gibbon, Edward. *The Decline and Fall of the Roman Empire* (abridged).* Ed. H. R. Trevor-Roper. New York: Washington Square Press, 1963.

Kayser, Wolfgang. *The Grotesque in Art and Literature.* Trans. Ulrich Weisstein. Bloomington, Ind.: Indiana University Press, 1963.

Kirchner, Walther. *Western Civilization to 1500.** New York: Barnes & Noble, 1960.

———. *Western Civilization since 1500.** 2nd ed. New York: Barnes & Noble, 1975.

Lucas, F. L. *The Decline and Fall of the Romantic Ideal.** New York: Cambridge University Press, 1948.

Pater, Walter. *The Renaissance.** New York: New American Library (Mentor), 1959.

Runciman, Steven *The Fall of Constantinople, 1453.* New York: Cambridge University Press, 1965.

## Fine Arts

Amiliani, Andrea (ed.) *Early Christian to Medieval Painting.* Vol. V of *Art of the Western World.* New York: Golden Press, 1963.

Ashton, Dore. *The Unknown Shore.* Boston: Little, Brown & Co., 1962. (This author is enthusiastic about Abstract Expressionism. See Huntington Hartford for the opposite view.)

Banham, Reyner. *The Age of the Masters: A Personal View of Modern Architecture.** New York: Harper & Row (Icon), 1975.

Bazin, Germain. *The Loom of Art.* Trans. Jonathan Griffin. New York: Simon & Schuster, 1962.

Canaday, John. *Keys to Art.* New York: Tudor Publishing Co., 1962.

Cichy, Bodo. *The Great Ages of Architecture.* New York: G. P. Putnam's Sons, 1964.

Clark, Kenneth. *Landscape into Art*. Rev. ed. New York: Harper & Row, 1976.

Delevoy, Robert. *Early Flemish Painting*. New York: McGraw-Hill Book Co., 1963.

*Dictionary of Modern Sculpture*. Ed. F. Hazan. New York: Tudor Publishing Co., 1960.

Fitch, James M. *Architecture and the Aesthetics of Plenty*. New York: Columbia University Press, 1961.

Gombrich, E. G. *The Story of Art*.* 12th ed. New York: Phaidon Art Books, 1974.

Grant, Michael (ed.). *The Birth of Western Civilization: Greece and Rome*. New York: McGraw-Hill Book Co., 1964.

Grohmann, Will. *The Expressionists*. New York: Harry N. Abrams, 1961.

Guitton, Jean. *The Madonna*. New York: Tudor Publishing Co., 1963.

Hall, R. J. *Dictionary of Subjects and Symbols in Art*.* New York: Harper & Row (Icon), 1974.

Hart, Ivor B. *The World of Leonardo da Vinci*. New York: Viking Press, 1962.

Hartford, Huntington. *Art or Anarchy*. New York: Doubleday & Co., 1964. (This author is opposed to the moderns except for Dali. See Dore Ashton for an opposite view.)

Horizon Magazine (eds.). *The Light of the Past*. New York: Simon & Schuster, 1965.

Janson, H. W. *History of Art*. Rev. ed. Englewood Cliffs, N.J.: Prentice-Hall, 1969.

Lieberman, William S. (ed.). *Pablo Picasso*. New York: Harry N. Abrams, 1952.

McClinton, Katharine. *Christian Art through the Ages*. New York: Macmillan Co., 1962.

Panofsky, Erwin. *Early Netherlandish Painting*. Cambridge, Mass.: Harvard University Press, 1954. Vol. I text; Vol. II, plates.

Pevsner, Nikolaus. *Outline of European Architecture*.* Baltimore, Md.: Penguin Books (Pelican), 1960.

Pope-Hennessy, John. *Italian Renaissance Sculpture*. 3 vols. Greenwich, Conn.: New York Graphic Society, 1958.

*Praeger Encyclopedia of Art*. 5 vols. New York: Frederick A. Praeger, 1971.

Richardson, Tony, and Stangos, Nikos, eds. *Concepts of Modern Art*.* New York: Harper & Row (Icon), 1974.

Richter, Gisela M. *Handbook of Greek Art*. 4th ed. Greenwich, Conn.: New York Graphic Society (Phaidon), 1960.

Symonds, J. A. *The Renaissance in Italy*.* 4 vols. New York: G. P. Putnam's Sons (Capricorn), 1960.

Wehle, Harry B. *Art Treasures of the Prado Museum*. New York: Harry N. Abrams, 1954.

Wölfflin, Heinrich. *Classic Art: Introduction to the Italian Renaissance*. 2nd ed. Greenwich, Conn.: New York Graphic Society (Phaidon), 1953.

Young, G. F. *The Medici*. New York: Random House (Modern Library), 1930.

## Music

Allen, Warren D. *Philosophy of Music History*.* New York: Dover Publications, 1963.

Apel, Willi. *Harvard Dictionary of Music*. 2nd rev. ed. Cambridge, Mass.: Harvard University Press, 1969.

Bernstein, Leonard. *The Joy of Music*.* New York: New American Library (Mentor), 1967.

*An Elizabethan Song Book*.* Ed. Noah Greenberg, W. H. Auden, and Chester Kallman. Garden City, N.Y.: Doubleday (Anchor), 1956.

Ewen, David. *Encyclopedia of the Opera*. Rev. ed. New York: Hill & Wang, 1963.

Gal, Hans. *Johannes Brahms: His Work and Person*. Trans. Joseph Stein. New York: Alfred A. Knopf, 1963.

Grove, George. *Dictionary of Music and Musicians*. 5th ed. by George Grove and Denis Stevens. New York: St. Martin's Press, 1961.

Hodeir, André. *Since Debussy: A View of Contemporary Music*.* Trans. Noel Burch. New York: Grove Press (Evergreen), 1961.

Howard, John Tasker. *Our American Music*. 4th ed. New York: Thomas Y. Crowell Co., 1965.

Lang, Paul Henry (ed.). *One Hundred Years of Music in America*. New York: G. Schirmer, 1961.

———. *Problems of Modern Music*.* New York: W. W. Norton & Co., 1962.

———, and Bettmann, O. L. *Pictorial History of Music*. New York: W. W. Norton & Co., 1962.

Lockspeiser, Edward. *Debussy, His Life and Times*. 2 vols. New York: Macmillan Co.; Vol. I (Collier),* 1962; Vol. II, 1965.

Machlis, Joseph. *Introduction to Contemporary Music*. New York: W. W. Norton & Co., 1961.

Miller, Hugh M. *History of Music*.* 4th ed. New York: Barnes & Noble, 1972.

Parrish, C. C. (ed.). *Treasury of Early Music*.* New York: W. W. Norton & Co., 1958.

Reese, Gustave. *Music in the Middle Ages*. New York: W. W. Norton & Co., 1940.

Rolland, Romain. *Essays on Music*.* Ed. David Ewen. New York: Dover Publications, 1959.

Sessions, Roger. *The Musical Experience of Composer, Performer, Listener*.* New York: Atheneum Publishers, 1965.

Weinstock, Herbert. *Tchaikovsky*. New York: Alfred A. Knopf, 1943.

## Literature

Adams, N. B., and Keller, J. E. *Brief Survey of Spanish Literature*.* 3rd ed. Totowa, N.J.: Littlefield, Adams & Co., 1974.

Babbitt, Irving. *Masters of Modern French Criticism.*\* New York: Farrar, Straus & Giroux (Noonday Press), 1963.

Bowra, C. M. *The Creative Experiment.* New York: Grove Press, 1958.

Brée, Germaine. *Albert Camus.* New York: Columbia University Press, 1964.

Brooks, Cleanth (ed.). *Tragic Themes in Western Literature.*\* New Haven, Conn.: Yale University Press, 1955.

————, and Heilman, Robert B. (eds.). *Understanding Drama.* New York: Holt, Rinehart & Winston, 1948.

Brustein, Robert S. *The Theatre of Revolt: An Approach to the Modern Drama.*\* Boston: Little, Brown & Co., 1964.

Cazamian, Louis. *A History of French Literature.*\* New York: Oxford University Press, 1955.

Cohen, J. M. (ed.). *Penguin Book of Spanish Verse.*\* Baltimore, Md.: Penguin Books, 1960.

Cummings, E. E. *Poems, 1923–1954.* New York: Harcourt, Brace & World, 1954.

Deutsch, Babette. *Poetry in Our Time.*\* Garden City, N.Y.: Doubleday (Anchor), 1963.

Downer, Alan S., ed. *American Theater Today.* New York: Harper & Row, 1967.

Ellmann, Richard, and Feidelson, Charles, Jr. (eds.). *The Modern Tradition: Backgrounds in Modern Literature.* New York: Oxford University Press, 1965.

Farnham, Willard. *The Medieval Heritage of Elizabethan Tragedy.* New York: Barnes & Noble, 1957.

Flores, Angel (ed.). *Anthology of French Poetry from Nerval to Valéry.*\* Rev. ed. Garden City, N.Y.: Doubleday (Anchor), 1962.

————. *Anthology of German Poetry from Hölderlin to Rilke.*\* Garden City, N.Y.: Doubleday (Anchor), 1960.

Gassner, John. *Directions in Modern Theatre and Drama.* Rev. ed. New York: Holt, Rinehart & Winston, 1965.

Greaves, Margaret. *The Blazon of Honour: Studies in Medieval and Renaissance Magnanimity.* New York: Barnes & Noble, 1964.

Hamburger, Michael. *Reason and Energy: Studies in German Literature.*\* New York: Grove Press (Evergreen), 1957.

Headings, Philip R. *T. S. Eliot.*\* New Haven, Conn.: College and University Press Services, 1964.

Heller, Eric (ed.). *Studies in Modern French Literature.* New Haven, Conn.: Yale University Press, 1960.

Henn, T. R. *The Lonely Tower: Studies in the Poetry of W. B. Yeats.*\* 2nd ed. New York: Barnes & Noble, 1965.

Hoffman, Frederick J. *The Modern Novel in America, 1900–1950.*\* Rev. ed. Chicago: Henry Regnery Co. (Gateway), 1964.

Holbrook, David. *Dylan Thomas and Poetic Dissociation.* Carbondale, Ill.: Southern Illinois University Press, 1964.

Kay, George (ed.). *The Penguin Book of Italian Verse*. Baltimore, Md.: Penguin Books, 1958.

Levin, Harry. *The Gates of Horn: Study of Five French Realists.** New York: Oxford University Press (Galaxy), 1963.

Litz, A. Walton (ed.). *Modern American Fiction: Essays in Criticism.** New York: Oxford University Press (Galaxy), 1963.

Loomis, Roger Sherman. *A Mirror of Chaucer's World*. Princeton, N.J.: Princeton University Press, 1965.

Matthiessen, F. O. *American Renaissance: Art and Expression in the Age of Emerson and Whitman.** New York: Oxford University Press, 1968.

Murry, John Middleton. *William Blake.** New York: McGraw-Hill Book Co., 1964.

Rennert, Hugo A. *The Spanish Stage at the Time of Lope de Vega.** New York: Dover Publications, 1963.

Scott, Wilbur S. (ed.). *Five Approaches of Literary Criticism*. New York: Macmillan Co., 1963.

Shapiro, Karl. *In Defense of Ignorance.** New York: Random House (Vintage), 1960.

Slonim, Marc. *Outline of Russian Literature.** New York: New American Library (Mentor), 1959.

Staël, Madame de. *De L'Allemagne.** Philadelphia: Chilton Books, 1956.

Taubman, Howard. *The Making of the American Theatre*. New York: Coward-McCann, 1965.

Trilling, Lionel. *The Experience of Literature.** Brief ed. New York: Holt, Rinehart & Winston, 1969.

Warren, Robert Penn, and Erskine, Albert (eds.). *Short Story Masterpieces*. New York: Dell Publishing Co., 1963.

Weston, Jessie L. *From Ritual to Romance* (influence of Oriental mysticism on Christian religious practices).* New York: Doubleday (Anchor), 1957.

Whitfield, J. H. *A Short History of Italian Literature.** Baltimore, Md.: Penguin Books, 1960.

Wilson, Edmund. *Axel's Castle* (literary criticism for the period 1870–1930). New York: Charles Scribner's Sons, 1931.

# Glossary

**A cappella.** Originally, in the style of the (Sistine) chapel: i.e., singing without instrumental accompaniment.

**Abstract art.** Painting that portrays designs that are nonrepresentational: i.e., do not depict recognizable forms.

**Abstract Expressionism.** A twentieth-century art movement emphasizing color and form that do not represent visual reality.

**Alexandrine.** Verse of twelve-syllable lines in iambic hexameter, originally used in early French romantic poems about Alexander the Great. It is the leading verse form in French heroic poems, in epics, and especially in the classic drama of the eighteenth century. (*See* Meters.)

**Allegory.** Veiled presentation in figurative language, forming a story, of a meaning implied but not expressly stated.

**Allegretto.** A musical direction, in a cheerful, happy manner; in tempo between allegro and andante.

**Allegro sonata form.** The form of the first movement (and sometimes the last) of a classic symphony. It involves statement, development, and restatement usually of two contrasting motifs.

**Antependium.** An altar screen or hanging.

**Antiphonal.** In the manner of strophes of songs performed by alternating choirs.

**Apollonian.** From Apollo, Greek god of lyric poetry; restrained, poised, poetic.

**Apse.** The half-dome projection of a church which contains the high altar.

**Archivolt.** One of a series of moldings forming the heading of a round arch.

**Ars nova.** A form that originated in France with Machaut, who took the ancient dance-songs and combined them with polyphony, making a highly artistic secular and rhythmic composition. The Italian *ars nova*, originating with Landino, was an animated, delicate miniature.

**Atonality.** A musical style without feeling for or reference to key center.

**Atrium.** The open court in front of the entrance to basilican churches. There was usually a fountain in the center for ceremonial cleansing.

**Avant-garde.** The innovators of new styles and ideas, especially those who are decidedly unconventional.

**Ballata.** A dancelike song of the fourteenth century in which the melody determines the form.

372

**Basilica.** The earliest form of Christian church, a building style taken over from the Romans. It contained a wide center aisle, two lower side aisles, and a small half-dome apse for the altar.

**Basso continuo.** In music, continuous bass accompaniment; the foundation of the harmony in Mannerist and Baroque music.

**Bauhaus.** Originally, a modernistic building designed by Walter Gropius as an art school; now also applied to the art school itself, which emphasized functional architecture and the creative use of modern techniques.

**Bel canto.** Literally, "beautiful song." The Italian vocal technique especially of the eighteenth century, which emphasized beauty of sound and brilliance of performance rather than dramatic or emotional expression.

**Blank verse.** Verse without rhyme, in iambic pentameter, characteristic of English dramatic and epic poetry.

**Caccia.** Literally, "chase"; fourteenth-century Italian popular song, often humorous, in which the voices chase each other; an earthy natural form of Italian musical expression.

**Cacophony.** Harsh and discordant sound or noise, especially in language as a result of letter and syllable combinations.

**Cadence.** From Latin *cadere*—to fall; a melodic or harmonic formula marking the end of a phrase, section, or composition which gives the impression of a momentary or permanent conclusion.

**Cantata.** A composite vocal form, especially of the Baroque period, consisting of solos, recitatives, duets, and choruses, interspersed with instrumental interludes, based on a continuous narrative text.

**Cantilena.** Melody.

**Canzona.** A fourteenth-century Italian secular song, accompanying lyric poems by Petrarch and others, the predecessor of the madrigal. The instrumental *canzone* developed from the French contrapuntal *chansons,* and were usually arranged for lute or keyboard.

**Capital.** The top of a column, pillar, pier, or pilaster. The three orders as derived from the Greeks are: the Doric, a flat slab; the Ionic, shaped like a cushion; the Corinthian, decorated with stylized acanthus leaves.

**Caryatid.** A female figure used as an architectural support, as in the south porch of the Erechtheum.

**Catharsis.** Greek term for a purging of the emotions through art, particularly tragedy.

**Chiaroscuro.** Arrangement of light and shadow in painting.

**Chorale.** A strophic hymn tune used for congregational singing.

**Choreography.** The arrangement of dance patterns which bring out the story in ballet.

**Chromaticism.** The use of musical tones extraneous to the diatonic scale and hence nonharmonic.

**Closed form.** The design of a painting in which all details are kept within the picture frame and the eye is drawn to the center of interest.

**Coda.** The ending of a musical composition intended to give a feeling of completion and to underline the key.

**Collage.** A picture made by pasting objects of different textures onto a canvas. It may be representational or abstract. The Cubists combined collage with painting.

**Commedia dell'arte.** A type of popular comedy developed in sixteenth-century Italy in which over a conventional plot the actors improvised their lines. It emphasized complicated and absurd intrigues and type characters who wore appropriate masks. It influenced literary comedies such as those of Molière.

**Conceit.** In literature, a clever, fanciful, or quaint fancy or expression.

**Concerto.** A musical composition built up by contrasting bodies of sound, loud opposed to soft, performed by an orchestra with one or more solo voices or instruments.

**Concerto grosso.** In the Baroque period, the opposition of a small group of solo instruments (*concertino*) to a larger group (*tutti* or *ripieni*).

**Counterpoint (contrapuntal).** *See* Polyphony.

**Crossing.** In a church of cruciform design, the place where nave and transepts intersect.

**Cubism.** An art movement, founded in France in the early twentieth century, which reduced objects and people to geometric shapes.

**Dada (Dadaism).** An art movement, founded in Zurich in 1916, which aimed to suppress all relation between thought and expression.

**Da capo aria.** The typical solo song in opera and oratorio, in which the entire first section is repeated after the second section, thus making the form A B A. It reached its greatest perfection in the arias of Alessandro Scarlatti, Bach, and Handel.

**Denouement.** In drama, the unraveling of the plot, the outcome.

**Dialectic.** In philosophy, the process of intellectual discussion by logic or reason.

**Diatonic.** In music, stepwise, following the tones of the scale.

**Dionysiac.** From Dionysus, Greek god of wine and tragedy; hence dramatic and highly emotional, overwrought, uncontrolled.

**Discant (discantus, descant).** In music, a countermelody generally proceeding in contrary motion to the given melody.

**Dithyramb.** The early form of Greek choral drama, sung in honor of the God Dionysus; hence in Dionysiac style.

**Dominant.** The fifth of the diatonic scale, next in importance to the tonic (keynote).

**Dynamics** In music, intensity of sound, from *pp.* (very soft) to *ff.* (very loud).

**Eclectic.** Composed of elements selected from various sources.

**Entablature.** The upper portion of a building above the capital, held up by the columns. It consists of the architrave, the frieze (triglyph and metope), and the cornice.

**Epode.** The last of the three parts of the ancient lyric ode; it follows the strophe and the antistrophe.

**Equal temperament.** In music, the division of the octave into twelve equal semitones.

**Expressionism.** A type of art fostered by twentieth-century German and Austrian artists as a revolt against Impressionism. They aimed at a psychoanalytical effect of violent, sometimes distorted, forms and strong color.

**Fantasia.** A musical composition consisting of free flights of fancy rather than of organized forms.

**Fenestration.** Arrangement of windows in architecture.

**Flèche.** French, "arrow"; in a cruciform church, a slender spire above the intersection of nave and transepts.

**Flying buttress.** In a Gothic church, the outside supports built to take up the lateral thrust of the roof.

**Foreshortening.** Representation of objects or parts of the body as diminished from the point of view of the observer in such a way as to comply with the laws of perspective.

**Fresco.** Painting on wet plaster with water-soluble pigments; or a picture so painted.

**Frieze.** A long horizontal panel sculptured in low relief, like that extending around a Greek temple. (In the Parthenon the frieze depicts the Pan-Athenaic procession.)

**Frottola.** A late fifteenth- and sixteenth-century North Italian secular song that had a melody in the upper voice accompanied by simple chords. (Similar to the fourteenth-century *ballata* and the Spanish *villancico*.)

**Fugue.** A musical form chiefly for keyboard instruments, perfected in the Baroque era. The one theme appears in each of the several voices, and these entrances are separated by extraneous material called episodes.

**Genre.** Painting that depicts a realistic episode in daily life.

**Gregorian chant.** Medieval liturgical chant, used in the Roman Catholic Church.

**Groin vault.** Vault formed by the intersection of two barrel, or tunnel, vaults.

**Haiku.** A three- or five-line Japanese poem which suggests the poet's feeling about nature.

**Homophony.** Note-for-note counterpoint, based on the laws of tonality, with the melody in the upper part.

**Humanism** The Renaissance culture based on Greek and Roman ideals and centered on man as an individual.

**Icon.** A religious representation, such as a picture or mosaic, in the Eastern Orthodox Church, often richly ornamented and regarded as having miraculous power.

**Imagism.** A modern poetic cult dedicated to "free verse" and the expression of ideas and emotions through clear, precise word pictures.

**Impasto.** Thick paint which stands out from the canvas.

**Impressionism.** A musical and poetic school of the late nineteenth century which portrayed fleeting ideas and images. It aimed at subjective and suggestive effects rather than objective representation.

**Lantern.** In architecture, a small cupola at the top of a dome or spire.

**Largo.** A musical direction: in a very slow and usually very expressive manner.

**Laudi spirituali.** Religious songs of praise which arose among the followers of St. Francis and were sung by the common folk in the streets and at work.

**Leitmotif.** In Wagner's music a recurrent theme which stands for a character, object, or idea.

**Libretto.** The text of an opera or oratorio.

**Liturgy.** The form of public worship followed by a Christian church.

**Madrigal.** Originally, secular polyphonic song going back to the Provençal *pastourelle,* concerning the love adventures of the common people. A later subject was contemplation of nature. The late Renaissance madrigal had the same pattern, but it was a highly developed art form compounded of polyphony and homophony.

**Mass.** The service of the Eucharist, or Lord's Supper, in the Roman Catholic Church. The high Mass ordinarily has five musical portions: Kyrie, Gloria, Credo, Sanctus, and Agnus Dei.

**Melisma.** In music, a decorative passage of many notes to one syllable.

**Metaphor.** A figure of speech implying a comparison.

**Meter.** In poetry, measure of rhythm into feet per line as follows:
iambic: one short syllable followed by one long.
trochaic: one long syllable followed by one short.
anapestic: two short syllables followed by one long.
dactylic: one long syllable followed by two short.
Line length:
   trimeter: three feet.
   tetrameter: four feet.
   pentameter: five feet.
   hexameter: six feet.
Rhyme schemes:
   *terza rima:* aba bcb cdc, etc.
   Petrarchan sonnet: fourteen lines usually in iambic pentameter, abba abba cde cde.
   Shakespearean sonnet: fourteen lines in iambic pentameter, abab cdcd efef gg.

**Metope.** The plain opening between the ends of the roof joists (triglyphs) in a Doric frieze, usually decorated with a mythological scene.

**Minnesinger.** German poet and love singer of the late Middle Ages.

**Modal.** Referring to music based on the old medieval church scales, which derived from the Greek scales.

**Monody.** The style of solo song with a simple chordal accompaniment.

**Mosaic.** A surface decoration made by inlaying small pieces such as colored glass or stone in a pattern.

**Motet.** A religious polyphonic composition, which appeared first in the twelfth century when the cathedral church tended to supplant the monastery church and more elaborate music was needed. During the Renaissance it had a most elaborate polyphonic treatment. After this it developed into the Protestant anthem and cantata.

**Motif.** The smallest melodic element (sometimes only three or four notes) out of which a musical composition is fashioned.

**Mot juste.** French term meaning the one "right word" to express the meaning.

**Narthex.** The portico or vestibule leading to the nave of a church.

**Naturalism.** An ultrarealistic school of writers and artists of the late nineteenth century who strove to reproduce life as it is, emphasizing the forces of heredity and environment.

**Nave.** The central part of a cruciform church where most of the congregation worships.

**Nebulous.** Cloudy, vague, uncertain.

**Nemesis.** A Greek term, meaning just retribution.

**Neoplatonism.** A philosophy of the early Christian era that combined the teachings of Plato and Aristotle with Oriental ideas. It had a great influence on Christian mysticism.

**Nihilism.** Literally, "nothingness." The extreme form of pessimism.

**Open form.** The design of a painting in which details are cut off by the picture frame and the beholder is led to imagine what is going on outside the picture.

**Opera buffa.** Italian comic opera.

**Oratorio.** A lengthy religious composition consisting of solos, duets, choruses, orchestral interludes, etc. It is generally based on a Biblical theme or story and is similar to opera in construction, but not acted.

**Oratory.** A chapel for private devotions.

**Overture.** An instrumental piece that preceded an opera or play. The nineteenth-century concert overture is an independent instrumental piece on the same general lines as the operatic overture.

**Paradox.** A tenet that is opposed to common sense but in fact may be true.

**Parlando-rubato.** In music, speech rhythm rendered at the discretion of the performer.

**Passion.** The story of the sufferings of Christ between the Last Supper and his death on the Cross constructed in oratorio form for Holy Week services.

**Peripety.** A Greek term meaning "reversal." A sudden and complete change, usually from happiness to misery. One of Aristotle's requirements for tragedy.

**Philistinism.** A derogatory term applied by Matthew Arnold to the newly rich mercantile class who had no cultural background. Now referring to characteristics of crassness, materialism, and anti-intellectualism.

**Picaresque.** Referring to a narrative tale in which the hero is a lower-class rogue who lives by his wits.

**Pilaster.** A column which does not stand free of the wall and hence is decorative rather than functional.

**Plain chant (plain song).** *See* Gregorian chant.

**Platonic.** Derived from Plato's philosophy; hence maintaining the independent and eternal existence of ideas (beauty, truth, goodness, etc.).

**Polyphony.** Music built up by superimposed melodies that are independent but harmonize. Counterpoint. If the voices imitate each other the music is called imitative polyphony.

**Polytonality.** In music, the use of a number of keys at the same time.

**Portative.** A small organ which could be carried and played by one person and was important in Renaissance and Baroque religious processions.

**Portico.** The entrance porch or court of a church or public building.

**Realism.** In literature and art, the depiction of scenes or people as they are observed without reference to ideal standards.

**Refectory.** The dining room in a convent or monastery.

**Relief sculpture.** Sculpture which is not free standing but embedded in the background.

**Rib vault.** In architecture, a vault formed by the meeting of arches.

**Ricercare.** A musical composition based on Renaissance vocal forms in which each section was built on a different theme. From it developed the fugue, which is based on one theme.

**Rondeau.** A form of medieval French music, popularized by the *trouvères,* which reflected folk-dance elements.

**Rota.** The medieval name for a round (as in "Three Blind Mice").

**Rubato.** In music, fluctuation of tempo according to the discretion of the performer.

**Scherzo.** From the Italian, meaning "joke." A musical composition or movement in rapid, vigorous triple meter. Used by Beethoven as the third movement in his symphonies.

**Scholasticism.** A philosophical movement of the late Middle Ages which tried to reconcile Greek philosophy, Neoplatonic mysticism, and Christian theology.

**Sequence.** In the Middle Ages, a separate text fitted to a lengthy decorative passage interpolated between the notes of a Gregorian chant.

**Sonata.** From the Italian *sonare,* "to sound." Originally a composition to be played, in contrast to one meant to be sung. In the eighteenth century, a composition in allegro-sonata form for a solo instrument (piano sonata), or a solo instrument accompanied by piano.

**Stanze.** Italian, meaning "rooms."

**Stile concitato.** "Agitated style," in music, for increasing emotional tension, probably invented by Monteverdi. Generally represented by repeated groups of four sixteenth notes to the beat.

**Stringcourse.** A horizontal band used for design, usually between floors of a building.

**Strophe.** A stanza in chorus, folk song, hymn, or poem.

**Strophic.** Referring to several stanzas with the same tune or structure and a refrain of a different tune or structure.

**Stylobate.** The first continuous layer of the entablature held up by architectural columns.

**Surrealism.** Literally, "above the real"; a modern art movement, influenced by Freudian psychoanalysis which attempts to portray elements of the subconscious and the dream world.

**Symbolism.** In literature, the representation or suggestion of meaning by the use of signs or objects.

**Tempera.** A technique of painting much in vogue in the late Middle Ages which uses pigment soluble in egg or glue, applied in a series of hard varnishes rubbed to a high gloss.

**Terza rima.** A rhyme scheme (used by Dante in *The Divine Comedy*), represented by letters aba bcb cdc ded, etc. Each rhyme except the first appears three times.

**Theatricalism.** A term applied to drama in which the unreal atmosphere of the stage is stressed rather than hidden.

**Timbre.** In music, the quality of tone distinguishing voices or instruments.

**Toccata.** From Italian *toccare,* "to touch"; a keyboard composition consisting of big chords and runs in very free form.

**Tonic.** In music, the keynote or first degree of a scale.

**Transcendentalism.** A philosophy, originating in nineteenth-century New England, that emphasizes ideas received from visionary or sublimated sources and holds that man can attain knowledge that transcends appearance or observed reality.

**Transepts.** The parts of a cruciform church that represent the arms of the cross.

**Triptych.** An altar painting or carving in three sections, especially one in which the two wings, usually painted on both sides, fold so as to completely cover the central panel.

**Trompe l'oeil.** French meaning "fool the eye"; tricks in painting, to make objects or architectural features seem actual.

**Trope.** In the Middle Ages, similar to a sequence, except that the interpolated text made a comment on the meaning of the chant. (The custom was abused so that churchmen complained that every part of the Gregorian chant was being "troped.")

**Twelve-tone row.** An arbitrary arrangement of the twelve chromatic tones of the scale, used by some late nineteenth- and twentieth-century composers to unify a musical composition without tonality.

**Tympanum.** The space within an arch above lintel of door or window.

**Uomo universale.** Italian meaning "the universal man"; a Renaissance ideal.

**Villanella.** A sixteenth-century popular song, opposed to the refinements of the contemporary madrigal. It originated in Naples and was often humorous and clownish.

**Virelai.** From French *viver*, "to turn around" and *lai*, "song." (Also called *chanson ballade*.) A verse form derived from a dancing song in which chorus and soloist alternated, consisting of stanzas with alternating long and short lines and interlaced rhyme.

# A Few Superior Recordings

BENEVOLI, ORAZIO. *Festival Mass in Fifty-three Parts for the Dedication of the Salzburg Cathedral in 1628.* Musical Heritage Society 503.

BERLIOZ, HECTOR. *L'Enfance du Christ* ("Childhood of Christ"), Munch, Boston Symphony and New England Conservatory of Music Chorus. Two Victor records. VIC 6006.

CENTRAL MIDDLE AGES: TROUBADOURS, TROUVÈRES, MINNESINGERS. Adam de la Halle's *Le jeu de Robin et Marion*, pastoral play with music. Minstrel dances. Archive ARC 3002.

ECHOES FROM A SIXTEENTH-CENTURY CATHEDRAL. Josquin des Prez, Palestrina, Victoria, Viadana, and others. Roger Wagner Chorale Ensemble. Capital P8460.

GABRIELI, GIOVANNI. *Seven Canzonas for Brass Instruments.* Especially *Sonata Pian e Forte.* New York Brass Ensemble. Counterpoint 503.

HANDEL, GEORGE FREDERICK. *L'Allegro* and *Il Penseroso.* Setting of parts of Milton's poems. Illustrations by William Blake. Decca DXA 165.

HERITAGE OF THE BAROQUE. Praetorius, Gabrieli, Alessandro Scarlatti, and others. Telemann Society. Vox PL 16260.

LULLY, JEAN BAPTISTE. *Symphonies and Fanfares for the King's Supper.* Nonesuch Records. H 1009.

MONTEVERDI, CLAUDIO. *L'Orfeo.* First modern opera, 1607. Archive Production. ARC 3036. Two records.

MASTERPIECES OF MUSIC BEFORE 1750. Three records, from Gregorian chant through Bach and Handel. Danish soloists, ensembles, and the Chamber Orchestra of the Danish State Radio. Recorded in conjunction with W. W. Norton and Company. HS 9038, HS 9039, HS 9040.

MUSIC FROM THE COURT OF BURGUNDY. Dufay, Binchois, and others. Nonesuch Records. H 1058.

MUSIC OF THE MEDIEVAL COURT AND COUNTRYSIDE. Leonin, Dufay, and others. New York Pro Musica Society. Decca DL 9400.

PERGOLESI, GIOVANNI BATTISTA. *La Serva Padrona* ("The Maid as Mistress"). First comic opera, 1733. Vox OPX 380.

PURCELL, HENRY. *Dido and Aeneas.* Seventeenth-century English opera. Mermaid Theatre Company, London, with Kirsten Flagstad. Gramophone Company Ltd. R.C.A. LHMV 1007.

TWELFTH-CENTURY MUSICAL DRAMA. *The Play of Daniel,* composed by students of Beauvais Cathedral. New York Pro Musica Ensemble. Decca DL 9402.

# Prints

Reproductions of Painting,
Sculpture, and Architecture
Discussed in the Text.
Numbers refer to listings in the catalogue of
*University Prints*
15 Brattle Street
Cambridge, Massachusetts 02138
The four-digit numbers are colored.

The author has made the following selection of 236 prints to accompany this book.

## Chapter 3: The Greeks

| | |
|---|---|
| The Acropolis (restored) | G 39 |
| The Parthenon, West Front | A 135 |
| Three Fates, East Pediment | A 136 |
| "Apollo Belvedere" | A 272 |
| "Venus de Milo" | A 292 |
| Erechtheum, Porch and Caryatid | A 166 |
| "Nike Tying her Sandal" | A 170 |
| Lysippus, Statue of Alexander the Great | A 399 |
| "Venus dei Medici" | A 202 |
| "Victory of Samothrace" (Louvre) | A 302 |
| Pergamon Altar (reconstructed) | A 265 |
| "Laocoön" | A 270 |

## Chapter 4: The Romans and the Early Medieval Period

| | |
|---|---|
| La Tene Celtic Bronzes | M 188 |
| Etruscan Horsemen and Offering | 1507 |
| Colosseum, Rome | G 84 |
| Pantheon, Rome | G 87 |
| Busts of Caligula and Antoninus Pius | A 424 |
| Pompeii, Interior of a Home | 1511 |
| Hagia Sophia, Byzantium | G 110 |
| St. Apollinare in Classe, Ravenna | MG 167 |
| San Vitale, Apse, Ravenna | MG 169 |
| ———, Mosaics | 1603 |

## Chapter 7: Mannerism

## Chapter 8: The Baroque

## Chapter 11: Realism, Romantic Realism, and Naturalism

## Chapter 12: The Modern Period

| | |
|---|---|
| Ernst, "Two Children Menaced by a Nightingale" | E 342 |
| Albright, "That Which I Should Have Done, I Did Not Do" | H 237 |
| Mondrian, "Composition #10, Plus and Minus" | E 460 |
| Kandinsky, "Improvisation #35" | 1248 |
| Picasso, "Girl Before a Mirror" | 1266 |
| Braque, "Musical Forms" | E 469 |
| Picasso, "Les Demoiselles d'Avignon" | ME 70 |
| ————, "Three Musicians" | 1265 |
| Duchamp, "Nude Descending a Staircase" | E 336 |
| Dali, "Persistence of Memory" | 1267 |
| De Chirico, "Nostalgia of the Infinite" | E 339 |
| Chagall, "I and my Village" | E 335 |
| Klee, "Twittering Machine" | E 323 |
| Miró, "Person Throwing a Stone at a Bird" | E 343 |
| Picasso, "The Old Guitarist" | ME 68 |
| ————, "Harlequin's Family" | E 463 |
| ————, "Seated Woman Nude" | E 310 |
| ————, "The Lovers" | 1243 |
| ————, "She-Goat" | ME 156 |
| Blume, "The Eternal City" | H 245 |
| Feininger, "Steamer Odin II" | H 203 |
| Graves, "Bird Singing in the Moonlight" | H 247 |
| De Kooning, "Woman I" | H 124 |
| Pollock, "Autumn Rhythm" | H 125 |
| Marin, "Lower Manhattan" | H 169 |
| Tobey, "Tundra" | H 227 |
| Kline, "The Chief" | H 248 |
| Motherwell, "Elegy 1948" | H 298 |
| Hopper, "Early Sunday Morning" | H 186 |
| Shahn, "Handball" | H 294 |
| Wyeth, "Christina's World" | H 255 |
| Rodin, "The Kiss" | ME 19 |
| Lembruch, "Kneeling Woman" | ME 153 |
| Maillol, "Seated Woman" | ME 61 |
| Brancusi, "Bird in Space" | ME 149 |
| Moore, "Family Group" | MF 27 |
| Duchamp-Villon, "The Great Horse" | ME 151 |
| Lipton, "Thunderbird" | H 328 |
| Wright, Kauffmann House | GM 366 |
| Gropius, The Bauhaus | GM 205 |
| Saarinen, M.I.T. Chapel and Auditorium | GM 387 |
| Van der Rohe, Seagram Building | GM 391 |
| Le Corbusier, Apartment Building, Marseilles | GM 176 |
| Nervi, Exhibition Hall, Turin | GM 499 |

# INDEX

# Index

This index has been compiled with the aim of making it useful for reference and review. Most entries are in the following order: topic or name, dates, brief identification, one or two representative examples or works, and page number on which primary discussion begins.

# 410 / Index